Light & Glory

Light & Glory

The Transfiguration of Christ in Early Franciscan and Dominican Theology

Aaron Canty

The Catholic University of America Press
Washington, D.C.

The paper used in this publication meets the minimum requirements
of American National Standards for Information Science—
Permanence of Paper for Printed Library Materials, ANSI Z39.48-1984.
∞

Designed by Kachergis Book Design of Pittsboro, North Carolina.
Printed by Thomson-Shore of Dexter, Michigan.

LIBRARY OF CONGRESS CATALOGING-IN-PUBLICATION DATA
Canty, Aaron M.
Light and glory : the transfiguration of Christ in early Franciscan and
Dominican theology / Aaron Canty.
p. cm.
Includes bibliographical references (p.   ) and index.
ISBN 978-0-8132-1795-6 (cloth : alk. paper)   1. Jesus Christ—
Transfiguration—History of doctrines—Middle Ages, 600–1500.
2. Franciscans—Theology—History—To 1500.   3. Dominicans—
Theology—History—To 1500.   I. Title.
BT410.C38 2011
232.9'56—dc22   2010022119

TO KAREN

Contents

Acknowledgments

Many people are responsible for making this volume possible. Joseph Wawrykow encouraged me to explore the topic of Christ's transfiguration in scholastic theology, and he has been a constant source of support throughout my writing and research. I am grateful for his careful guidance, constructive criticism, and remarkable insights into scholastic Christology. Thomas Prügl warmly communicated to me his enthusiasm for medieval theology and for scriptural exegesis, in particular. His willingness not only to examine manuscripts with me, but also to help procure two of them with his own resources, was a great kindness that made the scope of this study possible. Brian Daley, SJ, generously provided numerous suggestions for making connections between authors, including those from the Early Church, and for improving my translations. Larry Cunningham also provided his expertise by asking probing questions about my research, especially on the transfiguration's spiritual importance for medieval theologians, and by helping me articulate more effectively the broader contours of this study.

In the Medieval Institute at the University of Notre Dame, Marina Smyth assisted me with the preliminary location of the relevant manuscripts for this study and shared with me her own scholarly interest in the early medieval interpretations of Christ's transfiguration. Linda Major also provided invaluable help as I located manuscripts in the Ambrosiana Collection.

In addition, I must extend my gratitude to the reviewers for the Catholic University of America Press and to Parker Ladwig; they all demonstrated a keen interest in my research and offered valuable comments and suggestions for the improvement of the manuscript.

Abbreviations

CCSA
Corpus Christianorum.
Series Apocryphorum. Turnhout.

CCCM
Corpus Christianorum.
Continuatio Mediaevalis. Turnhout.

CCSL
Corpus Christianorum.
Series Latina. Turnhout.

DS
Dictionnaire de spiritualité ascétique et mystique: doctrine et histoire. Paris.

LexMA
Lexikon des Mittelalters.
München-Zürich.

LThK
Lexikon für Theologie und Kirche.
3rd ed., Freiburg.

PL
Patrologia Latina. Paris.

SC
Sources chrétienne. Paris.

Light & Glory

INTRODUCTION

The Christian tradition, from a very early period, recognized in the transfiguration of Jesus an event of inexhaustible doctrinal and spiritual richness. The Fathers of the Church examined the scriptural passages that describe the event from a number of vantage points and highlighted several Christological, soteriological, eschatological, and ascetical themes that emerge. Patristic reflections on the transfiguration were recorded in exegetical works and in doctrinal and spiritual treatises, and they were incorporated into the liturgies of the Early Church.

Although the Christian tradition in the East gave a more central place to Christ's transfiguration than the tradition in the West, not only in theology but also in liturgy, art, and architecture, it is nevertheless true that Christian theologians in the West also appropriated the transfiguration for various theological purposes and commented on its significance numerous times. This fact may be somewhat surprising given that the soteriological interests of many of the Latin Fathers laid the foundation for the medieval emphasis on Christ's atoning passion. The medieval emphasis on Jesus' death, however, did not preclude sustained contemplation of those events in Christ's life that manifested His divinity, such as His transfiguration, miracles, and resurrection. The monastic tradition in the West, for as long as it maintained its vigor, kept the theophanic dimensions of Christ's divinity firmly in mind. With the rise of scholasticism, however, Christ's transfiguration and the events of Christ's life in general lost the centrality they had possessed earlier. This trend of scholastic theology—at least as articulated in those systematic treatises that have been printed or edited—continued throughout the Middles Ages with only a few exceptions.

The most notable exception to this trend was Thomas Aquinas,[1] but there were other theologians as well, who found Christ's life and the transfiguration in particular to be important subjects for theological reflection.

This study will explore how one epoch of scholastic theology, that of the early Franciscans and Dominicans, addressed the theological significance of Christ's transfiguration. The period under consideration extends from the first scholastic theologians to address the transfiguration, Hugh of St. Cher and Alexander of Hales, whose reflections on Christ's transfiguration were written roughly between 1230 and 1240, to Thomas Aquinas, who died in 1274.[2] The study will examine seven theologians who addressed the transfiguration through synthetic works, biblical commentaries on the synoptic gospels, or sermons on the transfiguration. Three of these theologians, Alexander of Hales, John of La Rochelle, and Bonaventure of Bagnoregio were Franciscans; and four were Dominicans, namely Hugh of St. Cher, Guerric of St. Quentin, Albert the Great, and Thomas Aquinas. This study will examine similarities and differences among the theologians as well as the relative continuity and discontinuity of their output with the patristic era and with later medieval scholasticism. Special attention will be paid to the differences between the theologians under consideration and the scholastic theologians of the twelfth and early thirteenth centuries.

As precise dates of most of the works under consideration are not available, the chronological outline of this study is approximate. Still,

1. *Le Christ en ses mystéres: la vie et l'œuvre de Jésus selon saint Thomas d'Aquin*, 2 tt. (Paris: Desclée, 1999), t. 1, 14–20, and *Saint Thomas Aquinas, vol. 1: The Person and His Work*, translated by R. Royal (Washington, D.C.: The Catholic University of America Press, 1996), 261–66; Inos Biffi, *I misteri di Cristo in Tommaso d'Aquino* (Milan: Jaca Book, 1994), 23–29, and "I misteri della vita di Cristo nei Commentari biblici di S. Tommaso d'Aquino," *Divus Thomas* 79 (1976): 217–54; Leo Scheffczyk, "Die Stellung des Thomas von Aquin in der Entwicklung der Lehre von den Mysteria Vitae Christi," in *Renovatio et Reformatio: Wider das Bild "finsteren" Mittelalter*, edited by M. Gerwing and G. Ruppert, 44–70 (Münster, Ger.: Aschendorff, 1985); Gerd Lohaus, *Die Geheimnisse des Lebens Jesu in der Summa theologiae des heiligen Thomas von Aquin* (Freiburg im Breisgau, Ger.: Herder, 1985), 14–20; Alois Grillmeier, *Mit ihm und in ihm: christologische Forschungen und Perspektiven* (Freiburg, Ger.: Herder, 1975), 725–26.

2. Although Albert the Great died in 1280, works examined in this study antedate the last writings of Aquinas.

it will provide the reader a sense of the Christological and exegetical developments in the middle of the thirteenth century. This approach also has the advantage of better preserving the integrity of the authors' texts, and it will convey more clearly any influence one theologian may have had on another.

In addition to applying a chronological approach, this study will attempt to engage the whole of each author's views on Christ's transfiguration, insofar as this is feasible. In order to accomplish this goal, consideration of the whole range of scholastic discourse, including sermons, biblical commentaries, as well as disputed questions, *Sentences* commentaries, and *summae* is necessary. This study will draw from several genres of scholastic theology and integrate their respective teachings on Christ's transfiguration. Not all theological topics can benefit from this approach. For a number of theological questions, this approach may be either unfeasible because of the lack of editions or inapplicable because some theological topics (such as the metaphysics of the hypostatic union or of Christ's real presence in the Eucharist) tend to be addressed only in treatises and disputed questions. The theme of Christ's transfiguration, however, is not such a topic, and the study of High Scholastic views of this event can show that multiple genres of thirteenth-century theology are indeed "scholastic" and that in some cases a comparative study of their respective teachings may shed considerable light on theological questions, including the ones that are more metaphysically oriented.[3]

This methodology is not new with respect to Thomas Aquinas, whose sermons and biblical commentaries have gained increasing attention, nor have scholars entirely neglected approaching Bonaventure's theology in this way. There are, however, few studies that integrate on a sustained basis, a scholastic author's sermons and biblical commentaries with his synthetic works and disputed questions. This study will attempt to bridge the gap, which frequently exists between the multiple genres of scholastic literature, and it will bring to light many of the Christological views of several important theological

3. See Thomas' discussion of the hypostatic union in his commentary on the first chapter of John, for example. *Super evangelium S. Ioannis lectura,* edited by R. Cai (Turin, Italy: Marietti, 1952), 1, lect. 1–11.

masters from the mid-thirteenth century, including some who are well known and others who have remained obscure.

As to what a study on the transfiguration can produce, it should be said that besides a rare glimpse of medieval exegesis and comparisons between Eastern and Western theology and spirituality, this study will present additional insight into medieval perspectives on a number of central theological topics. The story of Jesus' transfiguration includes a Trinitarian dimension and raises a number of Christological issues, including the relationship between Christ's divinity and humanity and the nature of His body before and after His resurrection. The narrative placement of this event before Christ's passion, death, and resurrection invites reflection on soteriology and eschatology. The relationship between the Old Testament and the New Testament is important, not only because of the presence of Moses, Elijah, and three of Jesus' closest disciples, but also because the imagery used to describe the event has obvious parallels with several passages in the Old Testament. The presence of the representatives of the Law, the Prophets, and the Church and the significance of the event taking place on a mountain have implications regarding the nature of the Church in history and about Christian discipleship in general. In short, the story of Jesus' transfiguration unites a number of closely related themes in a short, dense, and very rich narrative.

Before providing an exposition of the writings of these early Franciscans and Dominicans, some theological and historical context is required to assess properly the relative continuity and discontinuity between the writings on the transfiguration of the early Franciscans and Dominicans and their predecessors. The following chapter contains a brief examination of how New Testament texts describe Christ's transfiguration, patristic interpretations of the transfiguration, and the theological treatment of it in the twelfth and early thirteenth centuries. However, an exhaustive analysis of the patristic and medieval writings on Christ's transfiguration will not be attempted here. Although scholars have written little on the transfiguration in the Middle Ages, readers may consult several excellent books addressing the transfiguration in the Early Church.[4] This chapter will be helpful not only in un-

4. Ysabel de Andia, *Mystiques d'Orient et d'Occident* (Bégrolles-en-Mauges, Fr.: Abbaye de Bellefontaine, 1994), 121–51, *Grâce de la transfiguration d'après les pères d'occident*, edited by

derstanding the exegetical tradition that shaped the early mendicant theologians, but also for appreciating their unique contribution in reflecting upon Christ's transfiguration and all related theological motifs identified by the friars.

M. Coune (Bégrolles-en-Mauges, Fr.: Abbaye de Bellefontaine, 1990), and *Joie de la transfiguration d'après les pères d'orient,* edited by M. Coune (Bégrolles-en-Mauges, Fr.: Abbaye de Bellefontaine, 1985); John Anthony McGuckin, *The Transfiguration of Christ in Scripture and Tradition* (Lewiston, N.Y.-Queenston, Ont.: Edwin Mellen Press, 1986); Georges Habra, *La transfiguration selon les Pères Grecs* (Paris: Éditions S.O.S., 1974). For a variety of spiritual reflections on the transfiguration, which draw extensively from patristic texts, see Raniero Cantalamessa, *Il mistero della trasfigurazione: quale immagine di Cristo per l'uomo del duemila?* (Milan: Ancora, 1999); Joseph Raya, *Transfiguration of Our Lord and Saviour Jesus Christ* (Combermere, Ont.: Madonna House Publications, 1992); Robert Wild, *His Face Shone Like the Sun: Encountering the Transfigured Christ in Scripture* (New York: Alba House, 1986); Johann Auer, "Die Bedeutung der Verklärung Christi für das Leben des Christen und für die Kirche Christi," in *Die Mysterien des Lebens Jesu und die christliche Existenz,* edited by L. Scheffczyk, 146–76 (Aschaffenburg, Ger.: Paul Pattloch Verlag, 1984).

1

CHRIST'S TRANSFIGURATION

The Early Church to the High Middle Ages

This chapter will trace the development of the Church's understanding of Christ's transfiguration in the period that extends from the New Testament to the High Middle Ages. It will examine the transfiguration narratives in the synoptic gospels and in 2 Peter, which also contains a passing reference to the transfiguration. Next, it will briefly outline the early Christian and Gnostic interpretations of those passages and the Early Medieval reception and development of those interpretations. The chapter will then prepare for the examination of early Franciscan and Dominican theologies of the transfiguration by discussing the relative absence of the transfiguration and other events of Christ's life from the scholastic Christology of the twelfth century. Finally, the chapter will provide a succinct overview of how thirteenth-century scholastic theologians explored Christ's transfiguration. This overview will constitute an introduction to the Franciscan and Dominican theologians studied in this work and will provide reference points for the fuller explorations in subsequent chapters.

The Transfiguration in the New Testament

Jesus' transfiguration is recorded in all three synoptic gospels; several common elements unite these Gospel narratives. The first common theme is that Jesus took Peter, James, and John to a mountain, where they witnessed his transformation: His garments became exceedingly white and shining. Moses and Elijah then appeared and conversed with Jesus. In all three Gospel accounts, Peter addressed Jesus, saying, "It is well [καλόν] that we are here," and he suggested building three booths: one for Jesus, one for Moses, and one for Elijah.[1] A cloud overshadowed the disciples, and a voice from the cloud proclaimed, "This is my Son . . . listen to him."[2]

The different emphases of each of the three synoptic gospels are too numerous to examine exhaustively in this section, but a few of the more important ones should be mentioned.[3] One apparent disparity

1. Mt 17:4, Mk 9:5, and Lk 9:33. All English translations of the New Testament in this chapter are taken from the RSV. The Greek texts of the New Testament are from Nestle-Aland, *Novum testamentum graece et latine*, 26th ed. (Stuttgart, Ger.: Deutsche Bibelgesellschaft, 1991).

2. Lk 9:35. All three Gospels have slightly different statements, among them Matthew's Gospel has the most full expression: "This is my beloved Son, with whom I am well pleased; listen to Him" (Mt 17:5).

3. The unique characteristics of each Gospel narrative have been the subject of numerous biblical studies. The following studies by no means exhaust the secondary literature on this topic: P. R. Baldacci, "The Significance of the Transfiguration Narrative in the Gospel of Luke: A Redactional Investigation" (PhD diss., Marquette University, 1974); Stephen C. Barton, "The Transfiguration of Christ according to Mark and Matthew: Christology and Anthropology," in *Auferstehung-Resurrection*, edited by F. Avemarie and H. Lichtenberger, 231–46 (Tübingen, Ger.: Mohr Siebeck, 2001); T. F. Best, "Transfiguration and Discipleship in Matthew" (PhD diss., Graduate Theological Union, 1974); Josef Blinzler, *Die neutestamentlichen Berichte über die Verklärung Jesu* (Münster, Ger.: Verlag der Aschendottschen Verlagsbuchhandlung, 1937); Rudolf Bultmann, *The History of the Synoptic Tradition*, translated by John Marsh (New York: Harper and Row, 1963), and *Theology of the New Testament*, translated by Kendrick Grobel, vol. 1 (New York: Charles Scribner's Sons, 1951); Eugène Dabrowski, *La transfiguration de Jésus* (Rome: Institut Biblique Pontifical, 1939); Augustín Del Agua, "The Narrative of the Transfiguration as a Derashic Scenification of a Faith Confession (Mark 9.2–8 par.)," *New Testament Studies* 39 (1993): 340–54; André Feuillet, "Les perspective propres à chaque évangéliste dans les récits de la transfiguration," *Biblica* 39 (1958): 281–301; Crispin H. T. Fletcher-Louis, "The Revelation of the Sacral Son of Man: The Genre, History of Religions Context and the Meaning of the Transfiguration," in *Auferstehung-Resurrection*, 247–98; Augustin George, "La transfiguration (Luc 9:28–36)," *Bible et vie chrétienne* 33 (1960): 21–25; Wolfgang Gerber, "Die Metamorphose Jesu (Mark 9, 2f. par.)," *Theologische Zeitschrift* 23 (1967): 385–95; John Paul Heil, *The Transfiguration of Jesus: Narrative Meaning and Function of Mark 9:2–8, Matt 17:1–8, and Luke 9:28–36* (Rome: Editrice Pontificio Istituto Biblico, 2000); Morna D. Hooker, "'What Doest Thou Here, Elijah?' A Look at St. Mark's Account of the Transfiguration," in *The Glory of Christ in the New Testament: Studies in Christology*, edited by L. D. Hurst and N. T. Wright, 59–70 (Oxford: Clarendon Press, 1987); Howard Clark Kee, "The Transfiguration in Mark: Epiphany or Apocalyptic Vision?" in *Understanding the Sacred Text: Essays in Honor of Morton S. Enslin on the Hebrew Bible and Christian Beginnings*, edited by John Reumann, 137–52 (Valley Forge, Pa.: Judson Press, 1972); Charles Masson, "La transfiguration de Jésus (Marc 9:2–13)," *Revue de théologie et de*

is the actual number of days between the occasion of one of Jesus' sayings and His transfiguration. In all three Gospels, Jesus claims that "there are some standing here who will not taste death" before the coming of the kingdom.[4] In all three Gospels the transfiguration narrative immediately follows that saying. In Matthew and Mark the saying begins, "And after six days Jesus took with him Peter and James and John"; while Luke says, "Now about eight days after these sayings he took with him Peter and John and James." Subsequent theologians will find it necessary to explain the disparity between Matthew and Mark's six days and Luke's "about [ὡσεὶ] eight days."

Another difference lies in the evangelists' description of the transfiguration. Although all three writers describe how Jesus' clothes became white,[5] Matthew and Luke specifically recount how Jesus' face was transformed.[6] Jesus' *metamorphosis,* His altered appearance rendered the disciples awestruck and terrified. In Mark and Luke, the evangelists attribute fearful Peter's suggestion to build booths for Jesus, Moses, and Elijah to his confusion about what to say; however, in Matthew fear plays a less prominent role in Peter's suggestion.

The conclusions of each Gospel narrative are also slightly different. The Gospels of Mark and Luke record that the disciples did not realize that Jesus was alone until after the voice from the cloud had spoken. Matthew adds that the disciples had fallen on their faces and that it was Jesus who came to them, touched them, and encouraged them,

---

philosophie Sér. 3, 14 (1964): 1–14; A. D. A. Moses, *Matthew's Transfiguration Story and Jewish-Christian Controversy* (Sheffield, U.K.: Sheffield Academic Press, 1996); Johannes M. Nützel, *Die Verklärungserzählung im Markusevangelium* (Würzburg, Ger.: Echter Verlag, 1973); Barbara E. Reid, *The Transfiguration: A Source- and Redaction-Critical Study of Luke 9:28–36* (Paris: J. Gabalda et Cie Éditeurs, 1993); Harald Riesenfeld, *Jésus transfiguré, l'arriére-plan du récit évangélique de la transfiguration de Notre-Seigneur* (Copenhagen: E. Munksgaard, 1947); Luis F. Rivera, "Interpretatio transfigurationis Jesu in redactione evangelii Marci," *Verbum Domini* 46 (1968): 99–104; Paulo Augusto de Souza Nogueira, "Visionary Elements in the Transfiguration Narrative," in *Apocalyptic in History and Tradition,* edited by C. Rowland and J. Barton, 142–150 (London: Sheffield Academic Press, 2002); Allison A. Trites, "The Transfiguration in the Theology of Luke: Some Redactional Links," in *The Glory of Christ in the New Testament: Studies in Christology,* 71–81. Additional studies can be found in the concluding bibliography.

4. Mt 16:28, Mk 9:1, and Lk 9:27.

5. They were "white as light" (Mt 17:2), "intensely white, as no fuller on earth could bleach them" (Mk 9:3), and "dazzling white" (Lk 9:29).

6. Matthew has τὸ πρόσωπον while Luke describes τὸ εἶδος τοῦ προσώπου.

saying, "Rise, and have no fear." At this point they noticed that Moses and Elijah had departed and that Jesus was alone.[7] Matthew and Mark relate that Jesus then instructed the disciples not to tell anyone what they had seen until the "Son of man" had risen from the dead,[8] while Luke notes merely that the disciples "kept silence and told no one in those days anything of what they had seen."[9]

Besides these three passages in the synoptic gospels, the only other canonical pericope in the New Testament to mention the transfiguration is 2 Peter 1:16–18. This passage is important because the author of 2 Peter is the first author other than the evangelists to make reference to it.[10] The text is as follows:

For we did not follow cleverly devised myths when we made known to you the power and coming of our Lord Jesus Christ, but we were eyewitnesses

7. Mt 17:6–7.

8. Mt 17:9 and Mk 9:9.

9. Lk 9:36.

10. The controversy regarding the dating and authorship of this epistle is complicated, perhaps the most complicated of any New Testament work. Most scholars date this work between the late first and early second centuries (see Richard J. Bauckham, *Word Biblical Commentary: Jude, 2 Peter* [Waco, Tex.: Word Books, 1983], 131–63; Fred B. Craddock, *First and Second Peter and Jude* [Louisville, Ky.: Westminster John Knox Press, 1995], 85–94; Hubert Frankenmölle, *1. Petrusbrief, 2. Petrusbrief, Judasbrief* [Würzburg, Ger.: Echter Verlag, 1990], 73–87; Eric Fuchs and Pierre Reymond, *La deuxième épitre de saint Pierre, L'épitre de saint Jude* [Neufchâtel, Fr.: Delachaux, 1980], 30–41; David Horrell, *The Epistles of Peter and Jude* [Peterborough, U.K.: Epworth Press, 1998], 135–42; Jonathan Knight, *2 Peter and Jude* [Sheffield, U.K.: Sheffield Academic Press, 1995], 15–36; Steven J. Kraftchick, *Jude, 2 Peter* [Nashville, Tenn.: Abingdon Press, 2002], 71–83; Ceslas Spicq, *Les épitres de saint Pierre* [Paris: Librairie Lecoffre, 1966], 1–36; Anton Vögtle, *Der Judasbrief, der 2. Petrusbrief* [Solothurn, Switz.: Benziger Verlag, 1994], 117–31). Other scholars, however, situate it in the middle of the second century (see Oscar Cullman, *Le Nouveau Testament* [Paris: Presses Universitaires de France, 1967], 104–7; Ernst Käsemann, "Eine Apologie der unchristlichen Eschatologie," *Zeitschrift für Theologie und Kirche* 49 [1952]: 272–96; Willi Marxsen, *Einleitung in das Neue Testament: Eine Einführung in ihre Probleme* [Gütersloh, Ger.: Gütersloher Verlagshaus Gerd Mohn, 1964], 204–8), while some claim a very early date or even Petrine authorship (see Michael Green, *2 Peter and Jude* [Leicester, U.K.: Inter-Varsity, 1987], 13–41, and *2 Peter Reconsidered* [London: Tyndale Press, 1961]; Everett F. Harrison, *Introduction to the New Testament* [Grand Rapids, Mich.: Eerdmans, 1964], 386–401). On the relation of 2 Peter to the Gospels, see G. H. Boobyer, "The Indebtedness of 2 Peter to 1 Peter," in *New Testament Essays: Studies in Memory of Thomas Walter Manson, 1893–1958*, edited by A. J. B. Higgins, 34–53 (Manchester, U.K.: Manchester University Press, 1959); Irénée Fransen, "Cahiers de Bible: Le feu de la gloire (2 Pierre)," *Bible et vie chrétienne* 33 (1960): 26–33; Robert J. Miller, "Is There Independent Attestation for the Transfiguration in 2 Peter?" *New Testament Studies* 42 (1996): 620–25.

of his majesty. For when he received honor and glory from God the Father and the voice was borne to him by the Majestic Glory, 'This is my beloved Son, with whom I am well pleased,' we heard this voice borne from heaven, for we were with him on the holy mountain.[11]

In this passage, the author places Jesus' transfiguration in an explicitly ecclesial and eschatological context. The transfiguration is a miraculous historical event, which authenticates the authority, preaching, and scriptural interpretation of the witnesses of Christ's "majesty [μεγαλειότητος]."[12] The experience with Christ on the "holy mountain" substantiates their proclamation of Christ's "power [δύναμιν]" and "coming [παρουσίαν],"[13] because the Father imparted "honor and glory [δόξαν]" to Christ and testified to it through a voice "borne to him by the Majestic Glory [μεγαλοπρεποῦς δόξης]."[14] The author chooses not to name all the witnesses on the mountain; but, in the general literary context of the whole epistle, with its admonition to virtue, denunciation of false prophets, and reminder of the end times,[15] it is important that those witnesses of Jesus' transfiguration were commissioned by God to be the true teachers of the Christian communities. The witnessing of the theophany on the mountain is itself the mandate to teach, and makes the witnesses the authentic teachers of scriptural prophecy. False prophets and false teachers are guilty of making private interpretations of scriptural prophecy,[16] immorality,[17] despising authority,[18] and apostasy.[19] If those addressed would turn from these false prophets who encourage the faithful to ignore the imminence of the coming "day of the Lord [ἡμέρα κυρίου]"[20] and instead "remember the predictions of the holy prophets and the commandment of the Lord and Savior through [their] apostles,"[21] they could prepare themselves for the Lord's coming.

11. 2 Pet 1:16–18.
12. 2 Pet 1:16.
13. 2 Pet 1:16.
14. 2 Pet 1:17.
15. See 2 Pet 3:1–13.
16. 2 Pet 1:20.
17. 2 Pet 2:2–3, 10–15.
18. 2 Pet 2:10.
19. 2 Pet 2:20–22.
20. 2 Pet 3:10.
21. 2 Pet 3:2.

The Interpretation of Christ's Transfiguration by the Fathers in the East and the West

Subsequent interpretations of the transfiguration by some early Christian and Gnostic communities in the second and early third centuries were removed from the ecclesial context of 2 Peter, but the eschatological and soteriological interest remained. Although this event of Christ's life was not treated by the so-called "Apostolic Fathers" and the apologists, it nevertheless found a place in apocryphal pseudepigrapha and Gnostic treatises.[22]

Early Christian writers first interpreted Christ's transfiguration in response to fantastic Gnostic accounts, in which either Christ's body changes drastically or His humanity is denied. Irenaeus of Lyons and Clement of Alexandria, in the second and early third centuries, were the first Christian theologians to reflect on the transfiguration in response to Gnostic accounts. Both writers tried to combine a spiritual reading of the Gospel narratives with an emphatic confession of Christ's true humanity. Irenaeus was the first theologian to interpret the transfiguration as a fulfillment of God's promise to Moses, that He would reveal His glory to him. In Exodus 33, Moses asks to see God's glory, and God promises to show Moses His "back parts" while Moses is in the "cleft of the rock."[23] According to this interpretation, humanity is allowed to see God, who by His nature is invisible, by His coming in the depth of the rock, which Irenaeus interprets typologically as Christ's flesh. Irenaeus thus interprets the presence of Moses and Elijah on the mountain with Jesus as the fulfillment of Moses' request to see God's glory.[24] Even in this interpretation, Irenaeus' anti-Gnostic

22. See Hermann Josef Sieben, "Transfiguration du Seigneur: Les commentaires spirituels," DS 1151–53. All of the following contain transfiguration narratives: The *Apocalypse of Peter,* in *Your Eyes Will Be Opened: A Study of the Greek (Ethiopic) Apocalypse of Peter,* edited and translated by Dennis D. Bucholz, 157–265 (Atlanta: Scholars Press, 1988); the *Acts of Peter* [*Actus Petri cum Simone*], 2 pts., edited by R. A. Lipsius and M. Bonnet (Darmstadt, Ger.: Wissenschaftliche Buchgesellschaft, 1959); the *Acts of John* [*Acta Iohannis*], edited and translated by E. Junod and J.-D. Kaestli, 2 vols. CCSA 1–2); and the *Treatise on the Resurrection* [*De resurrectione (Epistula ad Rheginum)*], edited by M. Malinine et al. (Zürich: Rascher Verlag, 1963).

23. Ex 33:19–23.

24. See Irenaeus, *Contre les hérésies, Livre IV,* 2 tt., edited by A. Rousseau et al., SC 100; IV, 20:9–10.

polemic is evident. Christ brings salvation to the temporal order, not through knowledge according to the spirit, but through vision according to the flesh. Clement of Alexandria also tried to emphasize the importance of the Incarnation and Christ's true flesh in anti-Gnostic passages.[25]

In the third century, Origen introduced a more pronounced spiritual dimension to the transfiguration. Reappropriating and recasting a theme from some of the Gnostic literature, Origen emphasized that Jesus appeared differently to different people, according to their spiritual capacities. Thus, Origen asserted that only Peter, James, and John were capable of seeing Christ in his glory.[26]

From the fourth century, Eastern theologians tended to interpret the glory of the transfiguration principally as a manifestation or foreshadowing of Christ's kingdom, a revelation of His divinity perceived as such by close followers who themselves were being transfigured. The revised Office of Readings for the Feast of the Transfiguration in the Liturgy of the Hours presents an extract from Anastasius of Sinai, which expresses these themes beautifully:

> Upon Mount Tabor, Jesus revealed to his disciples a heavenly mystery. While living among them he had spoken of the kingdom and of his second coming in glory, but to banish from their hearts any possible doubt concerning the kingdom and to confirm their faith in what lay in the future by its prefiguration in the present, he gave them on Mount Tabor a wonderful vision of his glory, a foreshadowing of the kingdom of heaven . . . Jesus goes before us to show us the way, both up the mountain and into heaven—I speak boldly—it is for us now to follow him with all speed, yearning for the heavenly vision that will give us a share in his radiance, renew our spiritual nature and transform us into his own likeness, making us forever sharers in his Godhead and raising us to heights yet undreamed of.[27]

25. See *Extraits de Théodote*, edited and translated with an introduction by F. Sagnard, SC 23; 5, 3; and *Les stromates: Stromate VI*, edited and translated with an introduction by P. Descourtieux, SC 446; 16, 140, 3.

26. See the translated selection of Origen's *In Matthaeum Commentarii*, in John Anthony McGuckin's *The Transfiguration of Christ in Scripture and Tradition*, 156–57.

27. *The Liturgy of the Hours*, translated by the International Committee on English in the Liturgy, 4 vols. (New York: Catholic Book Publishing, 1975), 4:1285–87 (in the Proper of Saints). The full homily is in *Joie de la transfiguration d'après les pères d'orient*, edited by M. Coune (Bégrolles-en-Mauges, Fr.: Abbaye de Bellefontaine, 1985), 153–64.

In some Catholic Churches of the Byzantine rite and in the Greek Orthodox Church, the fifth tone for orthros or Matins on the Feast of the Transfiguration has the following troparion written by Cosmas of Jerusalem: "Today as He has promised Christ, shining on Mount Tabor, dimly disclosed to His disciples the image and reflection of divine brightness; and filled with godlike and light-bearing splendour, they cried out for joy: 'Let us sing unto God for He has been glorified.'"[28]

As early as the fourth century, Basil of Caesarea and Gregory of Nazianzus taught that the splendor which Christ radiates is His divinity (θεότης). While this opinion, at least expressed without qualification, is not unanimous in the East, it may be considered the consensus position among Eastern theologians in the Early Church. John of Damascus, in his famous *Oratio in transfigurationem Domini*, articulates this view several times. One finds the culmination of this interpretation in Gregory Palamas, who emphasizes both the identity of the Father's glory and the Son's kingdom and also the spiritual transfiguration of those who perceive Christ's divinity. Although the radiance of the transfigured Christ is perceived by both the spirit and the senses, the light itself is uncreated. The disciples "behold Christ in all his divine and ineffable radiance whose glory proceeds naturally from his godhead and on Tabor is revealed as common even to his body because of the oneness of hypostasis."[29]

In the West, in late Antiquity and the Early Middle Ages, the most influential interpretations of the transfiguration came from Jerome, Ambrose, Augustine, Leo the Great, Gregory the Great, Bede, and from John Chrysostom, whose writings were circulated in the West even in the early fifth century. Since the liturgical Feast of the Transfiguration did not exist in the West until the twelfth century, and it was not a universal feast until the fifteenth century,[30] the sermons and com-

28. *The Festal Menaion*, translated by Mother Mary and Archimandrite Kallistos Ware with an introduction by Georges Florovsky (London: Faber and Faber, 1969). See also *La prière des églises de rite byzantin*, 2 tt., edited by R. P. E. Mercenier (Monastère de Chevetogne, Belg.: Éditions de Chevetogne, 1948?–1953), t. 2, 1:391–408.

29. Gregory Palamas, *Homilia 34*, in McGuckin, 231. See also Palamas' interpretation of the transfiguration in *The One Hundred and Fifty Chapters*, edited and translated by Robert E. Sinkewicz (Toronto: Pontifical Institute of Mediaeval Studies, 1988), chap. 66, 146–50.

30. See Pierre Batiffol, *History of the Roman Breviary*, translated by Atwell M. Y. Baylay

mentaries of these authors provided the most influential interpretations of Christ's transfiguration in medieval Christianity. In general, the spiritual meaning of the transfiguration is articulated more profoundly in Eastern exegesis, but the Latin interpretations more frequently address exegetical difficulties, which the various transfiguration narratives pose, and are more interested in connecting the transfiguration both to Peter's confession of faith and to the Church in general.

Another significant difference concerns the explanation of Christ's glory. For several of these Latin writers, the glory of the transfiguration is not only Christ's divinity, but it also signifies the glory of Christ's humanity. Leo the Great's Lenten sermon on Matthew's transfiguration narrative resounds with striking affirmations of the glory of Christ's humanity. Christ revealed His divinity in the miracles that His disciples witnessed, and Peter confessed this divinity in proclaiming Christ to be "the Son of the living God."[31] Until the transfiguration, however, the disciples could not perceive the glory of Christ's humanity. As Leo explains:

For though they had witnessed in Him the power of the Divinity, yet they had not begun to know the power of the Body with which the Divinity was clothed.

And for this reason He had personally and clearly promised that some among the Disciples who had stood about Him would not taste death until they had seen the Son of man *coming in His Kingdom* (Mt xvi. 28), that is, till they had seen Him clothed in the royal dignity that rightly belonged to the human nature He had assumed, and which He now wished to make visible to these three men. For while they remained in the body they could never look upon and behold that unspeakable and inaccessible vision of the Divinity, which is laid up for the clean of heart unto life everlasting.

And so in the presence of these chosen witnesses the Lord unveils His glory, and clothes with such splendour the Body, which is His in common with all other men, that His face shines as the sun and His garments appear as white as snow.[32]

(London: Longmans, Green, 1912), 135, 169. After the feast was instituted, the two patristic interpretations found in the lessons of Matins were from John Chrysostom and Leo the Great. See also Cantalamessa, 7–8.

31. Mt 16:16.

32. *Sermo 51*, in *The Sunday Sermons of the Great Fathers*, translated and edited by M. F. Toal, 4 vols. (Swedesboro, N.J.: Preservation Press, 1996), 2:70 (italics are the translator's).

The transfiguration reveals Christ's divine nature, but this revelation is made possible only because of Christ's human nature, which acts as a sort of prism through which Christ's divinity is perceived. The humanity of Christ shares the divinity in a bodily way, so that the Church can realize the glory for which it hopes.[33] Bede also emphasizes the glorious humanity that Christ manifests on the mountain, and Ambrose Autpert even wonders how Peter could have denied Christ after beholding the glory of Christ's body.[34]

The Transfiguration in the Twelfth and Early Thirteenth Centuries

Christians in the Middle Ages received these Latin interpretations and a few Eastern interpretations (especially from Origen and John Chrysostom) through Gregory the Great, Bede, Ambrose Autpert, Rabanus Maurus, Remigius of Auxerre, and John Scotus Eriugena. Since most of these authors added their own questions, comments, and opinions regarding the transfiguration to their sermons and commentaries, exegetes in later centuries worked to separate earlier interpretations from later ones; they were not always successful.

In the glosses and histories of the High Middle Ages, patristic interpretations were gathered together along with the interpretations of Carolingian exegetes. Thus, the scholars of the twelfth century combined the exegesis of earlier centuries with their own interpretations to create a form of exegesis that possessed a high level of complexity and intertextuality. As it pertained to Christ's transfiguration, these scholars asked questions of every phrase and incorporated insights not only from the Fathers of the Early Church but from contemporaries as well. Twelfth-century interpretations of the transfiguration, which combined patristic and contemporary exegesis, include those of the *Glossa ordinaria,* and those found in the works of Peter of Blois, Bernard of Clairvaux, Peter Comestor, and Zachary of Besançon. The

33. Ibid.

34. Ambrose Autpert, *Homilia de transfiguratione,* in McGuckin, 311. For a short commentary on Bede's interpretation of the transfiguration, see Bertrand de Margerie, *Introduction a l'histoire de l'exégèse,* 4 tt. (Paris: Cerf, 1980–1990), t. 4, 220–24.

authors of these texts commented on the transfiguration in their sermons, biblical commentaries, and summaries of scriptural texts.

In the nascent scholastic theology of the cathedral schools, there was no interest in treating the events of Christ's life in a systematic way. Thus, Christ's transfiguration is not found in that genre of theological writing. The events of Christ's life—salvific actions, which had merited the contemplation of monks for centuries—did not capture the attention of theologians such as Hugh of St. Victor or Peter Lombard, who attempted to summarize the subject matter of Scripture and theology in a general way. Part of the reason for this omission may have been the broad parameters with which early scholastic theology had begun. These theologians began by discussing God, creation, and redemption. Christ's Incarnation and His death and resurrection were important events in this outline, but early scholastic theologians tended to omit discussion of the events of Christ's life between His birth and passion.

Thus, consideration of the transfiguration is almost entirely absent from the scholastic theology of the twelfth and early thirteenth centuries. Only passing references to it can be found in Anselm's *Cur Deus homo* and in Peter Abelard's *Sic et non*, for instance; and it is completely absent from Hugh of St. Victor's *De sacramentis christianae fidei*, the anonymous *Summa sententiarum*, and Peter Lombard's *Sentences*.[35] Likewise, in the early thirteenth century, Jesus' transfiguration is not treated in William of Auxerre's *Summa aurea*, William of Auvergne's *Magisterium divinale et sapientale*, Philip the Chancellor's *Summa de bono*, Roland of Cremona's *Summa*, or Alexander of Hales' *Glossae in IV libros sententiarum*.

As scholastic theology became more sophisticated and complex, however, theologians posed more questions and provided more elaborate answers. Eventually scholastic theologians found room to ask technical questions regarding Christ's life. Beginning with a theology of the Incarnation, theologians applied their various theories of the hypostatic union to questions pertaining to the events of Christ's life, including His death and resurrection. The transfiguration, in particu-

35. Peter, however, does discuss the transfiguration in his biblical commentaries. See *In totum Psalterium commentarii*, PL 191, 489.

lar, raised a number of important questions. In addition to vexing exegetical concerns; metaphysical, anthropological, and epistemological questions arose when theologians considered the glory witnessed by the disciples, the presence of the Father's voice and the bright cloud, and the presence of Moses and Elijah. For example, how do Jesus' human nature and its modifications at the time of His transfiguration compare with the human nature and modifications He assumed at the first moment of the Incarnation, and how does it compare with His humanity after His resurrection and ascension? What is the relationship between Christ's humanity and ours? Are the gifts *(dotes)* of Christ's transfigured body different from those of His resurrected body? What exactly did the disciples hear and see in the divine testimony regarding Christ's Sonship? Why were Moses and Elijah present, and how did the disciples know that the two men were Moses and Elijah? What eschatological significance does the transfiguration have for the Christian hope in the resurrection of the dead at the Last Judgment?

Theologians in the thirteenth century raised these questions both in exegetical genres, such as sermons and biblical commentaries, and in what is conventionally thought of as "scholastic" literature, for example, disputed questions, commentaries on Peter Lombard's *Sentences*, and *summae*. The Dominican Hugh of St. Cher, who taught at the Dominican *studium generale* in Paris around 1230, addressed numerous questions posed by the Gospels' transfiguration narratives in his *Postilla super totam Bibliam*. Not only does Hugh provide literal and spiritual interpretations of the transfiguration in his commentaries on Matthew, Mark, and Luke, but he also raises a number of speculative questions, which were typically addressed in disputed questions and theological manuals. Since each biblical commentary examined in this study, not only Hugh's but also those of Alexander, John, Albert, Bonaventure, and Thomas, contains abundant material, a thorough exposition of each scholastic biblical commentary would prove tedious. Thus, the focus here will be on Christ's appearance, the witnesses of the transfiguration, and any noteworthy spiritual interpretations.

The first thirteenth-century theologian to write a disputed question about the transfiguration was the Franciscan Alexander of Hales.

Alexander composed his question on the transfiguration while he was still a secular master, but his theological work paved the way for the influential *Summa fratris Alexandri* (compiled by several Franciscan theologians) and for later biblical commentaries as well.

Like Hugh and Alexander, the Dominican Guerric of St. Quentin also taught at the University of Paris in the 1230s, and like Alexander, Guerric wrote a disputed question on the transfiguration. This question consists of five inquiries with numerous arguments but short "determinations" or magisterial replies.

The most elaborate and involved treatment of Christ's transfiguration in the entire thirteenth century is from the pen of Alexander of Hales' fellow Franciscan, John of La Rochelle. Teaching at the University of Paris in the late 1230s and early 1240s, John wrote a detailed question on the transfiguration, which the compilers of the *Summa fratris Alexandri* (of which he was one) inserted into the *Summa*. These Franciscan compilers placed John's disputed question on the transfiguration, interestingly enough, in the treatise on Christ's resurrection. In this question, John addresses more questions on the transfiguration than anyone from this period, and he provides innovative responses regarding a number of topics. He also contributes significantly to the development of scholastic biblical exegesis in general and to the interpretation of the transfiguration in particular. His manner of dividing the scriptural text when interpreting various passages is much more elaborate than that of his predecessors, and the questions which he formulates as part of the commentary are more sophisticated than those of his predecessors as well.

Albert the Great interpreted Christ's transfiguration both in a textbook treatise and in commentaries on the synoptic gospels. He wrote his treatise on Christ's resurrection in the early 1240s, and like the editors of the *Summa fratris Alexandri,* Albert saw fit to address the transfiguration in the theological and literary context of that treatise. Although the analysis of the transfiguration in this treatise is not as complete as that found in the *Summa fratris Alexandri,* Albert's question, more than any other question on the transfiguration in the thirteenth century, applies logic and philosophy to this extraordinary event of Christ's life. In Albert's scriptural commentaries, which date from approximately the early-to-mid-1260s, the ecclesiological dimensions of the transfiguration are highlighted in a unique way, as is the Trinitarian dimension of the theophany.

Another theologian who first addressed Christ's transfiguration in the 1240s was Bonaventure of Bagnoregio. Bonaventure was a pupil of Alexander of Hales and of other Franciscan masters; his first major exegetical work was his *Commentarius in Evangelium S. Lucae,* which he wrote in the late 1240s and likely reworked at a later date.[36] In this commentary, Bonaventure treats Christ's transfiguration in a relatively conventional way, drawing heavily from patristic and earlier medieval commentators. In later sermons, Bonaventure becomes more creative, but even the interpretations of the transfiguration found there tend to be highly allegorical or spiritual. Unfortunately, Bonaventure left no technical scholastic discussion of Christ's transfiguration either in his disputed questions or in his *Sentences* commentary.

Thomas Aquinas also addressed Christ's transfiguration in several works. His teaching on the events of Christ's life in general constitutes the last sustained systematic reflection on this theme for the remainder of the thirteenth century. Thomas' first discussion of the transfiguration occurs in his *Sentences* commentary. Since Peter Lombard's *Sentences* does not address the transfiguration, it is somewhat surprising that a thirteenth-century commentator would choose to do so. Neither Albert the Great nor Bonaventure addresses the transfiguration in a *Sentences* commentary. Thomas incorporates a discussion of the transfiguration in his commentary on Book Three, distinction 16, which pertains to the passibility of Christ's body. Thomas also discusses the transfiguration in his exegetical works. The *Catena aurea* and the Matthew commentary, both from the 1260s, contain interpretations of the transfiguration narratives. Thomas' exegetical work contributes to his discussion of Christ's transfiguration in the Third Part of the *Summa theologiae.* Thus, as we shall see, Thomas' teaching on the transfiguration develops in several important ways from the early *Sentences* commentary to the *Summa theologiae.*

This preliminary sketch of the seven thirteenth-century theolo-

36. See Jacques Guy Bougerol, *Introduction a l'étude de Saint Bonaventure* (Tournai, Belg.: Desclée, 1961), 142–43.

gians should demonstrate that the choice of these Franciscan and Dominican theologians is not arbitrary. Hugh of St. Cher and Alexander of Hales, one a Dominican and the other a Franciscan, taught at their respective orders' conventual schools at the University of Paris and also wrote their major exegetical and theological works at nearly the same time. They are significant because they were the first theologians of the thirteenth century to address Christ's transfiguration on a sustained basis. Hugh's massive *postillae* and his other scriptural studies and Alexander of Hales' disputed question on Christ's transfiguration seem to be the first of their kind in the thirteenth century. Thomas Aquinas' work is the culmination of this study, not only because his writings on the transfiguration constitute the last sustained treatment of Christ's transfiguration in the thirteenth century, but also because, of all the theologians examined in this study, his synthesis of Greek and Latin patristic sources allows him to develop the most complex account of Christ's transfigured glory. Thomas, however, like his contemporaries Albert and Bonaventure, was aware of and drew from his predecessors while achieving his own theological expression. In their similarities and in their differences, these early Franciscan and Dominican theologians of the thirteenth century act as remarkable witnesses to the power and depth that the life of Jesus Christ, His transfiguration in particular, have for Christian theology.

2

HUGH OF ST. CHER

There is little information about the life of Hugh of St. Cher before he became a Dominican in 1225 or 1226.[1] At the time he entered the Dominican Order, he was a bachelor of theology and probably also a doctor in canon law. Like his own theological mentor, Roland of Cremona, Hugh taught theology at the Dominican *studium generale* in Paris from 1229 or 1230 to 1236. From the time he became a Dominican until 1244, when he became the first Dominican cardinal, Hugh wrote a commentary on Peter Lombard's *Sentences*[2] and, with the help of students and colleagues, collaborated on a number of notable exegetical projects, including commentaries on all the books of Scripture,[3] a list of variant readings of the Vulgate Bible called a *correctorium*, and an alphabetical concordance.[4] Hugh's group of scholars

1. See Jacques Verger, "Hugues de Saint-Cher dans le contexte universitaire parisien," in *Hugues de Saint-Cher († 1263) bibliste et théologien*, edited by L.-J. Bataillon, G. Dahan, and P.-M Gy, 13–22 (Turnhout, Belg.: Brepols, 2004).

2. On Hugh's *Sentences* commentary, see J. Fisher, "Hugh of St. Cher and the Development of Mediaeval Theology," *Speculum* 31 (1956): 57–69; Artur M. Landgraf, "Mitteilungen zum Sentenzkommentar Hugos a S. Charo," *Zeitschrift für katholische Theologie* 58 (1934): 391–400; K. F. Lynch, "Some Fontes of the Commentary of Hugh de Saint Cher: William of Auxerre, Guy d'Orchelles, Alexander of Hales," *Franciscan Studies* 13 (1953): 119–46.

3. On the various manuscript traditions and editions of these commentaries, see Patricia Stirnemann, "Les manuscrits de la *Postille*," in *Hugues de Saint-Cher († 1263) bibliste et théologien*, 31–42; Bruno Carra de Vaux, "La constitution de corpus exégétique," in ibid., 43–63.

4. See Beryl Smalley, *The Gospels in the Schools: c. 1100–c. 1280* (London: Hambledon Press, 1985), 125–43 and *The Study of the Bible in the Middle Ages* (Notre Dame, Ind.: University of Notre Dame Press, 1964), 270–74; Robert E. Lerner, "The Vocation of the Friars Preacher: Hugh of St. Cher between Peter the Chanter and Albert the Great," in *Hugues de Saint-Cher († 1263) bibliste et théologien*, 215–31; Mary A. and Richard H. Rouse, "La concordance verbale des Ecritures," in *Le Moyen Age et la Bible*, edited by P. Riché and G. Lobrichon,

probably compiled the biblical commentaries in the early to mid-1230s, and they likely completed the commentaries on the synoptic gospels before Alexander of Hales wrote his postillae on the Gospels, which were roughly contemporaneous with Hugh's.[5]

This chapter will explore Hugh's interpretation of the transfiguration as found in the commentaries on each of the synoptic gospels. As mentioned in the last chapter, since each biblical commentary contains a wealth of interpretive insight, not all of which can be neatly categorized, the focus will be on Christ's appearance, the witnesses of His glory, and any noteworthy spiritual interpretations of the transfiguration.

Postilla super Matthaeum

In the commentary on the Gospel of Matthew, the *Postilla super Matthaeum,* Hugh and his colleagues (who henceforth will be referred to collectively as "Hugh") deliver an insightful treatment of Christ's transfiguration by drawing on the work of earlier exegetes and by linking the transfiguration narrative to a number of biblical passages, some of which are quite surprising. The exegesis demonstrates a strong reliance not only on the early twelfth-century *Glossa ordinaria* but also on later authors such as Zachary of Besançon and Richard of St. Victor.[6]

Although Hugh manifests a number of interests in his commentary on the transfiguration narrative, he focuses far more on Matthew 17:2 ("And he was transfigured before them, and His face shone like the sun, and His garments became white as light") than on any other verse. He begins the commentary on this verse by situating the transfiguration within the context of Christ's love and its broader Trinitarian implications. Hugh's lone gloss on Christ's transfiguration in front

---

115–22 (Paris: Beauchesne, 1984); C. Jerman, "Hugh of Saint-Cher," *Dominicana* 44 (1959): 338–47. For more on Hugh's Matthew commentary in particular, following largely Smalley's research, see Kevin Madigan, *Olivi and the Interpretation of Matthew in the High Middle Ages* (Notre Dame, Ind.: University of Notre Dame Press, 2003), 22–28.

5. See Smalley, *The Gospels in the Schools: c. 1100–c. 1280,* 144–-69. For more information oin Hugh's life and works, see Rainer Berndt, "Hugo von St. Cher," LThK: 310–11; and M. Gerwing, "Hugo von St. Cher," LexMA: 176–77.

6. See Paul F. Stuehrenberg, "The Medieval Commentary Tradition: The Glossa Ordinaria, Hugh of St. Cher and Nicholas of Lyra and the Study of the Bible in the Middle Ages," *Journal of Religious and Theological Information* 1 (1993): 91–101.

of His disciples is from the second half of John 14:21, and Hugh uses it to emphasize the presence of the disciples, not Christ's transfiguration. Hugh had already indicated that Jesus had taken Peter, James, and John on account of their "preeminence."[7] The passage taken from John, "He who loves me will be loved by my Father. . . . I will manifest myself to him," shows that Christ's transfiguration is an event that testifies to the love that the three disciples have for Christ and to the love that the Father has for them. This unique manifestation of Jesus is characterized by His shining face, which, following a long tradition, Hugh interprets as a mark of Christ's divinity. It is this face, namely Christ's divinity, which Moses could not see on Mount Sinai; however, Moses does see His back, that is, His humanity, on the mountain of transfiguration.[8] Hugh interprets the characterization of Jesus' face shining like the sun as evidence of the limited nature of the theophany. The gloss accompanying that part of the verse is from John Chrysostom's *Homily 56*, where, representing a recurring theme in the Eastern tradition, Chrysostom asserts that Jesus revealed only as much glory as the disciples could bear to see.

Hugh next proceeds to comment on the last part of Matthew 17:2, "and His garments became white as snow." It is particularly noteworthy that Hugh writes more than one-quarter of the commentary on the entire transfiguration narrative just on this brief clause. Hugh is interested primarily in how the transfiguration relates to Christ's humanity. His opening comments, which offer an allegory of the story of Jacob and Esau, seem irrelevant at first glance to the transfiguration story. Hugh says that "the garments by which Jacob was covered when he was blessed by his father are Christ's humanity. And just as the splendor of the sun exceeds the splendor of the snow infinitely, so too does the splendor of His divine nature exceed the splendor of His humanity."[9] It may be difficult to see how Jacob's garments relate to Christ's transfiguration, but Hugh's subsequent commentary implies

7. "praeeminentiam," *Postilla super Matthaeum*, in *Opera omnia in universum Vetus et Novum Testamentum*, 8tt. (Lyons, 1645), t. 6, fol. 59ra.

8. *Postilla super Matthaeum*, fol. 59rb.

9. "Vestimenta, humanitas Christi quibus indutus Iacob benedicitur a patre. Et sicut solis splendor in infinitum splendorem nivis excedit, ita splendor deitatis splendorem humanitatis," *Postilla super Matthaeum*, fol. 59rb.

that Jacob's garments represent the members of the Church, Christ's body, and it is their sweet smell, which elicits the Father's blessing. Isaac's blessing, which occurs only after Jacob has transformed himself by putting on goat skins, is a foreshadowing of the Father's blessing of His Son, which occurs only after the Son is transfigured. The transfiguration is not only of His proper body, but also of His entire mystical body.

Although Christ's transfiguration held explicitly ecclesiological connotations dating back to the Early Church, especially in the works of Augustine and Gregory the Great, Hugh's commentary signifies an important development in both terminology and emphasis. After citing a gloss from Zachary of Besançon, which Hugh erroneously attributes to Bernard of Clairvaux, Hugh encourages his readers to "note, however, that in this transfiguration is signified the transfiguration of the mystical body."[10] Hugh is the first theologian to describe the transfiguration's effect on the Church using the increasingly popular language of the "mystical body" of Christ, which became current in the late twelfth and early thirteenth centuries. Indeed, he is the only theologian in this study to use the phrase "transfiguratio corporis mystici."

In the transfiguration of the mystical body, there are two affected parts. They are not "Head" and "members," to use the traditional vocabulary, but rather the "face" and "garments." Although this language certainly follows the biblical narrative, Hugh's characterization of these two elements is interesting. The face of the body corresponds to the clerics, "because, just as a human is recognized by his face, so too ought Christ to be recognized in His clerics."[11]

Hugh goes on to juxtapose two verses, one from the Old Testament and one from the New Testament. The first verse is Leviticus 21:17, "Whoever should have a blemish may not offer bread to his God"; the verse indicates God's desire that His priests, for reasons of ritual purity,[12] have a certain physical integrity. Such integrity is necessary be-

10. "Nota autem, quod in hac transfiguratione significatur transfiguratio corporis mystici," *Postilla super Matthaeum*, fol. 59rb.

11. "quia sicut per faciem cognòscitur homo, sic per clericos debet cognosci Christus," *Postilla super Matthaeum*, fol. 59rb.

12. See Lv 21:23.

cause, as Hugh says, "in no part of the body is a blemish so unbecoming as in the face."[13] The face of the mystical body, which the clerics constitute, must undergo a transformation or transfiguration so as to be configured to the Head of the body. Hugh cites Revelation 1:16 to show how the clerics should be transfigured. In the opening chapter of Revelation, John sees "one like the Son of Man" whose face was like the sun "shining in its power," which Hugh interprets to mean "at midday, when it is warm and bright. Thus [the clerics] ought to shine with knowledge and burn with love."[14]

Once he has established the clerics as the face of the mystical body, Hugh comments on the garments of the mystical body, the laity. Hugh first associates the laity with the builders of Zion, mentioned in Isaiah 49:17–18. In that passage, God says to Zion that He will clothe her with all those who have gathered and come to her "as with an ornament."[15] The Lord forms a garment from the laity, who "ought to be sewn together by the unity of faith and charity."[16] Like Christ's garments on the mountain, the garment that is the laity has its own character apart from the face: "It is sufficient for this tunic to be white and clean in itself, but it is not sufficient for the face, which, on the contrary, should illuminate others as does the sun."[17] The laity preserves its whiteness, cleanliness, and unity by not separating itself or anyone else from the garment, and by imitating Christ.[18] It is the imitation of Christ that allows the garment to fit Christ perfectly.

As Hugh reflects on Isaiah 13:10, "the sun will be dark at its rising," he notes that the sun can be eclipsed at times. When this happens the garments do not share in the light of the sun, and they "appear discolored."[19] This changed appearance occurs in those people who can-

13. "in nulla parte corporis ita indecens est macula, sicut in facie," *Postilla super Matthaeum*, fol. 59rb.

14. "in meridie quando calet et lucet. Sic debent lucere per scientiam, ardere per amorem," *Postilla super Matthaeum*, fol. 59rb.

15. Is 49:18.

16. "debent consui unitate fidei et charitatis," *Postilla super Matthaeum*, fol. 59rb.

17. "Sufficit huic tunicae quod fit alba in se, et munda, sed hoc non sufficit facie, imo oportet, ut alios illuminet, sicut sol," *Postilla super Matthaeum*, fol. 59rb.

18. See *Postilla super Matthaeum*, fol. 59rb.

19. "discolorata apparent," *Postilla super Matthaeum*, fol. 59rb.

not be transfigured. The inability to be transfigured is not absolute but results from sinful transformations. Hugh differentiates among three types of people: those who change themselves (such as those who have adorned themselves for adultery),[20] those who disfigure themselves (such as the hypocrites who contort their faces while they are fasting),[21] and those who transfigure themselves from one form into another (such as those who boast about themselves). Hugh's discussion illustrates that transfiguration is not intrinsically good unless it is patterned after Christ's transfiguration.

These reflections on how sin can obscure one's capacity to be transfigured act as a transition from the ecclesiological allegory of the face and garments to a more spiritual allegory. Here Hugh uses the number six, representing both the number of days between Jesus' prophecy and the transfiguration and the number of people present at the transfiguration, to describe the transfiguration of the human soul. Hugh then deepens the allegorical symbolism by relating the six days mentioned in the Gospels of Matthew and Mark and the six people present at the transfiguration with the six days of creation.[22] These interwoven symbols describe the transfiguration of the entire person.

On the first day light was made, which signifies the knowledge by which man knows himself; Psalm 81 says "they have not known nor understood, they walk in darkness." To this work corresponds Peter, who is interpreted as "knowing." On the second day the firmament was made, and the waters were divided from one another. This happens when man separates his heart from the delights of the flesh. The firmament represents the heart which ought to be firm. The waters under the firmament represent the delights of the flesh, while the waters above the firmament represent spiritual delights. To this corresponds James, who is called "wrestler," for we need to accomplish this through great struggles. On the third day, the earth brought forth the green herb yielding seed. This represents the good works with which man adorns himself after attaining knowledge of himself and restraining himself

20. Hugh cites Is 57:9 as a reference.

21. Hugh cites Mt 6:16 as a reference.

22. In the *Postilla super Marcum,* Hugh ascribes this connection between creation and transfiguration to John Chrysostom, but I have not been able to locate the text to which he refers (see *Postilla super Marcum* on Mk 9:2, in *Opera omnia in universum Vetus et Novum Testamentum,* t. 6, fol. 103vb).

from the delights of the flesh. John corresponds to this. For just as the earth is not able to produce without seed, neither can the heart produce without grace. On the fourth day lights were made to rule the day and the night. This is because the human heart is illuminated by wisdom concerning what is divine, which is designated by the sun, and by knowledge of earthly matters, which is designated by the moon and the stars. For, after man knows himself, separates himself from delights, and performs good works, he is given these two gifts. Hence Isaiah 28, "To whom will the Lord teach knowledge, and to whom will he explain what is heard? Those who are weaned from the milk, those who are torn away from the breast." Elijah corresponds to this. Ecclesiasticus 48 says, "Elijah the Prophet arose like a fire," insofar as he kindled a knowledge of what is divine, illuminated, and rose to superior things; "His word burned like a torch," insofar as he imparted knowledge of inferior things. On the fifth day fishes and birds were made from the water, because by the reasoning knowledge mentioned above, man disdains temporal things and desires eternal things. A bird never descends to earth except out of necessity. To this work corresponds Moses, who was taken from the waters. On the sixth day man was made in the image and likeness of God. In this is shown that everything which preceded ought to take place according to reason, for in this man is like God, who made all things according to number, weight, and measure. Jesus corresponds to this, because there is equality in the Son, as Hilary and Augustine say. If anyone should have those six things, he will be thoroughly transfigured, and his face will be like the sun. The inner part of a person is represented by the face, for if someone's face is ugly, all of him is ugly, since he is known by his face. Psalm 44 says, "All the glory of the king's daughter . . . ," And His garments, that is, His body, were white, like snow; Ecclesiastes 9 says, "Let your garments be white at all times." Garments are works which provide warmth and cover and embellish nakedness, as clothes are wont to do. Clothes, moreover, should not be exceedingly long in winter, lest they become dirty; so too our works ought not be lengthened in order to be seen.[23]

23. "Prima dies lux facta est, quae significat cognitionem ut homo cognoscat se, *Psalm.* 81. Nescierunt neque intellexerunt, in tenebris ambulant. Huic operationi adaptatur Petrus, qui agnoscens interpretatur. In secunda die factum est firmamentum, et divisae sunt aquae ab aquis. Hoc fit quando homo separat cor suum a deliciis carnis. Per firmamentum cor quod debet esse firmum. Per aquas quae sub firmamento, deliciae carnis. Per aquas quae sub firmamento, spirituales deliciae intelliguntur. Huic Iacobus respondet, qui luctator dicitur: ad hoc enim faciendum magna lucta indigemus. Tertia die protulit terra herbam virentem facientem semen. Haec est bona operatio, ad quam homo post cognitionem sui et delectationum carnalium refrenationem se accingit. Huic respondet Ioannes. Sicut enim terra sine semine fructi-

This remarkable passage describes the transfiguration of the whole person. The first three stages of the ascent to transfiguration concern the person considered in himself, apart from his relationship with God or with other creatures. There is a movement from self-knowledge to the role of the will in curbing desire for sensual pleasures, and from there the movement culminates in good works. The second three stages depict a more explicit movement from the individual to God. The fourth stage, like the first, concerns the intellect. Here self-knowledge gives way to knowledge of earthly matters and wisdom pertaining to what is divine. The fifth stage, like the second, concerns the will. The curbing of desire for sensual pleasures liberates the will so that, freed from those desires and all those that pertain to this life, it can firmly desire what is eternal. The final stage in the ascent is transfiguration. It is not just the intellect and the will that are transformed, but the body as well, especially the face. Although only the face shines like the sun, the transfiguration of the whole person is reflected in the garments, or good works.

The transfiguration of the human person, however, is not solely an individual phenomenon. It begins with Christ and emanates through

---

ficare non potest, sic nec cor sine gratia. Quarta die facta sunt luminaria, ut praesint diei, et nocti. Hoc est quod cor humanum illustratur sapientia de divinis quae per solem designatur, et scientia de terrenis quae per Lunam, et stellas. Postquam enim homo seipsum cognovit, et a delectationibus se separavit, et in bonis operibus execitatus est, cum his duobus donis ordinatur. Unde *Isa* 28.c. Quem docebit Dominus scientiam et quem intelligere faciet auditum? Ablactores a lacte, avulsos ab uberibus. Huic respondet Elias, *Eccles.* 48.a. Surrexit Elias Propheta quasi ignis, hoc quantum ad cognitionem de divinis quae inflammat, et illuminat, et trahit ad superiora, verbum ipsius quasi facula ardebat, quantum ad scientiam de inferioribus: Quinta die fiunt pisces et aves de aqua, quia habita cognitione praedicta homo fastidit temporalia et desiderat aeterna. Avis nunquam descendit ad terram nisi propter necessitatem. Huic operationi respondet Moyses, qui sumptus ab aquis, sexta die homo factus est ad imaginem et similitudinem Dei. In hoc significatur quod omnia praecedentia secundum rationem debent fieri. In hoc enim homo est similis Deo, qui omnia fecit in numero, pondere, et mensura. Huic respondet Iesus, quia in filio aequalitas, ut dicit *Hilarius* et *August.* Si homo habeat illa sex, recte transfiguratur, et facies eius erit sicut sol. Per faciem homo interior: Si enim facies hominis turpis, et ipse totus turpis: Per faciem enim cognoscitur homo. *Psal.* 44. Omnis gloria eius filiae regis. Et vestimenta eius erunt candida, sicut nix, id est, corpus. *Ecclesiast.* 9.b. Omni tempore vestimenta tua sint candida. Vel vestimenta sunt opera quae calefaciunt, turpitudinem tegunt et ornant, sicut vestes. Praeterea vestes non debent multum elongari in hyeme, ne lutum contrahant, sic opera nostra non debent elongari, ut videantur," *Postilla super Matthaeum*, fols. 59rb–59va.

His apostles. Hugh interprets Jesus' warning to His disciples not to tell anyone about the transfiguration, "until the Son of man is raised from the dead," to mean that they should not proclaim the transfiguration until they themselves are transfigured. The preaching of the transfiguration follows Christ's resurrection because it is that event that effects the disciples' own transfiguration. Just as Jesus rises from the dead, so too "the preacher must rise from the dead, so that there is something new both in one's soul and in one's outward behavior."[24] Hugh goes on to say that this personal transformation is "a perfect transfiguration, so that the face of the mind may be radiant to God and the garments to one's neighbor."[25] It is this transfiguration of the disciples that allows their preaching of the transfiguration to be efficacious. Personal transfiguration must precede the preaching of Christ's transfiguration so that the disciples "manifest in themselves visually what they preach to their listeners."[26] Christ's transfiguration, then, affects Peter, James, and John immediately, but it effects a fuller personal transfiguration only after the resurrection. Their own preaching of the transfiguration then is efficacious in such a way that it transfigures others. In this way, all personal transfiguration, no matter how isolated it may appear, leads back to Christ's transfiguration through the preaching of His apostles.

In this commentary, Hugh gives the three apostolic witnesses a significant function, but what about the witnesses from the Old Testament, Moses and Elijah? How does their presence shed light on Christ's transfiguration? Although Moses and Elijah make only a brief, symbolic appearance in Hugh's description of the personal ascent to transfiguration, Hugh ascribes more significant roles to them, as well. With Jesus, they comprise a triumvirate of representative figures. Together with Jesus, they symbolize the Gospel, the Law, and the Prophets; and their number corresponds with the three tabernacles, which Peter of-

24. "praedicator debet resurgere a mortuis, ut nouus sit in anima, et exteriori conversatione," *Postilla super Matthaeum*, fol. 59vb.

25. "Haec est perfecta transfiguratio, ut splendeat facies mentis Deo, et vestimenta proximo," *Postilla super Matthaeum*, fol. 59vb.

26. "ostendunt in se ad videndum, quod praedicant auditoribus," *Postilla super Matthaeum*, fol. 59vb.

fers to build, and with the three Persons of the Trinity. The symbolic correspondence of parts of Scripture, tabernacles, and the Trinitarian Persons may seem obscure, but Hugh's citation of a quotation ascribed to Bernard of Clairvaux proves helpful here. This text, which actually comes from Bede's *Commentary on Luke* and is reproduced in Zachary of Besançon's *In unum ex quatuor,* states that no one should separate the Law, Prophets, and Gospel, since "they by no means flourish when they are separated from one another."[27] Just as the Trinitarian Persons are inseparable, so are the Law, Prophets, and Gospel; and their nexus, their own point of inseparability, as suggested not by Hugh's abridged citation of the text but by the original passage in Bede, occurs within the one tabernacle, the Church.[28]

The analogy of the parts of Scripture to the Persons of the Trinity, another spiritual interpretation, is a powerful image of unity, but Hugh never loses sight of who actually gives Scripture its unity. The presence of Moses and Elijah bears witness to the unity of salvation history, which Christ achieved through his life and work. The living Elijah, who comes down from heaven, and the dead Moses, who appears "by a certain ineffable power known only to God,"[29] talk with Jesus about His "departure" or "exodus."[30] The fact that the prophet is living and the lawgiver is dead point to the full reality of Christ's *excessus,* which encompasses both death and victorious resurrection.[31]

After Christ's resurrection, the full import of Moses' and Elijah's

27. "haec nequaquam valeant ab invicem separari," *Postilla super Matthaeum,* fol. 59va.

28. Hugh's citation of this text also fails to convey the sense of foolishness the original text imputes to those who would separate these three parts of Scripture. See Bede, *In Lucae evangelium expositio,* PL 92, 455; and Zachary of Besançon, *In unum ex quatuor,* PL 186, 292.

29. "quadam ineffabili virtute soli Deo cognita," *Postilla super Matthaeum,* fol. 59va. The text ascribes this kind of mysterious appearance to Elijah, but this could be an editor's mistake. In the *postillae* on all three synoptic gospels, Moses is dead and Elijah is living. Hugh found this interpretation of Moses' appearance in the third book of John Scotus Eriugena's *Periphyseon* (see *Periphyseon III,* edited by E. A. Jeauneau, CCCM 163, 62). This interpretation, cast in more philosophical language, is given by John of La Rochelle in the *Summa fratris Alexandri*'s interpretation of Moses' appearance (see below, pp. 111–14). Beryl Smalley noted the presence of this gloss in Hugh's Luke commentary, but did not point out the difference between the wording of the gloss and the original (see *The Gospels in the Schools: c. 1100–c. 1280,* 130).

30. The Vulgate text of Luke 9:31 has "excessum."

31. See *Postilla super Matthaeum,* fol. 59va.

testimony becomes apparent. Hugh finds Luke 24:44–45, which contains the words of the resurrected Jesus, to be important in this context. Although Hugh cites only a short clause, the full passage helps to explain Hugh's exegesis of the transfiguration:

> Then he said to them, "These words are my words which I spoke to you, while I was still with you, that everything written about me in the law of Moses and the prophets and the psalms must be fulfilled." Then he opened their minds to understand the Scriptures, and said to them, "Thus it is written, that the Christ should suffer and on the third day rise from the dead, and that repentance and forgiveness of sins should be preached in his name to all nations beginning from Jerusalem."

Jesus' unveiling of the disciples' eyes and opening the Scriptures to them after the resurrection is anticipated symbolically in the transfiguration. The disappearance of the bright cloud and of Moses and Elijah signifies the removal of the shadow of the Law and Prophets. After the cloud disappears, the only person the disciples see is Jesus. The Law and Prophets, the testimony of the Old Testament, covered the eyes of the disciples (whose Jewish identity Hugh acknowledges). It is the light of the Gospel, which remains and disperses the shadows of the Law and Prophets.

This emphasis on the disunity between the Old and New Testament stands alongside of Hugh's previous description of their unity, or, to be more precise, of the unity of the Law, Prophets, and Gospel. These parts of Scripture were, in another gloss, as inseparable as the Persons of the Trinity, and in this interpretation, the Law and Prophets are shadowy prefigurations. In both cases, Moses and Elijah, in their presence and in their absence, point to Christ. In order for the transfiguration to be intelligible to Christ's disciples, Moses and Elijah must disappear so that the testimony from the cloud, the voice of the Father, clearly refers to Christ.[32]

Only then can the Father's words, "This is my beloved Son, with whom I am well pleased; listen to him,"[33] convey their full meaning. Hugh appropriates Genesis 6:6, "And the Lord was sorry that he had

32. See *Postilla super Matthaeum*, fol. 59vb.
33. Mt 17:5. See also Mk 9:7 and Lk 9:35.

made man on the earth, and it grieved him to his heart," and Moses' words in Deuteronomy 18:15, "The Lord your God will raise up for you a prophet like me from among you, from your brethren—him you shall heed," to interpret the Father's testimony. The Father's happiness with His "beloved Son" contrasts with His regret about the creation of the human race.[34] He fulfills both His plan of salvation and the prophecy of Moses, which suggested how it might be accomplished, by sending His Son as a prophet.

Beyond this meaning, however, the Father's words show the profound unity of the Trinitarian Persons. Hugh draws from a rich interpretation, which he ascribes to a certain Gilbert,[35] but which is actually from Richard of St. Victor's *Beniamin minor.* This exegesis is based on a literal interpretation of the Vulgate text of the Father's testimony at Jesus' baptism and at His transfiguration. Richard interprets "Hic est filius meus dilectus in quo mihi bene complacui," as "This is my beloved Son in whom I have been very pleasing to myself." The passage Hugh cites concludes, "Certainly if the Son was other than the Father, the Father could not be pleasing to Himself in the Son. What does it mean to say, 'I am pleasing to myself,' except 'Just as I am pleasing to myself in myself, so I am pleasing in the Son.'"[36] Although this exegesis may sound odd, it is at least partially inspired by another passage, which contains the words "dilectus," "meus," and the dative "mihi," namely Song of Songs 2:16: "Dilectus meus mihi, et ego illi . . . ." This passage conveys a sense not only of the difference between the lover and the beloved, but also of their union, whose description using the dative "mihi" and "illi" suggests a movement, or at least an orientation of the two toward each other.

Using this passage in the Song of Songs as a lens through which to read the Father's testimony, Hugh's interpretation becomes clearer. For

34. Hugh articulates the Adam-Christ typology to fit better with the Father's testimony: "E converso Adam sibi displicuit," *Postilla super Matthaeum,* fol. 59vb.

35. Beryl Smalley allows for the thesis, advanced by N. Häring, that this gloss may come from Gilbert of La Porrée, but she also points to a possible Cistercian influence (see *The Gospels in the Schools: c. 1100–c. 1280,* 131–32).

36. "Certe si filius aliud esset, quam pater non posset pater in filio sibi complacere. Quid est dicere, complacui mihi, nisi sicut placui mihi in meipso, ita placui in filio," *Postilla super Matthaeum,* fol. 59va.

the Father to be pleasing to Himself "in" the Son suggests their complete union and inseparability. Although Richard suggests a number of other readings of the Father's testimony, Hugh's primary interest in his appropriation of "Gilbert" is to follow Richard's interpretation that the passage expresses "an identity of essence and the diversity of Persons."[37] Hugh's own interpretation broadens this conclusion beyond Richard's suggestion. Richard's exegesis focuses on the Father and the Son, but Hugh extends it to include the Holy Spirit as well: "Just as the Father is pleasing to Himself in the Son, so too is He pleasing to the Holy Spirit in the Son."[38]

The voice of the Father then is both loving and overpowering. Indeed it is overpowering in its love. The end of Chapter 82 of *Beniamin minor,* which Hugh does not cite but probably had in mind, describes how the voice, which utters the mystery of the Trinity, overpowers both sense and reason, and the hearers of the voice must fall down, as did the disciples. Although the incomprehensibility remains, Jesus removes the fear and allows the disciples to approach the Father. Hugh's sole gloss on Jesus' coming to the disciples is simply John 14:6, "No one comes to the Father, but by me." The approach of the Son allows the disciples to approach the Father, whose voice Hugh descries in the Song of Songs, "let your voice sound in my ears, for your voice is sweet, and your face beautiful" [2:14]. Hugh cites this verse immediately after he refers to the voice as "the voice of grace, knocking and speaking in the heart."[39] The Father's voice causes the disciples to fall down, but by testifying to the *consolatio,* which Jesus offers and which Jesus Himself is, the voice also gives Jesus' disciples the grace to approach the Father through the Son they adore.[40]

37. "identitas essentiae, et diversitas personarum," *Postilla super Matthaeum,* fol. 59vb. Richard's text seems to express the unity of the mystery more profoundly: "unitatem substantiae in diuersis personis," *Les douze patriarches ou Beniamin minor,* edited and translated by J. Châtillon and M. Duchet-Suchaux with an introduction by J. Longère, SC 419, 328.

38. "quomodo complacet patri in filio, sic in filio complacet spiritui sancto," *Postilla super Matthaeum,* fol. 59vb.

39. "vox gratiae pulsantis, et loquentis in corde," *Postilla super Matthaeum,* fol. 59va.

40. See Hugh's comments on Mt 17:7.

Postilla super Marcum

In the *Postilla super Marcum,* Hugh returns to the theme of the six days. Whereas in the *Postilla super Matthaeum* Hugh linked Christ's transfiguration to creation and personal transfiguration within the context of His garments, interpreted either as the Church or as the laity, in the *Postilla super Marcum* Hugh addresses the theme of the six days when commenting on the first verse of Mark's transfiguration narrative, "And after six days Jesus took with Him Peter and James and John . . . ." Hugh ascribes the first gloss on this text to John Chrysostom, whose description of a spiritual ascent is similar to the interpretation Hugh offered in the *Postilla super Matthaeum.* In that passage there were six stages: self-knowledge, a curbed desire for sensual pleasures, good works, knowledge of earthly matters and wisdom pertaining to what is divine, firm desire of what is eternal, and finally, complete transfiguration. In this passage, there are seven stages and an explicit link both to the six days of creation and to the Sabbath rest. The first stage is self-knowledge, but the remaining six stages differ from Hugh's interpretation in the *Postilla super Matthaeum.* The remaining stages are attrition, reflection on one's state in life, confession, satisfaction, and contemplation.[41] The passage ends simply, "The Lord indeed will rest on the seventh [day]."[42] Unlike the first ascent Hugh describes, which possesses a sapiential orientation, this ascent, while beginning like the first, leads to a sacramental dimension that prepares the soul for contemplation.

Hugh's subsequent addition of a passage from Richard of St. Victor, interspersed with comments not found in the Victorine's text, deepen the symbolic significance of the six days and the Sabbath rest. Although Richard links Christ's transfiguration with contemplation in a number of passages throughout both the *Beniamin minor* and the *Beniamin maior,* Hugh transforms Richard to make this connection more profound.

The six days are six kinds of contemplation, on the seventh of which, the Lord is seen transfigured. The first is in the imagination according to the

41. See *Postilla super Marcum,* fol. 103vb.
42. "Dominus vero in septimo requiescet," *Postilla super Marcum,* fol. 103vb.

image, when, namely, the image of visible things is considered with wonder and veneration of the Creator. The second is in the imagination according to reason, when, namely, the mind, having perceived reason in the imagination, seeks and finds with the imagination. The third is in reason according to imagination, when, namely, the mind is raised to the speculation of invisible things through the likeness of visible things. The fourth is in reason according to reason, when, namely, the mind in visible things gathers some things through the experience of language and other invisible things which it does not know through experience. The fifth is above reason but not beyond reason, when the soul is raised through the elevation of the mind, because it transcends the limits of its capacity and because reason, by the power of the intellect, alludes to it by its testimony. The sixth is above reason and beyond reason or even against reason. In this the soul truly rejoices and dances when it recognizes by the illumination of a divine gift those sublime things against which all human reason protests. Such are all those things which we are commanded to believe concerning the persons of the Trinity. In this kind [of contemplation] Jesus is transfigured on the mountain, but with the testimony of Moses and Elijah, that is, of the Scriptures, without which revelation of this sort would be suspicious. Here the hearer falls at the thunder of the divine voice, that is, human reason falters. The failure of sense, memory, and reason is shown through the fall of the three disciples. There Rachel dies in the birth of Benjamin (Genesis 35). Rachel is "vision," that is, reason seeing; Benjamin is "the son of the right hand." The seventh step of contemplation is when the Son is seen at the right hand of the Father. With the Lord speaking, a bright cloud overshadowed [them]—a "cloud" on account of the mind being driven back and "bright" on account of the illumination of the intellect.[43]

43. "Sex dies sunt sex genera contemplationum, in quorum septimo videtur Dominus transfiguratus. Primus est in imaginatione secundum imaginem, quando, scilicet, visibilium imago consideratur cum admiratione et creatoris veneratione. Secundus est in imaginatione secundum rationem, quando, scilicet, mens imaginatione sensus rationem quaerit et cum imaginatione invenit. Tertius est in ratione secundum imaginationem, quando, scilicet, mens per rerum visibilium similitudinem, in rerum invisibilium speculationem sublevatur. Quartus est in ratione secundum rationem, quando, scilicet, mens in visibilibus per experientiam vocis alia et alia invisibilia colligit quae per experientiam non novit. Quintus est supra rationem, non tamen praeter rationem, quando animus per mentis sublevationem ita sublevatur, quod metas capacitatis transcendit, et quod per intelligentiae aciem ratio ei sua attestatione alludit. Sextus est supra rationem et praeter rationem seu etiam contra rationem, in hoc animus veraciter exultat atque tripudiat, quando illa sublimia ex divini muneris irradiatione agnoscit, quibus omnis humana ratio reclamat. Talia sunt omnia quae de personarum Trinitate credere iubemur. In hoc genere transfiguratur Iesus in monte, sed cum attestatione Moysi et Eliae, id

Although Richard does indeed appropriate the transfiguration narrative to describe the movement from reason to contemplation, Hugh's citation of Richard is not from any one text, but rather from at least two different passages from Richard and perhaps one from Pseudo-Anselm (of Canterbury).[44] The beginning of the passage that Hugh cites is obviously from *Beniamin maior* I, 6, but Hugh or an unknown source he is following adds the reference to the "six days" and to Christ's transfiguration. The description of the six kinds of contemplation, as described in the abridged text supplied by Hugh is somewhat difficult to follow, since he omits much of Richard's text and adds a few of his own comments.[45] He then emphasizes the relation of contemplation to the transfiguration by drawing from *Beniamin minor* 74 and 82, both of which describe the death of Rachel in giving birth to Benjamin as the transition from sense, memory, and reason to ecstatic contemplation.

The seventh step of contemplation, which corresponds to the seventh day of creation—the day on which God rested—and the transfiguration are completely absent from these passages. The only text from Richard that implies these connections is *Beniamin maior* IV, 22, which describes Moses' entrance into the cloud on Mount Sinai (see Exodus 24).[46] Hugh either based the creation-contemplation-

est, Scriptuarum, sine quibus suspecta esset huiusmodi revelatio. Hic ad tonitruum divinae vocis auditor cadit, id est, humana ratio deficit. Et per casum trium discipulorum, sensus memoriae, rationis defectus ostenditur. Ibi moritur Rachel in partu Beniamin. *Gen*.35.c. Rachel visio, id est, ratio videns: Beniamin, filius dexterae. Septimus gradus contemplationis, cum filius ad dexteram patris videtur, Domino loquente, nubes lucida obumbrat, sed nubes propter mentis reverberationem, lucida propter intelligentiae illustrationem," *Postilla super Marcum*, fols. 103vb–104ra.

44. In a sermon on the transfiguration, Pseudo-Anselm's description of the sun dazzling the eyes may have suggested to Hugh the image of the bright and impenetrable cloud thwarting the gaze of the mind, since their respective passages use "reverberatio" and "reverberationem" (see *Homilia IV*, PL 158, 608).

45. Compare Hugh's text to Richard's (*Benjamin major*, PL 196, 70–72).

46. "Ejusmodi vero montem nubes tunc tegit, quando exteriorum omnium memoria menti excidit. In hoc monte Moyses sex diebus moratur, et in septimo de medio nubis ad Domini colloquium vocatur. Sex diebus, ut notum est, opera nostra peragimus, et in septimo requiescimus. Quasi sex ergo dies transigimus in hoc monte, quando cum multo labore, magnaque animi industria in ejusmodi sublimitatis statu assuescimus diutius permanere. Tunc autem quasi ad septimum diem venitur, quando tanta mentis sublevatio, menti in oblectamentum vertitur, et sine ullo labore subitur. Quasi ad septimum jam diem pertingitur, quan-

transfiguration trichotomy on this passage (and other hints in Richard such as *Beniamin maior* I, 5 and V, 2) or drew from an unknown source. In either case, Hugh transformed Richard's theology to make the connection between spiritual transformation and Christ's transfiguration more explicit than would have been the case if Richard's text stood alone.

Although Hugh wrote much on the theme of personal or mental transfiguration, both in the *Postilla super Mathaeum* and, as we have just seen, in the *Postilla super Marcum,* as well, until this point Hugh had written almost nothing on Christ's transfiguration considered in itself, apart from its effects on the members of His body. In the *Postilla super Marcum,* Hugh examines for the first time Christ's transfiguration itself. The comments, glosses, and opinions that Hugh compiles in this text are rather brief, but are expanded upon significantly in the *Postilla super Lucam.* This passage is significant also because several comments, closely woven together, will serve as key texts for other authors in their disputed questions and synthetic works.[47]

The first important set of comments relates to Christ's clarity.[48] Here Hugh mentions four opinions about how clarity inhered in Christ's pre-glorified body. He first asserts that "someone wanted to say that the Lord had all the gifts *(dotes)* from the beginning."[49] Hugh never disclos-

do in illo sublimitatis statu, tandem aliquando, ad summam animus tranquillitatem componitur, ut non solum omnem curam et sollicitudinem deponat, imo universas pene humanae passibilitatis metas excedat. Ad colloquium Domini, Domino vocante, admittitur, quando ex divina inspiratione et revelatione," (*Benjamin major,* PL 196, 165).

47. Here arises the question of the chronological priority of Hugh's and Alexander of Hales' respective Mark commentaries and Alexander's *De transfiguratione Christi.* The only pertinent observation that can be made here is that the *De transfiguratione Christi* contains a very high proportion of passages from the *Glossa ordinaria,* starting a trend that continues through Guerric and John of La Rochelle in the *Summa fratris Alexandri.* The mode and nature of citing authoritative texts changes somewhat with the *Summa fratris Alexandri,* which cites authoritative texts in different ways, including the quotations of longer passages not found in the *Glossa ordinaria.*

48. For the purposes of this study *claritas* will be translated as "clarity." Although more descriptive words such as "splendor," "brilliance," or "radiance" might be better in many instances, those words fail to convey the notion that ultimately *claritas* is a property that can exist visibly and invisibly. The metaphysical and anthropological implications of *claritas* as a property emerge more clearly from less exegetical and more technical discussions of the transfiguration in disputed questions, *Sentences* commentaries, and *summae.*

49. "Voluit dicere quidam quod Dominus omnes dotes ab initio accepit," *Postilla super Marcum,* fol. 104ra.

es the identity of this "someone" (indeed the author of this opinion will remain nameless until Aquinas erroneously refers to him as "Hugh of St. Victor"), but the opinion is basically that of Innocent III, which posits Christ having subtlety, agility, clarity, and impassibility from the first moment of the Incarnation.

As opposed to the first opinion, which may have been advanced by only one person or had only one person as its source, judging by the singular "voluit," the other three opinions may have been more widespread. The first of these opinions is that Jesus "naturally was impassible, immortal, and radiant." The second is that the radiance of the transfiguration was only in the air surrounding Christ's body. The third posits that the radiance was actually in Christ's mortal body. Hugh never gives an explicit response to these opinions, but judging by the two glosses that he provides, he seems to prefer the last. Immediately after giving the last opinion, he cites one of Jerome's texts designated "in originali," which states that, "The transfigured Savior did not put off the substance of true flesh, nor did He assume an aerial body, but He showed to creation the glory of His true resurrection."[50] He later quotes a similar interpretation of Bede, specifically designated "in Glossa," which essentially repeats Jerome's statement, but adds that the way the transfigured Christ appeared to His disciples is how "He will appear to all the elect after the Judgment."[51] Both these glosses affirm the reality of Christ's pre-glorified human body and link the glory of the transfiguration with the eschatological events of the resurrection and Last Judgment. This effort to preserve the tension between the reality of Christ's pre-glorified humanity and the eschatological significance of Christ's glory will be important in later discussions of the transfiguration by other theologians.[52]

50. "Transfiguratus Salvator non substantiam verae carnis amisit, nec aereum corpus assumpsit, sed gloriam creaturae suae verae resurrectionis ostendit," *Postilla super Marcum*, fol. 104rb.

51. "talis post iudicium cunctis apparebit electis," *Postilla super Marcum*, fol. 104rb.

52. For more on Hugh's Christology, see Wilhelm Breuning, *Die hypostatische Union in der Theologie Wilhelms von Auxerre, Hugos von St. Cher und Rolands von Cremona* (Trier, Ger.: Paulinus Verlag, 1962), 163–215; Manuel Cuesta Leyva, *Salvacion y cruz, un capitulo de la soteriologia de Hugo de Saint-Cher* (Granada, Sp.: Facultad de Teologia, 1980); Walter H. Principe, *Hugh of St. Cher's Theology of the Hypostatic Union* (Toronto: Pontifical Institute of Mediaeval Studies, 1970).

For the most part, Hugh's glosses on the presence of the witnesses are fairly conventional. Peter, James, and John represent faith, hope, and charity, on the one hand, and married people, virgins, and Church leaders, on the other. There are, however, a couple of unique interpretations. One interpretation concerns Moses and Elijah. There is, not surprisingly, a connection to the Law and the Prophets, but Hugh also links Moses and Elijah to baptism and penance. Moses represents the baptized, Hugh says, because he was taken from the water, and Elijah represents those doing penance because of his austerity. Hugh also links the presence of Moses and Elijah to two passages in the synoptic gospels, which precede the transfiguration. The first is Jesus asking His disciples who people say that Jesus is. The disciples respond that some say Elijah, John the Baptist, or one of the prophets. In light of this response, Elijah's presence at the transfiguration shows that Jesus and Elijah are not identical. Also, Moses' presence shows that Jesus did not hold the Law in contempt as some of the Pharisees had believed. In the second passage, Jesus exhorts those who want to follow Him that they must first deny themselves and take up their crosses and then follow Him.[53] Hugh states that Moses and Elijah followed Jesus in just this way. Both Moses and Elijah renounced their possessions and risked their lives on behalf of their people, who were often ungrateful.[54]

Moses and Elijah not only testify to Christ's salvific mission, they also teach by their presence. Their appearance, for example, the one living and the other dead, teaches Jesus' disciples that He "has the power of death and life."[55] Hugh claims that Jesus uses their presence to show the disciples how to be gentle like Moses and zealous like Elijah.[56] Also, their lives of prayer are examples for the disciples, who will soon become leaders of Christ's Church.

Hugh's second interpretation examines the relationship between Christ's transfiguration and His preaching. He says that Christ taking his disciples onto a mountain is analogous to "the Lord [leading]

53. See Matthew 16:24, Mark 8:34, and Luke 9:23.

54. See *Postilla super Marcum*, fol. 104rb.

55. "mortis et vitae habet potestatem," *Postilla super Marcum*, fol. 104rb.

56. See *Postilla super Marcum*, fol. 104rb.

good preachers to the excellence of life and knowledge."[57] In offering a "moral" interpretation, Hugh asserts that "a preacher and a prelate"[58] ought to have this superior life and knowledge.

The later commentary on Mark 9:8 conveys the way in which Christ imparts this life and knowledge, "And as they came down from the mountain, He charged them not to tell anyone what they had seen, until the Son of man should be risen from the dead." It is not surprising that Hugh links ascending the mountain to contemplation, but he also links descending the mountain to preaching. What must happen to the disciples on the mountain before they can come down and preach? In the *Postilla super Matthaeum*, Hugh says that the disciples must be transfigured before they can preach about Christ's transfiguration. This personal transfiguration is founded on Christ's resurrection, the event that His transfiguration foreshadows. Hugh returns to the same theme here, but the emphasis on the resurrection in the *Postilla super Matthaeum* is somewhat muted. The personal "transfiguration" articulated in this context is not just one ascending process, but rather it requires a number of unfolding "transfiguring" processes. Here is Hugh's account of the *multiplex transfiguratio:*

There is, moreover, a multifaceted transfiguration by which the Lord's disciples ought to be transfigured before they can be ready to preach the Lord's transfiguration. The first [aspect] is in baptism, so that they may be transfigured from children of wrath into children of grace, "everything transfigured became subject to your grace which nourishes all things," (Wis 16). The second [aspect] is in confession, so that children of God may be made from children of the devil, "being conformed to His death, if by any means we may attain the resurrection from the dead," (Phil 3). The third [aspect] is in the advancement of doctrine, so that teachers may be made from the unlearned, "Follow me, and I will make you become fishers of men," (Mt 4). The fourth [aspect] is in despising the things of the world, where the burden is laid aside in order to run swiftly, "Behold, we have left everything and followed you," (Mt 19). And then, as though they were impassible, are they first ready to preach the transfiguration.[59]

57. "Dominus bonos praedicatores ducit ad excellentiam vitae et ad excellentiam scientiae," *Postilla super Marcum*, fol. 104ra.

58. "praedicator et praelatus," *Postilla super Marcum*, fol. 104ra.

59. "Est autem multiplex transfiguratio, qua debent transfigurari discipuli Domini ante-

In this account of the preacher's transfiguration, there are four transfiguring events a disciple must experience before he is able to preach Christ's transfiguration efficaciously. Hugh builds on and expands the sacramental resonance of the transfigurative ascent recounted by the gloss ascribed to Chrysostom and of the interpretation of the presence of Moses and Elijah. Thus, there is more than attrition, confession, and satisfaction, the various elements associated with the sacrament of penance. It is the sacrament of baptism that begins this transfigurative process. Next, confession continues the transfiguration but does not exhaust it. Only after advancing in doctrine and finally by turning from the world does the disciple rise from the fields to the mountaintop, only to descend again to recapitulate the process in other disciples through preaching.

This process of transfiguration is not merely cyclical, in the sense of an indeterminate process of ascending and descending, but there is a cumulative effect related to the whole mystical body. The individual members of Christ's mystical body may ascend and descend, but once the glorified Christ leads the elect to the mountaintop by His transfiguration there is a sense that the whole body rises from the fields to the mountaintop to stay. The consummation of the transfiguration will occur when all Christ's garments, His members, are radiant at the end of time.[60]

Postilla super Lucam

Hugh's *Postilla super Lucam* is quite lengthy compared to his other two commentaries on the synoptic gospels. Although the length of

---

quam sint apti praedicare Domini transfigurationem. Prima est in baptismo, ut de filiis irae transfigurentur in filios gratiae. *Sap. cap.* 16.d. Omnia transfigurata omnium nutrici gratiae tuae deserviebant. Secunda est in confessione, ut de filiis diaboli fiant filii Dei. *Philip. cap.* 3.c. Configurati morti eius, si quo modo occurramus ad resurrectionem quae est ex mortuis. Tertia est in profectu doctrinae, ut de idiotis fiant doctores. *Matth. cap.* 4. Venite post me, faciam vos fieri piscatores hominum. Quarta est in contemptu terrenorum, ubi deponitur onus ad bene currendum. *Matt. cap. decimonono,* d. Ecce nos reliquimus omnia et secuti sumus te. Et tunc primo sunt apti ad praedicandum transfigurationem Domini, quasi facti impassibiles," *Postilla super Marcum,* fol. 104va–b.

60. On Christ's garments, Hugh says, "Vestimenta Domini splendentia, sunt omnes electi glorificati, quibus in futuro quasi vestimento pulcherrimo vestietur," *Postilla super Marcum,* fol. 104rb.

the transfiguration narrative in Luke is no longer than the passages in Matthew and Mark, Hugh's commentary on Luke is about as long as the other two commentaries combined. Hugh does repeat some of the glosses he included in the previous two commentaries, but he provides a number of additional interpretations as well, including some lengthy tropological interpretations. In addition, Hugh makes greater use of anagogical or "mystical" interpretations. This section will look at a few of the exegetical motifs found in the other commentaries that Hugh has expanded upon in this work.

One problem in Luke's transfiguration narrative that challenged many earlier exegetes is its reference to "about eight days" between Jesus' promise that some would not "taste death" before seeing "the kingdom of God" and the transfiguration. Hugh provides a typical response, which goes back to Augustine, that Matthew and Mark note the six days intervening between Jesus' announcement and the transfiguration, while Luke's eight days include the day of the announcement, the day of the transfiguration, and the six days between them. Hugh also provides an allegorical interpretation without citing his sources. This interpretation, from Bede and reproduced in the *Glossa ordinaria,* argues that the "after six days" of Matthew and Mark refers to the rest from all work after the six ages of the world. Luke's reference to eight days "suggests by an eighth age the resurrection of the dead."[61]

Hugh does not abandon the significance of the number eight after he has finished commenting on the "eight days." Reminiscent of his commentary on Matthew, that motif reappears rather significantly in Hugh's commentary on the transformation of Jesus' garments. In giving a "moral" or tropological interpretation of this transformation, Hugh claims that there is a threefold transfiguration that corresponds to the three disciples whom Jesus took up the mountain and before whom He was transfigured. The three transfigurative processes build on one another in a way far more complex than any transfigurative ascent Hugh has described thus far. In the two previous commentaries, Hugh was content to find ascents of six stages, which existed parallel

61. "octava aetate innuit resurgendum," *Postilla super Lucam,* in *Opera omnia in universum Vetus et Novum Testamentum,* 8tt. (Lyons, 1645), t. 6, fol. 186va.

to one another. Here, three ascents interlock to form one long ascent of twenty-four stages.

Hugh's outline of this detailed, personal threefold transfiguration (the whole account takes up half a folio), is as follows:

> The first is doing penance, by which there occurs a passing from the state of guilt to the state of grace; this is for those who are beginning. The second is advancement in justice, by which there occurs a passing from virtue into virtue; this is for those advancing. The third is the searching of contemplation, by which there occurs a passing from the world to the cloister; this for the perfect. In the first, a beast is transfigured into a human. In the second, a boy is transfigured into an old man. In the third, a human is transfigured into an angel. Each of these transfigurations occurs after eight days.[62]

While the language Hugh uses to describe the overall transfiguration may seem hyperbolic, it serves the purpose of showing to what extent each person must undergo a transfiguration in order to transcend one's sinful human nature. In sin, humanity is, in some sense, less than human; hence, the rhetoric of changing from beast to human. Once in grace, man is "human," but he is still not at the condition to which God has called him. Only by becoming an "angel" does man transcend the limits of reason and begin to see God.

Although the first transfiguration, that of penance, has eight stages, Hugh is still able to link it with the six days of creation that is reminiscent of his previous two commentaries. The first six stages, which correspond to the days of creation, are examination of oneself, contrition of the heart, the resolution to do good, confession of the mouth, satisfaction by works, and the assistance of Providence against the tricks of the devil and lapses into evil.[63] The seventh stage is "contempt for all earthly things."[64] Once the six days are completed, so to speak, one can "rest" from what is earthly, just as "God rested from all the time which

62. "Prima est susceptio poenitentiae, per quam fit transitus de statu culpae ad statum gratiae. Haec est incipientum. Secunda est profectus iustitiae, per quam fit transitus de virtute in virtutem: Haec est proficientum. Tertio est inquisitio contemplationis, per quam fit transitus de mundo ad claustrum: Haec est perfectorum: In prima transfiguratur bestia in hominem. In secunda transfiguratur puer in senem. In tertia transfiguratur homo in angelum. Quaelibet istarum transfigurationum fit post octo dies," *Postilla super Lucam*, fol. 186va.

63. See *Postilla super Lucam*, fols. 186va–b.

64. "Contemptus omnium terrenorum," *Postilla super Lucam*, fol. 186vb.

he had brought to completion."[65] The eighth day consists of "freedom of mind, delight of the heart, and serenity of conscience."[66] Only by reaching this state can one truly be transfigured, and only at this point does one see Christ transfigured.[67]

The second kind of transfiguration that Hugh describes relates to justice. Hugh links this transfiguration in no way with creation, but rather with a text from 2 Peter, which is not mentioned in Hugh's other two commentaries. This passage is 2 Peter 1:3–8, and it contains a number of points, which relate it to Hugh's first transfiguration:

> His divine power has granted to us all things that pertain to life and godliness, through the knowledge of him who called us to his own glory and excellence, by which he has granted to us his precious and very great promises, that through these you may escape the corruption that is in the world because of passion, and become partakers in the divine nature. For this very reason make every effort to supplement your faith with virtue, and virtue with knowledge, and knowledge with self-control, and self-control with steadfastness, and steadfastness with godliness, and godliness with brotherly affection, and brotherly affection with love. For if these things are yours and abound, they keep you from being ineffective or unfruitful in the knowledge of our Lord Jesus Christ.

Unfortunately Hugh cites only a part of this passage, noting briefly that one is transfigured and sees Christ transfigured on the "eighth day," that is when one has love. It is not difficult, however, to see why Hugh was attracted to this passage. Some of its importance derives from the fact that it occurs almost immediately before 2 Peter 1:16–18, the only passage outside of the Gospels to refer to the transfiguration. The text's author mentions that Christ calls humanity "to his own glory and excellence," a phrase easily associated with the transfiguration. Also, escaping "the corruption that is in the world," correlates with other interpretations of moral transfiguration and the ascent to

65. "Dominus requievit ab omni tempore, quod patrarat," *Postilla super Lucam*, fol. 186vb.

66. "mentis securitas, cordis iocunditas, conscientiae tranquillitas," *Postilla super Lucam*, fol. 186vb.

67. *Postilla super Lucam*, fol. 186vb. Hugh also describes an interesting concomitant circumincession of spiritual qualities, which occurs at this state: "Quae se invicem complectuntur hoc modo: Secura iocunditas atque tranquillitas. Item iocunda securitas, atque tranquillitas. Item tranquilla securitas atque iocunditas," *Postilla super Lucam*, fol. 186vb.

contemplation. More importantly, however, is the exhortation to "become partakers in the divine nature," and to "supplement . . . faith with virtue." Although the first transfiguration does not mention faith, it does describe the transition from sin to grace. In order to continue the transfigurative process, one must advance in grace through virtue. Indeed virtue is the first stage of a new transfiguration that leads to love. In between the beginning and the end of this process, the believer rises through the six stages so that there are eight in total. Because the moral ascent that this passage describes has eight stages and because of its contextual relation to a description of the transfiguration, Hugh could not resist interpreting it in light of the "eight days," which is unique to the Gospel of Luke.

The third transfiguration pertains to contemplation. Hugh's account of the contemplative ascent is somewhat surprising in his use of Richard of St. Victor. As noted above,[68] Richard describes only six kinds of contemplation: in the imagination according to imagination alone, in the imagination according to reason, in reason according to imagination, in reason and according to reason, above but not beyond reason, above reason and seeming to be beyond reason.[69] In the *Postilla super Marcum,* Hugh adds a seventh kind of contemplation, one that occurs "when the Son is seen at the right hand of the Father."[70]

In the account of contemplative transfiguration in the *Postilla super Lucam,* Hugh drops this account of a seventh kind of contemplation and adds two more, at the first and at the eighth stages. Instead of Richard's "in the imagination according to imagination alone," the first stage of contemplation is now knowledge "in the senses according to imagination, which uses the world as a mirror to gain knowledge of God, as when one reflects with wonder and reverence upon the creatures of the world and observes in them the power, wisdom, and mercy of the Creator."[71] Although Richard does talk about the mind

68. See above, pp. 34–36.

69. See *Benjamin major,* PL 196, 70.

70. "filius ad dexteram patris videtur," *Postilla super Marcum,* fol. 104ra.

71. "in sensu secundum imaginationem, quae utitur mundo ad Dei cognitionem tanquam speculo, ut quando considerat creaturas mundi, et in illis speculatur potentiam, et sapientiam et clementiam creatoris cum admiratione, et veneratione," *Postilla super Lucam,* fol. 186vb.

acquiring images of corporeal objects from a "corporeal sense,"[72] contemplation for him never occurs "in the senses," but rather in the imagination, in reason, or above reason. Hugh may not seem justified in reinterpreting Richard's order, but Richard does distinguish between when "the form of these visible things and their image are brought into consideration" and when "our contemplation is engaged in imagination and is formed according to imagination alone."[73] This latter condition is met when "our mind freely wanders here and there wherever wonder takes it in these kinds of displays."[74] Hugh seems to be separating the consideration of the forms of visible objects and the first kind of contemplation in order to fit the eight-step schema he has proposed.[75]

Hugh also needs to move beyond Richard's contemplative schema to discern an eighth step. The eighth kind of knowledge is "ecstasy" or "rapture," the vision in a cloud of what is divinely revealed.[76] Interestingly, Hugh's concept of this ecstatic state is derived not from Richard's understanding of contemplation in the *Beniamin maior,* but from his articulation of the mind rising above itself in the *Beniamin minor.* When Richard describes this movement, in chapter 82 of the *Beniamin minor,* there is no reference to an eighth day or stage of contemplation. What makes this passage attractive for Hugh, however, is that when the pursuit of wisdom ends (signified by Rachel's death), ecstasy begins (signified by Benjamin's birth). The *Beniamin maior* and *Beniamin minor* do not actually disagree, but the passage from *Beniamin minor* gives a stronger sense of reason failing and the mind going outside of itself in its vision of the Trinity. The latter also contains an ongoing meditation on the transfiguration, which culminates at the point

72. "sensu corporeo," *Benjamin major,* PL 196, 70.

73. "rerum istarum visibilium forma, et imago in considerationem adducitur . . . contemplatio nostra in imaginatione versatur, et secundum solam imaginationem formatur," *Benjamin major,* PL 196, 70.

74. "libera mens nostra huc illucque discurrit, quo eam in hoc spectaculorum genere admiratio rapit," *Benjamin major,* PL 196, 70.

75. Hugh has prepared for this kind of interpretation by saying, "Octo dies tertiae transfigurationis sunt octo genera cognitionum," *Postilla super Lucam,* fol. 186vb. Distinguishing between knowledge and contemplation—something Richard does not do in the cited passage from the *Beniamin maior*—allows Hugh to interpret the forms of visible objects as a sort of preamble to actual contemplation.

76. *Postilla super Lucam,* fol. 186vb.

where reason must be abandoned, namely beholding the unity of the divine substance and the diversity of the Trinitarian Persons.

Another interpretation that receives significant elaboration and organization, when compared to his previous commentaries, is that of the witness of Moses and Elijah. In the *Postilla super Matthaeum* and the *Postilla super Marcum,* Hugh's interpretation of their presence is fairly lengthy, providing several reasons why their presence is appropriate. Hugh's exegesis emphasizes their testimony regarding Christ's divinity and the unity of Scripture, while also acknowledging their significance for Jesus' disciples. In the *Postilla super Lucam,* Hugh compiles a list of fifteen succinct reasons for Moses' and Elijah's appearance with Jesus. Although many of the reasons are also found in the other commentaries, this list expands the number and the range of the interpretations while providing an enumeration absent in his other accounts.[77]

Hugh also provides interpretations, which he specifically designates as "mystical." One good example concerns the Trinitarian theophany on the mountain. Hugh first addresses the significance of the cloud. He points out that the cloud motif, both in the Old Testa-

77. "Ecce multae rationes quare cum Domino apparuerunt Moyses, et Elias. Prima, quia pro plebe se morti exposuerunt. Secunda, quia simplices fuerunt; tertia, quia omnibus abrenunciauerunt. Quarta in testimonium, alter de caelo, alter de inferno, tertius testis fuit de terra, scilicet Apostoli. Et omnes isti venient ad iudicium, de caelo, de inferno, de mundo. *Phil.*c.2.b. Ut in nomine eius omne genu fluectatur [*sic*], caelestium, terrestrium et infernorum. Quinta ratio est, quia turbae dixerant Christum esse, alii Eliam, alii Ioannem Baptistam, *sup. eodem.* Sexta, ut appareat servorum, et Domini differentia. Septima, quia dicebant Christum esse transgressorem legis quasi inimicum Moysi, et ideo legislator Moyses, et legis zelator Elias quasi testes, et amici cum eo apparuerunt. Octava, quia volebat Apostolos fieri mansuetos, ut Moyses, et zelantes, ut Elias. Nona, ut discerent Apostoli ipsum Christum mortis, et vitae habere potestatem, ideo unus vivus, et unus mortuus cum eo apparuerunt. Decima, ut ostenderetur Christus moriturus, et iterum victurus, ideo unus vivus, et alter mortuus apparuerunt. *Apoc. cap.* 1.d. Ego sum vivus, et fui mortuus, et ecce sum vivens in saecula saeculorum. Undecima, ut nos si voluimus esse cum eo in monte simus vivi, et mortui simul, vivi Deo, mortui mundo. *Coloss. cap.* 3.a. Mortui estis, et vita vestra abscondita est cum Christo in Deo. Duodecima, quia uterque oravit pro peccatoribus, et persecutoribus suis. Moyses: *Num. cap.* 12.d. Elias 3. *Reg.* 18.g. Tertiadecima, quia Moyses, et Elias omnes regeneraturos significant, Moyses mortuus, iam mortuos Elias vivos illos qui vivi reperientur. Quartadecima, quia significant duas regenerationes. Moyses enim aquaticus interpretatur, et significat illam, quae fit in aqua baptismi. Elias interpretatur ascendens Dominus, et significat secundum, quae fiet in fine mundi, in qua omnes boni ascendent cum Domino. Quintadecima, ut doceret quales socios debent habere praelati. *Psalm.* 100. Ambulans in via immaculata, etc. *Seneca.* Cum his versare qui te meliorem facturi sunt," *Postilla super Lucam,* fol. 187rb.

ment and in the New Testament, signifies God's manifestation to His people. At Mount Sinai, the Lord comes to Moses "in the darkness of a cloud" so that the Israelites hear God speaking to Moses.[78] In Isaiah, God reveals that He will enter into Egypt on a "swift cloud" in order to bring punishment.[79] A cloud takes the ascending Jesus out of the apostles' sight,[80] and Hugh also notes a couple of psalms that refer to clouds in the context of God's presence and self-manifestation.[81]

After citing these biblical passages, Hugh adduces four more texts to illustrate four reasons why clouds really designate Christ's flesh.

> The first [reason] is because a cloud arises from something greater, and Christ's flesh arose from Mary, *Behold a little cloud arose* [*out of the sea*] *like the foot of a man* (3 Kgs 18). Second, because a cloud diminishes the sun's heat by placing itself between [us and the sun], and Christ's flesh restrained the Father's anger by means of its opposition [to it], because in [His flesh] He sustained the blow, *the chastisement of our peace was upon him, and by his bruises we are healed* (Is 53). Third, because rain comes from a cloud, and a twofold rain came from Christ's flesh, a rain of water for our ablution and a rain of blood for our redemption, *a remedy of all is the speedy coming of a cloud* (Eccles. 43). Also, a fourth reason is because, just as the sun is concealed by a cloud, so too is Christ concealed in the flesh, *truly you are a hidden God, the God of Israel, the Savior* (Is 45).[82]

Christ's flesh, in this schema, mediates between the sun, that is the Father or Christ's divinity, and the rest of humanity. Like a cloud, it arises *de mari* (from the sea, but also interpreted as, from Mary) and shields us from the heat of the sun, which represents the Father's anger. When Christ's flesh is beaten ("we have thought him as it were a leper, and as one struck by God and afflicted"),[83] it is like a cloud that

78. Ex 19:9.

79. Is 19:1.

80. Acts 1:9.

81. See *Postilla super Lucam*, fol. 187vb.

82. "Prima est, quia a maiori oritur nubes, et caro Christi de Maria 3. *Reg. cap.* 18.g. Ecce nubecula parva quasi vestigium hominis. Secunda, quia nubes ardorem solis mitigat per sui interpositionem, et caro Christi iram patris compescuit per suam oppositionem, quia in se sustinuit ictus. *Isa. cap.* 53.b. Disciplina pacis nostrae super emanat, et a carne Christi duplex pluvia emanuit. Pluvia aquae ad nostram ablutionem, et pluvia sanguinis ad nostram redemptionem. *Ecclesiast. cap.* 43.c. Medicina omnium in festinatione nebulae. Quarta etiam ratio est, quia sicut sol sub nube absconditur, ita Christus in carne, *Isa.* 45.c. Vere tu es Deus absconditus, Deus Israel Salvator," *Postilla super Lucam*, fol. 187vb.

83. Is 53:4.

bursts. Hugh's image of the "twofold rain" evokes the image of Christ's pierced side, which showers down water and blood. This "rain" from Christ's flesh washes us and redeems us by means of Christ's "cooling grace."[84]

Of course the cloud also represents the Holy Spirit. The other Gospel narrative that the transfiguration recalls is Jesus' baptism. A Trinitarian manifestation occurs there because of the Father's voice and the Spirit "descending as a dove."[85] In the transfiguration, the Father's voice comes from the cloud saying, "This is my beloved Son, listen to him."[86] There is no dove, but the cloud takes the place of the baptism scene's dove.

Hugh tries to connect baptism and transfiguration even more explicitly. He notes that it is at their baptism that Christians first publicly confess their faith in the Trinity.[87] The transfiguration, in a way, intensifies the Trinitarian theophany at Jesus' baptism because it foreshadows the resurrection, when the faithful do not merely confess their faith in the Trinity but actually behold the Trinity. As an intermediate step between faith and beatific vision, the transfiguration appropriately incorporates the cloud motif, which reveals and conceals simultaneously.

When the Father's voice and the cloud disappear, along with Moses and Elijah, the disciples find Jesus alone. Hugh carefully notes the sequence of events in order to extract a mystical interpretation. First, Jesus was alone with His disciples. Then, He was with Moses and Elijah, and after the voice and the cloud, Jesus was alone again. The sequence can be interpreted in two ways according to Hugh. One way is to see Christ as both the beginning of the Law and Prophets and their end. Another way is to emphasize Christ's solitude. There is one Christ, and all the witnesses of Christ's divinity and all the faithful are taken into Him. This unity is achieved through faith in Christ's divinity,[88] a faith that is preached by Jesus' disciples when they have

84. "gratia refrigerans," *Postilla super Lucam*, fol. 187vb.

85. Mt 3:16. See also Mk 1:10 and Lk 3:22.

86. Lk 9:35.

87. See *Postilla super Lucam*, fol. 188ra.

88. "Omnes fideles in fide Christi uniuntur," *Postilla super Lucam*, fol. 188ra.

been fully transfigured. In this context, Hugh points to Saint Paul's statement, "Therefore as we have borne the image of the earthly, let us bear also the image of the heavenly,"[89] to show that conformity to the celestial image, to which the transfiguration calls Christ's followers, is something that must be realized personally before it can be communicated.[90] It is this ongoing personal appropriation of Christ's transfiguration and its subsequent visual and verbal communication that effects in the present and will consummate in the future the transfiguration of Christ's mystical body.[91]

Conclusion

In these postillae on the synoptic gospels, Hugh ably combines available patristic texts and twelfth-century commentary and infuses his own interests. His primary interest in the transfiguration is both exegetical and spiritual. That is to say, he is interested in resolving difficulties in the transfiguration narratives through recourse to spiritual interpretations. Except for a brief *quaestio* on Christ's clarity in his Mark commentary, there is a general attempt to relate Christ's transfiguration to the spiritual development of the reader or student. Hugh sees the transfiguration as an exemplar for personal transformation that occurs through an ascent to contemplation, through an advance in virtue, and through the sacraments. This last description of personal transfiguration, through the sacraments, also shows an innovative desire to link Christ's transfiguration not only to the individual but to the whole Church, or the whole mystical body, whose Head is transfigured first as an exemplar. This ecclesial emphasis will influence later theologians, especially Albert the Great.

The intertextuality of the commentaries is very rich and far more complicated than that of the *Glossa ordinaria*. Many scriptural texts from both the Old and New Testaments are woven into the commentary, and some are even used as glosses. In addition to applying commentary, Hugh also poses questions to elicit the full meaning of the

89. 1 Cor 15:49.
90. See *Postilla super Lucam*, fol. 188ra.
91. See *Postilla super Matthaeum*, fol. 59rb.

scriptural text. Although his *quaestio* on Christ's clarity is relatively short, the opinions Hugh presents are some of the primary ones to shape the future discussion of Christ's clarity in the later synthetic literature. The later scriptural commentaries from the middle of the thirteenth century are more complicated than Hugh's, manifesting a greater interest in the literal sense of Scripture and a more sophisticated *divisio textus;* similarly, the later arguments concerning Christ's clarity are more complicated. However, Hugh's postillae on the synoptic gospels address most, if not all, details of the transfiguration narratives, and, as collections of interpretations and opinions, they constitute an important reference work for theologians from this period.

3

ALEXANDER OF HALES

Although Hugh's postillae addressed a number of points pertaining to the exegesis of the transfiguration narratives and the spiritual implications of the transfiguration, little attention was given to how the transfiguration affected Jesus. Later commentaries by Albert the Great and Thomas Aquinas, for instance, address more specific questions such as what the word "transfiguration" signifies and what exactly happened to Jesus during the transfiguration; the disputed question, however, was a scholastic genre ideally suited to asking these sorts of questions. Before 1230 no theologian examined the events of Christ's life between the Incarnation and passion in this genre. The first disputed question to contain an extensive analysis of Christ's transfiguration in particular is from Alexander of Hales, who wrote it around 1230, before he became a Franciscan.

Alexander, a secular theologian for most of his career, was a contemporary of Hugh's, and as in the case of Hugh, little is known of Alexander before his entrance into the Franciscan Order in 1236 or 1237. One important difference between the two theologians, however, is that Alexander was a regent master at the University of Paris when he became a Franciscan, while Hugh was a student when he entered the Dominican Order. Alexander's position as regent master was important for the Franciscans, because when he entered the order, his chair in theology became part of the Franciscan school.[1]

1. On Alexander's life, work, and entrance into the Franciscan order, see M. Mückshoff, "Alexander von Hales," LexMA: 377–78; Elisabeth Gössmann, "Alexander von Hales," LThK: 362–64; John Moorman, *A History of the Franciscan Order from Its Origins to the Year 1517* (Oxford: Clarendon Press, 1968), 117–18, 131–32, 240–42.

This chapter will explore Alexander's interpretation of the transfiguration as found both in his disputed question on the transfiguration and in his commentaries on the synoptic gospels, especially his *Postilla super Matthaeum*. The other commentaries on Mark and Luke are less helpful on this subject either because of their similarity with Hugh (in the case of the *Postilla super Marcum*) or because of the paucity of exegetical content (in the case of the *Postilla super Lucam*).

De transfiguratione Christi

Alexander divides his disputed question on the transfiguration into two parts: the first part addresses the type of change Jesus underwent, and the second addresses the appearance of Moses and Elijah. Alexander begins the first part by making a number of inquiries into the nature of Christ's transfiguration and the types of attributes Christ had before and after the transfiguration. Alexander's first concern is to clarify what "transfiguration" means. Properly speaking, a transfiguration is a change from one figure or shape into another. Alexander claims that since Christ's figure remained the same and only His appearance changed, there was no transfiguration properly speaking, but only in a qualified sense. Christ's transfiguration was a change "from the appearance of a non-glorified body as though into the appearance of a glorious body."[2]

One of the most important of Alexander's investigations probes the issue of Christ's clarity during the transfiguration. Clarity is one of the four *dotes* or gifts of a glorified body, and it seems that Christ was endowed with a certain brightness or clarity during the transfiguration before His body was glorified. Can Jesus have had the gift of clarity before His body was glorified?

Alexander makes several distinctions here to ascertain the kind of clarity Jesus possessed. He claims there are four different kinds of clarity:

2. "a specie corporis non gloriosi quasi in speciem corporis gloriosi," Alexander of Hales, *Quaestiones disputatae "antequam esset frater,"* edited by Pp. Collegii S. Bonaventurae, 3 vols. (Grottaferrata, Italy: Collegio S. Bonaventura, 1960), vol. 3, q. 67, n. 16 (hereafter *De transfiguratione Christi*).

> One kind of clarity is of a corruptible and non-glorified body; another kind is of an incorruptible and non-glorified body; another kind of clarity is of an incorruptible and glorified body; and another kind is of a corruptible body but in the manner of a glorified one. An example of the first is fire; an example of the second is the sun; and an example of the third will be glorified bodies. The fourth kind of clarity, however, is what is designated here, because [Christ] has the truth of a mortal body. For His body was both mortal and corruptible, and nevertheless it had a clarity similar to glorious clarity; because a mortal body is quite able to be subordinate or subject to clarity, but a mortal body is not able to be subordinate to immortality. Hence He reveals clarity to them in the manner of the appearance of a glorified body, or in the manner of a glorious appearance. But was this clarity just like that which is in a corruptible and non-glorified body? I say no. But was it just like that which is in a glorified and incorruptible body? I say no, but that it is less than the latter and greater than the former. Hence the Gloss: [The sun] does not have it more brightly than He to whom it is compared.[3]

The problem for Alexander is that Jesus' clarity is not like the clarity of other objects. Jesus' body is clearly mortal or corruptible at the time of His transfiguration, and yet His clarity is far different from that of other corruptible objects. Since His body is not yet glorified, He does not have the kind of clarity the elect will have in virtue of Christ's resurrection. This latter kind of clarity, the clarity of a glorified body, is what Alexander considers to be a gift, properly speaking; thus the clarity of Christ's transfigured body cannot be classified as a gift.[4] Since the clarity of Christ's transfigured body does not fit the usual catego-

3. "Est autem quaedam claritas corporis non glorificati corruptibilis; item quaedam corporis non glorificati incorruptibilis; item quaedam claritas corporis glorificati incorruptibilis; item quaedam corporis corruptibilis per modum glorificati. Exemplum primi in igne; exemplum secundi in sole; exemplum tertii erit corporum glorificatorum. Quarta autem claritas est de qua hic dicitur, quia veritatem corporis mortalis habuit. Corpus enim eius mortale fuit et corruptibile, et tamen claritatem habuit similem gloriosae; quia bene potest corpus mortale subditum esse sive subiectum claritati, sed non potest esse mortale subditum immortalitati. Unde claritatem ostendit eis per modum speciei corporis glorificati, sive per modum speciei gloriosae.—Sed numquid haec claritas fuit sicut in corpore corruptibili non glorificato? Dico quod non.—Sed numquid fuit sicut in corpore glorificato non corruptibili? Dico quod non, sed citra istam, et ultra illam. Unde Glossa: 'Non habet clarius cui comparet,'" *De transfiguratione Christi*, n. 17.

4. "dos est proprie corporis glorificati," *De transfiguratione Christi*, n. 17.

ries, Alexander designates it as the clarity of a corruptible body in the manner of a glorified body.

Alexander is clear, however, that this clarity is not that of a glorified body existing in a non-glorified body. It is only like that of a glorified body. The reason for this qualification, Alexander argues, is that "the clarity of the future resurrection is not able to be revealed to bodily eyes."[5] The disciples, Peter, James, and John, do see the glory of the resurrection, not in Christ's transfigured body, which does not possess clarity as a gift, but only by the "eye of the intellect," which is all their capacity allows.[6] This explanation based on the disciples' capacity has a long exegetical tradition, but Alexander cites no *auctoritas* here to support this argument.

In the next response, Alexander does respond to an authority. One of the early objections of the question cited Jerome's commentary on Matthew, although it appears that the text Alexander has in mind may actually be Bede's. The text states, "Just as He appeared then [during the transfiguration], so will He appear to all the elect during the Judgment."[7] Alexander qualifies this assertion with another phrase that he claims is "in the original," namely that Christ "will appear then to the elect and the reprobate in the form of a servant."[8] This modification allows Alexander to reassert that the kind of clarity manifested at these two events, the transfiguration and the Last Judgment, is similar but not the same.

Alexander responds next to a lengthy objection based on a consideration of the most fitting way for Christ to appear to His disciples. The objection states that Christ revealed the glory of His resurrection in the most fitting way possible, and that is to reveal it under a glorious

5. "claritas futurae resurrectionis non posset ostendi oculis corporalibus," *De transfiguratione Christi*, n 18.

6. "Dico ergo quod ostendit gloriam futurae resurrectionis secundum capacitatem illorum quibus ostendebatur; unde non fuit claritas gloriosi corporis, quia illa non fuit capabilis ab oculis corporalibus, licet gloriam resurrectionis futurae capiebant oculo intellectus," *De transfiguratione Christi*, n. 18.

7. "Talis apparuit tunc, qualis in iudicio cunctis electis apparebit," *De transfiguratione Christi*, n. 5.

8. "dicitur in originali quod 'in forma servi tunc apparebit ipsis electis et reprobis,'" *De transfiguratione Christi*, n. 19.

appearance while Christ Himself remained in a non-glorified body.[9] Drawing from an interpretation given by Gregory the Great, the argument continues that "just as after the resurrection, existing in a glorious form, Christ shows Himself under a non-glorious form in order to encourage faith, so too, in a contrary manner, does Christ show a glorious appearance while remaining mortal. Therefore, just as that was the most fitting manner after the resurrection, so too was that the most fitting manner before the resurrection; He, therefore, remaining non-glorified, showed a glorious form or appearance in order to encourage [the disciples] to have faith in the resurrection."[10]

Alexander first responds that Jesus' revealing the glory of His resurrection under a glorious appearance can be either "under the truth [sub veritate]" or "under a likeness [sub similitudine]."[11] He argues that if Jesus' glorious appearance is understood as *sub veritate,* that understanding is false, but if it is understood as *sub similitudine,* it is correct. Reiterating his earlier arguments, Alexander is concerned to show that Christ's clarity at the transfiguration is not the gift of a glorified body, but only the appearance of a gift.

Alexander's second response expands on his notion of the "truth" of Christ's glorious appearance. He says that "to bodily vision, the likeness of a glorified body appeared with respect to clarity, but the truth of glorification did not; in the intellect, moreover, [the disciples] perceived the glory of the future resurrection through that likeness of clarity which they saw with their bodily eyes, and through this it appeared to them there."[12] The "truth of glorification" exists when there is a resurrected body with a "glorious form." Only a resurrected body can have this form, which is linked to the gift of clarity. Before a body

9. *De transfiguratione Christi,* n. 6.

10. "Ergo, sicut post resurrectionem, existens in forma gloriosa, ostendit se sub forma non gloriosa ut invitaret ad fidem, ita hic a contrariis ostendit speciem gloriosam, manens mortalis. Sicut ergo ille modus convenientissimus fuit post resurrectionem, ita iste convenientissimus fuit ante resurrectionem; ergo ipse manens non glorificatus, ostendit formam sive speciem gloriosam, ut invitaret eos ad fidem resurrectionis," *De transfiguratione Christi,* n. 6.

11. *De transfiguratione Christi,* n. 20.

12. "visui corporali apparuit similitudo corporis glorificati quoad claritatem, sed non veritas glorificationis; in intellectu autem perceperunt gloriam futurae resurrectionis per illam similitudinem claritatis quam oculis corporalibus viderunt et per hoc quod ibi illis apparebat," *De transfiguratione Christi,* n. 21.

is resurrected, it can have only the likeness of clarity or the likeness of future glory.

Alexander acknowledges, however, that the likeness of clarity can be called clarity itself, although only in an analogous sense. He says that the clarity manifested in the transfigured Jesus existed so that "through this likeness, the intellect was led through faith to believing the truth of glory."[13] Drawing on his own earlier distinctions between different kinds of clarity, Alexander proceeds to describe two different manifestations of clarity in the transfigured Jesus that differ from the gift of clarity. Clarity was present both in Christ's face and in His garments, but these manifestations of clarity do not constitute the gift of clarity. Applying a useful analogy, Alexander claims that "there was clarity in His body and garments but in different ways: because just as there is clarity in snow and in the sun but the clarity of the sun is not proportionate to the clarity of the snow, so too was the clarity of His body not proportionate to that of His garments. Neither the clarity of His face nor that of His garments was that true and glorious clarity which will be in the future."[14]

Alexander next assesses the disciples' vision of the transfiguration and how the clarity they beheld affected them. The basis for this investigation is Luke 9:27, "But I tell you truly, there are some standing here who will not taste death before they see the kingdom of God," and a gloss on that text that links the kingdom of God with the glorification of bodies.[15] Alexander explains that there are two different kinds of seeing: "Because there is seeing with the bodily eye, and there is seeing with the eye of the intellect which surpasses vision. For there is seeing the glorification of bodies of the future resurrection by the intellect which surpasses the vision of the likeness of that glory; and thus this

13. "per hanc similitudinem ducebatur intellectus per fidem ad credendum veritatem gloriae," *De transfiguratione Christi*, n. 22.

14. "Unde fuit claritas in corpore et in vestimentis, sed differenter: quia sicut in nive est claritas et in sole, sed improportionabilis est claritas solis claritati nivis, ita claritas corporis fuit improportionabilis claritati vestimentorum. Neutra tamen claritas, neque faciei neque vestimentorum, fuit claritas illa vera et gloriosa quae erit in futuro," *De transfiguratione Christi*, n. 22. Both Hugh and Thomas Aquinas use this analogy of the sun and the snow in their accounts of Christ's clarity; for Hugh, see above, p. 23, and for Thomas, see below, pp. 220–21.

15. *De transfiguratione Christi*, nn. 14, 23. The key part of Alexander's Latin text reads, "Donec videant regnum Dei."

[phrase] is understood to mean, 'they will see the kingdom of God, that is the glorification of bodies,' not that that bodily vision should go beyond the glorification which will exist in the future."[16] Alexander's point here is that, during the transfiguration, the disciples' seeing is merely a bodily phenomenon and not a vision of the glory of the future resurrection, which can be "seen" only by the intellect.

Alexander's emphasis on the bodily dimension of the disciples' vision requires further examination. If the clarity of Jesus' transfigured body was so intense that it was brighter than the clarity of the sun, how could the disciples see it, since the human eye can hardly bear to look at the sun? Alexander claims that although the clarity of Jesus' transfigured body is greater than that of the sun, it has a far different effect on the eye. He says, "that clarity was an excellent and unique vision; it did not damage vision, however, because that clarity did not generate that heat which consumes the humor which is in the eye (because there is a watery substance in the eye) through rays proceeding from it, just like the clarity of heaven; but that clarity, which generates the kind of heat which destroys the humor in the eye, damages vision, and the eye is not able to endure it, just like the clarity of the sun, which generates heat."[17] The difference between solar and heavenly clarity is that solar clarity consumes the watery humor in the eye, which allows vision to occur, whereas heavenly clarity, despite its brightness, allows the watery humor to remain intact.

The exegetical basis for this interpretation of the clarity of Christ's body is Matthew 17:4, Peter's statement, "Lord, it is well that we are here." The clarity could not be so physically overpowering if Peter, James, and John were pleased to be witnesses of Jesus' transfiguration.

16. "quia est videre oculo corporali, et est videre oculo intellectus, praecedente visu. Videre enim est intellectu glorificationem futurae resurrectionis corporum, praecedente visu similitudinis illius gloriae; et ita intelligitur hoc: 'videbunt regnum Dei, id est corporum glorificationem,' non quod ipse visus corporalis transiret super glorificationem quae erit in futuro," *De transfiguratione Christi*, n. 23.

17. "Dico [etiam] quod illa claritas fuit excellens et disgregans visum, non tamen corrupit visum, quia illa claritas non aggeneravit calorem consumentem humorem qui est in oculo (quia in oculo est substantia aquosa) per radios procedentes ab ea, sicut claritas caeli. Sed claritas illa quae est aggenerativa caloris corrumpentis humorem qui est in oculo, illa corrumpit visum, et illam non potest oculus sustinere, sicut claritas solis, quae est aggenerativa caloris," *De transfiguratione Christi*, n. 24.

In fact, Alexander seems to believe that Peter's words "signify that they were delighted in [Christ's clarity], and thus they easily endured it."[18] The only other reason that Alexander offers as an explanation for Peter's statement is that Peter, either by himself or with James and John, perceived the clarity of the future resurrection through the clarity that he beheld through his bodily vision.[19]

After answering questions regarding the physical nature of clarity and its effect on the disciples, Alexander concludes the first part of the investigation of Christ's transfiguration with a series of questions about clarity as a special quality of Christ's body. He begins by alluding to an objection that compares clarity to the other gifts or qualities of a glorified body. On the premise that Christ's transfiguration is a prefiguration of the resurrection, pedagogically oriented for the benefit of Peter, James, and John, the question asked is why Jesus showed the glory of the resurrection only by means of clarity and not by means of other possibly more effective qualities. The problem with clarity is that it is "a common disposition of other bodies; impassibility is truly a quality of glorified body, as is agility."[20] In his response, Alexander phrases the question even more strongly, "Why does Christ show the glory of the resurrection through clarity, since other qualities are more certain signs?"[21]

Alexander's response draws from 1 Corinthians 15:41, "There is one glory of the sun, and another glory of the moon, and another glory of the stars; for star differs from star in glory." In this text, Alexander claims that Paul "shows the resurrection through clarity, not through other dispositions, because that disposition is first which is in our bodies in some way as a capacity; because in our bodies there are four elements, and some power flowing from a fifth body, by reason of which

18. "per quod significatur quod delectati fuerunt in ea, et ita bene sustinebant illam," *De transfiguratione Christi,* n. 24.

19. "Vel potest dici dixit Apostolus hoc, *bonum est* etc., ratione claritatis illius quam intelligebat per illam quam vidit sensu corporeo sive oculis coporeis," *De transfiguratione Christi,* n. 24.

20. "claritas est communis dispositio aliorum corporum; impassibilitas vero est proprietas corporis glorificati, et similter agilitas," *De transfiguratione Christi,* n. 13.

21. "quare per claritatem ostendit gloriam resurrectionis, cum aliae proprietates sint certiora signa," *De transfiguratione Christi,* n. 25.

power there is a capacity for clarity, and by reason of the one soul there is a capacity for greater clarity."[22]

This somewhat nebulous answer becomes clearer with the example of Moses. When Moses came down from Mount Sinai the second time, after receiving the Law of God again from the Lord, his face possessed such radiance that it seemed to have horns and the Israelites could not look at his face. Alexander, citing Saint Paul's understanding of this event, as found in 2 Corinthians 3:7, believes that the Israelites could not look at the face of Moses, "on account of the clarity which existed from the union [of the divine nature] to his soul."[23] When Saint Paul says, "even that which was illuminated in this part was not glorified on account of the surpassing glory," (2 Cor 3:10), Alexander interprets that to mean he "wants to say that Christ had clarity which does not cease; Moses, however, had clarity which ceases. How much more was the capacity in the body of Christ from the union of the divine nature to His flesh."[24]

Alexander's reference to 1 Corinthians 15:41 in another disputed question on the gifts of a glorified body provides additional information on the uniqueness of clarity as a gift. In this question Alexander claims that the distinction of varying degrees or different kinds of clarity implied by the verse has an epistemic value. He says that "clarity is first among the gifts, because the others are consequently ordered to it. For clarity refers to appearance, because clarity in bodies is ordered towards knowledge in spirits."[25] This knowledge has an eschatological dimension because of its relation to the gift of vision, which the

22. "ostendit resurrectionem per claritatem, non per alias dispositiones, quia illa dispositio est prima quae aliquo modo per possibilitatem est in corpore nostro; quia in corpore nostro quatuor sunt elementa, et aliqua virtus influens de quinto corpore, ratione cuius virtutis est possibilitas ad claritatem, et ratione unius animae ad maiorem claritatem," *De transfiguratione Christi,* n. 25. For more on the elements and the "fifth body," which Alexander derives from Aristotle's *De caelo,* see Alexander's q. 65 (Quid resurget in corpore glorificato), in *Quaestiones disputatae 'antequam esset frater,'* vol. 3, 1307–11, and his *Glossa in quatuor libros Sententiarum Petri Lombardi,* edited by Pp. Collegii S. Bonaventurae, 4 vols. (Quaracchi, Italy: ex Typographia Collegii S. Bonaventurae, 1951–1957), II, d. 20, n. 3.

23. "propter claritatem quae fuit ex unione [deitatis] ad animam," *De transfiguratione Christi,* n. 25.

24. "vult dicere quod Christus habuit claritatem quae non cessit; Moyses autem habuit claritatem quae cessit. Multo magis autem fuit potestas in corpore Christi ex unione deitatis ad carnem," *De transfiguratione Christi,* n. 25.

25. "dicendum quod prima inter dotes est claritas, quia ad eam aliae consequenter ordi-

blessed in heaven possess. Commenting on a gloss of Psalm 90:16, Alexander notes that "clarity in itself is ordered to vision, in which will be the whole reward; by speaking of the saints who will be in heaven, [the Apostle] rightly makes a comparison between the resurrected bodies of the saints according to clarity."[26] This explanation helps to explain that clarity is given priority in Alexander's question on the transfiguration because of its implied comparison to the other gifts. Of all the gifts (agility, subtlety, clarity, and impassibility), only clarity is a quality that can be seen in itself. The other gifts can be perceived by the intellect only through inferences drawn from visual evidence.

After Alexander resolves the problem of why Christ manifested the glory of His resurrection through clarity, he explores the question of how Christ possessed that quality, whether He had it by nature, as asserted in a gloss on Matthew 17:2, or whether He had it by a special dispensation. This question is important because it sheds light on Christ's human nature and its relation to the rest of humanity.

Alexander first acknowledges a distinction between what Christ possesses according to His human nature and what He possesses by way of a special dispensation. Alexander then suggests similarities and differences between Christ's humanity and that of other humans:

> Just as now the operation of the four elements appears in us, and the operation of the fifth body is hidden, although this will be reversed in the future, so too there were some things in Christ's body insofar as it was of a nature united to the divine nature, and similarly there were some things by dispensation, insofar as he came to redeem those things, namely the consequences of sin, for which it was fitting to have a redeemer. Hence on account of its union to the divine nature it had a greater disposition for clarity than we have . . . . But from this it does not follow that it was fitting for it to appear constantly, because weakness, which He assumed by dispensation, impeded it; but it appeared when it was necessary.[27]

---

nantur. Claritas enim ad speciem refertur, quia claritas in corporibus ordinatur ad cognitionem in spiritibus," Alexander, q. 66 (De dotibus corporis gloriosi), in *Quaestiones disputatae "antequam esset frater,"* vol. 3, n. 32. In nn. 6–9 of this question, Alexander also briefly discusses clarity at the transfiguration.

26. "Quia ergo claritas per se ordinatur ad visionem, in qua tota merces, loquendo de sanctis qui erunt in patria, recte fecit comparationem inter corpora sanctorum resurrecta secundum claritatem," q. 66 (De dotibus corporis gloriosi), n. 32.

27. "Sicut in nobis modo apparet operatio quatuor elementorum et latet operatio quinti

The union of Christ's body to the divine nature allows for its greater capacity for receiving and manifesting clarity. However, Alexander attributes the lack of clarity in Christ's body throughout His pre-resurrection life to the weakness of the assumed human nature, which prevented the clarity of His body from being revealed in its fullness. Although he allows for that clarity to be revealed "when it was necessary," Alexander provides no explanation for why it would be necessary for that clarity to appear.

Christ's greater capacity for clarity than other humans possess raises the question of whether other humans can be transfigured. Alexander acknowledges that God has the power to transfigure another person, but the key question for him is whether the bodies of other humans are "transfigurable,"[28] that is, whether they have the natural capacity to be transfigured. Alexander claims that the reason Christ's body is transfigurable and other people's bodies are not is because Christ's body is united to the divine nature. As for the bodies of most people, he claims "although there is a capacity for clarity on account of the union to the soul, the greater disposition which was in Christ from the conjunction, or rather, from the union to the divine nature, is lacking."[29] Christ's body derives some clarity because of its union with its soul, but it possesses a superior capacity for clarity because of its union to the divine nature. The fact that Christ's body is united both to His soul and to His divine nature accounts for the uniqueness of clarity among the other properties of His body.[30]

After these reflections on Christ's body, Alexander begins the sec-

---

corporis, sed e converso erit in futuro, ita in corpore Christi erant quaedam quantum est de natura unita deitati, et similiter erant quaedam ex dispensatione, quoad hoc scilicet quod venerat ad redimendum, scilicet poenalitates quas decuit habere redemptorem. Unde propter unionem ad deitatem habuit ulteriorem dispositionem ad claritatem quam nos habeamus . . . Sed ex hoc non sequitur quod illam oportuit semper apparere, quia infirmitas, quam assumpsit ex dispensatione, impedivit illud; sed apparuit quando fuit necessarium," *De transfiguratione Christi*, n. 26.

28. "transfigurabile," *De transfiguratione Christi*, n. 27.

29. "licet sit possibilitas ad claritatem propter unionem ad animam, deest tamen ulterior dispositio quae fuit in Christo ex coniunctione, immo ex unione divinae naturae," *De transfiguratione Christi*, n. 27.

30. "Ad hoc quod obiciture, quare per claritatem ostendit, dico quod quia prima dispositio fuit quae fuit ex unione [corporis] ad animam et ad deitatem," *De transfiguratione Christi*, n. 28.

ond part of this disputed question. As mentioned above, this part inquires into the appearance of Moses and Elijah. Alexander composes a series of interesting objections with the basic argument that neither the body nor the soul of Moses and Elijah appeared, but rather that angels assumed bodies to create the impression that Moses and Elijah were truly present.[31]

Alexander's opening reply, however, addresses only the possibility that the disciples' vision of Moses and Elijah was imaginary. Matthew 17:8 seems to contradict this thesis, "they lifting up their eyes, saw no one, but only Jesus." This passage, Alexander argues, shows that there was a bodily vision,[32] but Alexander also argues that Moses and Elijah did in fact appear and that their appearance was accomplished through the ministry of angels. Angels played a part in the vision because "the assumption of a body is neither fitting nor possible for souls."[33] However, since Scripture describes Moses and Elijah talking with Jesus, Alexander must acknowledge that they were truly there "because falsehood is lacking from the highest truth."[34]

Alexander first addresses the question of the how the bodies were formed and how they related to their souls. He affirms that the souls of Moses and Elijah did not assume their bodies again, but rather that God effected a conjoining of their souls with their bodies. Alexander seems to think that the bodies that appeared were formed from the ashes of the prophets' decomposed bodies, "the gathering of ashes does not occur by the power of souls, but by the ministry of angels. For to gather is of angels, but to form, however, is of God; afterwards there is a conjunction."[35]

For Alexander, *coniunctio* refers to only two different modes of joining soul to body. The first is *ad tempus* for the purpose of communicating.[36] This mode of conjunction is "not like that of form with

31. *De transfiguratione Christi,* n. 30.

32. "corporalis visio," *De transfiguratione Christi,* n. 35.

33. "sumptio corporis non convenit sive non competit animabus," *De transfiguratione Christi,* n. 35.

34. "quia absit fictio a summa veritate," *De transfiguratione Christi,* n. 35.

35. "collectio cinerum non est animarum, sed ministerio angelorum. Colligere enim est angelorum, formare vero Dei," *De transfiguratione Christi,* n. 36.

36. *De transfiguratione Christi,* n. 36.

matter, but like that of a mover with something moved, just as the angels assumed bodies in the Old Testament."[37] The second mode of conjunction is what Alexander calls *resuscitatio*. This conjunction occurs when God unites body to soul for the purpose of meriting. The latter mode occurred when Lazarus was raised from the dead, while the former mode, *coniunctio ad tempus* was present in the apparition of Moses and Elijah with the transfigured Christ.[38] In this way, the souls of Moses and Elijah were truly present in their own bodies (whose ashes had been gathered by angels and formed by God), but they were no longer able to alter their eternal punishment or reward through sin or merit.

Alexander next addresses an objection ascribed to John Chrysostom, which argues that the souls of those who are already in hell may not leave until Christ Himself has descended there.[39] The solution Alexander provides affirms the premise of the objection, namely that souls cannot see God before Christ's death, but he rejects its conclusion and affirms simultaneously that the soul of Moses could be, and in fact was, united to a body during the transfiguration. The solution rests on Alexander's understanding of hell and limbo. He claims that "hell is said in one way to be lacking the vision of God, and one understands it as such there. For wherever there will be a separated soul, since it does not see God, it is said to be in limbo, if it was created for seeing, just as the demons are somewhere under punishment."[40] Since Moses, during his conversation with the transfigured Christ on the mountain, lacked the face-to-face vision of God, possible only after Christ's death and His harrowing of hell, Moses could be in hell or limbo and on earth at the same time.[41] This position implies that "on

37. "non sicut forma cum materia, sed sicut movens cum moto, sicut angeli assumebant corpora in Veteri Testamento," *De transfiguratione Christi*, n. 36.

38. *De transfiguratione Christi*, n. 36.

39. "Item Chrysostomus: 'Nulla anima in inferno locata inde exiit, nisi Christo ad inferos descendente,'" *De transfiguratione Christi*, n. 37.

40. "dico quod infernus dicitur uno modo carentia visionis Dei, et de hoc ibi intelligit. Ubicumque enim fuerit anima abstracta, cum non videt Deum, dicitur esse in limbo, si nata sit ad videndum, sicut daemones in poena ubicumque sunt," *De transfiguratione Christi*, n. 37.

41. In this passage, Alexander does not seem to make a distinction between *in inferno* and *in limbo*.

earth" refers to the spatial location of Moses' body, (which is united to his soul), and "in hell" refers to the condition of his soul.

Another objection about the condition of Moses' soul is that uniting it to a body for the purpose of communicating would seem to disturb the quietude of his soul. This is evident in an allusion to 1 Samuel 28:5–25. In the story related there, King Saul consults a medium or witch to summon the spirit of Samuel. She does so and sees the appearance of an old man; and, as Scripture relates, "Samuel said to Saul, 'Why have you disturbed my rest, that I should be brought up?'" Saul explains that he needs advice, since he is beset by enemies and God seems to have abandoned him. In the formulation of the objection, Alexander cites a commentary on this passage from Augustine's *Ad Simplicianum*. Augustine believes that Samuel's soul was not in fact "awakened from his rest,"[42] but rather that the apparition of Samuel was an illusion of the devil. Alexander, working from this interpretation, shows two ways in which souls can be taken from their rest (which he equates with Abraham's bosom):

> It is one thing to be removed or recalled for the manifestation of glory, another thing for the manifestation or the effect of sin. The first case was that of Moses, because in this the rest of Moses' soul was not diminished; but in the case of Samuel, if [his soul] had been separated, his rest would have been diminished, because his being recalled was for the work of sin. In this other recalling, however, there was no diminution, but a certain anticipation, as it were. It was otherwise in the case of Elijah, however, because he comes to prefigure a greater rest, and besides, he was not dead.[43]

Moses and Elijah, not the apparition of Samuel's soul, exemplify the two ways in which souls can be recalled from their rest. The appearance of both their souls testifies to Christ's glory, in the case of Moses, and the glory of the resurrection, in the case of Elijah. Although it ap-

42. "a requie sua suscitatus est," *De transfiguratione Christi*, n. 34.

43. "Aliud est extrahi sive revocari ad ostensionem gloriae, aliud ad ostensionem vel opus peccati. Primo modo fuit in Moyse, quia in hoc requies non diminuebatur animae Moysi; sed in Samuele, si abstracta fuisset, diminuta fuisset requies sua, quia fuit illa revocatio ad opus peccati. In alia autem revocatione non fuit diminutio, sed quasi quaedam praelibatio. Secus autem fuit de Elia, quia ipse venit ad praefigurationem maioris quietis, et etiam ipse non erat mortuus," *De transfiguratione Christi*, n. 38.

pears that the witch of Endor had summoned Samuel, this must be an illusion since Samuel's appearance leads to no manifestation of glory.

Alexander also finds the conversation of Jesus and the prophets to bear theological significance. All three synoptic gospels record that Moses and Elijah spoke with Jesus, but only Luke relates what they were talking about: "And behold, two men talked with him, Moses and Elijah, who appeared in glory and spoke of his departure, which he was to accomplish at Jerusalem."[44] Alexander cites this passage specifically and says that their "conversation was of the resurrection,"[45] and that "through the transfiguration it is signified that man ought to hope for the glory of the resurrection; through the apparition of those two, however, is signified the testimony that [Christ] was going to communicate such glory to humans."[46]

Alexander concludes his disputed question on Christ's transfiguration with an insightful inquiry into how the disciples knew that the two men who appeared were in fact Moses and Elijah. He gives two possibilities. One is that the disciples knew the identity of the two men through scriptural descriptions. The other, and for Alexander, more preferable explanation is that "they knew through revelation, just as the prophets knew."[47] This revealed knowledge of the prophets' identity is not an end in itself, but a means to deeper faith in Christ. Alexander returns to Moses' and Elijah's conversation with Jesus to explain that it was not for the benefit of their own faith, which had been confirmed during their earthly lives, "but to confirm the disciples, and us in the disciples."[48]

Alexander's disputed question, although brief, raises a number of interesting questions. In its investigation of the nature of transfiguration and its different levels of meaning, the question assumes a metaphysical and semantic dimension. It also has an accentuated anthropo-

44. Lk 9:30–31.

45. "locutio fuit de resurrectione, sicut dicitur 9 Luc., 31," *De transfiguratione Christi*, n. 39.

46. "Per transfigurationem enim significatur quod homo debet sperare gloriam resurrectionis; per apparitionem autem illorum duorum significatur testimonium quod erat communicaturus cum hominibus talem gloriam," *De transfiguratione Christi*, n. 39.

47. "Ex revelatione cognescebant, sicut Prophetae cognoverunt," *De transfiguratione Christi*, n. 40.

48. "sed ut certificarent discipulos, et nos in discipulis," *De transfiguratione Christi*, n. 40.

logical emphasis in its investigation of the human body's capacity for glory in different stages of the economy of salvation, of Christ's body in its relation to the divine nature to which it is joined, and of the human person's bodily capacity to perceive the glory of another. These more philosophical considerations should not obscure Alexander's overarching engagement with the scriptural narratives and the sources from the tradition, who have supplied authoritative interpretations of these passages. Many of the questions that Alexander asks are explicitly exegetical, and he makes frequent recourse to the *Glossa ordinaria,* (which he cites ten times in this short question) and to earlier exegetes such as Jerome, Augustine, John Chrysostom, and Bede. While some of Alexander's questions and responses may seem curious to our sensibilities, the last sentence of his question shows that, in addition to providing grist for theological and philosophical speculation, Christ's transfiguration has great significance for the life of the Christian.[49]

Postilla super Matthaeum

Alexander also reflected upon Christ's transfiguration in his three commentaries on the synoptic gospels, which, although unedited, survive from the Middle Ages in three manuscripts.[50] His *Postilla super Matthaeum,* like his other postillae, probably dates from the mid- to late 1230s. Compared with the *Postilla super Matthaeum* of Hugh of St. Cher, Alexander's commentary possesses a much more even distribu-

49. For more on Alexander's Christology, see the following studies, most of which address his theory of the hypostatic union: Norbert de Amato, *Doctrina Summae Fratris Alexandri de Hales de ipsa natura a Verbo assumpta* (Rome: Casa Editrice Herder, 1956); Marie Lamy de la Chapelle, "Fils jusque dans la chair. Le mystère de l'Incarnation dans la pensée de S. Albert le Grand, Alexandre d'Halès, S. Bonaventure et S. Thomas d'Aquin," *Doctor Communis* 33 (1980): 149–57; Jean Châtillon, "L'union hypostatique chez les théologiens du début du XIIIe siècle: Guillaume d'Auxerre et Alexandre de Halès," *Cahiers de civilisation médiévale* 12 (1969): 161–64; Francisco Martínez Fresneda, *La gracia y la ciencia de Jesucristo: Historia de la cuestión en Alejandro de Hales, Odón Rigaldo, Summa Halensis y Buenaventura* (Murcia, Spain: Editorial Espigas, 1997); Kenan B. Osborne, "Alexander of Hales: Precursor and Promoter of Franciscan Theology," in *The History of Franciscan Theology,* edited by Kenan B. Osborne, 1–38 (St. Bonaventure, New York: The Franciscan Institute, 1994); Walter H. Principe, *Alexander of Hales' Theology of the Hypostatic Union* (Toronto: Pontifical Institute of Mediaeval Studies, 1967).

50. In Mss. Assisi Biblioteca Comunale 355, Reims BM 162, and Durham A II.22.

tion of commentary. That is, Alexander comments on more phrases but does not give as much attention to each phrase. He does spend much more time than Hugh discussing the importance of the "six days," but in general, there are few sustained passages of exegesis here as compared to Hugh.[51]

Particularly interesting is comparing Alexander's treatment of the transfiguration in his disputed question, which we have just looked at, with the way he addresses Jesus' transfiguration in his commentaries. In the disputed question, Alexander focused on what transfiguration actually signifies, along with concomitant considerations of the bodily gift of clarity, and some brief reflections on the appearance of Moses and Elijah. The types of questions Alexander asked in the disputed questions, addressing the meanings of words and how things could be, are largely absent in the commentary. In the commentary, Alexander's emphasis is on the actual events and the allegorical, moral, and mystical significance of those events.

In addressing Christ's transfiguration, Alexander raises an important point that Hugh neglected: how the word "transfiguration" functions elsewhere in Scripture. Alexander notes that Saint Paul refers to Satan as transfiguring himself "into an angel of light."[52] The active voice of the verb contrasts sharply with the *transfiguratus est* of Christ's transfiguration. Alexander says, "In the passive [voice] there is humility, in the active [voice] pride. Similarly in Isaiah 14, [Satan says] 'I will ascend to heaven, and I will be like the Most High.'"[53] Christ's trans-

51. The problems associated with dating these texts and establishing their relationship to Hugh of St. Cher's *postillae* are rather complicated. In the recent literature on Alexander's exegetical works, Ignatius Brady first suggested a broad window between roughly 1220 and 1236 ("Sacred Scripture in the Early Franciscan School," in *La Sacra Scrittura e i Francescani*, 65–80 (Rome: Antonianum, 1973). Beryl Smalley, who compared shared material in Alexander and Hugh of St. Cher, suggested that Alexander depended on Hugh for some of his exegesis or at least that the two shared a common unknown source. Dependence on Hugh would put Alexander's postillae in the middle-to-late 1230s, perhaps after his entrance into the Franciscan order (see *The Gospels in the Schools: c. 1100–c. 1280*, 122–23). More complex evaluation of the evidence, which supports Smalley's thesis, is provided by Abigail Ann Young, "Accessus ad Alexandrum: The *Praefatio* to the *Postilla in Iohannis Euangelium* of Alexander of Hales (1186?–1245)," *Mediaeval Studies* 52 (1990): 3–23; and Hubert Philipp Weber, *Sünde und Gnade bei Alexander von Hales: Ein Beitrag zur Entwicklung der theologischen Anthropologie im Mittelalter* (Innsbruck, Aust.: Tyrolia, 2003), 34–36.

52. 2 Cor 11:14.

53. "In passiva humilitas, in activa superbia; similiter Is. xiiii, *ascendam* in caelum et *ero*

figuration demonstrates that the power to effect His transfiguration comes from another, and Alexander ascribes this power to the entire Trinity.

Surprisingly, Alexander spends little time discussing how Christ's transfiguration appeared to the disciples. He notes, however, as did Hugh, that the white garments represent the saints in some way. He also picks up on something Hugh missed in his lengthy gloss on this passage, namely that Christ's garments "became as white as snow."[54] The comparison to snow is significant, Alexander argues, because snow is white and falls from the sky. There is a spiritual parallel with the saints, since they are made white by grace descending from heaven. Although this grace does not make them white, it does effect a cleansing, which is what the color white signifies. This cleansing affects the whole person, since it transforms each saint's exterior and interior.[55]

Alexander, like Hugh, also writes very little on the appearance of Moses and Elijah. He is content to follow the *Glossa ordinaria*'s interpretation that "the dead Moses signifies the dead, and Elijah signifies those who will be found living."[56] He also makes two observations made neither by the *Glossa ordinaria* nor by Hugh. One is a spiritual interpretation, namely that the lawgiver, Moses represents those who are active, and Elijah, who was taken to heaven in a fiery chariot, represents contemplatives. The other interpretation relates to Moses' and Elijah's forty days of fasting.[57] After the forty days, Moses received the Law from God, and Elijah heard God in a "still, small voice." Their presence, then, at the transfiguration manifests how spiritual transformation, prepared and accompanied by asceticism, precedes God's revelation.

Alexander's commentary on the voice and the cloud, is lengthier than his discussion of Moses and Elijah and seems more independent. He links the voice present at the transfiguration with the Father's voice

similis altissimo," Ms. Assisi Biblioteca Comunale 355, fol. 47vb. Italicized words here and in other citations from the unedited biblical commentaries are from scriptural texts.

54. Mt 17:2.

55. Ms. Assisi Biblioteca Comunale 355, fol. 47vb.

56. "Moyses mortuus mortuos significat, et Elias illos qui vivi invenientur," Ms. Assisi Biblioteca Comunale 355, fol. 47vb.

57. See Ex 24:18 and 1 Kgs 19:8.

at Jesus' baptism and notes how both events signify the "twofold effect of Christ's coming."[58] Baptism signifies the removal of original sin, while the transfiguration signifies the glory of the world to come. The Father's presence is signified in both events by the voice, and His words, "This is my beloved Son," present in both narratives, signify the same nature shared by the Father and the Son.

Even more profound is Alexander's account of the Holy Spirit. The disparate forms taken by the Holy Spirit—a dove at Jesus' baptism, a bright cloud at Jesus' transfiguration, and tongues of fire at Pentecost—reveal a spiritual ascent. The grace given at baptism is for "simple knowledge."[59] From there, one progresses to more advanced knowledge, which is signified by the bright cloud of the transfiguration. Finally, one ascends to charity, signified by the tongues of fire at Pentecost. The Holy Spirit is expressed as love, not only at Pentecost, but also during the transfiguration. What expresses this dimension of the Spirit is not the bright cloud, but the Father's characterization of the Son as "beloved." The word "beloved" signifies "the communion of love which is between the Father and the Son, that is the Holy Spirit, as in John 17, that they 'may be one even as we are one.'"[60]

The words of the Father, "with whom I am well pleased," refer both to Christ's humanity and to His divinity. They show, in one sense, that Christ's human will is in conformity with the Father's will. Moreover, they show the unity of the Father and the Son. Alexander, like Hugh, follows Richard of St. Victor's reading of this verse, which is, "in whom I am pleasing to myself."[61] Hugh had attributed this reading to a certain Gilbert, but Alexander merely ascribes it to an anonymous "expositor."[62] The Victorine influence, although unstated, goes further than that, however, since according to Alexander, the Father's last words, "listen to him," when heard at Christ's baptism, refer to renunciation of the devil, while during the transfiguration, they refer to the fact that

58. "duplicem effectum adventus Christi," Ms. Assisi Biblioteca Comunale 355, fol. 48ra.

59. "simplicem cognitionem," Ms. Assisi Biblioteca Comunale 355, fol. 48ra.

60. "communio dilectionis quae est inter Patrem et Filium, quae est Spiritus, scilicet Ioan. xvii, ut ipsi *sint unum sicut et nos unum sumus*," Ms. Assisi Biblioteca Comunale 355, fol. 48ra.

61. See Richard of St. Victor, *Beniamin minor*, chap. 82.

62. See Alexander of Hales, Ms. Assisi Biblioteca Comunale 355, fol. 48ra.

"man hears ineffable things when his soul is taken up to the highest contemplation of God."[63]

Postilla super Marcum

In his commentary on Mark, Alexander's notes on the transfiguration, as found in Assisi Biblioteca Comunale 355, are nearly the same as those in Hugh's commentary in his *Postilla super Marcum*. The texts of the two commentaries are similar enough to raise the question not only of influence, but also whether they are, in fact, the same commentary. Unfortunately this manuscript does not contain the commentary on the entire Gospel of Mark. It begins with the opening of Mark 6 and ends toward the conclusion of Mark 14. A comparison of Hugh's text with Assisi Biblioteca Comunale 355 shows that they are very similar, but not identical. The commentary on Mark 6 includes some passages in Hugh's text, but it is not the same as Hugh's commentary. The commentary on Mark 7, however, becomes markedly similar to Hugh's postilla, and the commentary on chapters eight through fourteen are nearly the same as Hugh's commentary. An examination of the other two manuscripts (Reims BM 162 and Durham A II.22) may provide further clues about Alexander's potential dependence on Hugh. If indeed Hugh compiled his postilla first, as Beryl Smalley suggests, Alexander's "commentary" would exemplify the importance and the extent of Hugh's influence.[64]

Postilla super Lucam

Alexander's commentary on the transfiguration in his commentary on Luke is quite short compared to his *Postilla super Matthaeum*. One side of a folio contains the entire passage and commentary, which is evenly distributed into little glosses. Unlike his Mark commentary, which almost duplicates Hugh of St. Cher's interpretations, Alexander's Luke commentary evinces little influence of Hugh's commentary;

63. "homo audit ineffibilia quando capitur ad contemplationem Dei summum anima," Ms. Assisi Biblioteca Comunale 355, fol. 48ra–b.

64. See Smalley, *The Gospels in the Schools: c. 1100–c. 1280*, 160–71.

and, although there is little original material on Moses and Elijah or the Trinitarian theophany, Alexander's postilla does in fact reflect one position on the transfiguration that he outlined in his disputed question. The question is whether the clarity manifested during Christ's transfiguration was a "gift" *(dos)*, properly speaking. In the *De transfiguratione Christi,* Alexander had argued that Christ's transfigured clarity was not a gift, because a gift by definition is a quality that inheres in a glorified body.[65] Alexander reaffirms that position and explains that the dazzling whiteness of Christ's garments occurred through a "condensation of light."[66]

This brief commentary also illustrates how a different dimension of the transfiguration may be emphasized by a theologian, depending on the genre of literature. Although Alexander displays his interest in Jesus' clarity and its manifestation to the disciples in both the disputed question and the biblical commentary, he omits the spiritual interpretation of the garments that clothe Christ's body in the disputed question. In the disputed question, Christ's garments are simply the clothes Jesus was wearing, but in the *Postilla super Lucam,* Alexander asserts that the radiant clothes of the transfigured Christ show that Christians can be transfigured with Christ and acquire His glory just as His clothes did.[67] Although this commentary does not demonstrate a marked dependence on Hugh, many of Alexander's interpretations, such as the one about the garments, can be found in patristic texts or twelfth-century glosses.

Conclusion

Alexander of Hales is the first theologian of the thirteenth century to treat Christ's transfiguration both in a disputed question and in scriptural commentaries. The disputed question on Christ's transfiguration, although the first of Alexander's writings on the transfiguration, is his fullest and most independent treatment of that event. Written before Alexander became a Franciscan, this question focuses

65. *De transfiguratione Christi,* n. 17.

66. "condensatio lucis," Ms. Assisi Biblioteca Comunale 355, fol. 122va.

67. Ms. Assisi Biblioteca Comunale 355, fols. 122va–b.

primarily on the status of Christ's humanity during the transfiguration and secondarily on the presence of Moses and Elijah on Mount Tabor.

His teaching on Christ's humanity is linked to the question of whether the clarity manifested during the transfiguration is a *dos,* or gift, properly speaking. His fundamental position is that a gift is necessarily a property of a glorified body. Because Christ's transfigured body was not yet glorified, it could not have the same clarity as He would have after the resurrection; even when Christ's resurrected body communicated no glory, it still possessed clarity as a gift in a way that even His transfigured body did not. All the remaining theologians in this study will affirm this basic teaching, although some will introduce some additional distinctions.

Although the clarity of the transfiguration is only the appearance of a gift in a non-glorified body, this clarity is not like that of other non-glorified bodies. Alexander distinguishes between the normal clarity, which all corruptible bodies possess and the unique clarity of Christ's mortal body during the transfiguration. This clarity, although it exists in a non-glorified body, nevertheless exists "in the manner" of a glorified body. This unique clarity exists because of the body's union with the divine nature. Christ's assumption of "weakness," which was fitting for His salvific mission, prevents His clarity from radiating throughout His life. Although Alexander claims that this clarity can emerge when "necessary," he fails to indicate what would constitute such a necessity.

Alexander's explanation of the clarity of the transfiguration maintains an incarnational emphasis throughout the disputed question. Although Alexander maintains that the clarity of the transfiguration foreshadows the clarity of the resurrection, there is an important difference between the two. The clarity of the transfiguration, which was pleasant for the disciples to behold, was a bodily clarity, which the disciples could perceive according to their capacity. The clarity of the resurrection will be a quality perceived only by the intellect. From that point of view, the clarity that will appear bodily in the resurrection need not be much different from that of the transfiguration. The main difference between the clarity of the transfiguration and the clarity of Christ's resurrected body lay more in the renewed state of Christ's immortal body than in the bodily appearance itself. Albert the Great, in particular, will depart from Alexander's teaching in this regard.

The second topic for consideration in this disputed question concerns the appearance of Moses and Elijah. Alexander believed that the souls of both Old Testament figures appeared with their bodies with the assistance of angels (especially in the case of Moses). This union of soul and body was only *ad tempus,* and it did not allow for the possibility of meriting reward or punishment.

Alexander also treated Christ's transfiguration in his commentaries on the synoptic gospels. His *Postilla super Matthaeum,* although clearly drawing from Victorine sources, is his most independent and most insightful commentary. In that work, Alexander shows little interest in Christ's appearance. Instead, Alexander focuses on the spiritual implications of the transfiguration, especially the preparation of fasting (symbolized by the experiences of Moses and Elijah), which must precede union with God. Alexander also focuses more on the term "transfiguration" than he does in the disputed question, and he especially highlights the role of the Trinitarian Persons in the transfiguration narrative.

In this way, Alexander's commentary on Matthew neatly supplements his teaching in the disputed question. There is no contradiction between them; indeed, their discussions of clarity parallel each other in several ways. What is most important to note, however, is how the theology found in one genre is developed and expanded by the theology of the other. The disputed question emphasizes the nature of Christ's glory, while the commentary highlights how that glory permeates the Church as a whole and each member individually. The commentary also touches on questions, which are neglected in the disputed question. Alexander's theology of the transfiguration, moreover, especially as found in the disputed question will be influential for later theologians. His treatment of clarity as a gift and of the various categories pertaining to clarity will provide a basic framework for future discussions of Christ's transfiguration.

4

GUERRIC OF ST. QUENTIN

The first Dominican to take up Christ's transfiguration in the form of a disputed question was Guerric of St. Quentin, who taught at the University of Paris from 1233 to 1242. Little is known about his life, but he left a number of exegetical and systematic works, most of which remain unedited.[1] Because no commentary on any of the synoptic gospels remains, and because Guerric does not take up Christ's transfiguration in his quodlibetal questions, Guerric's theology of the transfiguration can be derived only from one of his disputed questions.[2] This brief disputed question on Christ's transfiguration is similar in style to Alexander's. While Alexander had one larger inquiry and one smaller one, Guerric's question consists of six brief inquiries, in which he tends to adduce terse objections and responses with brief *solutiones.*[3]

1. On Guerric's life and work, see Palemon Glorieux, *Répertoire des maitres en théologie de Paris au XIIIe siècle,* 2 tt. (Paris: J. Vrin, 1933–1934), t. 1, 54–58; Thomas Kaeppeli, *Scriptores Ordinis Praedicatorum Medii Aevi,* 4 vols. (Rome: Ad S. Sabinae, 1970–1993), vol. 2, 61–70; F. M. Henquinet, "Les écrits du Frère Guerric de Saint-Quentin, O.P.," *Recherches de théologie ancienne et médiévale* 6 (1934): 184–214, 284–312, 394–410, and "Notes additionelle sur les écrits de Guerric de Saint-Quentin," *Recherches de théologie ancienne et médiévale* 8 (1936): 369–88. Henquinet notes that there may be a fragment of Guerric's Luke commentary in Ms. Assisi Biblioteca Communale 131; see his "Les écrits du Frère Guerric de Saint-Quentin, O.P.," 193.

2. See Jean-Pierre Torrell's introduction to Guerric of Saint-Quentin, *Quaestiones de quolibet,* edited by Walter H. Principe, 3–177 (Toronto: Pontifical Institute of Mediaeval Studies, 2002). Torrell reviews Guerric's exegetical works on 9–13.

3. Guerric outlines only five questions in the prologue to the question, but the two parts of the last question are not directly related.

Quaestio de transfiguratione Domini

The first inquiry, which is the longest, asks whether Christ assumed true clarity or only a likeness of clarity. Guerric opens the question with fourteen arguments, eight in favor of the position that Christ did indeed assume true clarity and six arguing against it. A full half of these brief arguments are taken from various glosses, and nearly all are exegetical in nature. Most of the arguments for true clarity, which derive from glosses, tend to emphasize that the transfiguration is a foretaste of Christ's heavenly kingdom, which He will establish at the Last Judgment. Another argument compares the transfiguration to the vision of Paul, as recorded in 2 Corinthians 12, concluding that if "Paul, while he was yet mortal, sees the true glory of [His] soul, which is greater than the glory of the body . . . how much more, therefore, were Peter and the others able to see the true glory of [His] body."[4] The two most compelling arguments, however, allege that it would be inappropriate for Christ to manifest the glory of His future resurrection by means of a likeness to that glory or for Him to confirm the apostles' faith by means of a likeness and not the true glory itself. The arguments suggesting a likeness of Christ's clarity emphasize the temporal and qualitative difference between Christ before His resurrection and Christ after His resurrection. If the transfiguration is a sign and example of Christ's future glory, it should be distinct from that glory. The transfiguration is not an instance of future glory, but merely a foreshadowing.

Guerric's solution is based primarily on a gloss (later attributed to Bede by John of La Rochelle), which asserts that Christ's mortal body cannot be subject to immortality. Here is Guerric's solution in full:

Some say that Christ is the first-fruits of those who are asleep and the first-born of the dead and that His resurrection is the cause of ours: It was fitting that, while He was still in His mortal body, He should manifest that excellence in His body. Hence they say that He assumed the true clarity

4. "Paulus adhuc mortalis vidit veram gloriam animae, quae maior est quam gloria corporis . . . ergo multo magis Petrus [et] alii potuerunt videre veram corporis gloriam," *Quaestio de transfiguratione Domini*, edited by Thomas Marschler in Marschler, *Auferstehung und Himmelfahrt Christi in der scholastischen Theologie bis zu Thomas von Aquin*, 2 vols., 81–86 (Münster, Ger.: Aschendorff Verlag, 2003), 2:81.

of a glorified body for a time and three other [gifts] before His passion: subtlety in His nativity, agility when He walked on water, and impassibility at the supper, when He gave Himself in an edible form to the apostles without suffering or injury.

Against this is that gloss: "He did not manifest immortality in His mortal body," etc. He assumed, therefore, neither that [clarity] which belongs to immortality nor the other [gifts].

Again, the fact that there was no subject in which this [clarity] could be shown and other related arguments sufficiently show that [Christ] revealed to them a likeness, not the truth. Again, [someone] might say that this was imaginary, and this easily would be of that heresy which said that Christ did not suffer truly, but only apparently.[5]

The gloss Guerric appropriates emphasizes the mortality of Christ's body and implies that opposite qualities cannot exist simultaneously in the same subject. Indeed, the fuller text cited later by John of La Rochelle is far more explicit, "He manifests clarity similar to that of future immortality, just as afterwards, He manifested to His disciples not mortality, but a form like that of mortality in His immortal body. For a mortal body is not subject to immortality nor is an immortal body subject to mortality."[6] If Guerric had cited this text in its entirety as John of La Rochelle had done, his argument would have been more persuasive. In any event, he seems to be aware of the dangers of taking

5. "Quidam dicunt, quod Christus est primitiae dormientium et primo et primogenitus ex mortuis, et sua resurrectio causa est nostrae: Decuit ut adhuc vivens in corpore mortali istam principalitatem ostenderet in corpore in corpore suo. Unde dicunt quod tunc ad tempus assumpsit veram claritatem corporis glorificati, et ante passionem alias tres [dotes]: subtilitatem in nativitate; agilitatem quando ambulabat super aquas; impassibilitatem in cena, quando Apostolis se comestibilem tradidit sine sui passione vel laesione.

Contra hoc est illa glossa: In corpore mortali ostendit non immortalitatem etc. Ergo non tunc assumpsit, quod est immortalitatis. Ergo nec alias.

Item, quia subiectum non erat in quo ostendi posset, et aliae rationes, quae ad hoc sunt, satis ostendunt, quod similitudinem, non veritatem eis ostendit. Item [aliquis] dicere hoc posset esse phantasticum, et cito illius haeresis [renoveretur], quae dixit, quod Christus non est vere passus, sed phantastice," *Quaestio de transfiguratione Domini*, 82–83.

6. "Ostendit claritatem similem futurae immortalitati, sicut post in corpore immortali ostendit discipulis suis non mortalitatem, sed formam similem mortalitati. Non enim corpus mortale subditum est immortalitati nec immortale mortalitati," John of La Rochelle, in Alexander of Hales, *Summa theologica*, 4 tt., edited by Pp. Collegii S. Bonaventurae (Quaracchi, Italy: Ex Typographia Collegii S. Bonaventurae, 1924–1948), III, pt. 1, t. 6, q. 2, tit. 1, chap. 1 (hereafter *Summa fratris Alexandri*).

either position; if Christ did assume true clarity for a short period, the implication may be that there were two subjects (one to possess mortality and one to possess immortality). However, if Christ assumed only a likeness of clarity, that might suggest that the transfiguration was only an imaginary event.

Because Guerric writes only one response to the fourteen opening arguments, one can discern his primary concern. He responds to the objection about the parallels of Peter's and Paul's visions of Christ's glorified body and soul, respectively. Guerric finds any close parallel misleading because one vision occurred before the resurrection and one took place after the resurrection. The temporal sequence of these events makes a difference to Guerric for two reasons. First, what can behold the glory of Christ's soul is a soul "being restored from sin."[7] Guerric seems to mean that only someone who has received the grace that proceeds from Christ's resurrection can see the glory of Christ's soul. In this sense, anyone can perceive the glory of Christ's soul through grace, but to perceive the glory of Christ's body requires Christ's body to be truly glorious, a quality absent during the transfiguration. The latter part of this explanation constitutes the second reason Guerric offers for the significance of the difference in temporal sequence between the visions of Peter and Paul. Before His resurrection, Christ's body did not share in the glory of His soul, but afterwards it did share in that glory. Guerric says that "the glory of a soul is able to be manifested and seen in one imparting it . . . but the glory of a body is not [able to be manifested and seen] except in the one receiving it."[8] Since Christ's soul was always imparting glory, its glory could always be seen; but since Christ's body did not share in that glory until after the resurrection, the true glory of His body could not be seen until after the resurrection. Guerric's emphasis on the role of Christ's glorified soul in mediating clarity from the divine nature to Christ's body stands in contrast to Alexander's explanation, which neglected to attribute a mediating role to Christ's glorified soul.

The second inquiry of Guerric's question asks whether the disciples

7. "resurgens a peccato," Guerric of St. Quentin, *Quaestio de transfiguratione Domini*, 83.

8. "gloria animae potest ostendi et videri in dante . . . sed gloria corporis non nisi in participante," *Quaestio de transfiguratione Domini*, 83.

saw the glory of the transfiguration naturally or miraculously. The central problem for Guerric in this question is that the glory of the transfiguration and the light that radiated from Christ exceeded the capacity of the disciples' vision. A secondary problem is a text attributed to Augustine, which claims that the disciples could not see Christ when He was transfigured.

Although he never gives a direct answer to the opening question, Guerric acknowledges that the light radiating from the transfigured Christ exceeded the ocular capacity of the disciples. Thus, he interprets the text attributed to Augustine to mean not that the disciples did not behold Christ at all, but rather that they saw Him in an imperfect or incomplete manner.[9] The overwhelming glory and light of the transfiguration, which Guerric, in opposition to Alexander of Hales, seems to believe caused the disciples at least some discomfort, if not pain, give witness to the ineffability and incomprehensibility of His divinity and to the glorious humanity the resurrected Christ will possess. Even though the bodily glory of the transfiguration is not the same as the glory of the future resurrection, nevertheless, through this likeness of future glory, Christ is trying to lead the disciples to "what is incomprehensible."[10] Although the frailness of the disciples caused them to be terrified in the presence of such glorious light, Christ used this revelation to impart a greater understanding and a stronger faith before His suffering and death.

After establishing that the glory of Christ's transfigured body exceeded the natural capacity of the disciples, Guerric proceeds, in the third inquiry, to examine whether Christ's clarity was natural or miraculous. The point of departure in this question is a gloss on Matthew 17:2, which Guerric divides into two parts, "The clarity which He had, He manifested through nature . . . that nature did not cease to be true, etc."[11] Guerric uses the first part to suggest that Christ possessed

9. "Verum est, quod improportionalis erat illa lux oculis eorum, nec eam viderunt plene. Quod vult Augustinus dicere in illa auctoritate. Unde plenitudinem et perfectionem visionis intendit ab eis removere," *Quaestio de transfiguratione Domini*, 83–84.

10. "Quod autem imperfecte et incomplete eam viderunt, patet quia aliter non duceret eos in incomprehensibile," *Quaestio de transfiguratione Domini*, 84.

11. "Claritatem, quam habebat, per naturam ostendit . . . eadem non veritatem amittens etc.," *Quaestio de transfiguratione Domini*, 84. The Rusch edition of the *Glossa ordinaria* (*Biblia*

clarity through nature, and the second part he cites to show that, if Christ indeed had clarity through nature, He would have had both clarity and opacity, two opposite qualities, simultaneously.[12]

Guerric, in his own brief solution to the problem, affirms both parts of the gloss, by specifying the meaning of "through nature" and "miraculously":

> [Christ] had that clarity through nature, that is through a natural disposition, because He was especially disposed to it, not only on account of the union with a glorified soul, but also on account of the union with the divine nature. Nevertheless, because that union was miraculous, in this sense can Christ be said to have had [clarity] through a miracle. For, since a new power was added, both the accumulation of powers is miraculous, and its act or its use is miraculous.[13]

From the first moment of the Incarnation, Christ's body possessed this "disposition" to clarity, but at the transfiguration it acquired, by virtue of its union with Christ's glorified soul and with the divine nature, clarity itself. Thus, for Guerric the disposition to clarity is natural, and the body's actual possession of it during the transfiguration is miraculous.

The fourth inquiry consists of two brief questions and answers. The first question addresses why Christ manifested His future glory through clarity rather than through the other gifts. To this question Guerric simply responds, "because more than all the other qualities of the body, clarity most completely reveals itself. Besides, it is the most noble of the gifts."[14]

---

latina cum glossa ordinaria: Facsimile Reprint of the Editio Princeps Adolph Rusch of Strassburg 1480/81, introduction by Karlfried Froehlich and Margaret T. Gibson, 4 vols. [Turnhout, Belg.: Brepols, 1992]) has this marginal gloss, with slightly different wording: "Speciem quam habebat per naturam ostendit: non amittens carnem quam assumpserat voluntate," 4:57 (hereafter *Glossa ordinaria*). The latter part of the gloss is replicated, with slight variations, in corresponding glosses on Mark and Luke (4:112, 174).

12. *Quaestio de transfiguratione Domini*, 84.

13. "Per naturam, id est per naturalem dispositionem, habuit illam claritaten, quia maxime erat dispositus ad hoc, tum propter unionem ad animam gloriosam, cum propter unionem ad divinitatem. Tam[en], quia illa unio fuit miraculosa, quantum ad hoc potest dici per miraculum habuisse. Cum enim confertur nova potentia, et collatio potentiae est miraculosa, et actus vel usus eius est miraculosus," *Quaestio de transfiguratione Domini*, 84.

14. "quia claritas super omnes corporis qualitates maxime se manifestat. Item, quia inter dotes ipsa est nobilior," *Quaestio de transfiguratione Domini*, 84.

The second question Guerric asks is why Christ, after His resurrection, manifested His resurrection in more than one way. The purpose of this question is to compare Christ's transfiguration with His resurrection, and Guerric identifies two differences. The first difference is that Christ manifested His glory only to a few disciples to prepare them for their ministry, while after the resurrection, He manifested Himself to people according to their capacity. The second difference is that Christ, in the transfiguration, "intended to manifest one thing, namely the glory of those who are good," while after His resurrection, "He intended to show many things, that the resurrection was of Himself and not of another, that it was true and glorious, and many other things, as well."[15]

Guerric's fifth inquiry investigates the kind of change that took place in Christ's body. First, he asks if there was either motion *(motus)* or change *(mutatio)*. Guerric uses the term *motus* to signify the changing of one quality to another, while *mutatio* refers to the creation of a quality or the augmentation or intensification of an already existing quality. The problem with motion, with respect to the transfiguration, is the implication that Christ's mortal body, in acquiring an immortal quality before the resurrection, lost its mortal character. The problem with change is that the increase of the pre-existing clarity in Christ's mortal body resulted from a source outside it, in which case "there were opposite qualities in the same thing . . . or there were two qualities of the same appearance and in the same thing."[16]

Guerric characterizes what happened during the transfiguration as *mutatio*, that is "a coming into being of a quality, not, indeed, in the manner of generation, since it did not occur from the principles of the subject, but rather more like the manner of creation."[17] What comes

15. "intendebat unum ostendere, gloriam scilicet bonorum . . . multa intendebat probare, quia et resurrectionem veram et resurrectionem gloriosam et resurrectionem sui, non alterius, et alia multa," *Quaestio de transfiguratione Domini*, 85. See also Guerric's third disputed question on the resurrection (*Quaestiones de resurrectione Christi*, edited by Thomas Marschler in Marschler, *Auferstehung und Himmelfahrt Christi in der scholastischen Theologie bis zu Thomas von Aquin*, 2:98–99).

16. "essent contraria in eodem, vel . . . essent duae qualitates eiusdèm speciei et in eodem," *Quaestio de transfiguratione Domini*, 85.

17. "ingressus qualitatis in esse. Non quidem secundum viam generationis, quia non ex principiis subiecti fuit, sed secundum viam creationis potius," *Quaestio de transfiguratione Domini*, 85.

into being at the time of the transfiguration is a quality, which is similar to the clarity of a glorified body, and it exists along with the clarity of Christ's non-glorified body.

In articulating his solution, Guerric describes two alternative theories, which have problems in his view. The first theory is that there are two qualities, a principle external to Christ's body and one which is connatural to it, which effect Christ's transfigured body. This theory is problematic because the two qualities are not proportionate to one another and thus could not combine to effect one appearance. The second theory is that, since the qualities of a mortal body and an immortal body are contradictory and could not exist in the same subject, Christ's body remained mortal, while the adventitious clarity that the disciples saw was actually in the air surrounding Christ's body. Guerric dismisses this opinion by referring to the accounts of Matthew and Mark, which say that Christ Himself was transfigured.

Guerric maintains that the clarity perceived was an adventitious quality of Christ's body, coming to it in a way that is analogous to creation. If Christ's transfigured body was a pledge of future glory, radiant air would not truly show that glory, which is of a resurrected human body. The clarity radiated from Christ's body, but came from outside His mortal body's natural capacity and was not a product of two opposing qualities. The adventitious clarity of the transfiguration and the natural clarity of Christ's mortal body remain distinct and operate distinctly within the same subject. Guerric explains:

> Just as a glorified body penetrates a non-glorified one without change to either, so too can the quality of a glorified body or one similar to it exist with the clarity of a non-glorified body or in it without any change to either. Hence both those qualities were able to exist in Christ's body as in a subject, without one impeding the other, just as two bodies, one glorified and the other not glorified, can exist simultaneously without one impeding the other.[18]

18. "Et quemadmodum corpus glorificatum penetrat non glorificatum sine utriusque mutatione, ita qualitas corporis glorificati vel similis illi potest esse cum claritate corporis non glorificati, vel in illa sine utriusque aliqua mutatione. Unde poterant ambo illae qualitates esse in corpore Christi sicut in subiecto, una non impediente alteram, sicut duo corpora, alterum glorificatum, alterum non glorificatum, sunt simul, altero alterum non impediente," *Quaestio de transfiguratione Domini*, 85.

Guerric realizes that although this position explains the existence of the clarity seen by the disciples by allowing for the separate operation of two distinct qualities, it nevertheless appears to contradict his own concern about opposite qualities inhering in the same subject. His solution is to argue that both qualities are present in Christ, but in different ways. The clarity similar to that of a glorified body is in Christ's body "like something which forms through illumination," while the clarity connatural to Christ's mortal body is "like something which forms by taking root."[19] Guerric clarifies this statement by saying that one quality was in Christ according to His mortal condition, while the other quality was in Christ because of His body's union with His glorified soul.[20]

In this inquiry Guerric has demonstrated three primary concerns. The first is that Christ's body remained mortal despite the overpowering glory of His transfigured body. The second is that the adventitious clarity, present on account of the body's union with Christ's glorified soul, truly existed in Christ's body. The third concern is that both types of clarity maintain their separate characteristics and operations. In maintaining these positions, Guerric has recourse to the argument he made in the first inquiry, that the adventitious clarity, while it foreshadowed the glory of the resurrection, was not exactly the same as that of Christ's resurrected body.

Appended to the fifth inquiry and concluding the disputed question is a brief inquiry regarding the appearance of Moses and Elijah. The sole argument is a statement from Jerome that claims the actual bodies of Moses and Elijah did not appear; rather, other bodies were created for the purpose of speaking with Christ and testifying to His divinity. A one-sentence objection notes that if this position were true, Moses and Elijah would not be truly speaking nor providing the testimony for which they were summoned. Guerric's own position confirms the objection by repeating that if Moses and Elijah did not truly appear there would be no true testimony, and he explains Jerome's

19. "sicut informans per modum raditionis [*sic*] . . . sicut informans per modum radicationis," *Quaestio de transfiguratione Domini*, 86.

20. "Vel potest dici, quod non secundum idem erant ibi, quia secundum principia complexionis humanae erat ibi qualitas eius propria, secundum vero unionem corporis ad animam gloriosam etc.," *Quaestio de transfiguratione Domini*, 86.

gloss[21] by saying that the statement merely relates "an opinion or some disputed positions."[22]

Conclusion

In all the articles of this disputed question, Guerric is interested in the truth or reality of the transfiguration. According to Guerric, the mortality of Christ's non-glorified body necessitates that Christ's transfigured body must have been different in some way from His resurrected body, and that the clarity of the transfiguration must have differed from the clarity of the resurrection. Although Guerric allows the hypostatic union to play a central role in allowing for the clarity of Christ's soul and for His mortal body's capacity for clarity, it does not play the exclusive role that it did for Alexander of Hales. Christ's glorious soul mediates clarity to the body during the transfiguration and after the resurrection. For Guerric, Christ's mortal body has a natural capacity for clarity. Like all physical objects that reflect light, it possesses a natural clarity, and in addition to this clarity, another clarity comes into being during the transfiguration. The presence of this second clarity, which derives from His divine nature, is miraculous insofar as the body possesses it in a non-glorified state. The mortality of Christ's body, however, ensures that the bodily clarity perceived by the disciples, a clarity that exceeds their natural powers of vision, is not the same as the one Christ's resurrected body will have.

Although this disputed question is very brief, it makes notable contributions to the discussion of Christ's transfiguration. The most important point is the mediating role of Christ's soul in communicating clarity to His body. Later questions on the transfiguration, especially by Thomas Aquinas, will strive to account for the immediate relationship of Christ's bodily clarity to the divine nature and to Christ's glorified soul. Also, the notion of two coexisting clarities in Christ's body, although implied in the teaching of Alexander of Hales, receives a much more sophisticated treatment in Guerric's question. The distinc-

21. See *Glossa ordinaria* 4:175.
22. "appunctata vel opinionem recitat," *Quaestio de transfiguratione Domini,* 86.

tion between two clarities allows Guerric to refer to the one proceeding from Christ's glorified soul as "miraculous." Thomas Aquinas will utilize this distinction in his early commentary on Peter Lombard's *Sentences*. Finally, while Guerric emphasizes that Christ's transfigured clarity is only similar to that of His glorified body, he nevertheless believes that this clarity overpowered the senses of the disciples. While Alexander emphasized the pleasantness of the transfiguration, Guerric highlights the fear the disciples experienced.

The form of Guerric's disputed question is fairly primitive compared to those written in the second half of the thirteenth century, insofar as the articles tend to incorporate only terse, undeveloped arguments or have incomplete citations of authoritative texts. Still, this disputed question provides an interesting contrast and supplement to Alexander's. Guerric's question not only represents another view of the transfiguration from the 1230s or early 1240s, but it voices Christological positions that will be taken up and developed by Guerric's successors.

5

JOHN OF LA ROCHELLE

After Guerric's question on the transfiguration, the next systematic reflection on the transfiguration is John of La Rochelle's *Quaestio de transfiguratione*, a question that was inserted into the *Summa fratris Alexandri* by the original editors of that work, of whom John was one. Almost nothing is known of John's life before he became a Franciscan master of theology at the University of Paris. He seems to have studied under Alexander of Hales and later occupied the second chair of theology in the Franciscan *studium generale*. In addition to teaching, John worked closely with Alexander of Hales and other Franciscan theologians to compile the *Summa fratris Alexandri;* indeed he may have composed much of Book One (on God) and Book Three (on Christ) before he died in 1245.[1] Book Three contains John's question on the transfiguration; this question bears the distinction of being the longest and most exhaustive examination of Christ's transfiguration in the thirteenth century.

This chapter will examine in detail both the content and literary context of John's question and his exegesis of the transfiguration narratives of the synoptic gospels. All three of John's commentaries survive but have received little study. As this chapter will show, John made enormous contributions to the development of scholastic theology. Not only does his question on the transfiguration demonstrate unprecedented thoroughness, but the distinctions he makes and his

1. See Ludwig Hödl, "Johannes de Rupella," LexMA: 598. On John's various works in the *Summa fratris Alexandri*, see Victorin Doucet, *Prolegomena in librum III necnon in libros I et II "Summae fratris Alexandri,"* in Alexander of Hales, *Summa theologica*, t. 4, CCXI–CCXXVII.

method of exegesis are more sophisticated than those of a decade or so earlier. John's investigation of the transfiguration, along with that of Albert the Great, marks a new stage in theological reflection on this event of Christ's life.

De transfiguratione or *De demonstratione resurrectionis Christi*

In the question on the transfiguration, John drew from Alexander's teaching, but the format of John's question is very different from Alexander's. Compared to Alexander of Hales' *Quaestio de transfiguratione Christi,* this question is much longer and more thorough in its investigation and treatment of the transfiguration. Not only are many more questions raised, but John applies more sophisticated distinctions in his answers as well. Although not all of John's answers are as complex as those of subsequent theologians, the wide range of questions he poses render this the most complete treatment of the transfiguration in the thirteenth century.

Unlike Alexander's and Guerric's disputed questions, however, John's question on the transfiguration has a literary context. That is, it was inserted into a *summa,* which possessed a certain organization. Therefore, it is appropriate to situate this question within the literary structure of the whole *summa* before analyzing its content. Like the *Summa theologiae* of Thomas Aquinas, the *Summa fratris Alexandri* is composed of three main sections called books. The first two books are divided into two parts each, and the third book has three parts.

This organization of the *Summa,* however, as it exists in its unfinished state, does not reveal the full intention of the authors. The general structure of the *Summa* was to resemble that of Peter Lombard's *Sentences,* but with far more detail. The most illuminating passage of the *Summa,* the prologue to Book Three is so instructive that the editors appended it as a general prologue to the entire work.[2] Here are two key passages from that text:

2. See the editors' note on the general prologue in *Summa theologica,* t. 1.

> The whole discipline of the Christian faith pertains to two things: to faith and understanding of the Creator and to faith and understanding of the Savior. Hence Isaiah the prophet, speaking in the person of the Lord, says in 43:10–11, "that you may believe me, and understand that I myself am. Before me there was no God formed, and after me there shall be none. I am, I am the Lord: and there is no savior beside me." A catholic inquiry into those things which pertain to the faith is fourfold: the first part pertains to knowledge of the substance of the divine Trinity and Unity; the second to the works of divine creation; the third to the person of the Savior in His divine nature and human nature; but the fourth pertains to the sacraments of salvation and the works of future glorification.[3]

The stated motivation for organizing the theological topics is very different from Lombard's in its principles, namely things and signs, but the result is similar.[4] The prologue divides theological inquiry into two parts, one regarding the Creator and one pertaining to the Savior. Each part is then divided into two parts, the first of which addresses knowledge of God (as Creator and as Savior) and the second of which addresses knowledge of His work (of creation and of redemption). Although there is no Book Four and each of the first three books remains incomplete,[5] the *Summa* maintains this general organizational schema.[6]

3. "Tota christianae fidei disciplina pertinet ad duo: ad fidem et intelligentiam Conditoris et fidem atque intelligentiam Salvatoris. Unde Isaias Propheta, in persona Domini loquens, dicit, 43, 10–11: *Credatis et intelligatis quia ego ipse sum: ante me non est formatus deus et post me non erit. Ego sum, ego sum Dominus, et non est absque me salvator* . . . Inquisitio igitur catholica de iis quae pertinent ad fidem quadripartita est: prima pars pertinet ad cognitionem substantiae divinae Trinitatis et Unitatis; secunda ad opera divinae conditionis; tertia ad personam Salvatoris in natura divinitatis et natura humanitatis; quarto vero pertinet ad sacramenta salutis et opera futurae glorificationis," *Summa fratris Alexandri,* III, prol. (italics here and in subsequent citations from the *Summa fratris Alexandri* are the editors').

4. See Peter Lombard, *Sententiae in IV libris distinctae,* 2 tt., edited by Pp. Collegii S. Bonaventurae (Grottaferrata, It.: Editiones Collegii S. Bonaventurae ad Claras Aquas, 1971–1981), I, d. 1, chap. 1.

5. On the unfinished nature of this text see Doucet, *Prolegomena in librum III necnon in libros I et II "Summae fratris Alexandri,"* CCCXXIV–CCCXXXIX.

6. It should be noted that the *Summa* contains another organizational schema, which, although not necessarily contradicting the outline from the more specific prologue to Book Three, follows more closely the text as it currently stands. The opening of Book Two relates that "With the tractates on those things which pertain to the investigation of God, who is the Maker of every creature, complete, the tractate on those things which pertain to the consideration of the creature follows; and first, concerning those things which pertain to the creature itself, insofar as it is a creature, then concerning those things which pertain to its lapse or

The first book opens with introductory reflections on the nature of theology and the knowledge of God, possible in this life. The compilers of the text use Romans 10:10, "For, with the heart, we believe unto justice; but, with the mouth, confession is made unto salvation" as a basis for their *divisio textus* and divide the book into two main parts. The first part of the book discusses what Christians believe about God, and the second part addresses what Christians confess about God. The opening passage of the first part explains: "There is, therefore, a twofold inquiry into the Unity and Trinity of the divine nature: the first concerns that thing, which is the Unity of the Trinity, ordered to the belief of the heart; the second concerns the articulation of that belief, ordered to the confession of the mouth, that we may know what we believe, confessing with Catholic and true words."[7]

The second book, as noted above, is also divided into two parts. The first part is a lengthy treatment of creatures. It begins with creatures in general and then looks at angels and human beings. The subject of the second part is evil and sin, and, like the first part, it is rather lengthy.

The third book is "on the Person of the Son of God, who is the Head of our salvation, through the assumption of our humanity."[8] The first part of this book, which contains John of La Rochelle's question on the transfiguration, is on the Incarnate Word. The second part is on laws and precepts, and the third part is on grace and virtues.

The *Pars Prima* of Book Three, on the Incarnate Word, is comprised of eight tractates: the Incarnation and assumption of human nature; Christ's conception and nativity; the grace, knowledge, and power of Christ; Christ's will; Christ's passion and death; Christ's res-

---

deterioration, and third follows the tractate on restoration [Completis tractatibus de iis quae pertinent ad speculationem Dei, qui est factor omnis creaturae, sequitur tractatus de iis quae pertinent ad considerationem creaturae: Et primo, de iis quae pertinent ad ipsam creaturam, in quantum est creatura; deinde, de iis quae pertinent ad lapsum sive deteriorationem eiusdem; tertio, sequitur tractatus de reparatione]," *Summa fratris Alexandri*, II, t. 1, s. 1.

7. "Est igitur inquisitio bipartita de Unitate et Trinitate deitatis: prima de ipsa re, quae est Unitas Trinitatis ordinata ad credulitatem cordis; secunda de nominatione ordinata ad confessionem oris, ut sciamus quod credimus, confiteri locutionibus catholicis et veris," *Summa fratris Alexandri*, I, pt. 1.

8. "circa personam Filii Dei, qui est caput nostrae salutis per assumptionem nostrae humanitatis," *Summa fratris Alexandri*, III, prol.

urrection and proof of the resurrection; Christ's ascension into heaven and His sitting at the right hand of the Father; and Christ's coming in judgment. John of La Rochelle's question on the transfiguration is the first part of two main investigations of the antepenultimate tractate on Christ's resurrection and proof of the resurrection. The first investigation is on Christ's resurrection and answers questions pertaining to the necessity, causality, and time of the resurrection. The second investigation examines Christ's transfiguration and His post-resurrection appearances as proof of the resurrection. The following outline illustrates the literary structure of Book Three's *Pars Prima* and identifies the location of John of La Rochelle's disputed question on the transfiguration within that structure:

- Tractate 1. On the Incarnation and assumption of human nature
- Tractate 2. On Christ's conception and nativity
- Tractate 3. On the grace, knowledge, and power of Christ
- Tractate 4. On Christ's will
- Tractate 5. On Christ's passion and death
- Tractate 6. On Christ's resurrection and proof of the resurrection
  - Question 1. On the resurrection
  - Question 2. On the proof of the resurrection or on the transfiguration
    - Title 1. On the first proof or on the transfiguration of Christ
    - Title 2. On the second proof of the resurrection or on the reasons for Christ's appearance
- Tractate 7. On Christ's ascension into heaven and His sitting at the Father's right hand
- Tractate 8. On Christ's coming in judgment

An overview of the major divisions and subdivisions of this vast work shows how John's disputed question, which may have been written independently of the compilation of the *Summa*, acquires additional theological significance by its placement in the *Summa fratris Alexandri*. Instead of a question exclusively on Christ's transfiguration, it becomes an investigation into how Christ's resurrection was anticipated or revealed. Thus, John's question is framed not only by the work of other authors, including Alexander of Hales, but also by the theological vision of the *Summa*'s compilers. Because John himself was one of the collaborators of this ambitious theological project, his question on Christ's transfiguration will be treated, not as an isolated disputed question, but within the context of the *Summa*'s literary structure, which was largely composed by Franciscans other than himself.

The introductory portion of the question exemplifies how certain conceptions, not attributable to John—but possibly his—shaped the reception of John's disputed question in its original form. The introduction is as follows:

> It remains to inquire about the proof of the resurrection. The resurrection, moreover, can be proven in two ways: before it happened, on the mountain, to Peter, James, and John in Matthew 17:1–9, and several times after it happened with his disciples, "for forty days appearing to them," in Acts 1:3. The question, therefore, is about the first proof or manifestation of the glory of the resurrection, concerning which it is said in Matthew 17:1–2: "He was transfigured before them. And his face did shine as the sun: and his garments became white as snow," etc.[9]

This text is not part of John's question, and it reveals the perspective of the compilers. The transfiguration is not primarily an event confirming the faith of the disciples before Christ's passion and death, nor is it discussed within the context of all the events of Christ's life. It is viewed primarily as a proof of the resurrection, along with the appearances of Jesus after the resurrection.

John himself divides the question on the transfiguration into nine inquiries: whether Jesus underwent a transfiguration, whether His clarity was real or imaginary, whether the clarity was really in Christ's body or in the air surrounding Him, whether the clarity was glorious or only similar to glorious clarity, whether the clarity was natural or assumed, whether Christ's body alone was transfigurable, how Christ's appearances before and after the resurrection compare, how Moses

9. "Restat quaerere de demonstratione resurrectionis. Resurrectio autem demonstrata est bis: antequam fieret, in monte Petro, Iacobo et Ioanni, Matth. 17:1–9, et postquam facta est, pluries discipulis, *per quadraginta apparens eis*, Act. 1:3. Quaestio ergo versatur circa primam demonstrationem sive ostensionem gloriae resurrectionis, de qua dicitur Matth. 17:1–2: *Transfiguratus est et resplenduit facies eius sicut sol, et vestimenta eius facta sunt alba sicut nix* etc.," *Summa fratris Alexandri*, III, pt. 1, t. 6, q. 2, tit. 1, intro.

and Elijah were present, and how the apostles saw the vision.[10] In the course of the twofold divisions of Alexander of Hales' question, most of these inquiries are addressed, but John's order is very different.

Like Alexander, John begins his question with an inquiry into what "transfiguration" signifies and how it relates to Jesus' experience on the mountain. John, however, is interested not so much in the lexical meaning of "transfiguration," although he does presuppose it, but rather in what *figura* means. Citing different passages from Scripture, he argues that "figure" has three different meanings:

In one way, "figure" is said to be a distinction according to quantity, and this is properly said to be a figure; one reads in Wisdom 7:1: "In the womb of my mother I was formed." In a second way "figure" is said to be the same as "form," and by this way figure is spoken of according to quality . . . concerning this is what is found in 1 Corinthians 7:31: "the form of this world is passing away." In a third way "figure" is said to be the same as a sign of something; concerning this is what is found in 1 Corinthians 10:11: "Now all these things happened to them in figure." Therefore, since transfiguration can be a change of figure or according to figure, it can be a change of figure according to quantity or according to quality or it can be the manifestation of a sign. If, therefore, transfiguration should be said to be a change of figure according to quantity, in this way there was not a transfiguration in that appearance of Christ; but by speaking of transfiguration in the second way, that is according to that which is said to be a certain transformation and change into another form, concerning which it is also said in 2 Corinthians 11:14: "Satan transforms himself into an angel of light." In this way there was a transfiguration. By speaking also of the said transfiguration in the third way, in this way also there was a transfiguration.[11]

10. See *Summa fratris Alexandri*, III, pt. 1, t. 6, q. 2, tit. 1, intro.

11. "Uno enim modo dicitur figura distinctio secundum quantitatem, et haec dicitur proprie figura; de hac legitur Sap. 7, 1: *In ventre matris figuratus sum.* Secundo modo dicitur figura idem quod forma, et hoc modo dicitur figura secundum qualitatem . . . de hac habetur I Cor. 7:31: *Praeterit figura huius mundi.* Tertio modo dicitur figura idem quod signum rei; de hac habetur I Cor. 10:11: *Haec autem in figura contingebant illis.* Cum igitur transfiguratio sit mutatio figurae sive secundum figuram, potest transfiguratio esse mutatio figurae secundum quantitatem vel secundum qualitatem vel ostensio signi. Si ergo dicatur transfiguratio mutatio figurae secundum quantitatem, hoc modo non fuit transfiguratio in apparitione illa Christi; sed dicendo transfigurationem secundo modo, hoc est secundum quod dicitur quaedam transformatio et mutatio in formam aliam, de qua etiam dicitur II Cor. 11:14: *Satanas transfigurat se in angelum lucis,* hoc modo fuit ibi transfiguratio. Loquendo etiam de transfiguratione dicta

Of the three ways in which "transfiguration" can be understood, all founded on scriptural references and corresponding glosses, John finds that two appropriately describe what happened to Jesus. Although Christ underwent no quantitative change, the transformation of Christ's face and garments merits the designation "transfiguration." Also, transfiguration can mean that the transformation of Christ's face and garments was a sign that pointed to the future glory of the resurrection.

John's appropriation of scriptural passages leads him to agree with Alexander's contention that there is no transfiguration, properly speaking; but his twofold distinction between types of improper senses of "transfiguration" is more specific than Alexander's mere "mutatio secundum quid."[12] This distinction allows John to respond to an objection, which Alexander had not really answered, namely, how it is that Jesus' post-resurrection appearances are not referred to as transfigurations since His glorified body does not then have its proper appearance. Alexander discussed Jesus' post-resurrection state, but primarily within the context of the clarity of Christ's body, not its relation to the significance of the word "transfiguration."

John's response to the objection that if "transfiguration" refers to Jesus' glorious appearance in a mortal body, then his humble appearances in a glorified body can also be called the same, allows him to elaborate on what constitutes a transfiguration. A transfiguration is a "transformation and assimilation to something; but where there is a change or assimilation of something less noble to something more noble, that is properly said to be a assimilation or transformation, and not the reverse."[13] The reason, John claims, is that "just as a building in one's mind is not said to be like an actual building, nor is an artistic conceptualization said to be like a work of art, but, on the contrary, an actual building is said to be like its artistic conceptualization or like a

tertio modo, hoc modo etiam fuit ibi transfiguratio," *Summa fratris Alexandri*, III, pt. 1, t. 6, q. 2, tit. 1, chap. 1.

12. See Alexander of Hales, *De transfiguratione Christi*, n. 16.

13. "transfiguratio idem est quod transformatio et assimilatio ad aliquid; sed ubi est mutatio sive assimilatio ignobilioris ad nobilius, proprie dicitur assimilatio vel transformatio et non e converso," *Summa fratris Alexandri*, III, pt. 1, t. 6, q. 2, tit. 1, chap. 1.

building in one's mind."[14] John applies this analogy to the transfiguration and the appearances of Jesus after His resurrection. Since transfiguration properly refers to the likeness of something less noble to something more noble, it is used appropriately of Christ's appearance with Moses and Elijah on the mountain. In this event Christ's mortal body truly acquires a likeness to a glorified body, whereas in His post-resurrection appearances, Christ's glorious body maintains a likeness to a non-glorified body.[15]

The next four chapters of this question on the transfiguration address the clarity of Christ's body. As noted above, the second inquiry asks whether the clarity of Christ's body is real or imaginary. This dimension of the transfiguration was not as significant for Alexander of Hales, whose succinct answer to this question was that the relationship between the clarity of Christ's body and that of His garments was like that of the clarity of the sun and that of the snow. The main point for Alexander is that although the clarity of Christ's garments was derived from His body, neither type of clarity was "that true and glorious clarity which will be in the future."[16]

John's examination of the question is more detailed. The first part of the second chapter examines an interpretation of Scripture. Responding to a gloss of Bede that states that the phrase "before they see the kingdom of God," (Luke 9:27) refers to the "glorification of the body in the transfiguration, that is the imaginary representation of future beatitude," John examines first the meaning of "imaginary" and its relation to the word *imago*.[17] Because an image is a likeness expressed either in a thing or in the mind, "a representation is therefore able to be called imaginary because of an image, according to which it has being through a likeness expressed in a thing or in the imaginary understanding."[18] Since the clarity of Christ's transfigured body is a likeness

14. "sicut domus in mente sive ars non dicitur similis domui in opere sive artificio, sed e converso domus in opere dicitur similis arti sive domui in mente," *Summa fratris Alexandri*, III, pt. 1, t. 6, q. 2, tit. 1, chap. 1.

15. See *Summa fratris Alexandri*, III, pt. 1, t. 6, q. 2, tit. 1, chap. 1.

16. Alexander of Hales, *De transfiguratione Christi*, n. 22.

17. "'Glorificationem corporis in transfiguratione, id est imaginariam repraesentationem futurae beatitudinis,'" *Summa fratris Alexandri*, III, pt. 1, t. 6, q. 2, tit. 1, chap. 2.

18. "Imaginaria ergo repraesentatio potest dici ab imagine, secundum quod habet esse

of "the clarity of future beatitude,"[19] it is an imaginary representation, in the sense of possessing a likeness that is expressed in a thing. John's understanding of *imago* and his definition of *repraesentatio* allow him to affirm simultaneously both the gloss that refers to the transfiguration as an "imaginary representation" and the reality of the clarity of Christ's body.

The second part of this chapter examines the relationship between the clarity of Christ's body and that of His clothes. John focuses on the reference in Luke 9:29 to Christ's clothing becoming "dazzling white." The question for John is how Christ's clothes become white. He gives two interpretations, both of which eschew the possibility that the dazzling whiteness comes from the clothes themselves. The first interpretation is that the clothes "seemed white from the surrounding splendor,"[20] the second, that the clothes "were shining, dazzling from the splendor of His face."[21] John points out not only that the second interpretation is more consonant with the word order of the Vulgate ("albus refulgens," not "refulgens albus"), but also that it accords better with the presupposition that Christ's clothes did not change color during the transfiguration.

John concludes the chapter with a reflection on the changes in Christ's face and garments, and this reflection approaches Alexander's ideas on this subject. The objection to which John responds contends that the changes in Christ's face and garments were nearly the same. John refutes this by saying, "That clarity which shone brightly in the face proceeded from an interior power, namely from the power of divinity, according to Augustine. But that which took place in the clothing, proceeded from the exterior; and only from the exterior was there a change in the clothing, namely from the splendor of the face."[22] In

per similitudinem expressam in re vel in comprehensione imaginaria," *Summa fratris Alexandri*, III, pt. 1, t. 6, q. 2, tit. 1, chap. 2.

19. "claritatis futurae beatitudinis," *Summa fratris Alexandri*, III, pt. 1, t. 6, q. 2, tit. 1, chap. 2.

20. "ex splendore circumfuso videbatur albus," *Summa fratris Alexandri*, III, pt. 1, t. 6, q. 2, tit. 1, chap. 2.

21. "refulgebat ex splendore vultus illius," *Summa fratris Alexandri*, III, pt. 1, t. 6, q. 2, tit. 1, chap. 2.

22. "Ipsa enim claritas, quae resplenduit in faciei, procedebat a virtute interiori, scilicet a virtute divinitatis, secundum Augustinum. Sed quod fiebat in veste, procedebat ab exteriori,

addition, only Christ's body is "glorifiable," not His garments, and thus only Christ's body can manifest the likeness, the true likeness, of a glorious body.

The third chapter of the question on Christ's transfiguration discusses whether the clarity of the transfiguration was in Christ's body as in a subject or in the surrounding air. At first glance, this question seems superfluous, given the teaching of the previous question, which affirmed that the clarity manifested in Christ's body proceeded from Christ's divine power. The first part presents arguments to support John's affirmations in the concluding lines of the previous question, namely that the clarity in Christ's body was real. The theological value of these first three arguments is that they specify that the clarity was in Christ "as in a subject,"[23] and they do so with more explicit evidence from scriptural texts and accompanying glosses.

The heart of the question is presented in the supporting arguments for the position that the clarity that appeared to be in Christ's body was really in the air surrounding His body. Although the opposite is implied in the previous chapter, this position gains not only more specificity here, but, more importantly, it acts as an opportunity for John to examine how Christ's pre-resurrected body could manifest clarity. The following is the lengthy first argument against the position that clarity was in Christ's body as a subject:

In the body of Christ, just as in other bodies, there was a twofold nature, namely an elemental one and a nature of the fifth body, that is a heavenly nature, which is the nature of light; but insofar as our body should have the capacity for clarity, this is not by means of the elemental nature, because, according to that, the body is corruptible, subject to contrariety, and dark; this exists, therefore, by means of the nature of light, which unites the elements in our body; the elemental nature, however, is thus related to the nature of light so that although one appears in bodies, the other is hidden, just as the elemental nature presently appears in our bodies, but the nature of light is hidden; but it will be the opposite in that glory in glorified bodies: because the nature of light will be revealed, and the elemental nature will be hidden.[24]

---

et solum ab exteriori erat mutatio in veste, scilicet a splendore faciei," *Summa fratris Alexandri,* III, pt. 1, t. 6, q. 2, tit. 1, chap. 2.

23. "ut in subiecto," *Summa fratris Alexandri,* III, pt. 1, t. 6, q. 2, tit. 1, chap. 3.

24. "In corpore Christi sicut in aliis corporibus erat duplex natura, scilicet elementaris

John goes on to apply this discussion of the "twofold nature" of human bodies to the transfiguration of Jesus. Jesus' body at the time of His transfiguration was not glorified. Thus, the "elemental nature" characterized His body, while the "nature of light" remained hidden. Since clarity must proceed from the "nature of light," which was hidden in Jesus' pre-glorified body, the clarity manifested during the transfiguration must be in something other than His body. Hence, it may be concluded that the clarity manifested "was in the air as in a subject and not in the body of the Lord."[25]

The second objection articulates a similar argument. Since the elemental nature of Christ's pre-glorified body existed "according to act," and because that nature always accompanies the darkness of such a body, it was impossible for clarity to exist "according to act" in Christ's body at the same time that the darkness of His body existed "according to act."[26] Since Christ's body could not be the subject of both brightness and darkness acting simultaneously, the clarity which was manifested must have come from the surrounding air.[27]

John begins his answer to the objections with Luke 9:29, "as he was praying, the appearance of his countenance was altered." This text, which John bolsters with a gloss from his Dominican contemporary, Hugh of St. Cher, shows that the transfiguration could not occur unless Jesus' face, itself, was actually "altered."

The reply to the first objection contains the core of John's understanding of the clarity of Christ's body. He begins by saying that the nature in Christ's body is "manifold," and that the various aspects of this nature to be considered include "the nature of the body insofar as

---

et natura quinti corporis, scilicet natura caelestis, quae est natura lucis; sed quod corpus nostrum habeat potentiam ad claritatem, hoc non est per naturam elementarem, quia secundum illam est corruptibile et subiectum contrarietati et opacum; ergo hoc est per naturam lucis, quae conciliat elementa in corpore nostro; sed sic se habet natura elementaris ad naturam lucis ut cum una apparet in corporibus, alia occultatur, sicut modo apparet in corporibus nostris natura elementaris, sed latet natura lucis; sed e contrario erit in ipsa gloria in corporibus glorificatis: quod natura lucis manifestabitur, et natura elementaris latebit," *Summa fratris Alexandri*, III, pt. 1, t. 6, q. 2, tit. 1, chap. 3.

25. "fuit in aëre ut in subiecto et non in corpore Dominico," *Summa fratris Alexandri*, III, pt. 1, t. 6, q. 2, tit. 1, chap. 3.

26. "secundum actum," *Summa fratris Alexandri*, III, pt. 1, t. 6, q. 2, tit. 1, chap. 3.

27. *Summa fratris Alexandri*, III, pt. 1, t. 6, q. 2, tit. 1, chap. 3.

it is a body, the nature of the body insofar as it is animated by a soul or the nature of the body insofar as it is united to a soul which is full of all grace, and the nature of the body itself as it is conjoined with the divine nature."[28] This "manifold" nature of Christ's body implicitly rejects the contention at the opening of the objection that the nature in Christ's body is "twofold." Insofar as Christ's body is considered as a body with no relation to anything else, its nature is "twofold," that is, it has a "dominant elemental nature and a hidden celestial nature."[29]

As such, Christ's body "acquires darkness and corruption,"[30] but Christ's body must also be considered under other aspects John outlines to obtain a more complete view of the properties possessed by Christ's body. Unfortunately, John writes little on the qualities of Christ's body, which follow from the body being united to a soul or a soul "full of all grace." He focuses instead on the fact that Christ's body is united to the divine nature. This union allows Christ's body to acquire a "habit which must surpass any corporeal creature, and from the nature of that union there belongs to [Christ's body] a capacity for agility, subtlety, and clarity."[31]

This account of the clarity in Christ's body is rather different from Alexander's in his question *De transfiguratione Christi*. Alexander understands Christ's bodily clarity in both incarnational and eschatological terms; Christ's bodily clarity derives from its union with the divine nature, but the clarity of the transfiguration also is "of a corruptible body, in the mode of a glorified one."[32] Christ's clarity is not that of a glorified body, but it is very much like it. It is true that Alexander

28. "naturam corporis secundum quod corpus, et naturam corporis secundum quod animatum anima rationali, vel corporis naturam secundum quod unitum animae quae est plena omni gratia, et naturam corporis ipsius prout coniunctum est divinitati," *Summa fratris Alexandri*, III, pt. 1, t. 6, q. 2, tit. 1, chap. 3.

29. "natura elementaris dominans et natura caelestis latens," *Summa fratris Alexandri*, III, pt. 1, t. 6, q. 2, tit. 1, chap. 3.

30. "sortitur opacitatem et corruptionem," *Summa fratris Alexandri*, III, pt. 1, t. 6, q. 2, tit. 1, chap. 3.

31. "habitum, qui debet praecellere omni creaturae corporali, et ex natura istius unionis inest ei potentia ad agilitatem, ad subtilitatem et ad claritatem," *Summa fratris Alexandri*, III, pt. 1, t. 6, q. 2, tit. 1, chap. 3.

32. "corporis corruptibilis per modum glorificati," Alexander of Hales, *De transfiguratione Christi*, n. 17.

also acknowledges that some things follow from the union of Christ's body to the divine nature, especially "a superior disposition to the clarity which we ought to have,"[33] but this union gives Christ only a "superior disposition," not a qualitatively different clarity from what other humans may possess.

John's account differs from Alexander's in several notable ways. First, there is no eschatological dimension whatsoever in John's understanding of Christ's clarity. It is the union of Christ's body with the divine nature, alone, which gives Christ's body its capacity for brightness and glory. Second, the clarity of Christ's body in the transfiguration is qualitatively different from the clarity other human beings can have. The union of Christ's body to the divine nature gives His body an "aptitude and capacity for things which are not fitting for the body of another man, namely clarity, subtlety, and agility."[34] Third, the properties clarity, subtlety, and agility are no longer *dotes*. It is not simply that only three qualities are mentioned (impassibility is omitted, perhaps because John does not consider these qualities *dotes* and because Christ's body, even when united to the divine nature, still has the capacity to suffer), but these qualities are also considered properties unique to Christ's body.

John must then answer how Christ's capacity for clarity relates to the "darkness" that characterized His body throughout most of His earthly life. The objection states that because the elemental nature was still operative in Christ's pre-glorified body and because bodily darkness "according to act"[35] always accompanies that nature, clarity "according to act" would have been impossible in Christ's body since contraries cannot exist simultaneously. John applies the distinction made in the reply to the first objection on the union of Christ's body to the divine nature. The union gives Christ's body the capacity for agility, subtlety, and clarity, but the elemental nature is still dominant. John explains:

33. "ulteriorem dispositionem ad claritatem quam nos habeamus," *De transfiguratione Christi*, n. 26.

34. "habilitatem et potestatem ad quaedam quae non conveniunt corpori alterius hominis, scilicet claritatem, subtilitatem et agilitatem," *Summa fratris Alexandri*, III, pt. 1, t. 6, q. 2, tit. 1, chap. 3.

35. "secundum actum," *Summa fratris Alexandri*, III, pt. 1, t. 6, q. 2, tit. 1, chap. 3.

In the departure of Christ's body from the womb of the Virgin there was subtlety according to act and bulk according to habit; similarly, when He was walking on the water there was agility in act but weight in habit; thus in the transfiguration there was clarity in act, which was from the union to the divine nature, and darkness in habit. In this way nothing prohibits opposites from existing simultaneously in the same subject.[36]

Without explaining why the potentialities for those qualities are reduced to act, without recourse to the "nature of light" whose operation is hidden in Christ's body before the resurrection, and without making any distinction between Christ's body before and after the resurrection, John affirms that Christ's body can manifest these qualities because of its union to the divine nature.

The fourth chapter of the question on the transfiguration, like the third, seems at first glance, superfluous. It asks whether Christ's clarity was glorious or only resembling glorious clarity. John already argued in chapter two, on the question whether Christ's clarity was real or imaginary, that the clarity manifested at the transfiguration was "a likeness of the clarity of future beatitude."[37] Although John had already provided, in this earlier chapter, some sort of answer to the question he poses in chapter four, he uses the current question as an opportunity to make further distinctions, which elucidate more clearly theological problems posed by Christ's transfiguration.

The question opens with two arguments, both drawn from glosses of Bede, which affirm that Christ's bodily clarity was not "glorious clarity ... but only similar to glorious [clarity]."[38] Then follow three glosses contending that the clarity of Christ's transfigured body was "glorious"; that is, it was the same clarity that the blessed will receive at the Last Judgment. In the opening of the *solutio*, John describes the

36. "in exitu corporis Domini ex utero Virginis fuit secundum actum subtilitas, et corpulentia secundum habitum; similiter ambulando super aquas fuit actu agilitas in ipso, sed habitu gravitas; sic in transfiguratione fuit claritas actu, et hoc ex unione ad divinitatem, et opacitas in habitu. Hoc modo nihil prohibet contraria simul esse circa idem subiectum," *Summa fratris Alexandri*, III, pt. 1, t. 6, q. 2, tit. 1, chap. 3.

37. "similitudo claritatis futurae beatitudinis," *Summa fratris Alexandri*, III, pt. 1, t. 6, q. 2, tit. 1, chap. 2.

38. "claritas gloriosa ... sed gloriosae similis," *Summa fratris Alexandri*, III, pt. 1, t. 6, q. 2, tit. 1, chap. 4.

former position as endowed with the authority of Bede, while the latter opinion, which maintains that Jesus assumed certain properties (including impassibility at the Last Supper) only for a short time, has the authority of Jerome.

John tries to articulate a middle position, which is based upon an examination of what the word "likeness" means and how it applies to the expression *similis gloriosae*. He makes two distinctions, the second of these is subdivided into two:

> In an object, something is an enigmatic likeness, which is of an altogether different kind, just as we say that faith in this life is similar to the vision in heaven or is assimilated to glorious knowledge. There is also a real likeness, and this is of things of the same kind; but this can be the case in two ways, either according to perfection or according to imperfection. If it is according to imperfection, in this way we say that love in this life is likened to love in heaven; for it is not likened to it in the same way as faith is to knowledge in heaven, because faith is likened to it enigmatically, because faith will be emptied, but the love of this life will be truly likened to the love of heaven, because the love of this life will not be emptied when that which is glorious comes, but it will be completed by it. It is, therefore, similar to it as an object, but nevertheless according to imperfection .... There is also a real likeness according to perfection, just as we say that a son is similar to a father, and that the love of Peter in heaven is similar to the love of Paul in heaven.[39]

John's application of these three distinctions, "enigmatic likeness," real and perfect likeness, and real and imperfect likeness to the transfiguration shows that although John believes that the clarity of Christ's transfigured body is only "similar" to that of "glorious" clarity, he never-

39. "Quaedam est similitudo aenigmatica in re, quae est omnino alterius generis, sicut nos dicimus quod fides hic in via similis est visioni in patria sive assimilatur cognitioni gloriosae. Est iterum similitudo realis, et haec est rerum eiusdem generis; sed haec potest esse dupliciter, quia aut secundum perfectionem aut secundum imperfectionem. Si secundum imperfectionem, hoc modo dicimus quod caritas in via assimilatur caritati in patria: non enim eodem modo assimilatur quo fides cognitioni in patria, quia fides assimilatur ei aenigmatice, quia fides evacuabitur, sed caritas viae [assimilatur] caritati patriae realiter, quia non evacuabitur caritas viae adveniente illa quae est in gloria, sed complebitur ab ea; est ergo ei similis in re, sed tamen secundum imperfectionem ... Est etiam similitudo realis secundum perfectionem, sicut nos dicimus quod filius est similis patri, et caritas Petri in patria caritati Pauli in patria," *Summa fratris Alexandri*, III, pt. 1, t. 6, q. 2, tit. 1, chap. 4.

theless does not want to make too sharp a disjunction between those two kinds of clarity. The "enigmatic likeness," which applies to things that differ in kind, does not apply; nor does the real and perfect likeness because that distinction implies an equality between two different things, which are of the same kind. The relationship between the clarity of the transfiguration and the "glorious" clarity of the Last Judgment is best described by John's notion of a real but imperfect likeness, in which, of two things of the same kind, one is completed or fulfilled by the other. From this point of view, the clarity of the transfiguration is similar to "glorious" clarity, and John even allows that "it was able to be called 'glorious' in some sense."[40]

The dissimilarity between the two kinds of clarity is rooted in the economy of salvation, or what John calls the *dispensatio*. This "dispensation" determined the qualities of Christ's body and soul, or rather, God determined those qualities with the Incarnation in mind. John claims that because of the union of body and soul to the divine nature, there was glory in both, but the presence of an "inferior power" in both body and soul limited the degree to which the "glorious" clarity could pervade the whole body and the whole soul. His concluding argument articulates concisely his views of the relationship of Christ's glory to His body and soul and its relation to the *dispensatio:*

Just as in Christ's soul, there was, in that which was united to the divine nature, glory in part although not in the whole, and this is according to the superior power and not according to the inferior power—indeed, according to the inferior part, there was in [His soul] passibility and misery and those things which do not attain glory, but there was glory according to the superior part, and that glory was not of another kind than that which it had afterwards, namely after the resurrection—so too in the dispensation in which the glory in His body was shown, since it was united to the divine nature just as the soul was, there was glory in part and not in part. And I say "in part," insofar as it was united to the divine nature, because just as that body was corruptible and dark by dispensation—and this on account of our liberation—so too it was due to the dispensation that it was shown before the resurrection in that clarity in which it ought to exist after-

40. "potuit dici gloriosa secundum quid," *Summa fratris Alexandri,* III, pt. 1, t. 6, q. 2, tit. 1, chap. 4.

wards—and this on account of the strengthening of our faith—and which it had from its union with the divine nature.[41]

Again, the glory in Christ's body exists only in the "superior" part of Christ's body as a result of its union to the divine nature. It is hidden during most of Christ's life so that His body, in its "inferior" part, can suffer for the salvation of humanity. The manifestation of glory during the transfiguration exists by dispensation, like the passibility of Christ's body; the special purpose of this unique event is to confirm the faith of Christ's followers. The clarity Christ reveals during the transfiguration is exactly the same kind of clarity that exists in His body after the resurrection, but because it permeates only the "superior" part of His body and not the "inferior," His body lacks the complete glorification that results after the resurrection. Although John provides an eschatological context for the clarity of Christ's transfigured body, he reaffirms its derivation from the union with the divine nature.

The emphasis on the union of Christ's body with the divine nature continues in the fifth chapter. John addresses two related questions in this chapter: the first is whether the clarity of Christ's body was natural or assumed, and the second, which presupposes that the clarity was natural, is whether it was always operating in Christ's body, even when it was not visible.

John's argument that Christ's clarity was natural is qualified, like the majority of his solutions. He begins his response by articulating the possible meanings of the word "natural" in relation to Aristotle's four causes:

41. "sicut in anima Christi, eo quod fuit unita deitati, fuit gloria secundum partem, licet non secundum totum, hoc est secundum vim superiorem et non secundum inferiorem—immo secundum partem inferiorem inerat ei passibilitas et miseria et ea quae non intrant gloriam, sed secundum partem superiorem erat gloria, et illa gloria non fuit alterius generis quam gloria quam post habuit, scilicet post resurrectionem—sic in dispensatione qua ostendebatur in suo corpore gloria, cum ipsum esset unitum deitati, sicut anima, poterat esse gloria secundum partem, et secundum partem non. Et dico secundum partem, hoc est secundum quod unitum deitati; quia, sicut ex dispensatione fuit quod corpus illud esset corruptibile et obscurum—et hoc propter liberationem nostram—sic ex dispensatione fuit quod ostenderetur in illa claritate ante resurrectionem, in qua debuit esse post—et hoc propter corroborationem fidei nostrae—quam habuit ex unione ad deitatem," *Summa fratris Alexandri*, III, pt. 1, t. 6, q. 2, tit. 1, chap. 4.

If, therefore, the nature in Christ's body should be considered from the point of view of its origin or in comparison to that from which it was produced, suffering is not natural to it, nor is passibility or mortality found in it. Hence Hilary, in *On the Trinity* 10: "Why do we judge the flesh which was conceived by the Holy Spirit by the nature of a human body? That flesh is from heaven." If, moreover, it should be considered in relation to the cause according to which it is flesh, that is, according to its perfection, namely from unity to the divine nature, I still say that, in this way, neither passibility nor those things which are opposed to glory is in Christ's body; and this is because of the nature of that perfection. In fact, from this, namely from the fullness of divine power, His body has power over all passions; therefore, according to the nature of its origin and perfection, passibility was not in His body. Understanding it, however, by comparison to that from which Christ's flesh was produced, passibility and those qualities which follow it are natural to it because it was assumed from the flesh of the Virgin: for, from our nature, He assumed a bulky nature composed from elements and subject to contrariety. Understanding it, moreover, according to the end for which it was produced, suffering and mortality are also natural to it because it was produced for our redemption so that He should redeem us through suffering.[42]

This disquisition is somewhat confusing; it concludes with John's affirmation of the naturalness of Christ's clarity in the first two senses of "nature" and his denial of it in the latter two senses. John seems to be saying that the Holy Spirit, the efficient cause of Christ's body, can convey only perfections, not impurities, to Christ's body. Likewise, the union of Christ's body to the divine nature, (which corresponds to Aristotle's

42. "Si ergo consideretur natura in corpore Christi a parte suae originis sive in comparatione ad illud a quo nata est, sic passio non est ei naturalis nec invenitur in ea passibilitas vel mortalitas. Unde Hilarius, in X *De Trinitate:* 'Quid per naturam humani corporis carnem de Spiritu Sancto conceptam iudicamus? Caro illa de caelis est.' Si autem consideretur secundum causam secundum quam est caro, id est secundum suum complementum, scilicet ex unione ad divinitatem, hoc modo adhuc dico quod non est in corpore Christi per naturam passibilitas nec ea quae opponuntur gloriae; et hoc per naturam illius complementi; sed ex hoc est corpus eius potestativum super omnes passiones, scilicet a plenitudine virtutis divinae; secundum ergo naturam originis et complementi non erat passibilitas in suo corpore. Accipiendo autem secundum comparationem ad illud de quo nata est caro Christi, secundum hoc est ei naturalis passibilitas et proprietates consequentes, quia de carne Virginis assumpta est: assumpsit enim de natura nostra naturam *corpulentam,* ex elementis compositam et contrarietati subiectam. Accipiendo autem secundum finem ad quem nata est, quia nata est redemptionem nostram, ut per passionem nos redimeret, sic adhuc est ei naturalis passio et mortalitas," *Summa fratris Alexandri,* III, pt. 1, t. 6, q. 2, tit. 1, chap. 5.

formal cause), would render it glorious. By a special dispensation, with a view toward the redemption of mankind, the Savior took flesh from the Blessed Virgin, whose own flesh contained defects such as passibility and mortality. The distinction between Christ's body according to its origin and its perfection, on the one hand, and according to a special dispensation, on the other, allows John to maintain that both clarity and passibility were natural to Christ's body, but in different ways.

John also applies this distinction in his response to the second question in chapter five: whether Christ's clarity was always operating in His body even when it did not appear. He bases his answer on a fundamental axiom, which states that "just as clarity of the soul belongs to the soul, so too does clarity of the body belong to the body."[43] John distinguishes this twofold clarity according to the body's and the soul's union with the divine nature and according "to the dispensation of our redemption."[44] According to both the union with the divine nature and to the dispensation, Christ's soul possesses "spiritual clarity"[45] or the "clarity of knowledge."[46]

Christ's body, however, by virtue of its union with the divine nature, possesses the capacity for clarity to be active constantly; however, by virtue of a general dispensation of the divine economy, it was not always active. If it had been constantly operative, Christ's body could not have suffered and thus could not have fulfilled the purpose of the Incarnation. The clarity, which could be active in both body and soul by virtue of their union with the divine nature, must be dormant[47] for Christ's suffering to be complete. Since, by dispensation, Christ's "soul ought to suffer in every power which it had in relation to the body, it is evident that His body, by dispensation, should suffer in the whole."[48]

43. "'sicut se habet claritas animae ad animam, ita claritas corporis ad corpus,'" *Summa fratris Alexandri,* III, pt. 1, t. 6, q. 2, tit. 1, chap. 5. This principle is cited in the first objection.

44. "ad dispensationem nostrae redemptionis," *Summa fratris Alexandri,* III, pt. 1, t. 6, q. 2, tit. 1, chap. 5.

45. "claritas spiritualis," *Summa fratris Alexandri,* III, pt. 1, t. 6, q. 2, tit. 1, chap. 5.

46. "scientiae claritas," *Summa fratris Alexandri,* III, pt. 1, t. 6, q. 2, tit. 1, chap. 5.

47. John uses the phrase "in potentia" to characterize the status of Christ's clarity by dispensation.

48. "eius anima debebat pati secundum omnem vim quam habebat per comparationem ad corpus, constat quod ex dispensatione fuit quod corpus eius secundum totum pateretur," *Summa fratris Alexandri,* III, pt. 1, t. 6, q. 2, tit. 1, chap. 5.

Having addressed four questions on Christ's clarity, John compares Christ's body to the bodies of other humans by inquiring into their relative transfigurability. Alexander of Hales addressed this question in one sentence, saying that only Christ's body, by virtue of its union to the divine nature, had the capacity to be transfigured and to receive clarity in the way that it did, although God could effect a transfiguration in another person if He willed it. John agrees with this position, but articulates it by making several interesting arguments and relevant observations.

John begins by proposing arguments that, besides Christ, at least two people were transfigured. The first is Moses, whose face shone after he spent forty days and forty nights with God and brought the Ten Commandments to the Israelites a second time. John says that "the 'face' of Moses appeared 'horned from the conversation of the Lord' because of its great brilliance; and it is said in 2 Corinthians 3:13 that 'the children of Israel' could not look 'on the face' of Moses because of its glory; and the Gloss says there that the clarity in his face was so great that it could not be greater."[49] Because the clarity in Jesus' transfigured body could have been greater, Moses' possession of a maximal degree of clarity should definitely qualify as a transfiguration.[50] Likewise, since Moses' face needed to be veiled because of the intense glory radiating from it, it seems that the manifestation of clarity in Moses' face was more intense than that emanating from Christ's face.

The second person, other than Christ, who seems to have been transfigured is the Blessed Virgin. The argument given here is rather surprising, "Again, on Matthew 1:25: 'He knew her not until she brought forth,' etc., the Gloss says 'Joseph was not able to see Mary face to face, whom the Holy Spirit filled.' From this it seems that the glorious Virgin was transfigured just as Christ's body was."[51] What is

49. "apparuit *facies* Moysi *cornuta ex consortio sermonis Domini* ex maximo splendore; et II Cor. 3, 13 dicitur quod non poterant *filii Israël* intendere *in faciem* Moysi propter gloriam vultus eius; et dicit Glossa ibi quod tanta fuit claritas in facie eius quod maior esse non poterat," *Summa fratris Alexandri,* III, pt. 1, t. 6, q. 2, tit. 1, chap. 6.

50. See *Summa fratris Alexandri,* III, pt. 1, t. 6, q. 2, tit. 1, chap. 6.

51. "Item Matth. 1, 25: *Non cognoscebat eam, donec peperit* etc., Glossa: 'Ioseph Mariam facie ad faciem videre non poterat, quam Spiritus Sanctus impleverat.' Ex quo videtur quod gloriosa Virgo fuerit transfigurata sicut corpus Christi." *Summa fratris Alexandri,* III, pt. 1, t. 6, q. 2, tit. 1, chap. 6.

interesting is not that the gloss takes the word "know" quite literally,[52] but that the objection takes the apparent meaning of the gloss, namely that Joseph did not see Mary until she gave birth, and intensifies it to mean that Joseph could not see Mary because she was somehow transfigured, a position John actually maintains, with some modifications, in the *solutio* of the question.

A concluding argument *ad oppositum,* drawing from the exegesis of Jerome, remarks that the Gospel of Mark's reference to Jesus' face shining like the sun (actually, only Matthew contains this passage) implies that Christ's bodily clarity was superior to that of Moses and the Blessed Virgin, and that only Christ experienced a true transfiguration.

In the body of the question, John has recourse to his distinction in chapter four on the different types of "likeness." In that discussion, John described the differences between "enigmatic likeness," real and perfect likeness, and real and imperfect likeness. Comparing the clarity of Moses, the Blessed Virgin, and the transfigured Christ to the clarity of glory, John claims that "the likeness of glory was in the face of Moses, in the Blessed Virgin, and in the body of Christ in different ways. In the faces of Moses and the Blessed Virgin, there was a likeness of clarity, which was simply of a different kind from the clarity of glory; hence it was an enigmatic likeness as was the likeness of faith to the vision of heaven."[53] John contrasts this "enigmatic likeness" of Moses' and Mary's clarity with that of Jesus, whose clarity in the transfiguration was of the same kind as the clarity of glory, even if, by dispensation, it did not permeate His entire body. The relationship between the two clarities is characterized by John's description in chapter four of the real and imperfect likeness according to which "the charity in this life is assimilated to the charity in heaven."[54]

52. The full text from the *Glossa ordinaria* reads: "Dicitur quod Ioseph Mariam facie ad faciem videre non poterat quam Spiritus Sanctus a conceptione impleverat penitus. Et ideo non cognoscebat facie ad faciem quam desponsaverat: donec uterus evacuatur. De quo hic non agitur" (4:7).

53. "aliter fuit similitudo gloriae in facie Moysi et in B. Virgine et in corpore Christi, quia in facie Moysi et B. Virginis fuit similitudo claritatis quae erat alterius generis simpliciter quam claritas gloriae; unde erat similitudo aenigmatica, sicut similitudo fidei ad visionem patriae," *Summa fratris Alexandri,* III, pt. 1, t. 6, q. 2, tit. 1, chap. 6.

54. "caritas in via assimilatur caritati in patria," *Summa fratris Alexandri,* III, pt. 1, t. 6, q. 2, tit. 1, chap. 4.

Ultimately the difference between Christ's clarity and the clarity of Moses and the Blessed Virgin rests in the union of His body to the divine nature. Moses and Mary have clarity "through grace following nature"[55] in different ways, from talking with God in the case of Moses and "from fellowship with God"[56] in the case of Mary, "who had [clarity] spiritually in her mind and also bodily in her flesh."[57] Christ's body, however, possessed clarity "through the grace which is produced in it . . . namely through the grace of union."[58]

Moses' clarity, which made his face impossible to look at, seems as though it may have been brighter than Christ's clarity, but the issue of relative brightness is irrelevant for John. In fact, John even uses the necessity for Moses' veil as evidence that Christ's clarity is actually superior. Christ's clarity was "delighting and strengthening the vision just like the clarity of glory, which strengthens and supports vision,"[59] and John even compares Christ's clarity with that of the heavenly Jerusalem in Revelation 21.

Concluding his reflections on this question, John addresses a final difference between Moses and the Blessed Virgin, on the one hand, and Christ, on the other. This difference lies in their respective bodily capacities for clarity apart from the supernatural origin of that property. Moses and the Blessed Virgin possessed in their bodies what John calls a "passive capacity" for clarity, while in Christ "there was a capacity called 'power'; this is an active capacity."[60] The difference between the "passive" and "active" capacities of a body reflects their "opposition to glory which results from sin,"[61] or, in the case of Jesus, the absence of

55. "per gratiam consequentem naturam," *Summa fratris Alexandri,* III, pt. 1, t. 6, q. 2, tit. 1, chap. 6.

56. "ex consortio Dei," *Summa fratris Alexandri,* III, pt. 1, t. 6, q. 2, tit. 1, chap. 6.

57. "quem habebat spiritualiter in mente, quem etiam habebat corporaliter in carne," *Summa fratris Alexandri,* III, pt. 1, t. 6, q. 2, tit. 1, chap. 6.

58. "per gratiam quae est ei natura . . . scilicet per gratiam unionis," *Summa fratris Alexandri,* III, pt. 1, t. 6, q. 2, tit. 1, chap. 6.

59. "delectans visum et confortans sicut claritas gloriae, quae confortat et corroborat visum," *Summa fratris Alexandri,* III, pt. 1, t. 6, q. 2, tit. 1, chap. 6.

60. "fuit potentia quae dicitur potestas, hoc est activa potentia," *Summa fratris Alexandri,* III, pt. 1, t. 6, q. 2, tit. 1, chap. 6.

61. "corpora nostra habent oppositionem cum gloria propter peccatum," *Summa fratris Alexandri,* III, pt. 1, t. 6, q. 2, tit. 1, chap. 6.

any opposition to glory. Although it is true that only Christ's body is truly transfigurable, on account of its unity with the divine nature, it is also true that only Christ's body, as a result of its immunity from sin, possesses an "active capacity" for clarity. John acknowledges that God's absolute power could produce the same kind of clarity in others as was produced in Jesus. Nevertheless, it remains true that the "passive capacity" of others' bodies is not a capacity for the clarity of glory, but rather a capacity for a non-glorious clarity that they can neither assume nor sustain on their own.[62]

The next chapter of the question on the transfiguration compares Christ's appearances before and after the resurrection, and it consists of two questions. The first question asks why the transfiguration, as a manifestation of the glory of the resurrection, was accomplished with clarity and not subtlety, agility, or impassibility. The second question asks why Christ did not manifest clarity to His disciples after the resurrection, but rather only subtlety.

Alexander of Hales answered the first question by claiming that subtlety, agility, and impassibility, as gifts of a glorified body, are ordered to the gift of clarity. John's response is the same, but he elaborates by providing the rationale for why clarity has a certain primacy over the other qualities:

> Since there are four qualities according to which glorification is manifested, clarity itself is the principal one after which the others follow. Subtlety follows on the nature of light: hence through its nature light has subtlety even for penetrating bodies, especially transparent bodies, as is well known from crystal, which is penetrated by light; agility, likewise, follows on it: hence its motion or change seems almost sudden; and impassibility follows on it, as well: hence it also does not suffer any impurity from others. Because, therefore, clarity presupposes all other qualities of glorified bodies, and no other one presupposes all the others, for that reason the manifestation of bodily glorification fittingly takes place through clarity.[63]

The notion that the presence of clarity implies the latent presence of the other three qualities is unique, and no other theologian from this

62. See *Summa fratris Alexandri,* III, pt. 1, t. 6, q. 2, tit. 1, chap. 6.

63. "cum sint quatuor proprietates secundum quas ostenditur glorificatio, ipsa claritas est

period provides this explanation, nor affirms that properties other than clarity were present in Christ's transfigured body.

The second question of this chapter addresses Christ's subtlety after the resurrection, a subject never discussed by Alexander in his disputed question. John provides an interesting argument to justify the order and significance of Christ's appearances as the Gospels record them. Because Christ reveals the glory of the resurrection to the senses and to the intellect, it is fitting that that manifestation correspond to the human process of knowledge, in which sense perceptions precede intellectual knowledge. Since, of the qualities that manifest glory, clarity is the only one that the senses can perceive, it is fitting that Christ first manifested the glory of the resurrection by means of clarity.

Once the disciples had perceived the glory of the resurrection in the transfiguration, they were prepared to perceive it by means of the intellect alone. Only subtlety could manifest the glory of the resurrection in this way, because only subtlety can be perceived by the intellect alone. When Jesus, after His resurrection, entered the room in which the disciples were staying (see John 20: 19–23), the disciples could not immediately perceive the glory of the resurrection because they saw only a man of flesh and blood, who showed to them the wounds in His hands and side (John 20:20). The disciples needed to infer the glory of the resurrection from the subtlety Christ manifested. John describes the disciples' process of ratiocination as follows, "the house was shut up and He entered with 'the doors being shut'; therefore He passed through the wall; therefore He is subtle."[64] This progressive manifestation of Christ's glory to the senses, first in the transfiguration and later to the intellect after the resurrection corresponds to the human cogni-

---

principalis ad quam consequuntur ceterae. Naturam enim lucis consequitur subtilitas: unde lux per naturam habet subtilitatem et ad penetrandum corpora et maxime corpora transparentia, sicut patet in lapide cristallino, qui penetratur a luce; similter ad ipsam consequitur agilitas: unde motus vel mutatio eius est quasi subdita; similiter ipsam sequitur impassibilitas, unde etiam nullum inquinamentum patitur ab aliis. Quia ergo claritas ponit omnes alias proprietates, quae sunt corporum glorificatorum, et nulla alia ponit omnes alias, ideo convenienter fit ostensio glorificationis corporis per claritatem," *Summa fratris Alexandri,* III, pt. 1, t. 6, q. 2, tit. 1, chap. 7.

64. "domus clausa erat et ipse intravit *ianuis clausis;* ergo transivit per murum; ergo subtilis est," *Summa fratris Alexandri,* III, pt. 1, t. 6, q. 2, tit. 1, chap. 7.

tive process and thus respects the proper *ordo*, which should govern the manifestation of glory.[65]

Chapter eight of John's question on the transfiguration pertains to the circumstantial details of the transfiguration. This chapter corresponds exactly to the second part of Alexander's question, and like the latter, it focuses on the presence of Moses and Elijah. John organizes this chapter with a series of four questions, the first two of which are closely related. In both the chapter's structure and content, John departs remarkably from the succinct answers of Alexander.

The first question, which is the longest, asks whether Moses and Elijah truly appeared or not. Alexander of Hales argued that if their appearance were imaginary, falsehood would have accompanied the truth of the transfiguration, and he claimed that their souls' conjunction with a body was necessary for them to speak. Although John's organization of the introductory objections is similar to Alexander's, his treatment of the question is much different.

He begins his *solutio* by describing two opposing opinions. One position, drawing from a gloss of Bede, which claims that angels assumed the personas of Moses and Elijah without appropriating their bodies, is that neither Moses nor Elijah truly appeared.[66] The other position is that Moses and Elijah did appear bodily. This opinion draws on the following gloss for support: "We have three witnesses from earth—the apostles—and three from heaven—Moses, Elijah, and the Father Himself."[67] This position, which argues that Moses took up his body "for a time,"[68] is basically Alexander's, although he did not appropriate the gloss that John cites.

Having juxtaposed these positions, John, again, argues for a middle

65. See the opening of the second part of the *solutio*.

66. The gloss John cites is: "Sciendum non corpora vel animas Eliae et Moysi apparuisse, sed in subiecta creatura illa corpora fuisse formata. Potest etiam credi ut angelico ministerio hoc factum esset, ut angeli eorum personas assumerent," *Summa fratris Alexandri*, III, pt. 1, t. 6, q. 2, tit. 1, chap. 8. The *Glossa ordinaria* (4:175) has "sed ex aliqua subiecta creatura . . . ."

67. "Tres testes habemus de terra: Apostolos; tres de caelo: Moysen et Eliam et ipsum Patrem," *Summa fratris Alexandri*, III, pt. 1, t. 6, q. 2, tit. 1, chap. 8.

68. "ad tempus," *Summa fratris Alexandri*, III, pt. 1, t. 6, q. 2, tit. 1, chap. 8. For Alexander, this qualification meant that God joined Moses' body with his soul for the purpose merely of communicating, not for meriting, as in the case of Jesus' raising Lazarus from the dead.

position. He cites a passage from Augustine's *De cura pro mortuis gerenda*,[69] a passage that Alexander had not incorporated into his question, and argues that although the souls of the dead may not appear in this world by virtue of their own power, they can appear by divine power. Augustine himself provides evidence for this fact by referring to the account of "trustworthy witnesses"[70] in Nola, who once saw the deceased Saint Felix, the third-century bishop of Nola, appear while the city was being attacked. For Augustine, this is one example of how "through divine power martyrs take part in the affairs of the living."[71]

John transforms this passage from Augustine on the participation of martyrs in the lives of the living and applies it to Christ's transfiguration. Nowhere in this passage from the *De cura pro mortuis gerenda* does Augustine refer to the transfiguration, nor does he clarify how the martyrs appeared. John, however, interprets the passage from Augustine to mean that when Saint Felix and other martyrs appeared, their souls appeared without a body. He goes on to link this mode of spiritual manifestation to the appearance of Moses' soul at the transfiguration.[72] It is especially interesting that, contrary to Alexander's opinion, which stated that Moses' soul was joined to his body for a time, John claims that we cannot know whether Moses' soul was joined to his body because that detail is not mentioned in Scripture:

> Whether Moses' soul took up its body again, we do not read, nor do we assert that; but we say that, just as Blessed Felix appeared to the citizens in his soul, through divine power, nor did he on account of this take up his body again, so too do we say that Moses' soul, through divine power, was there truly and appeared to them, namely the apostles, nor was it necessary that his body be resurrected. Concerning Elijah, however, who was alive, it must be acknowledged rightly that he appeared in soul and in body.[73]

69. John refers to this work as *De cura agenda pro mortuis, Ad Paulinum.*

70. "audivimus, non incertis rumoribus, sed testibus certis," *Summa fratris Alexandri*, III, pt. 1, t. 6, q. 2, tit. 1, chap. 8.

71. "per divinam potentiam martyres vivorum rebus intersunt," *Summa fratris Alexandri*, III, pt. 1, t. 6, q. 2, tit. 1, chap. 8.

72. See *Summa fratris Alexandri*, III, pt. 1, t. 6, q. 2, tit. 1, chap. 8.

73. "Utrum autem anima Moysi corpus resumpserit, non legimus nec istud asserimus; sed dicimus quod, sicut B. Felix apparuit aspectibus civium in anima per divinam virtutem nec propter hoc resumpsit corpus, sic dicimus quod anima Moysi ibi fuit vere et eis apparuit, scilicet Apostolis, per divinam virtutem, nec oportuit quod resurgeret corpus. De Elia autem,

Regarding the appearance of Elijah, John and Alexander both agree that Elijah was still alive, but John's opinion about Moses' appearance, positing the appearance of his soul alone, is far different from both that of his Franciscan colleague and his Dominican contemporary, Guerric of St. Quentin.

The second question in this chapter appropriately anticipates an obvious objection to the preceding line of argumentation. If only Moses' soul appeared, how could it do so, given that souls cannot be perceived by the senses? Here is John's reply:

> It must be said that a spiritual substance, namely an angel, can appear to the senses in two ways: one way is through an assumed body, the other way is through the likeness of a body alone, which it makes in the senses and through which it alters the senses. For just as an angel has power over bodies, so that it may assume a body to itself and appear to the senses through it, so too does it have the power to produce some likeness of a body in the eye and through it alter the eye, so that [the angel] may be perceived through it by the eye. Therefore, just as it is able to produce a likeness by which it is seen, both by means of a body and without a body, so too, I say that a holy soul, which is full of glory, has that power, and in this way Moses' soul could appear to the bodily eyes of the apostles without the assumption of a body, which we do not read about in Scripture; and thus it was perceived through the likeness of a body, which it produced in the senses. Besides, the soul is also naturally capable of this type of action, because the plan of the whole body is in the soul, as Augustine says. Hence it is related to the body not only as form, but also as exemplar; hence organs and bones which are in the body naturally are in the soul as in an exemplar, and therefore it is able to appear, by divine power, without a body through the likeness of a body.[74]

---

qui vivus erat, bene concedendum est quod apparuit in anima et in corpore," *Summa fratris Alexandri*, III, pt. 1, t. 6, q. 2, tit. 1, chap. 8.

74. "dicendum quod substantia spiritualis duobus modis apparet sensui, scilicet angelus: uno modo per corpus assumptum, alio modo per solam similitudinem corporis, quam facit in sensum et per quam immutat sensum. Sicut enim angelus potestatem habet supra corpora, ut sibi possit corpus assumere et apparere sunsui per illud, ita habet potentiam ut possit aliquam corporis similitudinem in oculo efficere et per illam oculum immutare, ut ab oculo per illam percipiatur. Sicut ergo mediante corpore potest facere similitudinem qua comprehenditur, ita et sine corpore, ita dico quod anima sancta, quae gloriosa est, habet istam potentiam, et hoc modo potuit anima Moysis apparere oculis corporalibus Apostolorum sine corporis assumptione, quam non legimus in Scriptura; et sic per similitudinem corporis, quam efficie-

This description of Moses' appearance at the transfiguration makes a number of interesting points that move beyond Alexander's opinion. Alexander, for example, describes the relationship between angels and their bodies as that between a mover and that which is moved. The angelic appearances in the Old Testament occurred in this way. John acknowledges that this can happen, but he also claims that angels and glorified souls can produce the "likeness" of a body. With regard to the biblical evidence for Alexander's and John's opinions, Alexander focuses on two distinct parts of the Gospel narratives, namely the apostles' vision of Moses and Moses' speaking with Christ, both of which imply bodily presences. John, however, emphasizes the fact that Scripture never mentions Moses' assumption of a body. John may have added the concluding part of the argument, which describes the exemplarity of the soul with respect to the body, because although Moses' soul may have had the passive capacity to effect the likeness of a body, nevertheless, because his soul was in fact not glorified, divine power was necessary to cause his soul to appear to the apostles. In any case, John's notion of the exemplarity of the soul, which gives it a certain natural capacity to appear without a body when actuated by divine power, is completely absent from Alexander's account.

The third and fourth questions, the last of this chapter, do not have parallels in Alexander's disputed question. The third question pertains to a gloss on Luke 9:31, "who appeared in glory and spoke of his departure, which he was to accomplish at Jerusalem," which refers to the testimony Moses and Elijah gave to show that Christ was the fulfillment of the Law and the Prophets. There was a time before God gave the Law to the Israelites, so why did not someone like Enoch appear as a representative witness from that period? John claims that it was fitting for representatives only of the Law and the Prophets to be present because it was only during those periods that humanity's salvation was prophesied explicitly with some indications as to how

bat in sensum, percipiebatur. Item, etiam ad hoc faciendum nata est anima, quia ratio totius corporis est in anima, sicut dicit Augustinus. Unde non solum comparatur ad corpus sicut forma, sed etiam sicut ars; unde membra et ossa, quae sunt in corpore naturaliter, sunt in anima sicut in arte, et ideo per divinam virtutem potest apparere per similitudinem corporis sine corpore," *Summa fratris Alexandri*, III, pt. 1, t. 6, q. 2, tit. 1, chap. 8.

that salvation would be effected. Since "Enoch was of that time before the Law, in which there was no explication of our redemption, namely whether it ought to be accomplished by man alone or by an angel, or by a God-man, therefore Enoch did not appear in the transfiguration to bear testimony, but only the Lawgiver and the Prophet."[75]

The final question of this chapter asks why Jesus commanded His disciples not to tell anyone what they had seen. John refers back to chapter seven, where he describes the fittingness of the order in which Christ revealed His glory in order to argue that although it was fitting for Christ to manifest the glory of His resurrection by means of the transfiguration before His passion and death, it was not fitting to proclaim it and make it universally known. The reason that the glory of Christ's resurrection needed to be preached after His resurrection is that the truth of His passion and death needed to be established first. If the disciples had openly related exactly how glorious Christ's transfigured body was before His passion and death, that "his face shone like the sun" (Mt. 17:2), people may have doubted whether Christ had really suffered and died. Doubt about the truth of Christ's passion would then obscure the truth of the glory of Christ's resurrection.

The final chapter of John's question on the transfiguration examines if the disciples could behold Christ's transfigured body with their bodily eyes. Unlike the previous chapter, in which John's opinion differed markedly from Alexander of Hales', in this chapter he follows Alexander's arguments while expanding on them. Like Alexander, John believes that the disciples truly saw Christ's transfigured body with their bodily eyes, and he adduces three reasons. The first reason is basically Alexander's argument, namely that Christ's clarity, although it exceeds that of the sun, does not generate heat, which would consume the liquid of the eye and thus obscure its vision. Christ's clarity was pleasant and delightful to behold because it did not generate the heat, which would lead to the bodily eye's discomfort.[76]

75. "Enoch fuit illius temporis ante Legem, in quo non erat explicatio nostrae redemptionis, an scilicet deberet fieri per hominem solum vel per angelum vel per Deum hominem, ideo non apparuit Enoch ad ferendum testimonium in transfiguratione, sed Legislator et Propheta," *Summa fratris Alexandri,* III, pt. 1, t. 6, q. 2, tit. 1, chap. 8.

76. See *Summa fratris Alexandri,* III, pt. 1, t. 6, q. 2, tit. 1, chap. 9; and Alexander of Hales, *De transfiguratione Christi,* n. 24.

John provides two additional arguments for the disciples' corporeal vision of the transfiguration, as well. The first argument, based partially on the *solutio* of the previous question, concerns the potential for a glorified body to be seen. John draws on the authority of Ambrose as cited by Augustine in one of his letters to the African laywoman, Paulina. John summarizes Ambrose's exegesis of Luke 1:11, "And there appeared to [Zechariah] an angel of the Lord standing on the right side of the altar of incense," in the following way:

> There is a difference between spiritual and bodily substances in that, with respect to bodily substances, it is in our power to see them if they should be present; hence those bodily substances are not able to prevent our seeing them, and it is necessary that we do see them. With respect to spiritual substances, however, it is in their power and will to be visible to us, and it is not in our power to see them; indeed they are quite able to prevent their being seen, and they are quite able to manifest themselves, as is obvious in the case of angels. In the power of a glorious, animated body, therefore, it is through the nature of the soul, by which it is living, and because it is spiritual that it may be seen, but it is not in our power or will that we see it.[77]

This answer moves beyond that of Alexander, who focused primarily on the clarity of Christ's transfigured body and the capacity of the eye to perceive it. John emphasizes not just the capacity of Christ's body for clarity (in chapters two through five), but also the capacity of Christ's soul to manifest itself through its body in different ways.

The second additional argument concerns the kind of light the disciples saw, and it builds on John's discussion of Christ's clarity. Light distorts the eye's vision whenever there is something in the object from which it emanates to oppose the multiform nature of the eye, which possesses humidity, heat, dryness, and coldness. John gives as examples, the light of fire, which is opposed to the humidity of the eye, and

77. "Differentia est in substantiis spiritualibus et corporalibus in hoc quod in corporalibus ita est quod in nostra potestate est videre ipsas, si praesentes sint; unde nec ipsa corporalia possunt prohibere quin videamus ea, et in necessitate habent hoc, scilicet quod videamus ea. Sed in spirtualibus ita est, quod in sua potestate et voluntate est quod a nobis videantur et non in nostra videre ipsa, immo bene possunt prohibere ne videantur et bene possunt se manifestare, sicut patet in angelis. In potestate ergo corporis gloriosi animati est per naturam animae, qua vivum est et quia spirituale est, quod videatur, sed non in nostra potestate vel voluntate quod ipsum videamus," *Summa fratris Alexandri,* III, pt. 1, t. 6, q. 2, tit. 1, chap. 9.

the light of the sky, which also opposes or is disproportionate to the capacities and properties of the eye.[78] The only light, which pleases the eye without qualification is light whose nature is "uniform"; that is, it exists without opposing any of the properties of the eye and in fact actually fortifies them. "Such is the light," John claims, "of the highest heaven, and such, similarly, is the nature of the light in a glorified body. It is just like that in the highest heaven because that is its region; hence it is proportionate to [the glorified body]."[79] Although the light of the transfigured Christ was intensely bright, even exceeding that of the sun, its heavenly provenance allowed it to be perceived by the bodily eyes of the disciples, who found it pleasant to behold.

Aside from the sheer length of this fascinating question on the transfiguration, it has a number of constitutive features that merit appreciation. First, John's question possesses a highly structured organization. The question forms a sort of treatise, which consists of nine questions; three have two or more sub-questions, and there is a general movement from definition of "transfiguration," to the property of clarity, to the capacity of Christ's body and its relation to God and to the bodies of other humans, to Christ's appearance and then that of Moses and Elijah, and finally to how those appearances were perceived by the apostles. Although the question possesses an elaborate structure, compared to the questions of Alexander and Guerric, the rationale for that structure is not always apparent. While the first part of Alexander's question begins with obvious tasks, such as clarifying the notion of transfiguration and investigating the property of clarity, the layout of the remainder of the first part, which includes questions about the fittingness of the transfiguration, Christ's bodily capacity for clarity, the disciples' vision, and the capacity of other humans to be transfigured (in that order) is not as easy to follow, especially since some questions, like that of the transfigurability of other humans, seem to arise somewhat spontaneously.

A second benefit of John's question is the number and kinds of

78. See *Summa fratris Alexandri,* III, pt. 1, t. 6, q. 2, tit. 1, chap. 9.

79. "talis est lux caeli empyrei, et talis similiter est natura lucis in corpore glorificato, sicut in caelo empyreo, quia est locus eius: unde ei proportionatur," *Summa fratris Alexandri,* III, pt. 1, t. 6, q. 2, tit. 1, chap. 9.

arguments raised. Although Alexander of Hales gives sustained answers to the objections he raised at the opening of his question, the objections themselves tend to be little more than authoritative glosses. John also relies on glosses, but many of his objections develop the implications of the glosses, or they are sustained arguments based on some stated principle. Also, John's *solutiones* are more sophisticated than Alexander's. Every question contains at least one key distinction, which John applies to formulate his response. Further, not only does John provide a greater number of possible opinions, some of which are quite lengthy, but he also tries clearly to articulate his own position, even portraying it as a mediating opinion between two opposite ones.

Another advantageous feature of this question is the range of authoritative material included. Compared to Alexander, John incorporates roughly twice as many scriptural citations from outside the transfiguration narratives and also about twice as many *auctoritates.* Although, with respect to the latter, John pulls many quotations from the *Glossa ordinaria,* his range of citations shows greater access to patristic works than Alexander may have had at the time he wrote the *De transfiguratione Christi.* A number of passages he cites are lengthy and are taken from patristic works themselves. In addition to including new passages from Augustine, John also alludes to authors not mentioned by Alexander, including Hilary of Poitiers, Boethius, and John of Damascus.[80]

These features show the remarkable transformation that had occurred in this genre of scholastic literature within the space of about ten years. In comparison with this question, Alexander's and Guerric's questions on the transfiguration are much less complex and detailed theological investigations of the transfiguration. Although some of the distinctions John makes in these numerous inquiries do not match the sophistication of his successors, this question remains not only an important stage in the development of scholastic Christology, but it is also the most complete scholastic treatment of Christ's transfiguration in the entire thirteenth century.

80. It is interesting to note that in these two disputed questions, the only reference to Ambrose, whom John of La Rochelle clearly regards as an authority, is to Augustine's quotation of Ambrose's Luke commentary.

Postilla super Matthaeum

John of La Rochelle probably wrote his commentaries on the Gospels in the early to mid-1240s, shortly before his death. Two pieces of evidence suggest this dating. First, there are similarities between the *Postilla super Matthaeum* and an exposition on the rule of the Franciscan Order, which he coauthored in 1240–1241,[81] and second, the organization of his commentaries is much more structured than that of Hugh of St. Cher and of Alexander of Hales in their commentaries.[82]

It may be true, as Beryl Smalley has argued, that John is a "conservative" postillator, like Hugh and Alexander, and uninterested in the literal sense of Scripture,[83] but this evaluation requires some qualification. John certainly drew heavily from the Fathers and from the allegorical, moral, and "mystical" interpretations of twelfth- and thirteenth-century commentaries, but John was also an exegetical innovator. He shaped his commentary by drawing insights from more recent interpreters, such as Anselm of Laon, Zachary of Besançon, Richard of St. Victor, Hugh of St. Cher, and Alexander of Hales and by asking his own questions regarding the text.[84] John's greatest contribution to scriptural exegesis, however, pertains to his style. The organization of his commentaries and his application of the *divisio textus*, the exegetical method of dividing the scriptural text for commentary, are much more sophisticated than those of his older Dominican and Franciscan colleagues. Girard Etzkorn, drawing from other texts of John's, has rightly noted John's "flair for organization and clear presentation."[85] The organization man-

81. See Smalley, *The Gospels in the Schools: c. 1100–c. 1280*, 181–82, 193.

82. For a list of manuscripts containing works by John, see Jacques Guy Bougerol, "Jean de La Rochelle. Les oeuvres et les manuscrits," *Archivum Franciscanum Historicum*, 205–15. I will be using Ms. Oxford New College 48 for John's *Postilla super Matthaeum*, Ms. Milan Biblioteca Ambrosiana D471 inf. for his *Postilla super Marcum*, and Ms. Milan Biblioteca Ambrosiana A211 inf. for his *Postilla super Lucam*.

83. See Smalley, *The Study of the Bible in the Middle Ages*, xiii, and *The Gospels in the Schools: c. 1100–c. 1280*, 190–96. For more on the "literal" sense of Scripture, see A. J. Minnis, *Medieval Theory of Authorship: Scholastic literary attitudes in the later Middle Ages*, 2nd ed. (Aldershot, U.K.: Wildwood House, 1988), 73–159.

84. On the exegetical development from Alexander of Hales to John of La Rochelle, see Gian Luca Potestà, "I fratri minori e lo studio della Bibbia. Da Francesco d'Assisi a Nicolò di Lyre," in *La Bibbia nel medio evo*, edited by G. Cremascoli and C. Leonardi, 269–90 (Bologna, Italy: Edizioni Dehoniane Bologna, 1996), 273–75.

85. Girard J. Etzkorn, "How to Read the Bible According to John of La Rochelle," in *That*

ifested in John's exegetical style represents a significant development from the exegetical methods employed in the 1230s.

The first thing to note about John's commentary on the transfiguration account in Matthew is what he thinks constitutes the transfiguration narrative. Unlike some exegetes, such as Thomas Aquinas, who locate the beginning of Matthew's transfiguration narrative at the opening of Matthew 17, John identifies it as beginning with Jesus' prophecy in Matthew 16:28, regarding some not dying before "they see the Son of man coming in His kingdom" and ending with Jesus' command in Matthew 17:9 that the disciples not tell anyone what they had seen. This pericope and the subsequent one, which runs from Matthew 17:10 until the end of the chapter, discuss the "confirmation of the established truth .... Just as our redemption was accomplished through [Christ's] passion and resurrection, so does [this passage] set forth a twofold confirmation by proceeding firmly here."[86] John explains further:

> First there is a certain confirmation of faith in the resurrection, and second there is confirmation with proof of faith in the passion, that is when "and His disciples asked Him" follows. Faith, however, is confirmed by a proof of the resurrection through the transfiguration. Hence, according to this, first there is a foretelling or promise of the transfiguration, next there follows a manifestation or display of the transfiguration before them, "and after six days Jesus took," etc. Third, there follows the concealment of the transfiguration, "and they lifting up their eyes saw no one," etc.[87]

In John's view then, three things pertain directly to the transfiguration: Jesus' announcement of the transfiguration with the words, "the Son

---

Others May Know and Love: Essays in Honor of Zachary Hayes, OFM, edited by M. F. Cusato and F. E. Coughlin, 159–64 (St. Bonaventure, N.Y.: The Franciscan Institute, 1997).

86. "confirmatio fundatae veritatis . . . sicut redemptio nostra factum est per passionem et resurrectionem, ita hic resolute procedendo ponit duplicem confirmationem," Ms. Oxford New College 48, fol. 178va.

87. "Primo quidam confirmationem fidei resurrectionis, secundo confirmationem fidei demonstratione passionis, id est cum sequitur *et interrogaverunt eum discipuli eius*. Confirmatur autem fides demonstratione resurrectionis per transfigurationem. Unde secundum hoc primo est praedictio sive promissio transfigurationis, deinde sequitur ostensio vel exhibitio transfigurationis ibi, *et post dies vi assumpsit*, etc. Tertio sequitur occultatio transfigurationis ibi, *levantes autem oculos neminem viderunt*, etc," Ms. Oxford New College 48, fol. 178va–b (italicized texts in all manuscript citations are from Scripture).

of man coming in His kingdom;"[88] the transfiguration itself; and Jesus' command to the disciples, exhorting them not to tell anyone what they had seen.

John further divides the text into what precedes the transfiguration (that is, Jesus taking Peter, James, and John up on the mountain), what accompanies or is contemporaneous with the transfiguration (that is, the transfiguration itself and the presence of Moses and Elijah there), and what follows the transfiguration (Peter's response and the theophany of the voice and cloud). The following outline illustrates John's division of the text:

I. Confirmation of faith in the resurrection
    A. Promise of the transfiguration
    B. Manifestation
        1. What precedes the transfiguration
            i. Time
            ii. Witnesses
            iii. Place
        2. What accompanies or is cotemporaneous with the transfiguration
            i. Act
            ii. Mode
            iii. Witnesses
        3. What follows the transfiguration
            i. Love
            ii. Fear
                a. Cause
                b. Feeling
                c. Consolation
                    Jesus' approach
                    Jesus' touch
                    Jesus' words
    C. Concealment
        1. In fact
        2. In word

88. Mt 16:28.

II. Confirmation of faith in the passion
    A. By example
    B. By a miracle
    C. By words

The second part of John's threefold division of the "manifestation," on what accompanies the transfiguration, is of special interest. The section of the pericope, which describes the transfiguration itself, Matthew 17:2–3,

> records first the act of transfiguration, second the mode of transfiguration, "and His face shone," and third it introduces the witnesses of the transfiguration, "and behold," etc., because the transfiguration is confirmed not only by the testimony of the apostles, but also by the testimony of the Law and the Prophets.[89]

The "act" of transfiguration refers simply to the words, "and He was transfigured before them," (Matthew 17:2). John's primary interest in this phrase is to discern the meaning of "transfiguration." In this way, he is following neither Hugh nor Alexander in his Matthew commentary, but rather, the line of questioning manifest in Alexander's *De transfiguratione Christi.* In his Matthew commentary, Alexander focused on the spiritual implications of being transfigured and the role of the Trinity in effecting Christ's transfiguration; in his disputed question, Alexander asked what transfiguration signifies and what happened to Christ's body when it underwent transfiguration.

John cites a passage ascribed to Jerome, most of which actually comes from Zachary of Besançon's *In unum ex quatuor,* in order to affirm two points. The first point derives primarily from Jerome and posits that Christ's appearance at His transfiguration will be like His appearance when He returns again in judgment. The second point the passage affirms is from Zachary, and states that Christ did not put aside the reality of His body at the transfiguration, nor "did He assume a spiritual body,"[90] but rather Christ "added splendor"[91] to His body

89. "Primo . . . notat actum transfigurationis, secundo modum transfigurationis, *et resplenduit,* tertio introducit testes transfigurationis, *et ecce,* etc., quia non solum confirmatur transfiguratio per testimonium apostolorum immo etiam per testimonium legis et prophetarum," Ms. Oxford New College 48, fol. 179vb.

90. "assumpsisse corpus spirituale," Ms. Oxford New College 48, fol. 179vb.

91. "splendorem addit," Ms. Oxford New College 48, fol. 179vb.

during the transfiguration. As confirmation of the truth that Christ did not lay aside His true body, John notes that the transfiguration account in Luke says merely that "the appearance of His countenance was altered," not that anything else changed. Like Hugh, John uses John 14:21, "He who loves me will be loved by my Father, and I will love him and manifest myself to him" as a gloss to show that Christ will reveal Himself to those whom He especially loves, those who love and obey Him.

The reference to Luke 9:29, which describes the appearance of Jesus' face being "altered" foreshadows the second division of the part of the narrative that describes the transfiguration itself, and that is what John refers to as the "mode" of transfiguration. The mode of transfiguration refers to Christ's appearance, both His face, which "shone like the sun" and His garments, which were "white as snow." Although John interprets Christ's face and garments allegorically, to signify Christ's divinity and humanity, respectively, he is also concerned about the reality of the event itself.

Because of Christ's divinity, John asserts that the Lord's face did not shine merely "like the sun," but that it exceeded the brightness of the sun, and he proceeds to ask how Christ's disciples could behold such radiance. John's answer is much like that of Alexander in his disputed question, where he claims that the light of the transfigured Christ is bright but not painful to behold. This response is based partly on John's reading of Exodus 33:18–23, where Moses beheld God's glory. Because Christ's face represents His divinity, and His garments represent His humanity, the glory radiating from Christ's face, or divinity, must exceed that of the created sun. Not only must Christ's glory exceed the sun's, but it must be exceedingly beautiful, as well. It is the beauty of Christ's divinity, which prompts Peter to say, "Lord, it is good for us to be here."

Christ's garments were really white as snow, as well, but what is more important is the holiness, which the whiteness symbolizes. John connects the transfiguration passages in Matthew and in Mark to illustrate powerfully the significance of the whiteness. In Mark, Christ's garments are described as extraordinarily white, "as no fuller on earth could bleach them."[92] John cites an explanation attributed to Bede (actually derived

92. Mark 9:2.

from Zachary of Besançon), which claims that the true Fuller is Christ, the one who "purifies souls from every impurity of flesh or spirit."[93] Although in both interpretations of Christ's radiance, the spiritual interpretation is primary, a literal interpretation is not excluded.

The final division of the narrative, specifically on the transfiguration, addresses the witnesses of the transfiguration. Here John collects a number of interpretations, largely from Hugh of St. Cher, to explain the significance of Moses' and Elijah's appearance and to explain how they appeared. Of great significance to John is the fact that Moses was dead and Elijah, having been taken to heaven, never died. The presence of these two representatives of the Old Testament, the former of the Law and the latter of the Prophets, thus represents the living and the dead, who will be present at the second coming of Christ in judgment.

Postilla super Marcum

John's treatment of the witnesses of the transfiguration is more profound in his Mark commentary, which, of all his commentaries on the transfiguration narratives, is the most original. John's treatment of the witnesses occurs within the framework of an elaborate *divisio textus,* similar to the one in his Matthew commentary. John claims that the transfiguration narrative provides evidence for both Jesus' resurrection and passion. He divides the text into two main sections, one from Mark 9:1–9, which addresses the foreshadowing of Christ's resurrection, and the other from Mark 9:10–13, which alludes to Christ's coming passion. The further divisions of the text parallel John's division of Matthew's text, but there are some differences:

I. Proof of the truth of the resurrection
- A. Promise of the manifestation of the glory of the resurrection
  - 1. What the promise signifies
  - 2. The promise pertains only to some people, not to everyone
  - 3. The promise must be fulfilled in the present time
  - 4. The promise concerns some great deed

93. "animarum mundator ab omni inquinamento carnis et spiritus," Ms. Oxford New College 48, fol. 180ra.

- B. Proof of the manifestation of glory
  - 1. Apostolic witness
  - 2. Legal and prophetic witness
  - 3. Divine witness
- C. Admonition to conceal the manifestation of glory

II. Proof of the truth of the passion

- A. Question pertaining to Christ's passion
- B. Christ's answer

This *divisio textus* is simpler than the one in John's Matthew commentary, and it has different emphases. In this commentary, John highlights the promise and the witnessing of future glory as central themes.

This division of the text, however, does not illustrate John's main interest. Although he outlines a number of themes here, the majority of John's commentary, roughly two-thirds of it, addresses the proof of the manifestation of Christ's glory, while only about one-tenth is devoted to elucidating the significance of the promise. John divides the manifestation of Christ's glory into three sections, as outlined above. The manifestation of Christ's glory is confirmed and communicated by three sets of witnesses: the apostles (Peter, James, and John); Moses and Elijah (representing the Law and the Prophets); and the Father, who acts as a divine witness. Each category of witnesses plays a different role. As John explains, "the apostolic witness, therefore, testifies to the glory of [Christ's] humanity, the prophetic and legal witness testifies to the dignity and the mystery of redemption, and the divine witness demonstrates the majesty of divinity in Christ."[94]

Although John applies allegorical interpretations to explain the presence of Peter, James, and John, he also discusses the importance of contemplation in his interpretation of the apostolic witnesses. Following Richard of St. Victor (as quoted by Hugh of St. Cher), John associates the six days between Jesus' promise and his taking Peter, James, and John up to the mountain as signifying six kinds of contemplation. However, he also discovers that the order of events reveals

94. "Testimonium ergo apostolicum est ad gloriam humanitatis, testimonium propheticum et legale ad dignitatem et mysterium redemptionis, testimonium divinum ad probandum in Christo maiestatem divinitatis," Ms. Milan Biblioteca Ambrosiana D471 inf., fol. 42va.

something about how the mind ascends to God. He notes the significance of the verbs used in Mark 9:2, "Jesus took . . . and led them." Jesus' taking *(assumpsit)* Peter, James, and John corresponds to Jesus "taking" human affection when humans experience devotion.[95] Jesus' leading parallels His leading human intellects through meditation. The fact that Jesus leads His disciples up to a mountain shows that this meditation is heavenly, and the mountain's height indicates the loftiness attained by invisible creatures in their meditation. That Jesus should lead them "apart" "signifies the removal of reason for meditating on the mystery of the Godhead," and their being by themselves shows that reason must leave behind all likenesses of creatures. Only after reason removes these likenesses from its purview, can the intellect be illumined by divine contemplation. At that point the intellect can discern the glorious divinity lying behind the appearances of creaturely images. Only then does there occur some sort of transfiguration in the realm of the intellect.[96]

John follows this exposition on the mind's ascent to God with a series of questions regarding Christ's transfigured glory. At times, the format of some of these questions is similar to that of a disputed question, and John's line of inquiry is very similar to the first part of the question on the transfiguration in the *Summa fratris Alexandri*. The first question he asks is whether Christ's glorious manifestation should be called a "transfiguration." Without any of the distinctions used in

95. Ms. Milan Biblioteca Ambrosiana D471 inf., fol. 42vb.

96. Here are John's exegetical arguments. Note the interweaving of Old Testament texts in this passage: "Nota hic ordinem transfigurationis. Primo enim assumit et inde ducit, deinde transfiguratum ostendit. In quo figuratur ordo contemplationis in qua primo assumitur affectus a Iesu per devotionem, Ps., *beatus quem elegisti et assumpsisti*. Item, *misi de* caelo *et accipit me, et assumpsit de aquis multis*. Deinde vero ducitur nostra ratio per meditationem, Ps. *etenim illic manus tua deducet me*, etc. Item, *in voluntate tua deduxisti me*. Et duci *in montem* significat celestium meditationem, Exod. xv, *introduces eos, et plantabis in monte haereditatis tuae*, etc., Ps., *Domine, quis habitabit in tabernaculo tuo, aut quis requiscet in monte sancto tuo?* Quod vero additur *excelsum*, significat rationis excelsum in meditatione creaturarum invisibilium, Bar. v, *Hierusalem, surge et sta in excelso*, Ps., *montes excelsi cervis*, etc., Is. xl, *super montem excelsum ascende tu*, etc. Quod vero subiungit *seorsum* significat abstractionem rationis ad meditandum divinitatis arcanum. Hinc dicitur Thren. iii, *sedebit solitarius, et tacebit*, supra vi, *venite seorsum in desertum locum*. Per hoc autem quod dicit *solos* significat abstractionem mentis ad meditationem primae veritatis cum exclusione omnium similitudinum creaturarum phantasmatum," Ms. Milan Biblioteca Ambrosiana D471 inf., fols. 42vb–43ra.

the disputed question, he makes a similar argument here, namely that transfiguration refers to a transformation from a less noble form to a more noble one.[97]

The second question asks whether Christ's glory was real or imaginary. In this investigation, John covers not only this particular question, but several others found in the *Summa fratris Alexandri*, including whether Christ's glory was in His body or in the air surrounding it, whether Christ's clarity was glorious or only similar to glorious clarity, how the transfiguration relates to Christ's post-resurrection appearances, and whether creatures can be transfigured.

John offers several opinions regarding the status of Christ's glory. He lists these opinions without any supporting biblical texts or patristic authorities, unlike in the *Summa*. The opinions, as John articulates them, simply point out certain problems posed by the description of the transfiguration in Scripture. These opinions and John's replies are an abridged form of the same investigation in the *Summa*.[98] The first opinion states that since the "glory of immortality" could not exist in a mortal body, the glory the disciples beheld was in the air surrounding Christ. The second argues that Christ assumed an immortal body during the time He was transfigured. The third is that Christ assumed an immortal body from the Blessed Virgin and that the effects of this immortality were hidden during Christ's earthly life. The fourth opinion is that the transfiguration was simply a miracle effected by divine power.[99]

John touches on these questions, either directly or indirectly, in chapters three, four, and five in his question on the transfiguration in the *Summa fratris Alexandri*. Indeed, the opening of John's response to these arguments in the Mark commentary, which claims that there was a "glorious form" in Christ, is nearly identical to his *solutio* in chapter three. In both responses John argues that Christ's transfigured glory

97. Ms. Milan Biblioteca Ambrosiana D471 inf., fol. 43ra. Cf. *Summa fratris Alexandri*, III, pt. 1, t. 6, q. 2, tit. 1, chap. 1.

98. On the relationship between the commentary on Mark and both the *Summa fratris Alexandri* and the Matthew commentary, see Constantino Nappo, "La Postilla in Marcum di Giovanni de Rupella e suoi riflessi nella Summa Halesiana," *Archivum Franciscanum Historicum*, 332–47. Nappo specifically addresses the transfiguration, as well. See Nappo, 345–47.

99. See Ms. Milan Biblioteca Ambrosiana D471 inf., fol. 43ra.

came from within Himself because His body was united to the divine nature, and that the radiance of His clothes derived from the splendor of Christ's face. The conclusion of John's response in his Mark commentary argues succinctly that Christ's clarity was only partly glorious. The core of this argument, which is that the clarity manifested during the transfiguration is truly glorious but also incomplete or imperfect, is also found in the fourth chapter in the *Summa* on whether Christ's clarity was glorious or only similar.[100]

There are also close parallels between John's Mark commentary and the *Summa fratris Alexandri* regarding the question of Moses' and Elijah's appearance. John's articulation of the true appearance of Moses, whose soul appears by divine power, and Elijah, who appears in his own body, is very close to the *solutio* in chapter eight in the *Summa.* He also relies heavily on Augustine's *De cura pro mortuis gerenda,* as he does in the *Summa.*[101] John also includes an explanation for how the apostles could recognize Moses and Elijah as themselves. In the Mark commentary, he cites an explanation by Zachary of Besançon, which argues that the disciples perceived the Lawgiver and the Prophet, as such, by means of a certain grace, which all the saints will receive after their resurrection. John addresses this question in the *Summa,* but there he locates the power to discern the identities of the mysterious figures not in a gratuitous power received by the disciples, but rather in the power of Moses' soul to appear to corporeal eyes without assuming a body.[102] What John excludes from the *Summa,* however, is any explanation for why Moses and Elijah appear. In his Mark commentary, John supplies numerous arguments, drawn mostly from Hugh of St. Cher, to explain why it is fitting for Moses and Elijah to witness the transfiguration of the Lord.

Another theme John omits from the *Summa* but includes in his Mark commentary concerns Peter's response to Jesus after he beholds his transfigured Lord and the venerable representatives of the Old Covenant. John returns to the theme of contemplation and notes that Peter's words manifest three effects of contemplation: love, wonder, and

100. See above, pp. 100–103.

101. See above, p. 112.

102. See *Summa fratris Alexandri,* III, pt. 1, t. 6, q. 2, tit. 1, chap. 8.

fear, which derives from love.[103] John astutely observes that when the Gospel of Mark records that Peter responded, no one had addressed him up until that time. In John's view, Peter "heard those glorious words concerning [His] passion and resurrection, and therefore, feeling almost like a lover, he responded as though someone had spoken to him."[104] Peter further conveys his feeling of love by saying, "Rabbi, it is good for us to be here." Peter expresses wonder in his words, "let us make three tabernacles . . . for he did not know what he said." John asserts that Peter's words show that he did not realize that the Law, the Prophets, and the Gospel cannot be separated; all three have one tabernacle, according to Bede, namely the Church.[105] The third effect of contemplation is fear, described by the words, "for they were struck with fear." John concludes his interpretation of the Old Testament witnesses with a "moral" interpretation, in which he allows for the existence of three tabernacles: the Church, the conscience, and heaven. Moses corresponds with the Church, because "he was taken from the baptismal waters."[106] Elijah's name means "the Lord God," according to John; combining this etymology with a passage from Job, "As I was in the days of my youth, when God was secretly in my tabernacle?" allows John to argue that the Lord is Lord in a unique way in the interior tabernacle, the conscience. Jesus more obviously corresponds to the tabernacle of heaven.

Next, John discusses the divine witness, which attests to Jesus' divinity. Although in his *divisio textus,* John ascribed this witness to the Father, he allows all three Persons of the Trinity to play a role. The Holy Spirit is present in the cloud. At Jesus' baptism the Holy Spirit descended from heaven in the form of a dove. The dove represented the "simplicity of affection,"[107] but the cloud shows that the Holy Spirit "tempers the gaze of contemplation."[108] The voice of the Father also

103. See Ms. Milan Biblioteca Ambrosiana D471 inf., fol. 43vb.

104. "audierat illa gloriosa verba de passione et de resurrectione, et ideo quasi amantis affectum respondet, quasi aliquis ei loqueretur," Ms. Milan Biblioteca Ambrosiana D471 inf., fol. 43vb.

105. Ms. Milan Biblioteca Ambrosiana D471 inf., fol. 43vb.

106. "assumptus est ex aquis baptismatis," Ms. Milan Biblioteca Ambrosiana D471 inf., fol. 44ra.

107. "simplicitatem affectionis," Ms. Milan Biblioteca Ambrosiana D471 inf., fol. 44ra.

108. "temperat aspectum contemplationis," Ms. Milan Biblioteca Ambrosiana D471 inf., fol. 44ra.

plays an important role. He tells those present what to believe about Jesus and admonishes them to be obedient to Him; every word the Father speaks is replete with meaning:

> Note that the special character of the Person is mentioned when He says, "This is Son [hic est Filius]," and so is the truth of the divine nature, when He says "my." The Psalm says, "You are my son, this day I have begotten you" . . . The exceeding excellence of the grace of [His] human nature is also mentioned, when He says "beloved": Colossians 1, "who has translated us into the kingdom of the Son of His love," and John 3, "The Father loves the Son, and He has given all things into His hand." Therefore listen to Him; here He shows the one who must be obeyed, as if He had said, "Here is that man whom Moses promised to you."[109]

The Son also plays a role in the divine witness. When the theophany recedes, that is, when the voice of the Father fades away and when Christ's revealed glory disappears along with the cloud and Moses and Elijah, the disciples behold Christ alone. Christ remaining alone signifies that contemplation must be "of the Savior alone."[110] The disappearance of Moses and Elijah affirms that the voice was speaking about Christ and not about either of them; it also shows that what they represent, the Law and the Prophets, is brought to fulfillment in Christ.

Although the theme of contemplation, so prominent in the commentary on Mark's transfiguration narrative, derives from Hugh of St. Cher, and before him, from Richard of St. Victor, John demonstrates considerable originality in his approach to various questions regarding Christ's clarity. The fact that the same objections and responses to some questions appear in both his Mark commentary and the *Summa fratris Alexandri* is evidence that by the 1240s, the biblical commentary was an appropriate genre for speculative lines of inquiry and for moral edification and spiritual direction.

109. "nota tanguntur proprietas personae, cum dicit *hic est Filius,* et veritas divinae naturae, cum dicit *meus,* Ps., *filius meus es tu, ego hodie genui te* . . . Tangitur etiam supereminentia gratiae ex parte humanae naturae, cum dicit *charissimus,* ad Col. i, *transtulit* nos *in regnum Filii dilectionis suae,* Ioan. iii, *Pater diligit Filium et omnia dedit in manu eius.* Ideo *audite illum.* Hic ostendit cui est obediendum, quasi diceret, hic est ille vir quem Moyses vobis promisit," Ms. Milan Biblioteca Ambrosiana D471 inf., fol. 44ra.

110. "solius Salvatoris," Ms. Milan Biblioteca Ambrosiana D471 inf., fol. 44rb.

Postilla super Lucam

If John's commentary on Mark offered interesting and original exegesis of the transfiguration narrative, John's commentary on Luke has the least original interpretations of the transfiguration. In addition to containing the least complicated *divisio textus,* it also is more reliant on previous interpreters, especially Hugh of St. Cher, than his other commentaries. John begins by separating Luke 9:27, "But I tell you truly, there are some standing here who will not taste death until they see the kingdom of God," from the rest of the transfiguration narrative. Hugh of St. Cher found in this verse an exhortation from the Lord to embrace martyrdom. John follows Hugh's interpretation and uses it to give the rest of Luke's transfiguration narrative an eschatological orientation. Since the glory of the transfiguration, which the disciples witness, occurs immediately after Jesus' prophecy, it may be interpreted as the promise of a future reward for those who follow Christ's example in suffering and death.

Although John borrows directly from Hugh for more than half of his commentary, the *divisio textus* seems original. The transfiguration narrative has five major sections, as follows:

I. Preamble
  A. The time of the transfiguration
  B. The persons Jesus took with Him
  C. The place of the transfiguration
  D. The reason the transfiguration occurred
II. The mystery of the transfiguration
  A. The alteration of Christ's face
  B. The alteration of Christ's garments
  C. The presence of the prophets
  D. The conversation between Jesus, Moses, and Elijah
III. The condition of the disciples
  A. The infirmity of their nature
  B. The assistance of grace
  C. The revelation of glory
  D. Love absorbing reason

IV. The divine witness
V. The concealment of the mystery

Hugh of St. Cher's exegisis appears in all of these sections, but the subsection in which John perhaps shows the greatest originality is in his explication of the conversation between Jesus, Moses, and Elijah.

According to the Gospel of Luke, "two men talked with [Jesus], and they were Moses and Elijah, appearing in majesty, and they spoke of His death, which He was to accomplish in Jerusalem."[111] Hugh of St. Cher noted that Christ's *excessus* was not only His death, but it was also an excess of sorts. Alluding to Philippians 2:8, Hugh claimed that *excessus* referred to "the excellence of His humility, by which He humbled Himself even to death on a cross."[112] John expands on Hugh's interpretation of *excessus* as excess to give fuller meaning to the text than might be had if one interprets *excessus* merely as "death." Not only is Christ's *excessus* an excess of humility, as Hugh noted, but it is also an excess of love. Here John adds depth to this interpretation by citing John 15:13, "Greater love has no man than this, that a man lay down his life for his friends," and Ephesians 2:4–5, "God, who is rich in mercy, out of the great love with which he loved us, even when we were dead through our trespasses, made us alive together with Christ."[113] John provides corresponding scriptural texts to show how Christ's *excessus* was also an excess of humility and sadness. He also claims that it is "an excess of the Godhead or an overflowing of justice and poverty. For something is said to overflow when it goes beyond its proper boundaries, as though a proper boundary of the Godhead is the Trinity, and the Son of God surpassed this boundary on account of the great charity by which He loved us."[114] There is an excess of justice because Christ surpasses the limits of justice, and rewards those who deserve

111. Lk 9:30–31.

112. "excellentem eius humilitatem, qua usque ad mortem Crucis se humiliavit," Hugh of St. Cher, *Postilla super Lucam*, fol. 187rb.

113. Ms. Milan Biblioteca Ambrosiana A211 inf., fol. 152rb.

114. "fuit excessus divinitatis seu transgressio iustitiae et paupertatis. Tunc enim dicitur aliquid transgredi quando exit extra proprios terminos quasi proprius terminus divinitatis est Trinitas, et hunc terminum transgressus est Filius Dei propter nimium caritatem qua dilexit nos," Ms. Milan Biblioteca Ambrosiana A211 inf., fols. 152rb–152va.

eternal punishment. The excess of poverty to which John refers pertains to Christ's exceeding poverty in his earthly life.

Although John's *Postilla super Lucam* is largely dependent on Hugh of St. Cher, this example provides a glimpse of John's exegesis of one part of Luke's transfiguration narrative with no parallel in Matthew or Mark. Almost every other section or subsection that John outlined is interspersed with commentary from John's Dominican contemporary, Hugh of St. Cher.

Conclusion

Although John of La Rochelle's question and commentaries on the transfiguration manifest evident engagement and dependence on his older mendicant colleagues, especially Alexander of Hales and Hugh of St. Cher, John advanced the investigation of the transfiguration in a number of ways. The following summary does not address all of John's contributions, but it does briefly describe the most important ones.

The first of John's contributions is the wide range of questions he poses. The range of questions and the thoroughness with which he treats them establishes his question on the transfiguration as the most complete investigation of the thirteenth century. The second contribution is the sophistication of his distinctions. His method of describing two opposing positions and finding a middle position is distinct from the methods of both Alexander and Guerric.

The third contribution is John's teaching, itself. Although Alexander of Hales is the probable source for John's almost exclusive emphasis on the Incarnation as the source for Christ's clarity, John develops this teaching considerably. There is, for example, almost no eschatological dimension to John's understanding of Christ's clarity, as there was in Alexander's account. The primary reminder that the transfiguration has a strong connection to the resurrection is not any teaching expressed in the question, but rather this question's literary placement in a treatise on the resurrection. Also, the soul plays no role in the communication of clarity, as it did for Guerric of St. Quentin.

John also applies numerous distinctions in his teaching on Christ's transfiguration. His understanding, for example, of the relationship between glorious clarity and that of the resurrected Christ as a "real but imperfect likeness" is unique among all the theologians in this study. This distinction allows John to maintain that Christ's bodily clarity is real, but it is neither a gift, properly speaking, nor does it have the same appearance as glorious clarity will have. In addition to this distinction between real and perfect likeness and real but imperfect likeness, John makes a distinction between the act and the habit of clarity. This distinction allows John to assert that there was in Christ's transfigured body the act of clarity, but not the habit. Christ's mortal body retains the habit of darkness or opacity, but it receives the act of clarity. John does not, however, explain the metaphysical or anthropological mechanism necessary for this condition to exist. This manifested clarity, while true clarity, does not possess the same brilliance glorious clarity will have. Albert the Great, who wrote his own question on the transfiguration at about the same time, makes a similar interpretation regarding the lack of intensity in Christ's transfigured clarity, as compared to the glorious clarity he will receive.

John's teaching is also innovative insofar as it relates to the appearance of Moses. Basing his teaching on a passage from Augustine, John argues that souls have the power to appear without a body. In the case of Moses' appearance on Mount Tabor, divine power permitted Moses' soul to be visible to the disciples, and God granted the disciples a singular gift to recognize Moses and Elijah.

John's fourth contribution to the discussion of the transfiguration is his exegetical method. More structured than that of his older peers, John's *divisio textus* contains multiple divisions and subdivisions of the biblical text. Although the content of John's scriptural commentaries is less innovative than that of his disputed question (especially in the *Postilla super Lucam,* which relies heavily on Hugh of St. Cher), John does incorporate teachings from his disputed question into his exegetical literature, and he does incorporate some twelfth-century scriptural commentaries, which Alexander and Hugh do not address.

These contributions to the theological investigation of various dimensions of Christ's transfiguration demonstrate that John was a talented theologian, despite being overshadowed by more famous colleagues such as Alexander, Albert the Great, Bonaventure, and Thomas

Aquinas. Still, despite John's innovative teaching on the transfiguration, it seems he had little influence on subsequent discussions of the transfiguration. As we will see, Bonaventure of Bagnoregio, John's younger colleague, never wrote a disputed question on the transfiguration and his only discussion of the transfiguration arises in sermons and a commentary on Luke (drawn predominantly from Hugh of St. Cher); and Albert the Great and Thomas Aquinas developed very different approaches to the transfiguration in their own writings.

6

ALBERT THE GREAT

While Alexander of Hales, Hugh of St. Cher, Guerric of St. Quentin, and John of La Rochelle were teaching at the University of Paris, another friar was teaching as *lector* in Dominican schools in Cologne, Hildesheim, Freiburg, Regensburg, and Strassburg during the 1230s. After teaching for about ten years, this friar, Albert, was sent to Paris to become a master of theology. Albert studied in Paris from 1241 to 1245. After he completed his studies, he taught in Paris until 1248. During the time in Paris Albert began writing his first *summa*. One of its treatises, the treatise *De resurrectione*, is important for this study because it contains a question on Christ's transfiguration.[1] Albert also wrote commentaries on the synoptic gospels in his later career.

This chapter will explore Albert's teaching on the transfiguration in the *De resurrectione* and in his scriptural commentaries, with particular attention given to the unique characteristics of his teaching and methodology. Since Albert's theological articulation of Christ's transfiguration differs not only according to its literary genre, but also according to the time period of its articulation, this chapter will discuss the significance of both these categories, in addition to highlighting Albert's application of philosophical terms and categories.

1. For more on Albert's early career, see Heribert Christian Scheeben, *Albertus Magnus* (Cologne, Ger.: J. P. Bachem, 1955), 21–58. For an introduction to his life and works, see Wilhem Kübel et al., "Albertus Magnus," LexMA: 294–99. The best guide to Albert's works is Winfried Fauser, *Die Werke des Albertus Magnus in ihrer handschriftlichen Überlieferung* (Aschendorff, Ger.: Monasterii Westfalorum, 1982).

De resurrectione

Albert probably began to write the *De resurrectione* in the mid-1240s. Judging by his own comments, this treatise, which remains incomplete, was conceived as part of a larger *summa* of six treatises, which was never finished.[2] Albert outlines the plan for this treatise in the brief prologue to the work. A study of the resurrection, Albert says, follows the investigation of the Incarnation, and it is to be divided into five parts. The first part is "of the Head, members, and those who are evil together; then of the Head alone; the third is only of those who are evil; the fourth is only of those who are good; and the fifth is of those things which accompany the resurrection, that is the judgment and renewal of the world."[3] Albert finished only the first three sections of the treatise and completed only a part of the fourth section.

Albert's discussion of the transfiguration occurs in the second part of the treatise, on what pertains to the Head alone. Although ten questions constitute the second tractate, Albert divides the investigation of Christ's resurrection into eight separate inquiries:

And because we now consider what Christ's resurrection is, what is asked first is whether it is the cause of our resurrection; second, what causality it may have in those who are good and in those who are evil; third, whether it is the cause of the resurrection of souls and what is the resurrection of souls; fourth, why the resurrection of all was not related to the resurrection of Christ as an effect to its cause; fifth, why the resurrection of souls is successive and the resurrection of bodies is simultaneous, since they are from one cause; sixth, what is to happen to all of us in the measure of the time of Christ's fullness; seventh, what are the proofs of His resurrection or of His

2. See Wilhelm Kübel's introduction to t. 26 of the Cologne edition of Albert's *Opera omnia (De sacramentis, De incarnatione, De resurrectione)*, edited by A. Ohlmeyer, I. Backes, and W. Kübel, v–xix (Monasterii Westfalorum, Ger.: Aschendorff, 1958). For the relationship of Albert's *De bono* to the *De resurrectione* and the four other treatises, see Bernhard Geyer's introduction to Albert's *De bono*, in *Opera omnia*, t. 28, edited by H. Kühle, C. Feckes, B. Geyer, and W. Kübel, ix–xxii (Monasterii Westfalorum, Ger.: Aschendorff, 1951).

3. "primo communiter ex parte capitis et ex parte membrorum et ex parte malorum; deinde ex parte capitis tantum; tertio ex parte malorum tantum; quarto ex parte bonorum tantum; quinto de his quae comitantur resurrectionem, idest de iudicio et innovatione mundi," *De resurrectione*, prol.

appearances; and eighth, what concerns His return to judgment and the handing over of His kingdom to God the Father.[4]

Albert divides the seventh section, on the proofs of Christ's resurrection, into four parts:

> What is considered first is what concerns the proofs before the resurrection and before [Christ's] death; second, what concerns those which were after death but before the resurrection; third, what concerns those which were after both; and fourth, what concerns the ascension, which was the proof of the glory of those risen from the dead.[5]

Albert's investigation of the transfiguration occurs in the first part of the seventh section, which is on proofs of the resurrection before Christ's death and resurrection, and it consists of most of question seven.

Since Albert's division of part seven of the second tractate is somewhat complicated, it may be helpful, before analyzing Albert's questions on the transfiguration, to illustrate how the questions and articles of the second tractate correspond to Albert's division of part seven. Of the eight separate inquiries that constitute the second tractate, each of the first six inquiries and the eighth comprise a discrete question. The seventh inquiry, however, on the proofs of Christ's resurrection is comprised of three separate questions. The first division of part seven, on the proofs of the resurrection before Christ's death and resurrection, corresponds to question seven, articles one through six. The second division, on proofs that occurred after Christ's death but before His resurrection, comprises a single article, the last one of question seven. Question eight is on Christ's appearances after the resurrection. Al-

4. "Et quia iam habitum est, quid sit resurrectio Christi, quaeritur primo, an sit causa nostrae resurrectionis; secundo, quam causalitatem habeat in bonis et malis; tertio, an sit causa resurrectionis animarum et quae sit resurrectio animarum; quarto, quare resurrectio omnium non fuit coniuncta resurrectioni Christi sicut effectus causae; quinto, quare resurrectio animarum est successiva et resurrectio corporum simul, cum sint ab una causa; sexto, quid sit nos omnes occurrere in mensuram aetatis plenitudinis Christi; septimo de argumentis resurrectionis eius sive de apparitionibus; octavo de reditu ad iudicium et quid sit tradere regnum deo patri," *De resurrectione*, t. 2, prol.

5. "Primo quaeritur de argumentis ante resurrectionem et ante mortem; secundo de his quae fuerunt post mortem et ante resurrectionem; tertio de his quae fuerunt post utrumque; quarto de ascensione quae etiam fuit argumentum gloriae resurgentium," *De resurrectione*, t. 2, q. 7, prol.

bert's fourth division, on Christ's ascension, corresponds to question nine. The following synoptic chart of tractate two illustrates the literary context of Albert's investigation of Christ's transfiguration.

Question 1. Whether Christ's resurrection is the cause of our resurrection
Question 2. What causality it has in those who are good and in those who are evil
Question 3. Whether it is the cause of the resurrection of souls
Question 4. Why the resurrection of all was not related to the resurrection of Christ as an effect to its cause
Question 5. Why the resurrection of souls is successive and the resurrection of bodies is simultaneous
Question 6. What is to happen to all of us in the measure of the time of Christ's fullness
Question 7. Of the proofs before the resurrection and before [Christ's] death
- Art. 1. Whether it was fitting for the resurrection to be proven
- Art. 2. What is transfiguration
- Art. 3. What is the starting point of the transfiguration
- Art. 4. What is the ending point of the transfiguration
- Art. 5. Whether Christ alone was transfigurable
- Art. 6. On the circumstances of the transfiguration
- Art. 7. On those proofs that occurred after death but before the resurrection

Question 8. On the appearances of Jesus Christ after His resurrection
Question 9. On the ascension
Question 10. On the return to judgment

From the outset of his investigation of the transfiguration, Albert gives the transfiguration an eschatological orientation by seeing it primarily as a proof of the coming resurrection of Christ. In q. 7, a. 1, Albert responds to objections that the raising of Lazarus and the apocalyptic events that occurred at Christ's death proved the coming resurrection. He says that "in the resurrection two things must be considered, namely the resurrection of the Head and of the members. Three things are found in either one, namely the power of rising, the act of resurrection, and the state of glory of those who have risen."[6]

Of these six distinctions, or the three-fold distinction applied to the resurrection of the Head and members, only the category of power designates which events can foreshadow a resurrection, which is yet to come. In the case of Christ's members, this foreshadowing occurred in the raising of Lazarus and others. These miracles do not prove that Christ will be resurrected one day, but they show that Christ possessed divine power. Albert refers to these miraculous events as *suscitationes,* or awakenings or resuscitations, not *resurrectiones.* The only event that properly illustrates Christ's capacity for being resurrected and thus foreshadows Christ's own resurrection, is the transfiguration. The act of resurrection is shown, with respect to Christ, in His post-resurrection appearances, and with respect to His members, in the resurrection of the dead, which occurs at Christ's death (see Matthew 27:51–53). The state of glory Albert mentions "is shown through the ascension of Christ and of those who ascended with Christ."[7]

After explaining how the transfiguration reveals Christ's capacity for resurrection, Albert addresses the meaning and significance of "transfiguration." The two objections that open the question take "transfiguration" to mean a change of figure or shape. In the first objection "figure" signifies a "termination of quantity," that is, a boundary beyond which the quantity of a sensible object does not extend. If Christ's figure changed during the transfiguration, that is, if His quantity contracted or dilated, it would do little to demonstrate His future resurrection, since resurrected bodies do not change their figure. The objection states that "either the resurrection is not demonstrated by the transfiguration or it should not be called 'transfiguration,'"[8] if Christ's figure indeed remained the same as it had been.

6. "in resurrectione duo attendenda sunt, scilicet resurrectio capitis et membrorum. In utroque istorum inveniuntur tria, scilicet potentia resurgendi et actus resurrectionis et status gloriae resurgentium," *De resurrectione,* t. 2, q. 7, a. 1.

7. "probatur per ascensionem Christi et eorum qui ascenderunt cum Christo," *De resurrectione,* t. 2, q. 7, a. 1. On Albert's theology of Christ's resurrection and ascension, see Ferdinand Haberl, *Die Inkarnationslehre des heiligen Albertus Magnus* (Freiburg im Breisgau, Ger.: Herder, 1939), 180–205.

8. "per transfigurationem vel non probetur resurrectio vel non sit transfiguratio vocanda," *De resurrectione,* t. 2, q. 7, a. 2.

In the second objection, Albert points out that, according to Aristotle, only a perfected or generated thing can undergo an "alteration," properly speaking, not its figure. What Aristotle seems to mean, in the passage which Albert cites from the *Physics*, is that, since an object's figure is intrinsically connected to certain sensible qualities, such as density and rarefaction, it cannot change on its own. Only when these sensible qualities change, can an object's figure change.[9] This principle applied to the transfiguration suggests that Christ's body changes, while its figure, understood as a "termination of quantity," remains the same.

To ascertain the appropriateness of the term "transfiguration," Albert first distinguishes between two senses of "figure." Figure can refer to the essence of a figure or to its role as a principle of knowing something that can be perceived by the common sense. In the former sense of the term, there can be no altered figure, as the second objection argued; but, in the latter sense, there can be change. Albert draws on Aristotle's epistemology by claiming that, in the act of recognizing something, the common sense discerns a particular object through that object's figure and those qualities perceptible to the particular senses alone, such as sight and touch. Although these latter qualities, such as color and odor, can change in an object, one can still recognize something for what it is. What allows for that recognition is the figure or shape of that object. Albert illustrates this process with an example:

> Elderly people, after they are known, are recognized immediately, even if they have been absent for a long time; children, however, are not, because the figure of children is changed through the extension and expansion of quantity, which does not happen with elderly people. We say, therefore, that figure, insofar as it is a principle of knowing, was altered [during the transfiguration], not that [Christ] could not be recognized to be the same by it, but that, by being joined to another quality, it could manifest another condition of the same person.[10]

9. See Aristotle's *Physics*, in *The Complete Works of Aristotle*, edited by Jonathan Barnes, 1:245b3–248a8 (Princeton, N.J.: Princeton University Press, 1984).

10. "senes, postquam noscuntur, statim discernuntur, etiam si multo tempore fuerint absentes, pueri autem non, quia in pueris per extensionem et dilatationem quantitatis mutatur figura, quod non contingit in senibus. Dicimus ergo, quod figura, inquantum est principium cognoscendi, alterata fuit, non quod non cognosceretur idem per ipsam, sed quod coniuncta alii qualitati ostenderet alium statum eiusdem," *De resurrectione*, t. 2, q. 7, a. 2.

As a principle of knowing, Christ's figure, which was perceived by the common sense rather than any one sense, was altered during the transfiguration, but not to the degree that He was no longer recognizable. He was still recognizable because His figure as a "termination of quantity," remained what it had been before the transfiguration. What changed were those qualities the individual senses perceive, and the change in what the disciples' senses perceived justifies the use of the term "transfiguration." In this explanation, Albert's familiarity with Aristotle's *De anima* allows him to overcome the difficulties that faced Alexander of Hales, who defined "transfiguration" by avoiding the term "figure." Albert employs the term "figure" but understands it to be more than just the shape of an object. By discussing "transfiguration" in terms of quality, as did John of La Rochelle, Albert is able to show that "transfiguration" is a proper term, if it is correctly understood.[11]

After establishing the veracity of the term "transfiguration" and its basis in the mutability of sensible qualities, Albert inquires into the starting point of the transfiguration. By "starting point," Albert means the point or condition from which the action of the transfiguration begins. In this question and in the next one, on the ending point of the transfiguration, Albert is concerned about explicating the relationship between Christ's transfigured but mortal body and His resurrected and glorified body.

Article three opens with three arguments that focus on whether Christ's bodily capacity for light is the starting point of the transfiguration. The first objection argues that Christ's body has a capacity for light, which makes the transfiguration possible and should be considered the starting point of the transfiguration. In one sense the body has a natural capacity for light. This capacity results from the fact that all human bodies are constituted, at least partially, by a heavenly power.[12] In addition, Christ possesses other capacities for light because of

11. John seems not to have been aware, however, of the difficulty posed by the *Physics*, 245b3 ff.

12. See *De resurrectione*, t. 2, q. 7, a. 3. This assertion is reminiscent of Aristotle's doctrine of "the transparent" or "the diaphanous," a power that exists in all bodies and whose activity, when in the presence of fire, is light (see *De anima* in *The Complete Works of Aristotle*, 1:418b4–25, and *De sensu et sensibilibus* in *The Complete Works of Aristotle*, 1:439a17–439b14). For Aristotle, however, the diaphanous does not derive from the heavenly fifth element, but

His will and because His body was united both to a rational soul and to the divine nature.[13]

An opposing objection argues that Christ's capacity for light cannot be a starting point of the transfiguration because a capacity by itself also signifies the absence of an act. If, moreover, Christ's bodily capacity for light is understood, in Aristotelian terms, as "that from which there is motion,"[14] capacity and act are opposites, which cannot coexist. In Christ's pre-resurrected body, however, a capacity for light did exist along with an actual manifestation of physical light; thus, this capacity cannot be a starting point, in the most precise sense of the term. Albert may be accused here of focusing exclusively on Aristotle's precise idea of "motion," as though there are no other kinds of motion, in a less technical sense; but Albert's point is expressed succinctly by his cited gloss, "A mortal body is not subject to immortality."[15] Albert uses this gloss to show that the bodily capacity for light of a mortal body is limited to the light that the elements can produce, and it cannot receive the glorious light of the resurrection.

The third objection also claims that Christ's bodily capacity for light cannot be a starting point for the transfiguration, and like the previous objection this argument relies on an Aristotelian concept of motion. Albert claims that the various capacities for light latent in Christ's mortal body are actualized only by that light, "which is the reward and blessedness of the body."[16] Since the light of the transfiguration is not the same as the light of the resurrection, it did not derive from Christ's bodily capacity for light as from a starting point; in other

---

rather it exists in the latter just as it exists in the other elements, although to greater or lesser degrees. The heavenly dimension to which Albert alludes may be either the fifth element itself or a Neo-Platonic vestige from al-Kindi and Abraham ibn Hasday, which Albert may have derived from his reading of the philosophical works of Isaac Israeli. See the latter's *The Book of Definitions*, chaps. 5–7 and *The Book of Substances*, frags. 3 and 4, in *Isaac Israeli*, translated by A. Altmann and S. M. Stern (Westport, Conn.: Greenwood Press, 1979), 39–48 and 83–90, respectively. John of La Rochelle, using more Aristotelian language, makes an argument similar to that of Albert in the *Summa fratris Alexandri*; see III, pt. 1, t. 6, q. 2, tit. 1, chap. 3.

13. See John of La Rochelle, *Summa fratris Alexandri*, III, pt. 1, t. 6, q. 2, tit. 1, chap. 3.

14. "quod est potentia, ut ex qua est motus," *De resurrectione*, t. 2, q. 7, a. 3.

15. "Non corpus mortale subditum est immortalitati," *De resurrectione*, t. 2, q. 7, a. 3.

16. "quod est praemium et beatitudo corporis," *De resurrectione*, t. 2, q. 7, a. 3.

words, despite the glory that Christ revealed in His transfigured body, His body still maintained a capacity for light. Only when movement exists between two opposites can there be a starting point and an ending point. Having applied Aristotle's discussion of the movement from black to white and white to black in the previous objection, Albert's opening second and third objections render the transfiguration a sort of gray between the black of Christ's bodily mortality and the white of His resurrected condition.[17]

In his solution to the question, Albert applies this Aristotelian definition of motion to determine the true starting point of the transfiguration. What changes in the transfiguration is not Christ's capacity for light, but merely the color of His body. Christ's mortal body possessed a particular color, which, during the transfiguration, was given a certain brilliance, resembling that of a glorified body. The color of His mortal body departed, and He attained a new or perhaps a better color; it took on a new intensity: The mortal condition of Christ's body remained, and His capacity for the light of the resurrection remained unchanged, still to be actualized by the resurrection itself. Albert explains:

> As it was objected, the state of the body, with respect to the nature of its mortality, was not changed, and since this capacity for light, which is in us because of a heavenly power or because of [the body's] union with a soul, is not able to exist in its own act of existence, it is proper for the elemental capacity to exist in active and passive qualities and the heavenly capacity to exist as though in potency until the resurrection. And this is what the Gloss says, that "there was clarity similar to that of immortality, but not that clarity itself." For it was not poured out throughout the whole nature of the body as the clarity of the resurrection will be poured out.[18]

17. See Aristotle, *Physics*, 229b14–22.

18. "Sicut enim obiectum est, status corporis quoad naturam mortalitatis non fuit mutatus, et cum hoc virtus, quae est ad lumen in nobis ex compositione virtutis caeli vel unione ad animam, non potest esse in actu suo, sed oportet, quod virtus elementalis in qualitatibus activis et passivis sit in actu et virtus caelestis quasi in potentia usque ad resurrectionem. Et hoc est quod Glossa, quod fuit claritas similis claritati immortalitatis, sed non ipsa claritas; non enim fuit profundata in tota natura corporis, sicut profundabitur claritas resurrectionis," (*De resurrectione*, t. 2, q. 7, a. 3). The gloss, which Albert cites and, which John of La Rochelle attributed to Bede (see III, pt. 1, t. 6, q. 2, tit. 1, chaps. 1, 4), has an unknown source. It may be, however, an allusion to or paraphrase of a gloss on Peter's words in Mark 9:4 ("Rabbi, it is good for us to be here,"): "Quamvis stupefactus insitum tamen affectum indicat; oblitus

This account of Christ's bodily capacity for light acknowledges only the composition of His body from earthly and heavenly elements and does not take into consideration the fact that it was united to a rational soul or to the divine nature. More so than in the first objection, it makes explicit that the "elemental" part of Christ's body provides a capacity for light, less than what the entire body possesses on account of the heavenly capacity. The capacity of the entire body is actualized only by the glory of the resurrection.

One question, which remains unclear at this point is whether Christ's body has a natural capacity to be transfigured. Albert concludes article three with an enigmatic postlude, which constitutes a response to the first objection. In it he says that the "dispositions" that result from Christ's body in its composition of earthly and heavenly elements, from its union to a rational soul, and from its union to the divine nature constitute Christ's capacity for light. This capacity, Albert avers, is for the light of the resurrection and not the light of the transfiguration.[19] How does the transfiguration occur? In article five, Albert will return to this question on Christ's transfigurability, but he does not satisfactorily answer the question there either.

The next article, however, asks what the ending point of the transfiguration might be. At first sight, this article seems superfluous. In the previous article, Albert established that only the surface of Christ's body, not His capacity for light, was effected by the transfiguration, and that the clarity that Christ manifested was not the same as that of His resurrected body. The ending point of the transfiguration, implied in article three and confirmed in article four, is the clarity Christ manifests in His transfigured body, a clarity that is similar to but not the same as that of His resurrected body. How does article four develop or clarify Albert's understanding of the transfiguration?

---

sanctis regnum promitti; non in terris sed in caelis; et se et coapostolos mortali carne indutos immortalis vitae statum subire non posse, domum manufactam necessariam non esse. Legi quoque et prophetis et evangelio tria tabernacula facere cupit; cum non possint separari, unum habentia tabernaculum, id est ecclesiam dei," (*Glossa ordinaria* 4:112). Judging by Albert's language in the next article, however, it seems more likely that it was in Albert's time a gloss on Matthew 17:1 and later dropped in subsequent copies and editions.

19. "dispositiones illae non dicunt potentiam nisi ad lumen resurrectionis et non transfigurationis," *De resurrectione*, t. 2, q. 7, a. 3.

The main purpose of this article is to distinguish more clearly the clarity of Christ's transfigured body from the clarity of His resurrected body. Albert's key authoritative text is the gloss he appropriated in article three, which asserts that the clarity of Christ's transfigured body was only similar to that of His resurrected body.[20] Using this text in his response to refute seemingly opposing glosses from the objections, Albert proceeds to make the following three distinctions with respect to the clarity of Christ's transfigured body:

> This clarity, which He assumed, can be considered according to intensity and according to the impression which it leaves in a subject, just as a certain philosopher, Averroes, has said that every quality leaves its impressions in a subject. And with respect to these two considerations, it has no likeness [to the clarity of a resurrected body], for the clarity of a resurrected body will be much greater. Likewise, the impression it leaves in a subject will be immortality or the glory of a body, which is not the impression of that which illumines nothing but the surface [of the body]. Clarity can also be considered according to act, which is to illumine or to shine according to its heavenly power, and thus it has some likeness [to the clarity of a resurrected body].[21]

Of the three distinctions Albert makes, only one corresponds to the clarities of both Christ's pre-glorified and His glorified body. Both kinds of clarity operate similarly, that is, by shining, but the glory of Christ's resurrected body will be much greater than that of His transfigured body, and the qualities or characteristics that Christ's glorified clarity conveys are those of an immortal body. By applying, in the *solutio* and in the reply to the second objection, the language of "gift" or "dowry"[22] to

20. In this question the gloss takes on two forms. The first is, "Non immortalitatem, sed claritatem similem immortalitati ostendit," and the second, which opens Albert's response, is "non assumpsit dotem, sed claritatem similem doti," *De resurrectione,* t. 2, q. 7, a. 4.

21. "Haec autem claritas quam assumpsit, potest considerari secundum intensionem et secundum impressionem, quam reliquit in subiecto, quia, ut dicit quidam philosophus Averroes, omnis proprietas relinquit impressiones suas in subiecto. Et quantum ad istas duas considerationes non habet similitudinem; claritas enim resurgentis corporis multo maior erit. Similiter impressio sua in subiecto erit immortalitas vel gloria corporis, quae non est impressio istius quae non illuminavit nisi superficiem. Potest etiam considerari ad actum, qui est illuminare vel fulgere secundum virtutem caelestem, et sic habet aliquam similitudinem," *De resurrectione,* t. 2, q. 7, a. 4.

22. Albert, following Alexander of Hales, applies the term *dos*. See also William of Aux-

Christ's final clarity and by denying any assumption of gifts before the resurrection, Albert further accentuates the difference between the clarity of the transfiguration and the clarity of the resurrection.

This question on the ending point of the transfiguration has, in addition to the purpose described above, a secondary goal, and that is to make sense of the seemingly contradictory authorities. The opening objections cite four different glosses (with one gloss cited twice) to argue for basically two opposing opinions. The first two objections assert that Christ brought the disciples to the mountain "to show the glory of His majesty,"[23] the clarity of which was to be what He would have at the Last Judgment.[24] The next two glosses argue that the clarity of the transfiguration was only similar to that of an immortal body and that Peter's words, "Lord it is good for us to be here"[25] and his offer to build three tabernacles show that Peter was "forgetting that the promised kingdom is not on earth but is in heaven and that those surrounding it cannot enter in mortal flesh."[26] Albert also adds an argument of his own, namely that the apostles, who saw Christ transfigured, could not see a truly glorified body with non-glorified eyes.

Albert's response to these seemingly contradictory statements is that those glosses that signify the "clarity of immortality"[27] refer to it "as a sign and not in itself absolutely. And it happens fittingly, that what is lesser is the sign of what is greater through some likeness, as is obvious with the signs of the sacraments."[28] This latter analogy of the sacraments aids Albert's effort to create distance between the transfiguration and the resurrection. The "likeness," which is common to both the clarity of Christ's transfigured body and His resurrected body is an act of illumination. However, since the intensity of the transfigured body and the characteristics of transfiguration that remain in Christ's

---

erre, *Summa aurea,* edited by J. Ribaillier, 4 vols. (Grottaferrata, Italy: Editiones Collegii S. Bonaventurae ad Claras Aquas, 1980–1985), IV, tr. 18, chap. 3, qq. 1–2.

23. "Gloriam maiestatis ostensurus," *De resurrectione,* t. 2, q. 7, a. 4.

24. See *De resurrectione,* t. 2, q. 7, a. 4.

25. Mt 17:4. Cf. Mk 9:4 and Lk 9:33.

26. "Oblitus regnum non in terra, sed in caelis esse promissum nec mortali carne circumdatos posse intrare," *De resurrectione,* t. 2, q. 7, a. 4.

27. "claritatem immortalitatis," *De resurrectione,* t. 2, q. 7, a. 4.

28. "ut signum et non in se absolute. Et bene contingit, quod minus est signum maioris per similitudinem aliquam, sicut patet in signis sacramentorum," *De resurrectione,* t. 2, q. 7, a. 4.

body do not approximate those of the clarity of immortality, Christ's transfiguration remains for Albert a sign pointing to the reality that will permeate the bodies of the elect, the clarity of immortality that is God's unique gift to His beloved.

Albert follows this question on the ending point of the transfiguration with a brief article on whether Christ alone is transfigurable. The opening objection follows from Albert's dictum in article four that "what is less is a sign of what is greater." It states the following:

> Our resurrection was revealed in others through the act of resurrection, and whoever can do something greater can do something lesser, and if something which is greater can be received, something which is lesser can be received, as well; but we are able to receive the act of resurrection, therefore how much more surely can we receive the act of transfiguration?[29]

As evidence for this assertion, the second objection cites the instance of Moses, who, after talking with God and receiving the Law a second time, came down alone from Mount Sinai with his face so radiant that he had to place a veil over it (see Exodus 34:29–35).

Albert's response is remarkably terse: "It must be said that God is able to transfigure anyone, but no one is transfigurable except Christ."[30] This appears to be basically the same answer that Alexander of Hales and John of La Rochelle proposed, but Albert's reply to the first objection provides a much different theological motivation. Albert claims that since the transfiguration is a proof of the resurrection, only He who is the "cause of our salvation and resurrection"[31] can bear in Himself the proof of the resurrection. Alexander and John attributed Christ's transfigurability to the union of Christ's body with the divine nature, but the eschatological orientation Albert gives to his overall investigation of the transfiguration is evident in this question, as well. Responding to Moses' apparent transfiguration in Exodus 34, Albert

29. "In aliis quibusdam per actum resurrectionis ostensa est resurrectio nostra, et qui potest facere maius, potest facere minus, et quod potest suscipere maius, potest suscipere minus; sed possumus suscipere actum resurrectionis, ergo multo fortius actum transfigurationis," *De resurrectione*, t. 2, q. 7, a. 5.

30. "Dicendum, quod deus quemlibet transfigurare posset, sed nullus est transfigurabilis nisi Christus," *De resurrectione*, t. 2, q. 7, a. 5.

31. "causa salutis et resurrectionis nostrae," *De resurrectione*, t. 2, q. 7, a. 5.

replies that "transfiguration," properly speaking, is a proof of the resurrection, and the radiance of Moses' face did not signify that. Albert is satisfied simply to remark that, "the clarity of his face signified the clarity of the truth of those things signified in the Law; the veil, however, which he placed over his face, signified the shadow of the ceremonial precepts and not the resurrection."[32] What matters, then, in determining how to classify a given manifestation of light is not its intensity or appearance, but rather its signification.

The soteriological and eschatological orientation that Albert gives the transfiguration continues in his last article on the transfiguration on some of the details surrounding Christ's manifestation of glory. This article is by far the longest of the six on the transfiguration, and it consists of seven separate inquiries: whether Moses was resurrected, why Moses and Elijah appeared, what they talked about with Jesus, the significance of their white vestments, the significance of the cloud, the importance of the Father's words, and the effect of the light on the disciples. In introducing these topics, Albert frames three of the questions in explicitly eschatological terms.[33]

The first question, and the central one from which the others follow, asks whether Moses was raised from the dead so he could appear with Jesus and Elijah. The importance of this question lies primarily in its introduction of the main theme of the whole article, namely the significance of the events surrounding the transfiguration. Three objections based on three different glosses,[34] argue that because of what Moses' presence signifies, he must have been resurrected. The key gloss to which Albert alludes is one on Matthew 17:3, which says, "Moses and Elijah signify all who are to reign with Christ; the deceased Moses signifies the dead, the living Elijah signifies those who are found liv-

32. "claritas vultus sui significabat claritatem veritatis significatae in lege, velum autem, quod imposuit faciei, significabat umbram caeremonialium et non resurrectionem," *De resurrectione*, t. 2, q. 7, a. 5.

33. The fourth question, for example, concerns Jesus' white garments, "cum in gloria non simus vestes habituri," and the fifth question is on the cloud, "cum nihil nubilum futurum sit in resurrectione," *De resurrectione*, t. 2, q. 7, a. 6.

34. The first two glosses are found in the same marginal gloss on Matthew 17:3, but Albert distinguishes between the first gloss, which is merely a "quaedam glossa," and the second gloss, which he refers to as a "glossa Rhabani longa," *De resurrectione*, t. 2, q. 7, a. 6.

ing."[35] The essence of all three objections is that if Moses is really to represent the resurrection from the dead or the glory of those resurrected from the dead, then he should himself be resurrected from the dead.

Although there are brief answers to all seven questions within article six, all of which address the significance of the circumstances surrounding Christ's transfiguration, the *solutio* of the article addresses exclusively how Moses' soul could appear without a resurrected body. The authority of Augustine allowed John of La Rochelle to argue that Moses' soul appeared by divine power, not only without a resurrected body, but without a body at all. Albert cannot maintain this position, but he also does not allow that Moses left hell. Albert's position is that Moses' soul assumed a body, so that both were present on Mount Tabor, but his soul remained in hell simultaneously. In order to maintain this opinion, Albert must sort the various powers of the soul to demonstrate how this situation could even be possible:

It must be said that Moses was not raised from the dead, but his spirit was there by means of an assumed body, by which it formed sounds which the disciples heard. If, however, it is asked how this could be, it must be said that the soul has a twofold power in relation to the body, namely a unitive or preservative power of the body, as it unites form to matter and preserves them together, and what follows this is the vivifying power and bodily life. It has another power, as well, a motive power of the body which operates by a movement proceeding through the whole body and by a movement of the organs for their proper operations, just as it moves the tongue to give utterances meaning and the hand to touch various objects. It has these conjoined powers with respect to its natural body, but the last one it only has with respect to a body that has been assumed, not naturally, but for a temporary use.[36]

35. "moyses et helyas significant omnes cum christo regnaturos. Mortuus moyses, mortuos, helyas vivus, eos qui vivi invenientur," *Glossa ordinaria* 4:57.

36. "Dicendum, quod Moyses non resurrexit, sed spiritus eius fuit ibi assumpto corpore, quo formabat voces ad auditum discipulorum. Si autem quaeritur, quomodo hoc potuerit esse, dicendum, quod in anima est duplex vis unitiva sive contentiva corporis, sicut unit et continet forma materiam, et hanc sequitur vis vivificativa et vita in corpore. Aliam habet vim motivam corporis motu processivo in toto corpore et motu organorum ad actus organicos, sicut movet linguam ad interpretationem loquelae et manum ad contrectationem rerum. Et has virtutes coniunctas habet respectu corporis naturalis, sed ultimam tantum habet respectu corporis assumpti non naturaliter, sed ad usum temporalem," *De resurrectione*, t. 2, q. 7, a. 6.

With such an understanding of the soul, Albert claims that a soul can unite itself only to the body to which it belongs, and it can give life only to that body. If it is joined to another body, it can move its parts only as an extrinsic cause.[37]

While the *solutio* of the article addresses how Moses' appearance is possible, Albert treats separately, in a reply to the objections listed above, why Moses was not raised from the dead. Albert acknowledges that Moses' appearance and the approach of all the witnesses of the transfigured Jesus to the light of the transfiguration signify "the approach of all the saints to the splendor of the clarity of the resurrected Christ,"[38] but from this premise it does not follow that those present at the transfiguration need to be resurrected themselves. Nor did Moses have to leave hell in order to appear on the mountain. Echoing a statement of Alexander of Hales, Albert argues that "hell" is a deprivation of the beatific vision, a condition Moses sustained while he beheld the clarity of the transfigured Christ. Beholding the transfiguration in no way compromised Moses' pre-redeemed condition because beholding the glory of the transfiguration is compatible with that condition, and it is far less than the glory of the beatific vision, which is the consummation of Christ's redemptive activity.

The remaining six questions address other details pertaining to the transfiguration story, and their order flows primarily from the narrative of the Gospel texts. The second question asks why Moses and Elijah, in particular, appeared. Albert finds one answer in the gloss cited at the beginning of the article, which, at one point, states that Moses and Elijah, "signify the oracles of the Law and the Prophets, which were fulfilled in the Lord."[39] Albert's explanation of this gloss focuses on how Moses and Elijah prefigure Christ's salvific work and how that work relates to Christ's glory. He says that the Law, which Moses gave and which expressed "the law of nature in moral laws and the form of

37. For more on the relationship between souls and bodies, Albert refers to a question on the angelic assumption of bodies in his own treatise; see *De IV coaequevis*, in *Opera omnia*, edited by A. Borgnet (Paris: Vivès, 1895), t. 34, q. 61, a. 2.

38. "occursus omnium sanctorum ad splendorem claritatis Christi resurgentis," *De resurrectione*, t. 2, q. 7, a. 6.

39. "significant oracula legis et prophetiae, quae in domino sunt completa," *De resurrectione*, t. 2, q. 7, a. 6. Cf. *Glossa ordinaria* 4:57.

future truth in ceremonial laws," will be fulfilled in the resurrection because in it, "nature will be in the highest beauty of justice, and the understanding will be in perfect knowledge of truth."[40] Albert's interpretation of Elijah's presence contains the oft-cited reason that he was the greatest of the prophets,[41] but Albert provides another interesting reason. As prophet, Elijah was considered by many theologians to be an important witness at the transfiguration, to the significance of Christ's mission. However, Albert makes no mention of Moses and Elijah as "witnesses," instead he relates two of the events of Elijah's life to Christ's glorified humanity.

In the first event, God twice sends fire from heaven to consume the soldiers who were sent to bring Elijah to King Ahaziah (see 2 Kings 1:1–17). In this episode, Albert sees a sign of the Last Judgment. The two groups of fifty signify "the twofold multitude of the condemned: for, as Augustine says, some people are condemned and not judged, and others are condemned and judged."[42] Albert envisions two categories of the damned. The first group consists of those who are not Christians and who, by rejecting Christ, are judged before the end of time (see John 3:18); the second group consists of those Christians who will be judged at the Last Judgment and condemned because of their evil actions. The second event in Elijah's life that Albert finds deeply significant is his journey to heaven by a fiery chariot. In this singular event, Albert sees a prefiguration of the "ascension of the saints into glory with Christ."[43]

The answer Albert gives to the question of why Moses and Elijah appeared, rather than others, is noteworthy, not only because of Albert's perspective and the singularity of some parts of the answer, but also because Albert decided not to connect the appearance of Mo-

40. "legem naturae in moralibus et figurationem veritatis futurae in caeremonialibus . . . natura in summo decore erit iustitiae et intellectus in perfecta cognitione veritatis," *De resurrectione*, t. 2, q. 7, a. 6.

41. See the interlinear gloss on Matthew 17:3 in *Glossa ordinaria* 4:57, and *Summa fratris Alexandri*, III, pt. 1, t. 6, q. 2, tit. 1, chap. 8.

42. "duplicem turbam condemnandorum: quidam enim, ut dicit Augustinus, condemnantur et non iudicantur et quidam condemnantur et iudicantur," *De resurrectione*, p. t. 2, q. 7, a. 6. The citation of Augustine is not from an authentic work.

43. "ascensionem sanctorum in gloriam cum Christo," *De resurrectione*, t. 2, q. 7, a. 6.

ses and Elijah to their roles as "witnesses" as Alexander of Hales and John of La Rochelle had done. In fact, Albert's interpretation of their significance makes no mention of the transfiguration at all. His emphasis is entirely eschatological. Of course, it is not surprising that a question on the transfiguration would have an eschatological perspective, but the fact that Albert's explanation for the significance of Moses and Elijah refers exclusively to the resurrection and the Last Judgment confirms the eschatological emphases that Albert articulated in earlier questions.

Albert's response to the next question on what the two Old Testament figures talked about with Jesus, continues this eschatological focus. As Albert notes, the key term is in Luke 9:31, where Moses and Elijah speak with Jesus about His "departure," which would take place in Jerusalem.[44] Albert, following a gloss of Rabanus Maurus cited at the beginning of the article (on Matthew 17:3), understands this departure to signify not only Christ's passion and death, but also His resurrection and glory.[45]

The fourth question, which asks about the significance of Christ's white garments, elicits an answer that shows how Christ communicates His glory. Following a familiar biblical and patristic motif, Albert associates Christ's garments with the saints. He explains that "the whiteness of His clothes signifies the refulgence which proceeds from Christ to the saints."[46] Albert uses the sun and its light as an analogy to portray Christ's glory and the saints' participation in it. Although it is true, as described in one of the Matthean parables of the kingdom, that "the righteous will shine like the sun in the kingdom of their Father," the glory of the saints pales in comparison to the glory of the Son, whose face also became like the sun during the transfiguration.[47]

44. Albert's Vulgate text has "excessu," although the Greek ἔξοδον is more suggestive.

45. "lectio eorum fuit de fine redemptionis, hoc est de passione, et de fine gloriae, hoc est de resurrectione gloriosa . . . exponit Rhabanus in glossa longa supra notata de excessu resurrectionis in gloria et de excessu passionis in redemptione," *De resurrectione*, t. 2, q. 7, a. 6.

46. "candor vestis significat fulgorem a Christo procedentem in sanctos," *De resurrectione*, t. 2, q. 7, a. 6.

47. Albert's answer may be inspired by Hugh of St. Cher (see above, pp. 23–25). Thomas Aquinas will provide a similar explanation in the *Summa theologiae*, in *Opera omnia iussu Leonis XIII P.M. edita* tt. 4–12 (Rome, 1886–1906), III, q. 45, a. 2.

Albert explains, "Just as the light from the sun is daylight, and on a surface it is pure and gleaming white, so too in Christ glory manifests itself as light, but in the saints it manifests itself as whiteness, not absolutely, but in relation to Him."[48] Both Christ and the saints will shine like the sun, but what the whiteness of Christ's clothes signifies is the communication of Christ's glory to the saints.

On the question regarding the significance of the voice from the cloud, Albert follows the narrative from Matthew because it is the only one that refers to the cloud as shining. This detail is significant because the brightness of the cloud, juxtaposed with its overshadowing of the disciples, creates a kind of narrative *chiaroscuro,* which invites theological reflection. Albert explains that the cloud signifies "the incomprehensible light that descended on Mount Tabor, which means 'mountain of light,' that is, upon the radiant Church, spiritually by the light of truth and corporeally by the clarity of physical beatitude."[49] Since the incomprehensible light of the theophany escapes the grasp of its beholders, Albert interprets the cloud's "overshadowing" as the utter transcendence of the infinite light and the necessity of its "being clothed with finite concepts which correspond to the intellects of the blessed."[50] Thus, the shadow that fell over the witnesses of the transfiguration was not a literal one, but an intellectual or spiritual one of a finite creature, which arose in the presence of the insuperable light of the Blessed Trinity.

Albert next addresses the voice from the cloud, the voice of the Father. Here Albert is content merely to place the Father's voice and His words, "listen to Him," within the context of other revelations of the Father within the economy of salvation. On the three occasions in the Gospels in which the Father reveals Himself by means of a voice,

48. "Sicut enim lumen in sole lux est, in superficie autem clara et pura candor, ita in Christo gloria est per modum lucis, sed in sanctis ad modum candoris non simpliciter, sed in comparatione ad ipsum," *De resurrectione,* t. 2, q. 7, a. 6.

49. "Ad aliud dicendum, quod nubes significant in circumscriptum et incomprehensibile lumen, quod tunc descendit super montem Thabor, qui interpretatur 'mons luminis,' idest super ecclesiam radiantem spiritualiter lumine veritatis et corporaliter claritate beatitudinis corporalis," *De resurrectione,* t. 2, q. 7, a. 6.

50. "vestiri determinatis rationibus congruentibus intellectibus beatorum," *De resurrectione,* t. 2, q. 7, a. 6.

the Father testifies to the unique relationship between Himself and Jesus. Albert notes that each occasion has a slightly different purpose:

> The first was at His baptism with respect to the obedience of the sacraments, the second was at Mount Tabor with respect to the obedience of the precepts and the law of the Gospel which were to be proclaimed by the disciples; for this reason, on both occasions the same voice added "Listen to Him." With the third testimony [the Father] confirmed the reward for those who were obedient before the passion, when he said "I have glorified it, and I will glorify it again," which means I have glorified it in grace and I will glorify it again in glory.[51]

Aside from the surprising application of this passage from the Gospel of John (12:28), in which the Father testifies that He has glorified and will glorify the Son's name, to the reward of the saints, this passage is noteworthy for its association of the transfigured Christ with the preaching of the apostles. The ecclesiological motifs that arise in this passage, regarding both preaching and the sacraments, will occur again in Albert's commentaries on the synoptic gospels.

The final response, in reply to the question of how the light of the transfiguration affected the disciples is the longest of the seven replies. Like Alexander of Hales and John of La Rochelle, Albert compares the effect of sunlight upon the human eye to the effect of Christ's luminous body. The light and heat of the sun, by consuming the watery humor in the eye, render vision impossible for one who looks directly at the sun; Albert expands on Alexander's explanation by claiming that the sun's heat consumes even the moistness and the liquid humor in the brain. The light of a glorified body and of Christ's transfigured body is much different from that of the sun, Albert claims. Since it is not subject to the elements, nor does it move the elements, it cannot overpower the senses. What happened then? How could the disciples perceive light which, by its nature, remains undetected by the senses?

It may be helpful at this point to recall Albert's teachings on Christ's

51. "primo in baptismo quoad oboedientiam sacramentorum; secundo in monte Thabor quoad oboedientiam praeceptorum et legis evangelicae, quae praedicanda fuerunt per discipulos; et propter hoc in utraque voce idem dixit subiungens: 'Ipsum audite.' Tertio testimonio suo confirmavit praemium oboedientibus ante passionem, cum dixit: 'Et clarificavi et iterum clarificabo,' hoc est clarificavi in gratia et iterum clarificabo in gloria," *De resurrectione*, t. 2, q. 7, a. 6.

transfiguration in previous articles. In article two, Albert explained that "transfiguration" does not mean that Christ's bodily shape changed, but rather that the sensible qualities of Christ's body changed, namely those qualities that allowed the disciples to recognize Jesus as Jesus. Which sensible qualities changed? Albert claimed in article three, on the starting point of the transfiguration, that nothing changed in Christ's body except the color of the surface of His body. In addressing the relationship between the clarity of the transfiguration and the clarity of the resurrection, Albert argued in article four that the only similarity between the two was their illuminating and resplendent quality. Christ's body radiated visible light, but not with nearly the same intensity as it will at the end of time.

Albert's emphasis on the spiritual nature of the light of Christ's transfigured body in article six in no way compromises his assertion regarding the corporeal light radiating from Christ's body. In this last question on the transfiguration, he wishes to emphasize that the spiritual light, which radiates from Christ's body, is much greater than the corporeal light. But what is this spiritual light, and how is it grasped by the minds of its beholders? Albert explains:

> If [the light] moves the senses, it will move them in relation to the mind, because the mind, having grasped what is sensible, is moved to wonder at the majesty shining in what is sensible or to consideration of the goodness shining in it, or to an understanding of the truth signified by what is sensible. And such was the case with the clarity of the Lord in the transfiguration. The apostles fell, therefore, not because of an opposition between what was sensible and the senses, but because of their amazement at the wonder which was perceived through what was sensible. And this is what Gregory says in an interlinear gloss on Matthew 17:6 ("the disciples, hearing this, fell"), "not only because of the Father, but also because of the majesty of the Son," and Gregory also says in the *Moralia* that we are in a miserable state since "we cannot bear [that light] which we were created to behold." It is obvious, however, that it is not corporeal light for which we were created, but rather spiritual light, which could be perceived through corporeal light.[52]

52. "Sed si movet sensum, movebit eum in comparatione ad rationem, secundum quod ratio ex sensibili apprehenso movetur in admirationem maiestatis refulgentis in sensibili vel in devotionem bonitatis refulgentis in eo vel in intellectum veritatis significatae per sensibile.

What the disciples perceived with their bodily eyes was "majesty" and "goodness," and through what they sensed, they perceived truth. Truth is the category to which spiritual light corresponds. Albert's response to the fifth question of this article, on what the shining cloud signifies, is persuasive. In that answer, Albert replies that the cloud signifies the infinite light, which descended upon the mountain, "spiritually by the light of truth and corporeally by the clarity of physical beatitude."[53] The light that permeates both the mountain and those who were chosen to behold the theophany, is one. It is the infinite and incomprehensible light of the Godhead. As this light is perceived by the created minds of its beholders, it manifests itself as truth, and as it is perceived by their bodily eyes, it is the glory of the transfigured Christ, made sensible to them through a change in His body. It is this corporeal light, moreover, of the body of the incarnate Word through which His disciples perceive the spiritual light they were created to behold.[54]

Albert's question on the transfiguration, written at about the same time as John of La Rochelle's question on the transfiguration or perhaps a little later, is notable for several reasons. First, Albert's account of the transfiguration maintains an eschatological focus throughout his question. Not only is Christ's resurrection the point of reference in the discussion of the transfiguration, but even when Albert discusses the circumstantial details of the transfiguration, such as the presence of Moses and Elijah, his explanations focus on bodily resurrection and the Last Judgment.

The only explicit role the hypostatic union plays with respect to

---

Et ita fuit in claritate domini in transfiguratione. Unde apostoli ceciderunt non ex contrarietate sensibilis ad sensum, sed ex stupore admirationis eius quod intelligebatur per sensibile. Et hoc est quod dicit Gregorius in Glossa XVII (6) Matth. super illud: 'et audientes discipuli ceciderunt,' interlineari: 'non solum de patris, sed et de filii maiestate,' et Gregorius in Moralibus: Miserae condicionis sumus, qui lumen 'ferre non possumus, ad quod videndum creati sumus.' Constat autem, quod hoc non est lumen corporale, ad quod creati sumus, sed lumen spirituale, quod per illud intelligebatur," *De resurrectione*, t. 2, q. 7, a. 6.

53. "spiritualiter lumine veritatis et corporaliter claritate beatitudinis corporalis," *De resurrectione*, t. 2, q. 7, a. 6.

54. Of all the thirteenth-century descriptions of Christ's transfigured clarity, Albert's, with its emphasis on the spiritual dimension of that clarity, most closely resembles the teaching of Gregory Palamas, although the latter may not share all aspects of Albert's eschatological interpretation of the transfiguration.

Christ's clarity is to give Christ an exceptional and unique capacity for clarity that no creature could possibly have. Only the very end of Albert's question makes it clear that Christ's divinity is always radiating glory, but this glory manifests itself fully in a bodily way only after the resurrection. From the first moment of the Incarnation until the resurrection, Christ's body has multiple capacities for clarity (e.g., a natural bodily capacity, a capacity resulting from His will, and capacities that derive from His body's union to a rational soul and to the divine nature), but the overall capacity of Christ's body for clarity is not "reduced to act" until the glorious clarity of the resurrection penetrates Christ's human nature completely. The transfiguration is only an important stage to this full divinization of Christ's humanity. The clarity manifested is similar to glorious clarity because of its radiance, but ontologically it is completely different from glorious clarity because it does not communicate immortality. The anticipatory stage that the transfiguration represents is rendered visible in the fact that only Christ's face, not his whole body, radiates glory. In his explanation of what changed in Christ, Albert never really explains how Christ's transfigured clarity radiates from His body, that is, whether it derives from His divine nature alone or is communicated by His soul. Albert's primary concerns are to affirm that Christ's body was mortal and passible during the transfiguration and that Christ's clarity was only a distant shadow compared to what He will have in His resurrected body.

Another notable feature of Albert's question on the transfiguration is the use of philosophical terms and concepts when describing the transfiguration. His use of Aristotle's epistemology to establish the change in "figure" as a principle of knowledge and the citation of Averroes in describing how properties act on subjects are just two examples of Albert's application of philosophy to the transfiguration. Nor should the terminology of his questions be forgotten. His use of phrases such as *terminus ex quo* and *terminus in quem* also testify to Albert's use of philosophy. Albert is unique in this regard, since no other theologian from this period has such explicit recourse to philosophical discourse in discussions on the transfiguration.

A third interesting feature is Albert's emphasis on the sacramental and ecclesial dimension of the transfiguration. Although Hugh of

St. Cher had made the connection between the transfiguration, on the one hand, and preaching and the sacraments, on the other, in his *Postilla super Marcum,* only Albert brings together these topics so forcefully in a disputed question. The full rationale for this connection will be brought out more fully years later in Albert's commentaries on the Gospels.

Super Matthaeum

Just as Albert's *De resurrectione* possesses numerous original insights, so too does his commentary on Matthew, written probably between 1257 and 1264.[55] What is immediately striking about Albert's treatment of Christ's transfiguration is the ecclesial dimension of his *divisio textus.* According to Albert, Matthew 17, which discusses both the transfiguration and Jesus casting a demon out of a young boy, is part of a larger portion of Matthew, which pertains to ecclesiastical power. This portion of Matthew is in turn one small subdivision among several others. Without providing a full synoptic outline of Albert's division of the whole Gospel of Matthew, we can trace the textual divisions Albert saw as pertaining to the transfiguration:

I. Matthew 1:1—title
II. Matthew 1:2–28:20—treatise
- A. Generation according to human appearance 1:2–2:23
- B. Our regeneration 3:1–28:20
  - 1. The sacrament of regeneration 3:1–4:11
  - 2. Illumination 4:12–25:49
    - i. Foretaste of what is to come 4:12–4:25
    - ii. Instruction and illumination pertaining to those who have been regenerated 5:1–25:46

55. See the *prolegomena* of B. Schmidt in Albert's *Super Matthaeum,* 2 vols., edited by B. Schmidt, in *Opera omnia,* t. 21 (Monasterii Westfalorum, Ger.: Aschendorff, 1987), vol. 1, xiii–xvi. See also Albert Fries, "Die Entstehungszeit der Bibelkommentare Alberts des Grossen," in *Albertus Magnus—Doctor Universalis 1280/1980,* edited by G. Meyer and A. Zimmerman, 119–39 (Mainz: Matthias-Grünewald-Verlag, 1980). For Albert's approach to Scripture, see Mikolaj Olsewski, "St. Albert the Great's Theory of Interpretation of the Bible," in *Albertus Magnus. Zum Gedenken nach 800 Jahren: Neue Zugänge, Aspekte, und Perspektiven,* edited by W. Senner, 467–78 (Berlin: Akademie Verlag, 2001).

- a. Matthew 5–9—Concerning a holy life
- b. Matthew 10–25—Teaching ministers for ecclesiastical ministry
  - aa. Matthew 10—The institution of prelates
  - bb. Matthew 11–25—The arrangement of the whole mystical body
    - Matthew 11—The order of the beginning of the mystical body
    - Matthew 12–25—The order of the Church's progression, or the ecclesiastical order
      - Matthew 12–15—All members without distinction
      - Matthew 16–17—The power by which prelates are ordered to their subjects
      - Matthew 18–20—The use of that power
      - Matthew 21–25—The order of the end of the Church

3. The sacraments of Christ 26:1–28:20

In this outline, Albert locates the transfiguration narrative in a larger section that pertains to the power by which prelates are ordered to their subjects. In order to show how Albert makes the connection between Christ's transfiguration and the hierarchy of the Church, a brief glimpse at his interpretation of Matthew 16 will be necessary.

Albert treats Matthew 16 and 17 together, arguing that both chapters address ecclesiastical power. Chapter sixteen addresses the power in the ministries of the Church, and chapter seventeen describes those events at the source of this power, including Christ's "passion, resurrection, and so forth."[56] Since chapter seventeen does not contain an account of Christ's passion or resurrection, Albert explains this enigmatic statement more completely in the opening of his commentary on chapter seventeen:

> Because it was said that the keys of the kingdom of heaven have been brought together in the ministers, here it is shown what that kingdom is

56. "passio et resurrectio et huiusmodi," *Super Matthaeum* vol. 2:451.

like, [and] what [the keys] open, just as it was promised in the preceding chapter. Two things are mentioned here: namely the glory of the resurrection following the merit of the passion and [its] effect, both on the harmful demon and with respect to the liberty of the children, which it will bring about most perfectly. These two things are contained in the second part of the chapter, as is obvious to anyone.[57]

The first part of chapter seventeen, on the glory of the resurrection, which is manifested during Jesus' transfiguration, has three parts: the circumstantial details, the mode of the manifestation, and the instruction of the disciples. The outline of this pericope, which Albert supplies, consists of the following:

I. Where, when, and for whom the transfiguration took place
II. Mode of the manifestation
  A. In the Lord
    1. In His body
      i. In a general way
      ii. In a particular way
    2. In His clothes
  B. In the witnesses
    1. The testimony of the fathers
    2. The testimony of the disciples
    3. The testimony of creatures
    4. The testimony of the Father
III. Instruction of the disciples
  A. From the transfiguration itself
    1. The return from exaltation
    2. Comfort from the Lord's consolation
      i. His approaching the disciples
      ii. His touch
      iii. His speech

57. "Quia dictum est, quod claves regni caelorum collatae sunt ministris, ostenditur hic, quale est regnum, quod reserant, sicut in fine praecedentis capituli est promissum. Tanguntur ergo hic duo, gloria scilicet resurrectionis sequens meritum passionis et effectus tam super daemonem impedientem quam etiam ad libertatem filiorum, quam perfectissime efficiet, et haec duo continentur in secunda parte capituli, sicut per se patet cuilibet," *Super Matthaeum* 2:466.

        3. Instruction from the passage from revealed glory
            i. The elevation of the disciples' eyes to the one teaching them
            ii. The significance of that action
    B. From Christ's words about the transfiguration
        1. Words of humility and mystery
        2. The solution to a question
            i. Jesus' question
            ii. Answer
                a. Concerning the coming of Elijah in person
                b. Concerning the coming of Elijah "in spirit and in power"
            iii. Perfect illumination

Considering that Albert's commentary occupies just over four pages in the critical edition, the complexity of this outline is impressive.

In discussing the transfiguration in his Matthew commentary, Albert begins by glossing the words, "And He was transfigured." Albert discusses first what "transfiguration" means. He notes, as he did in the *De resurrectione,* that Christ's shape *(figura)* did not change. In the *De resurrectione,* however, Albert focused on *figura* signifying a principle of knowing. As such, Jesus' figure did change. In his Matthew commentary, however, there is no mention of a principle of knowing. Instead, Albert merely notes that Jesus' appearance changed.

What is of particular interest in this brief passage (and in Albert's commentaries on Mark and Luke), however, is how Albert's theology of the transfiguration has changed from his earlier treatment in the *De resurrectione.* In the *De resurrectione,* Albert argued that during the transfiguration Christ assumed a type of clarity similar to the clarity resurrected bodies will have. The potential for clarity that Christ possessed as a result of His body's union with the divine nature and for other reasons is realized fully only by receiving that clarity that Christ will have after the resurrection. The hypostatic union plays no explicit role in the manifestation of bodily clarity. In Albert's later scriptural commentaries, however, he changes his articulation of the clarity's origin so that the Incarnation will play a much more important role in accounting for Christ's transfigured glory. In the Matthew commentary, for example, Albert's response heavily emphasizes the relationship between Christ's body and His divine nature, in a way reminiscent of John of La Rochelle. Albert says,

> because [His] body was divine, united to the divine nature and an instrument of a soul full of grace, and because the divine nature shines brighter than all light, as it says in Wisdom 7, "She is more beautiful than the sun and above all the order of the stars: being compared with the light, she is found before it," therefore that which appears in a divine body according to the power of the divine nature is a transfiguration into light.[58]

A transfiguration, then, is not so much the alteration of a principle of knowing, as it is in the *De resurrectione,* but rather it is "the act of a higher power" in Christ's body.[59]

Albert does follow the interpretation of Christ's garments that he gave in the *De resurrectione,* namely that they represent the saints, but he makes a couple of additional observations. He immediately refutes an interpretation found in Hugh's *Postilla super Matthaeum,* which asserted that the garments could be understood as Christ's humanity. Albert's distaste for this interpretation stems from the fact that Jesus is already human. He notes that the face that shone "like the sun" was a human face; thus, it is unnecessary to interpret Christ's face as His divinity and His garments as His humanity. The other point Albert makes here, which he neglected in his earlier work, concerns the significance of Jesus' garments being white "as snow." According to Albert, snow is "scattered, white, and soft."[60] Although he gives a brief meteorological account for this assertion, his primary goal is to make a spiritual interpretation. The scattered nature of snow signifies spirituality, its whiteness represents innocence and chastity, and its softness signifies tenderness and love.[61] Snow possesses certain qualities, which call

58. "quia corpus divinum fuit, unitatum deitati et organum animae plenissimae gratiae, et deitas radiat super omnem lucem, ut dicitur Sap. vii (29): 'Haec est speciosior sole et super omnem dispositionem stellarum; luci comparata invenitur prior': quod igitur secundum potestatem deitatis in corpore apparet divino, transfiguratio est in lucem," *Super Matthaeum* 2:467.

59. "actus altioris potestatis," *Super Matthaeum* 2:467.

60. "rara, alba et mollis," *Super Matthaeum* 2:467.

61. *Super Matthaeum* 2:467. The rationale for Albert's connection between the scattered snow and spirituality is a little obscure. In his *Meteororum,* Albert explains that precipitation is formed in various ways. When snow falls, a cloud turns into water and is frozen simultaneously.

to Albert's mind certain spiritual analogies. The purpose of the simile of snow, then, is to communicate something about the qualities of the saints, whom Christ wears like a garment.

One way in which Albert distinguishes himself from his contemporaries and predecessors is the way in which he accounts for the witnesses of the transfiguration. Like them, Albert sees Moses and Elijah as constituting one group of witnesses and the disciples as constituting another. However, by creating two more categories of witnesses, namely creatures and the Father, Albert introduces an entirely new category (creatures) and does away with any fully Trinitarian interpretation of the bright cloud and the voice. The "creatures" refer to the "bright cloud" itself, or rather the cloud and its light. The light "should express delight and the testimony of light, while the cloud should temper the excess of light, Isaiah 49: 'In the shadow of His hand He has protected me.'"[62] The voice is that of the Father, and His words, "my beloved Son," have Trinitarian implications for Albert, but without any reference to the Holy Spirit in his discussion of the theophany, the exegesis loses the fuller Trinitarian significance that it had in Hugh of St. Cher's interpretation.

Enarrationes in Marcum

Albert's commentary on Mark, which was probably written somewhere between the late 1250s and the late 1260s, shares some of the theological emphases found in his *Super Matthaeum*, but it possesses a less complicated *divisio textus* of the transfiguration narrative than his Matthew commentary. According to Albert, the transfiguration narrative describes "the establishment of the Church in glory."[63] The

The warmth in the cloud, however, expands the matter of the snow, thus causing the precipitation to scatter and to retain some warmth, as opposed to rime or hoar frost, which is colder and harder. The expansion of the matter (as well as the rarefaction of the air) corresponds to the "expansion" of an increasingly "spiritual" soul. See *Meteororum*, in *Opera omnia*, t. 4, edited by A. Borgnet (Paris: Vivès, 1890), l. 2, t. 1, 15–20.

62. "ingereret blandimentum et luminis testimonium, nubes autem temperaret lucis excessum. Is. xlix (2): 'In umbra manus suae protexit me,'" *Super Matthaeum* 2:468.

63. "Ecclesiae fundationem in gloria," *Enarrationes in Marcum*, in *Opera omnia*, edited by A. Borgnet, (Paris: Vivès, 1894), t. 21, 539.

narrative has two basic parts: the promise of glory (Mark 9:1) and the manifestation of glory (Mark 9:2–13).

The commentary on the latter part contains a number of interesting interpretations. The first one concerns the six days between Jesus' prophecy concerning the coming of the kingdom and the transfiguration. As we have seen, with the glosses of Hugh, the six days find analogues in the six days of creation and in Richard of St. Victor's six stages of contemplation. Albert also links these six days to creation and to the mysteries of Christ's life. He says that the six days can signify "six manifestations of grace . . . by which the Sun of Justice, Christ our God, illumines us."[64] The transfiguration in this schema completes earlier manifestations of grace:

> First, there is the sanctification of nature in the taking of human nature, second, there is the restoration of a cursed generation in His most pure and holy generation from the Virgin who was left intact, third, there was the condemnation of concupiscence in the circumcision, fourth, there was the cleansing of original sin in the sanctification of baptism, fifth, there was the defeat of our accuser the devil in the temptation, and sixth, there was the illumination of all souls in preaching and in the verification of teaching made through signs and examples.[65]

According to Albert, these events in Christ's life impart grace, and they prepare not only the disciples, but all Christians for the glory revealed in the transfiguration. The fact that Mark's text says that Jesus "took" Peter, James, and John shows that only Christ can initiate the glorification of humanity. Only when Christ brings human nature into the presence of His glory, can humanity overcome its weakness and behold the light of His divinity.[66]

64. "sex gratiae illustrationes . . . quibus Sol justitiae Christus Deus noster super nos illuxit," *Enarrationes in Marcum*, 540.

65. "primo, naturae sanctificatio, in humanae naturae susceptione: secundo, maledictae generationis reparatio, in mundissima et sanctissima sui de illibata Virgine generatione: tertio, concupiscentiae damnatio, in circumcisione: quarto, originalis peccati detersio, in baptismi sanctificatione: quinto, damnatoris nostri diaboli devictio, in tentatione: sexto, omnium animarum illuminatio, in praedicatione, et doctrinae per exempla et signa confirmatione," *Enarrationes in Marcum*, 540. Albert goes on to cite scriptural passages from both the Old and New Testaments to show how Christ's glory heals wounded human nature and elevates it through grace.

66. *Enarrationes in Marcum*, 541.

Another unique interpretation Albert offers concerns the role of Peter during the transfiguration. In his other commentaries on the synoptic gospels, Albert tends to follow the more conventional glosses on Peter's presence found in the *Glossa ordinaria* or in Hugh of St. Cher's postillae, but in his Mark commentary Albert elaborates on Peter's role and significance. In all three commentaries, Albert links Peter's receiving the keys of the kingdom of heaven with the transfiguration, which is a manifestation of the kingdom of heaven; but Albert significantly expands on this connection by referring not only to the kingdom of heaven, but also to Peter's relationship to the divine light of the transfiguration. According to Albert, Jesus took Peter "as the summit of the apostles and His vicar on earth, obliged to impart divine illuminations to all people and to scatter the shadows of hell by the power of his chains."[67]

Peter's unique role is bound up not only with the keys bestowed upon him, but more fundamentally on his profession of faith in the divinity of Christ and his corresponding martyrdom. Just as Jesus' Father revealed to Peter the divinity of His Son, so too Christ reveals His own divinity to Peter with the testimony of the Father's voice. In both Peter's confession and in his witnessing of the transfiguration, divine light shines on him in some way. It was light from the Father that illumined Peter's mind regarding Christ's identity, and during the transfiguration, Christ "transcended the shadows and the clouds of flesh and of human opinions, and now He transformed His appearance into a mass of eternal light."[68]

Albert's reverential treatment of Peter leads to a different interpretation of Peter's words to Jesus than is given in the glosses from the Fathers. The patristic interpretations included in the *Glossa ordinaria* and in Hugh's postillae tend to reproach Peter for being ignorant, forgetful, or selfish for wanting to stay on the mountain. Albert's interpretation is somewhat different. For Albert, Peter's error is not so

67. "Ut Apostolicum verticem, et suum in terra vicarium, illuminationes divinas omnibus conferre debentem, et inferni tenebras dissipantem suorum vinculorum potestate," *Enarrationes in Marcum*, 541.

68. "tenebras et nubes carnis, et humanarum opinionum transcenderat, et visum jam fixerat in globis aeternae lucis," *Enarrationes in Marcum*, 541.

much that he wants to remain in the presence of Christ's glory. That desire is legitimate, and anyone else having the same experience would wish the same. Peter's vice is fear. Albert links Peter's expression of joy on the mountain with his rebuke of Jesus in Matthew 16. After Jesus had given Peter the keys to the kingdom of heaven, Jesus began to discuss His own suffering and death with His disciples. The prospect of his master's death dismayed Peter, and he said that this suffering and death should not happen to Jesus. This rebuke was a manifestation of Peter's own fear to take up his cross and follow his Lord. Peter's words to Jesus on the mountain of transfiguration are a similar manifestation according to Albert. Albert interprets Peter's desire to stay on the mountain partly as an expression of fear of the Jewish leaders who wanted to persecute Jesus and of the crowds who might turn on Jesus.[69]

If Albert previously interpreted Peter's words, "Rabbi, it is good for us to be here,"[70] to signify both joy and fear, he now interprets the Gospel writer's words, "For he knew not what he said," in a charitable way, which differed from some patristic reproaches. Peter's not knowing what he said resulted not from selfishness, but rather from wonder and astonishment. Albert is careful to note that these words are immediately followed by "for they were struck by fear." "They," that is James and John, along with Peter, were afraid, not of something terrible, but of something terrifyingly glorious. Peter's fear was perfectly natural; Albert asserts that "the Evangelist . . . notes the cause of that wonder, knowing that they all were feeling the same thing with Peter."[71] Albert justifies his interpretation that the "fear" was caused by something wonderful by noting that the disciples were afraid only after Peter had said, "Rabbi, it is good for us to be here."

What follows in the Markan narrative is the entrance of the cloud (Mark does not say that it was a "bright" cloud) and the voice from the cloud. As in his Matthew commentary, Albert refrains from linking the cloud with the Holy Spirit. In that commentary, the cloud was a

69. See *Enarrationes in Marcum*, 544.

70. Mk 9:4.

71. "Causam . . . stupefactionis istius subjungit Evangelista, innuens quod omnes idem cum Petro sentiebant," *Enarrationes in Marcum*, 545.

creature that gave witness to Christ's divinity by tempering the exceeding brightness of the light that accompanied the cloud. In the Gospel of Mark, no mention is made of the cloud's brightness, so Albert does not suggest that two separate "creatures," the light and the cloud, act as witnesses. Albert does, however, maintain in his Mark commentary that the cloud is glorious and, as such, is a luminous witness of Christ's glory, "By its light [the cloud] portrays the figure of the clarity of eternity."[72]

The voice of the Father has a real, audible sound, but Albert gives the voice, and not only the words, a Trinitarian resonance. The voice of the Father "especially guarantees the certainty of eternal glory,"[73] and it is that voice "in which the Word was formed."[74] In all three of his commentaries on the synoptic gospels, Albert interprets the words spoken by the voice as expressing the relations among the Trinitarian Persons, but his explanation of the words is the most elaborate in the commentary on Mark. In his commentaries on Matthew and Luke, Albert emphasizes the consubstantiality of the Father and the Son signified by the words, "This is my most beloved Son;"[75] but in the commentary on Mark, Albert suggests that the Father's word "Son" refers to Christ both as Son of God and as Son of man. Albert also takes the opportunity to raise the question of the number of nativities and filiations in Christ. His interpretation (espoused also, with some qualifications, by Thomas Aquinas)[76] is that "Christ the man and Christ the God are one person in deity and in humanity; and in my judgment, although He has two nativities, one eternal and one temporal, He is Son by one and the same filiation."[77] The Father's word "my" signifies that the Son is the Image of the Father; and Albert, like Hugh before him, connects this saying of the Father with what occurred at Jesus' baptism. Whereas the Father gives the *forma naturae* to humanity by means of

72. "suo lumine figuram aeternae claritatis expressit," *Enarrationes in Marcum*, 545.

73. "maxime certificavit certitudinem aeternae gloriae," *Enarrationes in Marcum*, 545.

74. "in qua Verbum formatum est," *Enarrationes in Marcum*, 545.

75. Mk 9:6.

76. See *Summa theologiae*, III, q. 35, a. 5.

77. "Christus homo, et Christus Deus, una est persona in deitate et humanitate: et in meo judicio quamvis duas vere habeat nativitates, unam aeternam, et unam temporalem, cum una et eadem filiatione est Filius," *Enarrationes in Marcum*, 545–46.

the Son in creation, the Image imparts the *forma gratiae* through the regeneration of baptism and the *forma gloriae* through the beatitude represented in the transfiguration.

Albert's reflection on the Father's words, "most beloved" *(charissimus)* completes the Trinitarian exegesis of the theophany on the mountain of transfiguration in a very profound way. He says that that word, *charissimus* expresses the Love "by which the Father loves the Son and by which we are restored according to the form of love. And in it the Father Himself loves us because that same Love, the Holy Spirit, proceeds from the Father into the Son and from the Son into the Father and from both into us, who will be sanctified, illumined, and perfected."[78] In this articulation of the Trinitarian circumincession, the Holy Spirit acts as more than a static "bond." Since the Father cannot love the Son without the Love by which He loves the Son, there is some sense in which the Holy Spirit, or the relation signified by the word *dilectio,* must accompany the procession of the Son, or the relation signified by the word *filiatio.* The dynamism of the Holy Spirit's procession or spiration is captured by the description of Him proceeding from the Son into the Father. Whereas the Son proceeds from the Father and remains as the Image, who with the Father spirates the Spirit, the Spirit proceeds from the Father into the Son and returns into the Father by way of the Son's spiration. The dynamism of the Spirit's procession does not cease in His procession from and return to the Father. His procession, or passive spiration, has consequences for Christians in the economy of salvation. The Spirit's procession from the Father and the Son terminates in the dynamic redemption and perfection of the human person. The fact that the Spirit proceeds from the Father and the Son into the human person should not obscure the fact that both the Father and the Son, while not "proceeding into" the human person, are nonetheless intimately united to the human person at this point. The very *dilectio,* which is the Holy Spirit, is also that Love by which the Father loves humanity, and it is also that Love by which the Son effects the restoration of humanity.

78. "qua Pater diligit Filium, etiam nos reformamur ad formam dilectionis, et in ea nos ipse Pater diligit: quia ipsa dilectio, Spiritus sanctus, a Patre in Filium, et a Filio in Patrem, et ab utroque in nos sanctificandos, et illuminandos, et perficiendos," *Enarrationes in Marcum,* 546.

Enarrationes in Lucam

Albert's longest commentary on a transfiguration narrative is in his commentary on Luke. The *divisio textus* of this passage is fairly complicated and, as in the commentary on Matthew, Albert gives the transfiguration an ecclesiological orientation. Just as Albert had noted that, in Matthew, the transfiguration narrative follows Peter's confession of faith and Jesus' bestowal of ecclesiastical power on the apostles, so too does Albert see a similar literary structure in Luke 9. The chapter begins with Christ gathering the Twelve and granting them power "over all devils, and to cure diseases."[79] Christ then commands the Twelve "to preach the kingdom of God, and to heal the sick."[80] In Albert's reading of this chapter, Christ's admonition for the disciples to "take nothing"[81] is daunting and requires a miracle to fortify their resolve. The miracle is not the transfiguration, but the multiplication of the loaves, an event Christ uses to teach the apostles how they must exercise their episcopal power. They must comfort the crowds and learn to derive all their strength from Christ.[82]

Just as the miracle of the multiplication of the loaves is intended to strengthen the disciples, so too is the transfiguration. The transfiguration narrative follows a pericope in which Peter confesses that Jesus is "the Christ of God."[83] Jesus encourages His followers not to reveal this truth to anyone, and then He proceeds to prophesy His own suffering, death, and resurrection. Although the disciples will have to take up their own crosses in order to follow their Master, their reward for being configured to the crucified Christ is being configured to the resurrected Christ. Jesus decides to reveal the glory of the resurrection before His death to Peter, James, and John, who, in general, learn Christ's secret teachings before the other disciples.[84]

This glory that Jesus reveals comes from within Himself. In this commentary on Luke, Albert develops his position on the origin of

79. Lk 9:1.
80. Lk 9:2.
81. Lk 9:3.
82. *Enarrationes in Lucam*, in *Opera omnia*, edited by A. Borgnet (Paris: Vivès, 1894), t. 22, 623–35.
83. Lk 9:20.
84. See *Enarrationes in Lucam*, 652.

Christ's glory considerably from the earlier *De resurrectione*. Here, Albert is clear that the radiance of Christ's bodily clarity proceeded from His divinity. Albert is also certain, however, that nothing in Christ's human nature changed during the transfiguration, "He assumed nothing foreign and put off nothing proper to Himself and to us."[85] What changes then during the transfiguration? Albert says that before the transfiguration, Christ's "mortal exterior appearance"[86] concealed the glory of His divinity. During the transfiguration, Christ's exterior revealed that glory in such a way that "the interior radiance did not swallow up [His] mortal exterior appearance, but it covered it for a while."[87]

Albert introduces an interesting example to illustrate how the transfiguration might have appeared to the disciples. He says that the light that emanated from within Christ was like the light of a lamp, whose exterior *(pellis)* allows light to pass through it, although it does not lose anything proper to itself.[88] It is not clear what kind of lamp Albert has in mind, but it seems that he is thinking of a lamp with a translucent exterior. What is important for Albert is that Christ's humanity, both His "interior"—the ontological constitution of His humanity—and His "exterior" do not change. Albert insists that even the color of Christ's body does not change; it is just illuminated by the light that proceeds from His divinity. The same principle applies to Christ's garments, which receive the light passing through His body and become luminously white.

One interpretation Albert makes, which differs from the exegesis of his other commentaries, relates to the theophany on the mountain. In his commentaries on Matthew and Mark, Albert refrained from linking the cloud with the Holy Spirit, saying instead that it was a creature that gave witness to the divinity of the Son. In those commentaries, any Trinitarian resonances were bound up with the words of the Father. In Albert's Luke commentary, however, there is a connection between the cloud and the Holy Spirit. Albert maintains that

85. "nihil assumpsit alienum, nihil amisit sibi et nobis proprium," *Enarrationes in Lucam*, 657.

86. "mortalis species exterior," *Enarrationes in Lucam*, 657.

87. "fulgor interior consumpsit mortalem speciem exteriorem, sed obtexit ad horam," *Enarrationes in Lucam*, 657.

88. See *Enarrationes in Lucam*, 658.

the cloud is a creature, distinct from the Holy Spirit. Nevertheless, it is fitting for the Holy Spirit to be present in the cloud, testifying to Christ's divinity.

The fact that the Father's voice "came out of the cloud,"[89] shows the unity and harmony *(consonantia)* between the Father and the Spirit. The voice and the cloud do not, however, simply express the procession of the Spirit from the Father. They show how the Father and the Spirit relate to humanity. Albert says that "the harmony between the Father and the Spirit is shown in the fact that the Father is never heard except in a cloud. It is fitting that the Spirit, who must hear the Father's voice, should be hidden in a cloud because the Spirit bears the voice of the Father into the heart and reveals it [there]."[90] Albert bases this interpretation on a passage from Christ's last discourse to His disciples in the Gospel of John, "But when he, the Spirit of truth, is come, he will teach you all truth . . . and the things that are to come he shall show you."[91]

As in the Mark commentary, Albert prefers to base his Trinitarian reflections not on the cloud, but on the words, which proceed from the Father, and he focuses especially on the word "beloved." Albert cites a gloss from Augustine, which asserts that "love proceeds from the Son, as it does from the Father,"[92] but he also adds his own interpretation of "beloved," which is reminiscent of his unique articulation of the Trinitarian relations in the *Enarrationes in Marcum.* Particularly noteworthy is Albert's glossing the word "beloved" in a first-person discourse, "It also says "beloved," joined with me in the Holy Spirit, and with me He is one principle of the same Spirit or of love, because [the Spirit] flows back and forth by love from me into Him and from Him into me and from us into the world."[93] Albert interprets the theophany in dy-

89. Lk 9:34.

90. "Consonantia Patris cum Spiritu notatur in hoc, quod non sonat Pater nisi in nube. Oportet enim quod obumbretur nube Spiritus, qui audire debet vocem Patris: quia Spiritus vehit in cor vocem Patris, et docet eam," *Enarrationes in Lucam,* 666.

91. Jn 16:13.

92. "dilectio a Filio sicut a Patre procedit," *Enarrationes in Lucam,* 667.

93. "Dicit autem: *'Dilectus,'* in Spiritu sancto connexus mihi, et ejusdem Spiritus sive dilectionis mecum est unum principium: quia a me fluit in eum, et ab eo in me reciproca dilectione, et a nobis in mundum," *Enarrationes in Lucam,* 667 (italics are the editor's). Some of

namic Trinitarian terms. The way the theophany occurs, testifying to the same divinity Christ shares with the Father and the Spirit, allows Albert the opportunity to interpret it as a manifestation not only of Christ's divinity, but also as a manifestation in salvation history of the infinite vitality of the life and love that the Trinitarian Persons share.

Conclusion

Albert's theology of the transfiguration, as found in both the *De resurrectione* and the scriptural commentaries, is unique for several reasons. First, the explanation regarding Christ's clarity changes dramatically between the early *De resurrectione* and the later scriptural commentaries (especially as described in the *Enarrationes in Lucam*, which may date from the late 1260s). In the early question on the transfiguration, Albert had not really explained the cause of Christ's bodily clarity, but he made constant comparisons to the clarity of the resurrection. It was this clarity, which would realize the potential given to Christ's body by virtue of the hypostatic union. In the scriptural commentaries, especially those on Mark and Luke, Albert allows the Incarnation to explain the presence of glory in Christ's transfigured body. Although Albert fails to highlight the role Christ's soul may have had in the communication of clarity, his explicit acknowledgment of Christ's divinity as the source of clarity fills out the incomplete account of Christ's clarity, given in the *De resurrectione*.

A second characteristic of Albert's theology of the transfiguration is its ecclesial orientation. Not only does Albert associate "transfiguration" with preaching and the sacraments, as Hugh of St. Cher had done, but he is also careful to situate the transfiguration narratives of the synoptic gospels, especially those of Matthew and Luke, within the larger narrative frameworks of those Gospels. This careful linking of the transfiguration narratives with those pericopes situated both before and after the transfiguration narratives allows Albert to associate the transfiguration with Christ's bestowal of authority on the disci-

---

the dynamism of Albert's language is lost in the translation. In particular, *reciproca dilectione* connotes the constant movement of the love between the Father and the Son.

ples. One way in which this association is deepened is in Albert's positive interpretation of Peter's words and actions, an interpretation that differs significantly from many patristic and twelfth-century views of Peter on Mount Tabor.

A final characteristic of Albert's account of the transfiguration is the profound Trinitarian dimension it takes on in his scriptural commentaries. Although Albert's interpretation of the theophany on the mountain changes slightly from his earlier commentary on Matthew to his later Luke commentary, Albert nonetheless wants to link the Trinitarian dimension of Christ's transfiguration, in particular, with the Trinitarian dimension of the transfiguration of humanity, in general. In the Trinitarian theology Albert articulates in these passages, the procession of the Holy Spirit does not merely terminate in the passive spiration of the Spirit, but rather the Spirit is communicated by the Son back into the Father, who, with the Son, communicates the Holy Spirit into the world.

Of all the theologians examined in this study, Albert benefits most from an examination of both systematic and exegetical genres of scholastic literature, perhaps because the time span between his earliest work and his latest is so great (about twenty-five to thirty years). Not only do the styles in those two genres differ immensely, but Albert, in his later works, clearly manifests different theological priorities and even a more fully developed teaching regarding Christ's clarity. One characteristic that is constant in both the systematic and the exegetical genres is creativity. Albert articulates not only answers pertaining to the transfiguration, but also the questions themselves in unique ways that his peers and predecessors did not employ. His application of philosophical terms and categories is widespread. Also, he has little recourse to patristic exegesis, in general, and is content to glean interpretations from Carolingian exegetes and the *Glossa ordinaria,* which he cites infrequently, in any case. Often he simply uses other scriptural passages to illumine the text he is glossing. The combination of Albert's unique method and style, along with the insights of his teaching, renders Albert's theological investigation of Christ's transfiguration unique. Although Albert's treatment of the transfiguration may not be the most comprehensive of the thirteenth century, it is certainly one of the most original.

7

BONAVENTURE

While Albert was finishing his advanced theological studies at the Dominican *studium generale* in the mid-1240s, Bonaventure of Bagnoregio was just beginning his study of theology in the Franciscan school. His first teachers were Alexander of Hales and John of La Rochelle. After their deaths in 1245, he studied with Eudes Rigaud and William of Melitona. Once he had become a bachelor of theology, Bonaventure began lecturing on Scripture. During his studies to become a master of theology, Bonaventure wrote a commentary on Peter Lombard's *Sentences*. Once he became a master of theology, perhaps in 1254 or 1255, he wrote a series of disputed questions before he was elected Minister General of the Franciscan Order in 1257.[1]

It is somewhat surprising that Bonaventure omits any sustained discussion of the transfiguration in these scholastic works. Instead, one finds Bonaventure's theology of Christ's transfiguration in his scriptural exegesis and in his sermons. Because of this fact, Bonaventure's theology of the transfiguration is much more spiritual than that of his peers and predecessors. It is more spiritual in the sense that there is practically no interest in the metaphysics of the hypostatic union, nor is there much speculation about the transfiguration's relation to the glories of heaven. Instead, Bonaventure finds Christ's transfiguration to be a beautiful theme on which to teach his readers and listeners

1. For more on Bonaventure's life, works, and theology, see E. Longpré, "Bonaventure," DS 1768–1843; and Zachary Hayes, "Bonaventure: Mystery of the Triune God," in *The History of Franciscan Theology*, edited by Kenan B. Osborne, 39–125 (St. Bonaventure, N.Y.: Franciscan Institute, 1994). The best critical guide to Bonaventure's works is Balduinus Distelbrink, *Bonaventurae scripta, authentica dubia vel spuria critice recensita* (Rome: Istituto Storico Cappucini, 1975).

about how to advance closer to mystical union with God. This chapter will examine the places where Bonaventure articulates his understanding of the transfiguration and the details he highlights in his teaching about the contemplative ascent toward God.

Commentarius in Evangelium S. Lucae

Although Bonaventure mentions Christ's transfiguration in passing in such later works as the *Itinerarium mentis Deum,*[2] the *Lignum vitae,*[3] and the *Collationes in Hexaëmeron,*[4] Bonaventure's lengthiest sustained treatment of the transfiguration comes from the earliest part of his academic career. Bonaventure does not examine Christ's transfiguration in his *Sentences* commentary or in any of his disputed questions. The most exhaustive exegesis of the transfiguration occurs in his early commentary on Luke, which dates roughly from 1248–1250.[5] Bonaventure gives the transfiguration a highly spiritual interpretation, which differs markedly from that of Albert and even from that of his Franciscan master, Alexander of Hales. Bonaventure reflects extensively on the relationship between the transfiguration and contemplation in a manner reminiscent of some of the glosses of Hugh of St. Cher and John of La Rochelle (whose own commentary on Luke followed Hugh very closely). Bonaventure clearly relies on Hugh and perhaps John (and their appropriations of previous authors), but he also supplements their interpretations with his own reflections.[6]

2. See *Itinerarium mentis in Deum,* in *Opera omnia,* edited by Pp. Colegii S. Bonaventurae (Quaracchi, Italy: ex Typographia Collegii S. Bonaventurae, 1891), t. 5, 297.

3. See *Lignum vitae,* in *Opera omnia,* edited by Pp. Colegii S. Bonaventurae, (Quaracchi, Italy: ex Typographia Collegii S. Bonaventurae, 1898), t. 8, 73–74.

4. See *Collationes in Hexaëmeron,* in *Opera omnia,* edited by Pp. Colegii S. Bonaventurae (Quaracchi, Italy: ex Typographia Collegii S. Bonaventurae, 1891), t. 5, 22, 42.

5. See the introduction of Robert J. Karris to his translation of Bonaventure's *Commentary on the Gospel of Luke,* edited and translated by Robert J. Karris, 3 vols., vi–l (St. Bonaventure, N.Y.: Franciscan Institute Publications, 2001–2004), vol. 1, viii.

6. For more on Bonaventure's exegesis, see Robert J. Karris, "St. Bonaventure as Biblical Interpreter: His Methods, Wit, and Wisdom," *Franciscan Studies* 60 (2002): 159–208. For more on Bonaventure's dependence on earlier sources, especially Hugh, see the following articles by Karris, "A Comparison of the *Glossa Ordinaria,* Hugh of St. Cher, and St. Bonaventure on Luke 8:26–39," *Franciscan Studies* 58 (2000): 121–236; "Bonaventure's Commentary on Luke: Four Case Studies of His Creative Borrowing from Hugh of St. Cher," *Franciscan*

Before examining the content of Bonaventure's exegesis of the transfiguration narrative, it is appropriate to mention how his *divisio textus* compares with that of his peers and predecessors. Bonaventure divides the entire Gospel of Luke into four sections. Chapters one through three pertain to the mystery of the Incarnation, chapters four through twenty-one concern the office of teaching, chapters twenty-two and twenty-three describe the "medicine" *(medicamento)* of Christ's passion, and chapter twenty-four is about the "victory" *(tropaeo)* of the resurrection.[7] The second division, on teaching, has two main sections with multiple subdivisions:

Part Two
I. Jesus explains the truth
    A. The authentication of Christ's teaching
    B. The calling of the disciples
    C. The instruction of those called
    D. The delegation of those instructed
        1. The mission of the apostles
            i. The form of preaching
            ii. The way of advancing
                a. The difficulty of the way
                    Perfect knowledge of Christ through faith
                    Perfect imitation of Christ through the cross
                b. The sweetness of glory
                    Description of the promised glory to be revealed
                    Consideration of the revealed glory
                    Confirmation of what was revealed
            iii. The norm of presiding
        2. The mission of the seventy disciples
II. Jesus refutes falsehood
    A. He refutes the deceitfulness of the Jews
    B. He denounces their cruelty

Studies 59 (2001): 133–236; "St. Bonaventure's Use of *Distinctiones:* His Independence of and Dependence on Hugh of St. Cher," *Franciscan Studies* 60 (2002): 209–50.

7. Bonaventure, *Commentarius in Evangelium S. Lucae*, in *Opera omnia*, edited by Pp. Collegii S. Bonaventurae (Quaracchi, Italy: ex Typographia Collegii S. Bonaventurae, 1895), t. 7, 13.

C. He denounces their curiosity
D. He denounces their lack of faith

Luke's transfiguration narrative occurs within the section about "the delegation of those instructed." This section consists of chapters nine and ten, and the first part of chapter eleven of Luke's Gospel, and the section basically addresses Christ's sending His disciples to preach. Chapter nine discusses the "mission of the apostles," and chapter ten and the first part of chapter eleven describe "the mission of the seventy disciples."[8] Bonaventure divides the lengthy chapter nine into three main sections: on the form of preaching, the way of advancing, and the norm of presiding.[9] Luke's transfiguration narrative constitutes the second of three sections on the "way of advancing," or making spiritual progress. The first section (Luke 9:18–27), in which Christ predicts His suffering and death, addresses the difficulty of following Christ. The second section (Luke 9:28–45), the transfiguration narrative, describes the joy and the reward of following Christ, and the final passage of Luke 9 (verses 46–62) explains the mission of the Apostles after they beheld the transfigured Christ.

Two aspects of Bonaventure's *divisio textus* are worth mentioning. The first is that the transfiguration and Jesus' miracle of healing are grouped under the same heading, "the sweetness of glory." Bonaventure is the only author in this study to unite the transfiguration and the subsequent miracle or "confirmation" so closely. Alexander of Hales had applied a fairly simple *divisio textus,* which preserved the transfiguration narrative as a discrete unit. Hugh of St. Cher divided the ninth chapter of Luke into ten sections, but his *divisio textus* lacked the further subdivisions that characterize the later and more complex textual divisions arising in the 1240s.[10] In Hugh's division, the transfig-

8. "*missione Apostolorum,*" and "*missione septuaginta discipulorum,*" *Commentarius in Evangelium S. Lucae,* 216 (italics here and in subsequent citations are the editors').

9. "Prima pars continet praesens capitulum et habet tres partes, secundum tria quae explicat Evangelista necessaria Apostolis et praelatis ad praedicandum missis. Quorum primum est *forma praedicandi;* secundum est *via proficiendi,* quam explicat ibi: *Et factum est, cum solus esset orans;* tertium est *norma praesidendi,* quae describitur ibi: *Intravit autem in eos cogitatio, quis eorum* etc.," *Commentarius in Evangelium S. Lucae,* 216.

10. See Hugh of St. Cher, *Postilla super Lucam,* fol. 182va–b.

uration, which was the sixth of the ten sections in Luke 9, constituted a distinct narrative within the ninth chapter of Luke. Although John of La Rochelle's commentary on Luke followed Hugh of St. Cher very closely, John's *divisio textus* was much more sophisticated than Hugh's, as was Albert the Great's.[11] In the case of both John and Albert, Jesus' miraculous healing of the boy constituted a narrative separate from the transfiguration, even if it is a *confirmatio*. Bonaventure also describes the healing as a *confirmatio*, but by situating the narrative in the same section as the transfiguration, he makes the connection between the two events closer than his peers had done.

Another point, less apparent and less significant, is the fact that Bonaventure locates Jesus' promise that some would not "taste death" before they saw "the kingdom of God"[12] not in the section on Christ's glory, but in the earlier section on the difficulty of following Christ. This division of the promise from the event is not unusual—both Hugh and John had made that division—but it is different from Albert's approach, which sees the promise of the transfiguration and the transfiguration itself as constituting two parts of the same passage.

Bonaventure's exegesis of the transfiguration, then, begins with Luke 9:28, which describes Jesus' taking Peter, James, and John up to the mountain about eight days after His promise. Drawing from Hugh, Bonaventure, like his other peers, interprets the number eight primarily in terms of contemplation, the summit of which corresponds with the eighth day, that is, the resurrection. Bonaventure, however, develops this teaching by drawing not only on Richard of St. Victor, but also on Augustine and Brother Giles of Assisi.

Bonaventure clearly draws from Richard of St. Victor's teaching on contemplation, but as noted above, it is Hugh of St. Cher or an unknown author, who makes the connection between the six kinds of contemplation and the "six days" mentioned in Matthew 17:1 and Mark 9:1.[13]

11. The outline of John of La Rochelle's *divisio textus* of Luke's transfiguration narrative included in chapter 5 illustrates this point (see pp. 131–32).

12. Lk 9:27.

13. See above, pp. 34–37. When Bonaventure quotes Richard, the cited texts do not connect the six stages of contemplation with the transfiguration (see *Commentarius in Evangelium S. Lucae*, 231).

In any case, unlike Hugh, Bonaventure feels no compulsion to force the sexpartite matrix onto Luke's reference to eight days, or rather, "about" eight days. Bonaventure simply links Richard's account of contemplation to the transfiguration narrative in Matthew and then searches for other sources who can assist in his interpretation of Luke's eight days.

What is curious is that Bonaventure next refers to two separate septipartite ladders of contemplation, one from Augustine and one from "Brother Giles." The seven stages of contemplation, according to Augustine's *De quantitate animae* are animation, sensation, art, virtue, tranquility, initiation, and contemplation.[14] Bonaventure explains that "as [Augustine] says, 'The first step is of the body, the second through the body, the third about the body, the fourth toward itself, the fifth in itself, the sixth toward God, and the seventh with God.' And these steps designate not only the steps of contemplation, but they also are the means by which one arrives at contemplation."[15] Bonaventure also cites Brother Giles as an authority here, and he explains why:

> Now a certain Brother Giles, although simple in speech, but not in knowledge and of whom it was shown that he was most often rapt in contemplation, distinguished the steps, saying, "'There are seven steps of contemplation. The first is fire, the second is anointing, the third is ecstasy, the fourth is contemplation, the fifth is taste, the sixth is rest, and the seventh is glory. And after these nothing remains except eternal happiness."[16]

The significance of seven is partially that it is the penultimate number before eight, the number associated with the resurrection. Contemplation is the last stage of the soul before it reaches its final abode in heaven, but the "literal" basis for the significance of seven seems to have some basis in the Gospel narratives, even though the number seven is

14. See *Commentarius in Evangelium S. Lucae*, 231.

15. "Et ut dicit, 'primus est *de* corpore, secundus *per* corpus, tertius *circa* corpus, quartus *ad se ipsum*, quintus *ad se ipsa*, sextus *ad Deum*, septimus *apud Deum*.' Et hi gradus non tantum dicunt gradus contemplationis, sed quibus venitur ad contemplationem," *Commentarius in Evangelium S. Lucae*, 231.

16. "Quidam autem, licet simplici sermone, sed non scientia, frater Aegidius, quem frequentissime rapi probatum est, sic distinguit gradus dicens: Septem sunt gradus contemplationis: primus est *ignis;* secundus est *unctio;* tertius est *ecstasis;* quartus, *contemplatio;* quintus, *gustus;* sextus, *requies;* septimus, *gloria;* post quos non restat nisi *felicitas sempiterna*," *Commentarius in Evangelium S. Lucae*, 231.

never mentioned. Patristic interpretations, which tend to "harmonize" the accounts of Matthew and Mark, on the one hand, and of Luke, on the other, suggest that Matthew and Mark are counting the full days between the promise and the transfiguration, while Luke includes the days on which the promise and the transfiguration take place. The partial "days" of days one and eight together with the six full days equals roughly seven twenty-four hour periods. Bonaventure does not explicitly make this connection, but his allusion to the "completed order of the week"[17] suggests that this intermediary number between the six and eight does have some basis in the "harmonization" of the Gospels.

How does Bonaventure's interpretation of the relationship between contemplation and transfiguration compare to that of Hugh of St. Cher, who insisted on having six or eight stages of contemplation? Although Bonaventure's incorporation of two septipartite plans is puzzling at first, since no transfiguration narrative uses the number seven, this interpretation draws out more clearly than Hugh's the anticipatory character that contemplation has with respect to the beatific vision.[18] For Hugh, the summit of contemplation corresponds with the transfiguration and the resurrection; in Bonaventure's outline, however, the beatific vision transcends the seven days, which mark both the transfiguration and the seven stages of contemplation, as described by Augustine and Brother Giles.

After reflecting on the *antecedentia*[19] of the transfiguration, Bonaventure considers what actually happened while Jesus prayed.[20] The first thing that the Gospel of Luke notes is that Christ's face changed, and His clothes became white. Like Alexander of Hales, Bonaventure interprets the glory of the transfiguration through 1 Corinthians 15:40–42, "There are celestial bodies and there are terrestrial bodies; but the glory of the celestial is one, and the glory of the terrestrial is another. There is one glory of the sun, and another glory of the moon, and another glory of the stars; for star differs from star in glory. So it is

17. "revoluto ordine septimanae," *Commentarius in Evangelium S. Lucae,* 230.

18. As with Hugh's contemplative ascent, Albert the Great puts rapture or ecstasy in the eighth place. See his *Postilla super Lucam,* 654–55.

19. See *Commentarius in Evangelium S. Lucae,* 233.

20. See Lk 9:29.

with the resurrection of the dead." The clarity Christ manifests in His body conveys the glory of a resurrected body, although Christ Himself remains passible.

Unlike his Franciscan master, however, Bonaventure does not cogently differentiate between the clarity of His passible body and that of His impassible body. Alexander indicated that Christ's clarity during the transfiguration was not a gift, properly speaking. It was the clarity of a corruptible body "in the manner" of a glorified body.[21] Bonaventure, however, says that Christ "assumed [the gift of clarity] for a moment, but he did not, however, lose his own shape."[22] The analogy Bonaventure uses to illustrate his assertion is that of someone with a pale face blushing. The blushing is a transient action, which does not affect the habitual condition of the person blushing.[23] Christ's "earthly" body, says Bonaventure, was mortal, but during the transfiguration, His assumption of clarity made it "heavenly" for a brief duration.[24] Although this assertion sounds problematic, insofar as it seems to compromise Christ's passibility, Bonaventure also seems to argue that the clarity of the transfigured Christ is a "terrestrial" clarity, which lacks the overpowering radiance of "heavenly" clarity.

Bonaventure goes on to interpret more specifically the radiance of Christ's face, and just as he interpreted the time of the transfiguration in a spiritual way, so too does he interpret the radiance of Christ's face in a spiritual way. According to this explanation, Christ's face represents every human "face," or mind, which turns toward God and reflects His light. The radiant face of Moses, who came down from the mountain after speaking with God, is another prefiguration of this spiritual event.

The Gospel of Luke describes two other events, which occur during the transfiguration itself, namely the luminosity of Christ's garments and the appearance of Moses and Elijah. Bonaventure's in-

21. See above, pp. 54–55.

22. "ad tempus assumsit, propriam tamen effigiem non amisit," *Commentarius in Evangelium S. Lucae*, 233.

23. Bonaventure borrows this analogy from Aristotle. See the editors' comments in note 5 on p. 233 of *Commentarius in Evangelium S. Lucae.*

24. See *Commentarius in Evangelium S. Lucae*, 233.

terpretations of these narrative elements are fairly conventional. He interprets the garments allegorically as the saints and spiritually as their holy and spotless way of life. Likewise, Moses and Elijah serve typological functions, and their spiritual significance refers to the confirmation of the disciples' vision of Christ. Their discussion with Jesus of His *excessus* refers not only to His departure from the world, but also to His "excess" of humility, poverty, sorrow, and love.[25] Bonaventure borrows this interpretation almost entirely from John of La Rochelle, who himself had expanded on a gloss of Hugh of St. Cher.[26]

Bonaventure returns to the theme of contemplation in his discussion of the following section of the narrative on the "consideration of the revealed glory." The pericope runs as follows:

> Now Peter and those who were with him were heavy with sleep, and when they awoke they saw his glory and the two men who stood with him. And as the men were parting from him, Peter said to Jesus, "Master, it is good for us to be here; let us make three booths, one for you and one for Moses and one for Elijah," not knowing what he said. As he said this, a cloud came and overshadowed them; and they were afraid as they entered the cloud. And a voice came out of the cloud saying, "This is my Son, my Chosen; listen to him!" And when the voice had spoken, Jesus was found alone. And they kept silence and told no one in those days anything of what they had seen.[27]

According to Bonaventure, this passage describes a spiritual ascent. Peter, James, and John were sleeping while Moses and Elijah were present. The slumber of Jesus' disciples in the presence of their transfigured Master represents the weakness of their corporeal nature. To overcome this weakness, divine grace must allow the soul another kind of repose. This spiritual sleep begins when the soul withdraws from its external senses. When the soul has withdrawn from its external senses, it can focus on the eternal light more easily. In such a state, God can teach the soul more easily than when its senses are occupied with perceiving what is outside of itself.

At this point, grace can awaken the soul, kindling it with "the de-

25. See *Commentarius in Evangelium S. Lucae*, 234.
26. See above, pp. 132–33.
27. Lk 9:32–36.

sire and love of the Holy Spirit."[28] The disciples' awakening represents this awakening of the soul through watchful prayer. In this state of prayer, the soul sees God's majesty in creatures and God's humility in the Scriptures, which together constitute a "twofold book."[29]

Once the soul has entered into a contemplative state, it then progresses, and Peter's words to Jesus express that progress. Bonaventure interprets these words through the prism of Sirach 24:27, "For my spirit is sweet above honey . . . they that eat me shall yet hunger: and they that drink me, shall yet thirst." For Bonaventure, these words illustrate the true nature of the progressing contemplative soul. The advancing soul experiences both joy and desire simultaneously: "For through these two the soul in the act of contemplation is depicted, as one eating food to satiety and at the same time longing for more."[30] Peter's first words, "Master, it is good for us to be here," express "satiety," that is, the joy of being with Christ. Citing a number of scriptural passages, Bonaventure claims that the contemplative soul can enjoy Christ by waiting for Him, by tasting Him, or by rejoicing with Him.[31] These three stages ascend in order, and Peter's words express all three stages, "especially the way of joy."[32] Peter's last words, "Let us make three booths, one for you and one for Moses and one for Elijah," express "the desire for the gift to continue."[33] Peter wants to remain with the transfigured Christ, but he makes three errors in his desire:

> Peter was deceived first of all because he wanted to remain in a state from which one must move. For it is said in the last chapter of Hebrews [13:14], "Here we have no lasting city." Peter, however, wanted to remain here. In this some are indeed reprehensible. For as long as they want to ascend to the height of contemplation, they want to rest there, and they refuse to descend to the labor of action . . . . Secondly, he was deceived since he believed

28. "desiderium et amorem Spiritus sancti," *Commentarius in Evangelium S. Lucae*, 235.

29. "duplex liber," *Commentarius in Evangelium S. Lucae*, 235.

30. "Per haec enim duo anima in actu contemplationis figitur, sicut comedens in cibo per solatium simul et desiderium," *Commentarius in Evangelium S. Lucae*, 235.

31. See *Commentarius in Evangelium S. Lucae*, 235–36. It should be noted that "tasting" Christ has Eucharistic resonances, since Bonaventure refers to it as "viaticum," a term, which, even in the thirteenth century, was used to refer to the Eucharist as administered to the dying and the gravely ill.

32. "maxime ratione gaudii," *Commentarius in Evangelium S. Lucae*, 236.

33. *"desiderium de dono continuando,"* *Commentarius in Evangelium S. Lucae*, 236.

that the shadow had been fulfilled in this, although the Apostle could say in 1 Corinthians 13 [verse 12], "We see now in a mirror dimly." Also, he believed that the tent of glory was material, when, however, it is spiritual, according to the Psalm [41:5]: "I will enter into the place of the wonderful tabernacle." This is "the tabernacle which the Lord has set up, and not man," as it is said in Hebrews 8 [verse 2]. And contemplatives must be especially beware, lest they be deceived by obvious figures. Thirdly, he was deceived because he wanted to divide what was united, and he wanted to divide into three what was one. For there is one tabernacle in the glory of the saints according to John 17 [verse 24], "Father, I will that where I am, they may be with me." And Revelation 21 [verse 3] says, "Behold, the tabernacle of God with men, and He will dwell with them." And John 10 [verse 16] has: "There will be one fold and one shepherd."[34]

Although Peter's immediate desire was short-sighted, Bonaventure finds no fault with him because he was in ecstasy and did not know what he was saying.[35]

After Peter's words to Jesus, there is the theophany on the mountain, the cloud descending and the heavenly voice proceeding from it. For Bonaventure, this event reflects the summit of contemplation, which is perfected through the manifestation of divine majesty and the revelation of divine truth.[36] Citing numerous passages from the Old Testament, Bonaventure shows how the cloud is a common sign

34. "Petrus decipiebatur primo, quia *volebat manere in statu,* a quo est transeundum. Dicitur enim ad Hebraeos ultimo: 'Non habemus hic manentem civitatem'; Petrus autem volebat manere hic. In quo etiam reprehensibiles sunt quidam, qui, dum volunt arcem contemplationis ascendere, volunt quiescere et ad laborem actionis recusant descendere . . . . Secundo decipiebatur in hoc, quod *umbram credebat in hoc verificatam;* cum tamen dicat Apostolus primae ad Corinthios decimo tertio: 'Videmus nunc per speculum in aenigmate'; et tabernaculum gloriae credebat *materiale,* cum tamen sit *spirituale,* secundum illud Psalmi: 'Ingrediar in locum tabernaculi admirabilis'; hoc est 'tabernaculum, quod fixit Dominus, et non homo,' sicut dicitur ad Hebraeos octavo. Et hoc potissime cavendum est contemplativis, ne decipiantur in figuris ostensis.—Tertio vero, quia *dividere volebat unita,* et quod erat unum triplicare volebat. Unum est enim in gloria Sanctorum tabernaculum, secundum illud Ioannis decimo septimo: 'Volo, Pater, ut, ubi ego sum, et illi sint mecum'; et Apocolypsis vigesimo primo: 'Ecce, tabernaculum Dei cum hominibus, et habitabit cum eis'; et Ioannis decimo: 'Fiet unum ovile et unus pastor,'" *Commentarius in Evangelium S. Lucae,* 236–37.

35. "Haec autem deceptio non erat per iudicium et assensum, sed magis propter mentis excessum mentis, de quo secundae ad Corinthios quinto: 'Sive mente excedimus, Deo,' etc.; et Psalmus: 'Ibi Beniamin adolescentulus in mentis excessu,'" *Commentarius in Evangelium S. Lucae,* 237.

36. See *Commentarius in Evangelium S. Lucae,* 237.

of God's presence and grandeur. It can also signify Christ's humanity: "According to the mystical sense the flesh of Christ can be understood through the cloud."[37] This is fitting because the cloud both reveals and conceals light. Christ's humanity, in concealing the infinite splendor of the divine light, reveals it in such a way that it can be perceived by mortal humans, "It tempers the light of divinity for our eyes, so that we can see."[38] Using this reason and several others, Bonaventure explains the spiritual significance of the cloud by saying:

> From this contemplatives are taught that they should not only lift their eyes to the radiant light of the Deity, but also to the dark cloud of humanity. This was expressed figuratively in John 1 [verse 51] where the Lord said to Nathanael, "You will see angels," that is, contemplatives, "ascending and descending upon the Son of man," because divine majesty is hidden in his humanity.[39]

The revelation of divine truth occurs when the disciples enter the cloud and hear the voice saying, "This is my beloved Son; listen to him."[40] These words express the summit of contemplation and the point of departure from which the disciples will "descend" to the activity of apostolic preaching and ministry. In particular, Bonaventure focuses on "this," "my," and "beloved." "This" signifies that Christ's sonship is a personal property unique to Him. "My" shows that the Father, who is speaking, and the Son are of the same nature, and "beloved" expresses the coequality of the Father and the Son.[41] If the admonishment to "listen," "not only with the ear of the body, but also with the ear of the heart"[42] is heeded, the disciples will have the strength to teach what Christ commanded.

37. "Secundum *mysticum* autem sensum per *nubem* intelligi potest caro Christi," *Commentarius in Evangelium S. Lucae*, 237.

38. "contemperat lumen Divinitatis oculis nostris, ut possimus intueri," *Commentarius in Evangelium S. Lucae*, 237.

39. "Ex hoc erudiuntur contemplatavi, ut non tantum erigant oculos ad lucem Deitatis radiantem, sed etiam ad nubem humanitatis obumbrantem. Quod figuratum est Ioannis primo, ubi dixit Dominus Nathanaeli: 'Videbitis Angelos,' id est contemplativos, 'ascendentes et descendentes super Filium hominis,' quia in humanitate latet divina maiestas," *Commentarius in Evangelium S. Lucae*, 237.

40. Lk 9:35.

41. See *Commentarius in Evangelium S. Lucae*, 238.

42. "non aure solum corporis, sed etiam cordis," *Commentarius in Evangelium S. Lucae*, 238.

As mentioned above, this pericope, Luke 9:32–36, which describes the soul's advance in contemplation through the events of the transfiguration, is followed by another one that Bonaventure associates closely with the transfiguration itself. This pericope describes Jesus healing the son of a certain man who was among the crowd that He and His disciples encountered after they descended from the top of the mountain. In his commentary on this passage, Bonaventure never mentions the events or details of the transfiguration. For Bonaventure, the link between the healing and the transfiguration is not so much the glory of the transfiguration as the disciples witnessed it, but rather the relationship between action and contemplation, signified by the events of these passages. In short, it is not the literal interpretation of these passages that unites them so much as it is Bonaventure's spiritual interpretation of them. The transfiguration describes a spiritual ascent through "prayer, reading, the consideration of what is divine, and the revelation of secrets."[43] The descent from the mountain, including the encounter with the crowd and the healing of the boy, shows how "the prelate" must treat those under his care. His principle activities include "visiting, having compassion, reproving vices, and alleviating needs."[44]

Bonaventure's exegesis of the transfiguration narrative is not marked by novel insights regarding the literal meaning of the passage. He often follows interpretations from Bede or the *Glossa ordinaria* or Hugh of St. Cher. The Christology articulated in his reflections on the transfiguration is not entirely clear, either. There is little precision, for example, regarding either the relationship between Christ's divinity and humanity or the exact nature of the clarity that affected His body. Nevertheless, Bonaventure makes several contributions in his exegesis. First, his *divisio textus* is unique insofar as it closely connects Christ's healing with the events of the transfiguration. Secondly, more so than any of his peers and predecessors, Bonaventure extracts a spiritual theology from the transfiguration narrative. Much of his inspiration comes from Richard of St. Victor, as read in Hugh of St. Cher's postillae, but Bonaventure

43. *"oratio, lectio, contuitio divinorum* et *revelatio secretorum," Commentarius in Evangelium S. Lucae*, 239.

44. *"visitando, compatiendo, vitia increpando* et *necessitates relevando," Commentarius in Evangelium S. Lucae*, 239.

also articulates his own insights. A third contribution is the intertextuality, which his exegesis employs. To authenticate his interpretations, Bonaventure cites other scriptural passages, notably from the Wisdom Literature of the Old Testament. These exegetical elements provide for a rich, if not entirely innovative, interpretation of Christ's transfiguration.

Sermo dominicale 16

Much later in his career, probably during his tenure as Minister General of the Order, Bonaventure composed a series of sermons, which, in the manuscript tradition, were collected under a number of different titles, including *Sermones fratris bonaventure, Sermones bonaventure de tempore, Sermones compilati per bonaventuram, Collationes dominicales,* and *Sermones dominicales.*[45] This collection consists of fifty Sunday sermons for the liturgical year beginning in Advent. According to the medieval lectionaries, the transfiguration narrative, from the Gospel of Matthew, was read on the second Sunday of Lent, although it is possible that Bonaventure may have composed these sermons without having preached them.[46]

Bonaventure's sermon for that Sunday is notable, not only for its content, but also for its omissions. From Matthew's transfiguration narrative, Bonaventure comments on the following words, "Jesus took with him Peter and James and John, his brother, and led them up a high mountain apart. And he was transfigured before them." In choosing these words, Bonaventure leaves out the "six days," the transformation of Christ's face and garments, the presence of Moses and Elijah, Peter's words, the presence of the cloud and voice, and Jesus' words after the theophany.

45. See the introduction of Jacques Guy Bougerol to Bonaventure's *Sermones dominicales,* edited by Bougerol, 11–126 (Grottaferrata, Italy: Collegio S. Bonaventura Padri Editori di Quaracchi, 1977). On the dating of these sermons, which is disputed, see Timothy J. Johnson's summary of the evidence in his introduction to *The Sunday Sermons of St. Bonaventure,* edited and translated by Timothy J. Johnson, 11–58 (St. Bonaventure, NY: Franciscan Institute Publications, 2008), 22–30.

46. See, for example, the *capitulare evangeliorum* in the early medieval Lorsch Gospels. *The Lorsch Gospels,* introduction by Wolfgang Braunfels (New York: George Braziller, 1967), fols. 116r.–24v.

Just as contemplation was a significant theme in Bonaventure's Luke commentary, so it is in his sermon for the second Sunday in Lent. In fact, it is the central theme in this work. Beginning the commentary with Peter, James, and John also allows Bonaventure to give his theology of contemplation an ecclesial orientation, since each disciple represents a different facet of the Christian life. In a way the three disciples constitute the prism through which Bonaventure views contemplation and its relation to Jesus' transfiguration.

Bonaventure begins by linking the transfiguration to the resurrection. He says that because the resurrection is the element of human salvation most difficult to believe, Christ wanted to prepare His disciples (and all Christians) for that miracle through a similar event. The fact that the transfiguration prefigures the resurrection should not obscure the principle that spiritual transfiguration through contemplation must precede the glory of human resurrection, which will be accompanied by the vision of God. The brief passage Bonaventure chose for comment reflects this spiritual teaching:

> And since it is impossible to fix one's gaze on the glory of divine majesty, unless one is first chosen and preceded by divine grace, then prepared with the greatest diligence and elevated by the highest desire of love, the proposed text proceeds very methodically and in the proper order. For in the first place it records the divine grace of mystical assumption, secondly it records the devout preparation of love-filled elevation, and thirdly it records the manifestation of future glorification, which is a dispensation. First, therefore, it records the divine grace of mystical assumption when it says "Jesus took with him Peter and James and John." Secondly, it records the devout preparation of love-filled elevation when it adds, "and He led them up a high mountain apart," on which the Gloss says, "He ascends up the mountain to be transfigured, so that he could state that whoever awaits the resurrection should be raised up to a high place and persevere in continuous prayer." Thirdly, it records the manifestation of future glory, which is a dispensation, when it adds, "And he was transfigured before them."[47]

47. "Et quoniam impossibile est, aliquem figere aciem sui oculi in gloriam divinae maiestatis, nisi prius sit a divina gratia praeelectus et praeventus, deinde summa diligentia paratus atque summo desiderio amoris elevatus, ideo in verbo proposito valde ordinate et recto ordine proceditur. Nam primo notatur divina dignatio mysticae assumptionis, secundo notatur devota praeparatio affectuosae elevationis, tertio notatur dispensativa ostensio futurae glorificationis. Primo igitur notatur divina dignatio mysticae assumptionis, cum dicit: *Assumpsit*

The first part of the Matthean passage, which describes Jesus' initiative in taking the disciples to the top of the mountain, expresses the divine initiative that precedes the ascent to contemplation. The soul can ascend only when God "assumes" or takes it by means of grace. The second section of the passage describes the soul's response to God's initiative, and the third section describes the transformation of the human person.

Bonaventure gives this spiritual interpretation of the transfiguration an ecclesial orientation by emphasizing the presence of the three disciples, who represent the "threefold rank of the Church Militant, namely prelates, actives, and contemplatives."[48] Peter signifies the "prelates," James represents "actives," and John corresponds to "contemplatives." Christ called (or "assumed") all three disciples from one way of life and gave them new identities; their correspondence to one of the three ecclesiastical ranks is bound up with their respective missions.

The three ranks also act as a matrix through which one can see the development of spiritual life, signified by the disciples' ascension of the mountain. Peter, who represents prelates, has a particular responsibility because he is the first to receive the divine illumination. Bonaventure illustrates this assertion with the following example: "The sun first shines on the mountains, and then it illumines the valleys; thus prelates, like lofty mountains, ought to be the first to receive into themselves the illuminations of divine light, and then they transmit the example of a good life to those in their care, who are like valleys."[49] Prelates should possess a certain perfection "on account of the distinguished preeminence of their evangelical perfection,"[50] and Bonaven-

Iesus Petrum et Iacobum et Ioannem. Secundo notatur devota praeparatio affectuosae elevationis, cum subdit: *et duxit illos in montem excelsum;* Glossa: 'Transfigurandus in monte ascendit, ut innuat quod, qui resurrectionem exspectant, in excelsum debent elevari et continuis precibus insistere.' Tertio notatur dispensativa ostensio futurae glorificationis, cum subinfert: *et transfiguratus est ant eos,*" *Sermo 16* in *Sermones dominicales,* 244.

48. "triplicis status Ecclesiae militantis, scilicet praelationis, actionis et contemplationis," *Sermo 16,* 244–45. For more on this distinction see Bonaventure's *Collationes in Hexaëmeron,* 22, 17ff.

49. "Sol enim primo irradiat montes, deinde illuminat valles; sic praelati tanquam sublimes montes divinae lucis irradiationes debent primo in se recipere et deinde per bonae vitae exemplum in subditos tanquam in convalles transmittere," *Sermo 16,* 247.

50. "propter excellentem eminentiam evangelicae perfectionis," *Sermo 16,* 247.

ture denounces those ministers who fail to live up to Christ's example. Indeed, Bonaventure says that they lead Jesus up the mountain and "in the hearts of those in their care, they cast him down by their bad example."[51]

The ascent of those in the active life incorporates a "virtuous ability to endure every kind of tribulation."[52] In this context, the mountain is a location of winds and storms of temptation where the soul gains strength and fortitude. In the case of contemplatives, the mountain acts as a metaphor for those who receive refreshing rain from heaven and let it fall to the plains in streams and rivulets. They communicate the heavenly gifts "through the word of preaching and through the example of an upright life."[53]

Bonaventure also reads the act of transfiguration through the lens of the three ranks. This reading gives the transfiguration significance for both the "Church Militant" and for the soul. Bonaventure explains:

> Our Lord Jesus Christ wanted to be transfigured in front of those three, who represent prelates, actives, and contemplatives, and to show them his future glory, so that, speaking accurately, in Peter he should first illumine prelates, by the splendor of truth and understanding, secondly, in James he should confirm actives in the hope of awaited glory, and thirdly, in John he should inflame contemplatives by the love of charity and of kindness.[54]

The illumination of prelates helps them communicate the faith to those entrusted to their care. Thus, the transfiguration is intrinsically linked with faith, because Jesus underwent His transformation expressly to strengthen the disciples' faith.

It is in the context of the illumination of the prelates that Bonaventure clarifies a point that was poorly articulated in his commentary on Luke, and that is whether Christ assumed the gift of clarity. In his commentary on Luke, Bonaventure had claimed that Christ assumed the

51. "praecipitant eum in cordibus subditorum propter mala exempla," *Sermo 16*, 248.

52. "virtuosam tolerantiam omnimodae tribulationis," *Sermo 16*, 248.

53. "per verbum praedicationis, per exemplum honestae conversationis," *Sermo 16*, 249.

54. "Voluit Dominus noster Iesus Christus transfigurari coram istis tribus, per quos praelati, activi et contemplativi intelliguntur, et ostendere eis suam futuram gloriam, ut per hoc, appropriate loquendo, primo illuminaret in Petro praelatos splendore veritatis et intelligentiae, secundo confirmaret in Iacobo activos in spe exspectationis gloriae, tertio inflammaret in Ioanne contemplativos amore caritatis et benevolentiae," *Sermo 16*, 249.

gift of clarity for a brief time, during which His body became "heavenly." In this sermon, Bonaventure makes an advance by distinguishing between the gift of clarity and its act, as John of La Rochelle and Albert had done before him. Christ did not assume the gift of clarity, but, by divine dispensation, He assumed only the act of glorious clarity, and He manifested this glory to strengthen the disciples' faith, especially at the time of His crucifixion.[55] This articulation lacks the fullness of some of the writings of Bonaventure's peers. However, we learn from this account that Christ did not have the gift of clarity, and Bonaventure refrains from using the term "heavenly body," a term, which creates some confusion regarding Christ's passibility.

Next, Bonaventure examines the illumination of those in the active life and the contemplative life, represented by James and John, respectively. The transfiguration illumines those in the active life so that they can await the glory of the resurrection despite the sufferings endured in the "valleys" of this present life. The illumination of the transfiguration on those in the contemplative life inflames their hearts with love. Just as Christ's garments became exceedingly white, so too are contemplatives clothed with "the whiteness of chastity and of purity."[56]

III. *Sermones de tempore 200–203*

Bonaventure's *sermones de tempore* on the transfiguration narrative were also given on the second Sunday in Lent, but the dating of these sermons varies widely. The Quarrachi editors include them along with *Sermo dominicale 16*, but Jacques Guy Bougerol edited *reportationes* from a Milanese manuscript, Ambrosiana A 11 sup. In addition to editing the texts, Bougerol suggests possible dates for when Bonaventure may have preached the sermons in question and even who may have heard them. The *reportationes* are not always complete, and they sometimes differ from the Quaracchi text. For this reason and because they represent only one variant of the text, the exposition of the sermons here will be based on both the Quarracchi text and Bougerol's edition.[57]

55. See *Sermo 16*, 250.

56. "candore castitatis et pudicitiae," *Sermo 16*, 252.

57. See Jacques Guy Bougerol's introduction to his edition of Bonaventure's *Sermons de tempore* (Paris: Éditions franciscaines, 1990), 7–10.

Bougerol suggests that *Sermo 200*, which comments on the same passage from Matthew 17:1–2 as *Sermo dominicale 16* had done, may have been preached in 1257. Here we find the same distinction of prelates, actives, and contemplatives that Bonaventure made in the latter sermon, but, in addition to the spiritual interpretation he gave, he offers a different explanation of the mountain. In this sermon, Bonaventure interprets the mountain as the heavenly Jerusalem, "in which are seen the clarity of God and the face of Jesus Christ."[58] On this mountain, there is food for the soul, a beautiful view, safety, joy, and love.[59] There the face of Christ, which the soul gazes at, radiates clarity and light to all the elect whose home will be the mountain of God in heaven.

Sermo 201, which Bougerol suggests may have been preached two years earlier, in 1255, possesses a similar eschatological emphasis. Commenting again on Christ's radiant face and His white clothes, Bonaventure connects the transfiguration with the resurrection. Before God, the soul will receive divine light and radiate it. Bonaventure says that just as the sun is always glowing with light, so too will the beatified soul glow eternally.[60] The glorified soul will shine like snow "from the reception of the glorious gifts,"[61] but Bonaventure does not mean the gifts of a glorified body, but rather the special gifts of a glorified soul. These gifts include wisdom, a pure conscience, modesty, and love.[62] This spiritual interpretation of the transfiguration is like others he gives, but this one is unique because of how Bonaventure ascribes certain qualities to the "face" of the soul and others to its "garments." Like many of Bonaventure's spiritual interpretations, however, little rationale is provided for the classification of some qualities as pertaining to the "face" and others to the "garments."

In *Sermo 202*, Bonaventure focuses both on the disciples seeing only Jesus after the transfiguration and on the presence of Moses and Elijah. Bougerol suggests February 21, 1266, as a possible date for the

58. "in qua videtur claritas Dei et facies Iesu Christi," *Sermones de tempore, de sanctis, de B. Virgine Maria et de diversis*, in *Opera omnia*, edited by Pp. Colegii S. Bonaventurae (Quaracchi, Italy: ex Typographia Collegii S. Bonaventurae, 1901), t. 9, 219.

59. *Sermones de tempore, de sanctis, de B. Virgine Maria et de diversis*, 219.

60. See *Sermones de tempore, de sanctis, de B. Virgine Maria et de diversis*, 220.

61. "ex receptione dotum gloriosum," *Sermones de tempore, de sanctis, de B. Virgine Maria et de diversis*, 220.

62. See *Sermones de tempore, de sanctis, de B. Virgine Maria et de diversis*, 220.

preaching of this sermon. In this sermon, Bonaventure explains that "lifting" one's eyes might signify considering the world in its fallen state. When one considers the world in such a way, one sees "no one," as the disciples did. The fact that the disciples saw only Jesus after the transfiguration is a lesson that one must not only have contempt for the world, but one must also keep one's eyes fixed on the heavens, that is, on Jesus Christ.[63]

Bougerol claims that it is probable that *Sermo 203* was preached on March 1, 1271. In this sermon Bonaventure connects the illumination of Christ's radiant face to His illumination of the Church Militant. The Church and the spiritual soul love to gaze on Christ's face, which then imparts spiritual gifts. In addition to spiritual gifts Bonaventure mentions elsewhere, he includes confessing the truth, understanding Scripture, and experiencing ecstatic devotion.[64]

In all of these sermons, Bonaventure gives a completely spiritual interpretation of the transfiguration. Bonaventure is ordinarily fond of this method of interpretation; but in his commentary on Luke, he also asked questions about the gifts of Christ's body, the presence of Moses and Elijah, and the significance of the theophany. In these sermons, however, there is little interest in the events on the mountain of transfiguration. Bonaventure instead uses this event from Christ's life to illustrate the growth of the soul and to point out the direction it must take to attain perfection.

Conclusion

Bonaventure's primary interest in the transfiguration, both in the earlier commentary on Luke and in the sermons of his later career, is in its spiritual dimension, not in the transfiguration as a historical event. Although Bonaventure does address the nature of Christ's clarity, his teaching on how Christ's clarity radiated from His mortal human nature is not perfectly clear. The strength of Bonaventure's exegesis, however, lies in showing how the transfiguration recapitulates the transformation of the individual soul and the Church as a whole. Like

63. See *Sermones de tempore, de sanctis, de B. Virgine Maria et de diversis*, 221.
64. See *Sermones de tempore, de sanctis, de B. Virgine Maria et de diversis*, 221.

Albert, Bonaventure notices the ecclesial context of the transfiguration. However, he keeps more with the exegesis of the *Glossa ordinaria* and the postillae of Hugh, in focusing on the disciples as symbols for different dimensions of the Church. Like Albert, Bonaventure gives a sympathetic interpretation of Peter, but drawing from Hugh, he also applies the transfiguration to all people. In order to be deified, Christ must "assume" with grace the soul of the believer and the "Church Militant" and take them through six or seven stages of contemplation, after which they will experience the "eighth day," the beatific vision. This mystical ascent must be from the valleys of this world to the mountaintop of contemplation, where they will be transfigured into a glorious form. The illumination and transformation that the soul and the Church experience there constitute the penultimate stage of ascent before entering into heaven and the glory of the resurrection.

8
THOMAS AQUINAS

Thomas Aquinas wrote about Christ's transfiguration in a number of scholastic genres, including the *Sentences* commentary, biblical commentary, and *summa*. Interestingly, no extant sermon on the transfiguration remains. Given that Thomas' discussions of the transfiguration occur in a variety of literary contexts and given the relatively large amount of theological reflection on Christ's transfiguration, spanning much of his career, Thomas Aquinas provides the fullest account of the transfiguration in the thirteenth century. Thomas has this distinction also because he draws on a wider variety of patristic theology and offers more sophisticated philosophical and theological distinctions than most of his contemporaries and predecessors.

This chapter will look at both Thomas' synthetic works (his *Sentences* commentary and the *Summa theologiae*) and his relevant exegetical works (the *Catena aurea* and his commentary on Matthew). Like Albert, Thomas develops considerably the more speculative dimension of his theology of Christ's transfiguration in the course of his career. And like Bonaventure, Thomas provides a spiritual interpretation of the transfiguration, even though his is much more subdued than that of his Franciscan colleague.[1] Indeed, Thomas' ability to combine varying approaches to Christ's transfiguration, articulated further in the conclusion of the chapter, accounts in part for the profundity of Thomas' theology of the transfiguration.

1. For more on Thomas' career, the broad outline of which is well known, see Torrell, *Saint Thomas Aquinas, vol. 1: The Person and His Work.*

Scriptum super libros Sententiarum

Thomas Aquinas' earliest reflection on the transfiguration occurs in his commentary on Peter Lombard's *Four Books of Sentences,* which dates from the mid-1250s. The fact that Thomas includes a discussion of the transfiguration in his *Sentences* commentary is somewhat surprising. Peter Lombard nowhere discusses the transfiguration, either in the section on Christ in Book Three or in the section on eschatology in Book Four. Perhaps even more indicative of Thomas' originality here is the fact that Alexander of Hales, Bonaventure, and Albert make no effort to examine the transfiguration in their *Sentences* commentaries.

The place where Thomas chooses to write about the transfiguration is in his commentary on Book Three, distinction 16 of Lombard's *Sentences,* which examines whether Christ suffered and died out of necessity and what attributes Christ assumed from the various states of humanity.[2] The only part of Lombard's text that might invite consideration of the transfiguration is the second part, about the various states of humanity, but Thomas' contemporaries saw fit to focus on the first half of Lombard's text and to explore Christ's capacity to suffer.

Although Thomas devotes one question to each part of Lombard's text, the second question, which addresses what Christ took from the various states of humanity, only looks at Christ's bodily attributes that derive from the state of glory. After making the usual division of Lombard's text, Thomas states that there are two related questions. The first question concerns "the necessity of dying which Christ assumed from the second state," and the second concerns "those things which Christ had from the final state."[3] The reader does not find in question two, however, a general consideration of the gifts of a resurrected body, although that topic does arise briefly. Thomas decides to focus only on

2. Lombard, following some of the Fathers, distinguishes between humanity before sin and after sin and before grace, under grace, and in glory.

3. "de necessitate moriendi quam Christus ex secundo statu assumpsit . . . de his quae Christus habuit de ultimo statu," Thomas Aquinas, *Scriptum super libros Sententiarum,* edited by P. Mandonnet, (tt.1–2) and M. F. Moos (tt. 3–4), (Paris: Lethielleux, 1929–1947), III, d. 16 (hereafter *III Sent.*).

one of those gifts, namely clarity, and this gift is a quality that is manifested in Christ's earthly life only during the transfiguration. Thomas asks two questions about Christ's clarity, namely whether the clarity of Christ's transfigured body was real or imaginary and whether it was glorious, both with a view to explain how a glorious attribute could exist in Christ's mortal and passible body.

Compared with the more complex investigations of Alexander of Hales, John of La Rochelle, and Albert the Great, this question is rather brief, and Thomas' primary questions are determined primarily by Lombard's interests. Because of the structure of Lombard's text, Thomas is obliged at least to situate the glory of the transfiguration within the context of the passibility of Christ's body. This fact alone necessarily narrows the focus of an examination of Christ's transfiguration, but Thomas, perhaps foreshadowing his later prescription for brevity in the prologue to the *Summa theologiae*,[4] addresses almost all the questions of his peers and predecessors in the more condensed form of objection and reply.

Article one, which asks whether Christ's glory was real or imaginary, opens with five objections against the reality of Christ's clarity. Of the observations made and authorities cited in these five objections, all were made or alluded to by Thomas' peers and predecessors. The first objection cites a verse often commented upon during the Middle Ages, namely 2 Corinthians 11:14, "even Satan disguises himself as an angel of light." The Latin text of the Bible suggests a connection to the Gospel accounts of the transfiguration because of its language. Thomas' Bible has "angelus satanae transfigurat se in angelum lucis."[5] In order to form an objection, Thomas takes this verse to signify that "transfiguration" refers to something changing in such a way that its real nature is hidden. Just as Satan can appear as an angel of light, although he is evil, so too did Christ appear glorious during the transfiguration when he was not. It is interesting to note that Thomas' older contemporary, John of La Rochelle, cited this passage as well, but only to observe that

4. "Haec igitur et alia huiusmodi evitare studentes, tentabimus, cum confidentia divini auxilii, ea quae ad sacram doctrinam pertinent, breviter ac dilucide prosequi, secundum quod materia patietur," *Summa theologiae*, prol.

5. *III Sent.*, d. 16, q. 2, a. 1.

"transfiguration" can designate, among other things, a change in something's appearance.[6] Thomas juxtaposes Satan's "transfiguration" with Christ's to create an objection that suggests that Christ's glory hides or misrepresents "the truth which is in Him."[7]

The second objection is based on a gloss from Bede on Luke 9:27. In that passage Jesus says that "there are some standing here who will not taste death before they see the kingdom of God." The *Glossa ordinaria* contains an interlinear gloss on that verse that Thomas, perhaps following John of La Rochelle, erroneously ascribes to Bede,[8] and that links the kingdom of God to "the glorification of the body in an imaginary representation of future beatitude."[9] As John of La Rochelle had done before him, Thomas uses the adjective "imaginary" to object to the reality of Christ's bodily glory.[10]

The third objection Thomas lists is one common in scholastic questions on the transfiguration, namely how Christ's body can be both dark and radiant simultaneously. Because of its mortal nature, Christ's body should be unable to radiate light, so how can Christ's glory be explained?

The fourth objection is also a common one, and it addresses the question of how the disciples were able to behold Christ's glory. Instead of devoting an entire question to this problem, however, Thomas addresses it in one succinct objection. Following another erroneously ascribed gloss, this time one ascribed to Jerome,[11] Thomas crafts his objection to suggest that because Christ's face shone like the sun and because it did not hurt the eyes of the apostles, it could not be true

6. See *Summa fratris Alexandri,* III, pt. 1, t. 6, q. 2, tit. 1, chap. 1.

7. *III Sent.,* d. 16, q. 2, a. 1.

8. See *Summa fratris Alexandri,* III, pt. 1, t. 6, q. 2, tit. 1, chap. 2. In the *Glossa ordinaria* there is no ascription.

9. "glorificationem corporis in imaginaria repraesentatione futurae beatitudinis," *III Sent.,* d. 16, q. 2, a. 1.

10. See *Summa fratris Alexandri,* III, pt. 1, t. 6, q. 2, tit. 1, chap. 2.

11. Thomas may be following John of La Rochelle again. The gloss in question, on Matthew 17:2, states, "Deus non potest in hac vita tam clarum quid facere" (*Glossa ordinaria* 4:57). In the Gloss there is no ascription, and Alexander of Hales' disputed question does not provide one either. John of La Rochelle, however, claims, erroneously, that it is from Jerome (see *Summa fratris Alexandri,* III, pt. 1, t. 6, q. 2, tit. 1, chap. 6).

clarity. True sensible clarity hurts the eyes if it is too intense, and the disciples not only were not hurt, as evidenced by Peter's statement that "it is good for us to be here," but they found the experience pleasant.

The final objection against the reality of Christ's bodily clarity relates the appearance of Moses and Elijah to Christ's clarity. Thomas addresses a difficult gloss, which other theologians also found troublesome. It claims that "neither the bodies nor the souls of Moses and Elijah appeared there," and it suggests the possibility that angels impersonated Moses and Elijah by means of created bodies.[12] Thomas uses this suggestion to form an objection that argues that if angels could assume the appearances of Moses and Elijah and thus mislead their beholders, there is no reason to consider Christ's glory real.

The three opposing objections that follow do not constitute theoretical positions to be answered, but are rather facets of Thomas' own position, which argues for the objective reality of what is seen. Although Thomas' fellow theologians share the same concern, Thomas' own concern is particularly keen. He is the first of his peers to marshal in this context a text from Augustine's *Enarrationes in psalmos* that contains the claim that everything written about Christ in the Gospels is true. Augustine's text, which Thomas does not quote here, states:

> [Christ] assumed sorrow, just as He assumed flesh. Do not think that we believe that the Lord was not sorrowful. If we should say that He was not sorrowful, when the Gospel says, "My soul is sorrowful even unto death," it would follow that when the Gospel says, "Jesus slept," He did not sleep, and when the Gospel says, "Jesus ate," He did not eat, and so the worm of putrefaction creeps in and leaves nothing intact, so that it could be said that His body was not real and He did not have true flesh. Therefore, brothers, whatever was written of Him happened and is true.[13]

12. "non corpora vel animas Moysi vel Eliae ibi apparuisse," *III Sent.*, d. 16, q. 2, a. 1. Cf. *Glossa ordinaria* 4:175. The comment has no ascription in the *Glossa ordinaria*, and the only theologian from this period to provide one is Guerric of St. Quentin, who erroneously attributes it to Jerome.

13. "Sed tristitiam sic assumsit quomodo carnem. Nolite enim putare quia hoc dicimus, non fuisse tristem Dominum. Si enim hoc dixerimus, quia non erat tristis, cum euangelium dicat: *Tristis est anima mea usque ad mortem;* ergo et quando dicit euangelium: Dormiuit Iesus, non dormiuit Iesus; et quando euangelium dicit: Manducauit Iesus, non manducauit Iesus: subrepit uermiculus putredinis, et nihil sanum relinquit, ut dicatur quia et corpus non erat uerum, et carnem ueram non habuit. Quidquid ergo de illo scriptum est, fratres, factum

With respect to the transfiguration, Thomas summarizes this passage by saying, "if the clarity was not real, although the Gospel should assert this, it could be admitted that He did not really eat or that He did not truly suffer—which is heretical."[14]

The two remaining counterarguments confirm the contention that Christ's bodily clarity must be real. The first says that it was not fitting for the clarity manifested to deceive the disciples regarding its true nature. The final rejoinder cites a gloss claiming that both Moses and Elijah were witnesses from heaven. The argument concludes that Moses and Elijah could not truly be witnesses unless they were present, and they were witnesses because they beheld true clarity.

The response confirms Thomas' argument in these three objections: "It must be said that that clarity was sensible clarity, according to the truth existing in Christ's body, and its purpose was to manifest the clarity which He promised would be in the saints after the future resurrection, according to Matthew 13:43, 'The just will shine like the sun in the kingdom of their Father.'"[15] Thomas affirms here that the clarity was sensible, and the phrase "according to the truth existing in Christ's body" maintains that the revealed clarity in no way compromises Christ's passible and mortal body. Thomas' view that the clarity radiating from Christ's body also manifested the glory that "would be in the saints after the future resurrection" is significant because earlier discussions of the transfiguration tended to emphasize the difference between the clarity of the transfiguration and the clarity of the resurrection.[16] Although Thomas holds a different position in the later

---

est, verum est," *Enarrationes in psalmos,* edited by D. E. Dekkers and J. Fraipont, 3 vols. (Turnhout, Belg.: Brepols, 1956), CCSL 38–40, 2:93, 19 (italics are the editors').

14. "non fuit vera claritas, cum Evangelium hoc dicat, relinquitur quod non vere comederit nec vere passus sit: quod est haereticum," *III Sent.,* d. 16, q. 2, a. 1.

15. "Dicendum quod claritas illa fuit claritas sensibilis, secundum veritatem in corpore Christi existens, ad ostensionem claritatis quam promiserat in Sanctis post resurrectionem futuram, dicens: '*Fulgebunt justi tamquam sol in regno patris eorum,*' Mt xiii, 43," *III Sent.,* d. 16, q. 2, a. 1 (italics here and in subsequent citations are the editors').

16. Alexander, Guerric, and Albert insisted that the clarity of the transfiguration was only similar to that of the resurrection. John of La Rochelle, however, argued that the two clarities were of the same kind, but that the clarity of the transfiguration was less perfect than or incomplete with respect to the clarity of the resurrection. See *Summa fratris Alexandri,* III, pt. 1, t. 6, q. 2, tit. 1, chap. 4.

Summa theologiae, here he links the clarity of the transfigured Christ with that of the resurrected and glorified saints.

The replies to the five objections, which open the article, confirm this teaching by addressing the kind of clarity from different vantage points. The reply to the first objection argues that "transfiguration" in the case of Christ refers to the significance that His glorious body represents. "Christ is said to be transfigured," Thomas says, "because the clarity which He assumed for a time truly inhered in Him, as a figure of the future clarity which will be in the saints."[17]

The clarity Christ assumed is a sign of future glory, but how is it so? In the response to article one, Thomas claims that a figure or image either corresponds to what is "in the truth of a thing"[18] or it possesses only a relation to an object in the imagination. In article two, Thomas affirms, in response to Bede's gloss regarding the appearance of clarity as "an imaginary representation of future beatitude,"[19] that Christ's clarity was a figure that corresponded to the reality of the object signified. Thomas argues that Bede's troublesome adjective "imaginary" means "not that it is only in the imagination, but that it is an image and figure of something else."[20]

After addressing the significance of Christ's clarity, Thomas responds to the seeming impossibility of something being both dark and radiant simultaneously. He introduces two interesting analogies to explain how something intrinsically dark can acquire a light surface. The first analogy is that of a dull metal, which, after it is polished, acquires a shinier surface. The second analogy is that of an object, which, exposed to an extraneous light source such as the sun, becomes brighter in appearance. Thomas says that this latter analogy approximates what happened in Christ's transfigured body, although Christ's clarity "was added, certainly not by some radiant body, but miraculously by God Himself."[21]

17. "Dicitur autem Christus transfiguratus, quia claritatem sibi veraciter inhaerentem assumpsit ad tempus, in figuram futurae claritatis quae erit in Sanctis," *III Sent.*, d. 16, q. 2, a. 1.

18. "in rei veritate," *III Sent.*, d. 16, q. 2, a. 1.

19. "imaginaria repraesentatione futurae beatitudinis," *III Sent.*, d. 16, q. 2, a. 1.

20. "non quod est tantum in imaginatione, sed quod est imago et figura alterius," *III Sent.*, d. 16, q. 2, a. 1.

21. "non quidem superinducta ex aliquo corpore superlucenti, sed miraculose ab ipso Deo," *III Sent.*, d. 16, q. 2, a. 1.

The difference between clarity coming from the sun and from God Himself must be great, and although Thomas does not elaborate on this analogy, he conveys some sense of the difference in the next response, which pertains to the effect of Christ's clarity on the disciples' vision. Although Thomas says that the clarity of Christ's transfigured body was only similar to that of a glorified body, it has the same effect on non-glorified eyes. It "does not destroy vision but is pleasing."[22] Thomas links the clarity of Christ's transfigured body with the "clarity of God,"[23] which the heavenly Jerusalem possesses. Natural clarity can overpower vision, but the clarity that "comes from the spiritual clarity of the soul . . . does not destroy the relation of the eye to the power of the soul, but rather strengthens it."[24]

The final reply concerns the appearance of Moses and Elijah. Regarding the gloss that claims that Moses and Elijah were not present but were, rather, represented by angels, Thomas notes that this gloss "has been corrected by the masters."[25] The implication is that this gloss carries no authoritative weight because its original form was defective.[26] With other difficult glosses attributed to the Fathers, especially those with possible heterodox interpretations, Thomas usually attempts to provide an explanation consistent with the teaching of the Church, but with this gloss Thomas makes no such effort. He simply refutes it, asserting that Moses and Elijah were truly present. Elijah's presence is fairly easy to explain; both his body and soul were present. Thomas explains Moses' appearance, however, by allowing for either of two possibilities: Moses' soul assuming a body or his soul, by divine power, appearing to the disciples without a body. In the later *Summa theologiae*, as shown below, Thomas refuses to countenance the latter thesis.

22. "visum non corrumpit, sed demulcet," *III Sent.*, d. 16, q. 2, a. 1.

23. The Vulgate text of Revelation 21:10–11 reads, "Et sustulit me in spiritu in montem magnum et altum et ostendit mihi civitatem sanctam Ierusalem, descendentem de caelo a Deo, habentem claritatem Dei, et lumen eius simile lapidi pretioso, tanquam lapidi iaspidis, sicut crystallum."

24. "provenit enim ex claritate spirituali animae . . . non corrumpit proportionem oculi ad vim animae, sed magis confortat," *III Sent.*, d. 16, q. 2, a. 1.

25. "punctata est a Magistris," *III Sent.*, d. 16, q. 2, a. 1.

26. Thomas will provide a more specific reason for discarding this gloss in the *Summa theologiae*, namely its erroneous ascription to Augustine. See *Summa theologiae*, III, q. 45, a. 3.

Having shown that the glory of Christ's transfigured body was real and not imaginary, Thomas proceeds to the second article of this question, which asks whether Christ's clarity was glorious. At first glance this question seems unnecessary. In his reply to the fourth objection in the first article, Thomas had just remarked that Christ's clarity was similar to that of a glorious body. For Thomas' predecessors, with the notable exception of John of La Rochelle, "similar" implies difference in kind. Thomas' statement regarding similarity, however, must be balanced by his position that both Christ's transfigured clarity and the glorious clarity of the elect have the same effect on the vision of the non-glorified. One must also take into consideration his response, in which he stated that Christ's sensible clarity "manifested the clarity which He promised would be in the saints after the future resurrection."[27] From Thomas' discussion in the first article, it would seem that Christ's clarity is similar to glorious clarity, but it is also the same in some respects. Perhaps the specific nature of the question asked in article one prevented Thomas from providing a complete answer. In any case, Thomas thought this question on the relationship between the clarity of the transfiguration and glorious clarity important enough to devote a separate article to it.

Thomas begins the article with seven objections, and although rehearsing them all is unnecessary, since most are treated by one or more of Thomas' peers and predecessors, several observations should be made. First, Thomas lists an important gloss, which all of the authors examined in this study thus far, with the exception of Alexander of Hales, have used.[28] It says that Christ "showed in His mortal body not immortality, but clarity similar to the immortality of the future."[29] Since the clarity of immortality is glorious, Christ could not have had glorious clarity during the transfiguration.[30] The second objection Thomas lists, although not differing in substance from other similar objections, possesses a unique articulation. It says that Christ's body cannot be

27. "ad ostensionem claritatis quam promiserat in Sanctis post resurrectionem futuram," *III Sent.*, d. 16, q. 2, a. 1.

28. Alexander, however, addressed a number of similar glosses.

29. "In corpore mortali ostendit non immortalitatem, sed claritatem similem futurae immortalitati," *III Sent.*, d. 16, q. 2, a. 2.

30. *III Sent.*, d. 16, q. 2, a. 2.

"subject to punishments and to glory" simultaneously.[31] Since Christ's body could bear suffering, it could not have glorious clarity. The final objection is also unique. It says that because the clarity of Christ's garments was not glorious, neither was that of His body.

Three counter-arguments follow, and, like the counter-arguments of article one, they represent facets of Thomas' position that affirm the glorious nature of the clarity of Christ's transfigured body. The first counter-argument is a gloss on Philippians 3:21, "Who will reform the body of our lowness, made like to the body of His glory," cited by John of La Rochelle.[32] The gloss states, "we will be conformed to the clarity which He had in the transfiguration."[33] The next two arguments reaffirm the eschatological link between the transfiguration and the end times by connecting the transfiguration specifically to the Last Judgment and to the resurrection of the dead.

Thomas begins the response of this article by commenting on a difficult passage known to all the theologians of this period. Theologians before Thomas had refrained from attributing it to any one person, but Thomas ascribes it (erroneously) both here and in the *Summa theologiae* to Hugh of St. Victor.[34] This passage is the one that asserts that Christ assumed "subtlety in the nativity, when [Christ] came forth from the virginal womb, . . . agility when He walked on the waves of the sea, clarity in the transfiguration, and impassibility at the supper, when He gave His body to His disciples to eat without it being divided."[35] Although Thomas appropriates this passage to support his

31. "subjectum poenalitatis et gloriae," *III Sent.*, d. 16, q. 2, a. 2.

32. See *Summa fratris Alexandri*, III, pt. 1, t. 6, q. 2, tit. 1, chap. 4.

33. "Assimilabimur claritati quam habuit in transfiguratione," *III Sent.*, d. 16, q. 2, a. 2.

34. See *Summa theologiae*, III, q. 45, a. 2.

35. "subtilitatem in nativitate, quando est egressus de utero virginali . . . agilitatem autem, quando super undas maris ambulavit; claritatem in transfiguratione; impassibilitatem in coena, quando corpus suum ad edendum discipulis sine hoc quod divideretur dedit," *III Sent.*, d. 16, q. 2, a. 2. Although this passage is not from Hugh, indeed its first articulation seems to be in Pope Innocent III's *De sacro altaris mysterio* (PL 217, 864) or *Sermo XIV de tempore* (PL 217, 380–82), Hugh does indicate that Christ could assume and lay aside a quality such as mortality at will: "Quia ergo uoluntate non necessitate mortalis fuit ipsius mortalitatis proprietatem secundum quod ratio et ordo temporis postulabat priusquam eam per mortem totam exueret, aliquando ex parte quando uoluit deposuit. et rursum quando uoluit recepit. Vt in hoc ipso probaret quia in quantum eam sustinuit, ex necessitate non esset. qui sic pro potestate in quantum uoluit eam non habere. sustinere omnino non posset," *Hugonis de Sancto-*

position (in contradistinction to his treatment of this passage in the *Summa theologiae*), he brackets his summary of the text with two caveats. The first caveat, preceding the text, says that although "Hugh" allowed that Christ assumed "properties or gifts of a glorified body,"[36] these properties should not be understood as possessing the "character of a gift."[37] Thomas clarifies this statement in his concluding caveat, which says that the text of "Hugh" should not be interpreted to refer "to the qualities or habits of a glorified body, because they are opposed to the conditions and properties of a passible body."[38]

Thomas' primary concern in these explanations is to maintain that although Christ's transfigured body appeared to be glorious, it was nonetheless mortal and passible. He cites the argument, used by his contemporaries, that contraries cannot exist in the same subject simultaneously. If that argument is true, however, and the transfiguration does not manifest gifts of a glorified body, how does one classify the revealed properties since they do not have "the character of a gift"? Thomas eventually must say that Christ's body did not manifest "properties" at all, but rather the acts of the properties, which seemed to be manifested. How is Christ's body able to reveal an act of a property without the property itself? Thomas claims that "the acts of those properties were in it, not by proceeding from something inherent, but supernaturally by a divine miracle."[39]

In these answers, Thomas has argued that the clarity of Christ's transfigured body was truly glorious clarity, despite His body being mortal and passible. Nevertheless, the clarity of Christ's transfigured body exists only in act, whereas the clarity of a glorified body exists as a habit inhering in the body. Thomas does, however, want to make a further distinction between the clarity of Christ's transfigured body and that of glorified bodies. This distinction pertains to the brightness

Victore De sacramentis Christianae fidei, curo et studio R. Berndt (Monasterii Westfalorum, Ger.: Aschendorff, 2008), II, 8, 3.

36. "proprietates seu dotes corporis glorificati," *III Sent.*, d. 16, q. 2, a. 2.

37. "rationem dotis," *III Sent.*, d. 16, q. 2, a. 2.

38. "ad ipsas qualitates sive habitus gloriosi corporis, quia contrariantur conditionibus et proprietatibus corporis passibilis," *III Sent.*, d. 16, q. 2, a. 2.

39. "actus illarum proprietatem fuerunt in eo non quidem procedentes ex aliquo inhaerente, sed supernaturaliter divino miraculo," *III Sent.*, d. 16, q. 2, a. 2.

or radiance of Christ's body. "That brightness," Thomas says, "was of the same kind as that of glorified bodies, although not as perfect, just as charity in this life is likened to the charity of heaven."[40] Thomas may have derived this distinction between perfect and imperfect brightness from John of La Rochelle, who uses the same analogy and almost the exact formulation to describe the difference in clarity between Christ's transfigured body and a glorified body.[41] Both Thomas and John of La Rochelle maintain that Christ's transfigured and glorified clarities are of the same kind and that the transfigured clarity is imperfect with respect to the glorified clarity. Like John, Thomas cites Moses as a counter-example to illustrate how Christ's clarity is different from other manifestations of clarity. Moses' clarity was similar to glorious clarity, "just as faith [is similar] to vision [in heaven], although they are not of the same kind."[42] The clarity of the transfiguration, in contrast, is of the same kind as that of the resurrected Christ, but it lacks the same intensity. This difference exists because Christ's soul is glorified, unlike Moses' soul.

In this response, Thomas applies his two main contributions, namely the distinction between act and habit and the distinction between clarity and brightness. He responds to the first two objections, the gloss that describes "similar" clarity and the argument that contraries cannot exist in the same subject simultaneously, by saying that the clarity "similar" to that of a glorified body is explained by Christ's possession of the act of clarity. Although Christ's transfigured body lacked the habit of clarity, there was "an act of similar splendor,"[43] which Thomas believes had a different effect from the effect of the habit of clarity. This distinction between clarity and splendor allows Thomas to explain the relationship between Christ's glory and that of His garments as the relationship of clarity to its effect; Christ's body miraculously possessed the act of clarity, which radiated splendor all around Him. Thomas also notes that since there was no habit of clarity in Christ's transfigured

40. "ille fulgor ejusdem generis cum fulgore corporum glorificatorum, non tamen ita perfectus; sicut caritas viae assimilatur caritati patriae," *III Sent.*, d. 16, q. 2, a. 2.

41. See *Summa fratris Alexandri*, III, pt. 1, t. 6, q. 2, tit. 1, chap. 4.

42. "sicut fides visioni, non ejusdem generis," *III Sent.*, d. 16, q. 2, a. 2.

43. "fuit actus splendoris similis," *III Sent.*, d. 16, q. 2, a. 2.

but passible body, but rather only an act of clarity, the argument regarding contraries in the same subject is not valid.

This emphasis on the act of clarity in accounting for Christ's glory lends itself to a corresponding emphasis on divine power. How can an act exist without its habit? A miracle effected by God is an obvious answer. Although Thomas later will alter his opinion on this point, in the *Scriptum* he argues that the act of clarity and the acts of the other gifts did not derive from Christ's soul, which was still passible, but from divine power alone. Thomas ascribes the fact that the clarity of the transfiguration and the resurrection are of the same kind to Christ's glorified soul, but insofar as Christ's soul was passible, it could not communicate the habit of glorious clarity to His passible body. What allowed Christ to have glorious clarity during the transfiguration was a miraculous act of divine power.

Thomas' theological approach to the transfiguration in this brief passage is noteworthy on a number of accounts. First, as noted above, other commentaries on the *Sentences* omitted, for good reason, any discussion of the transfiguration. Second, Thomas' explanation focuses primarily on Christ's clarity and allows questions regarding the circumstantial details of the transfiguration to be peripheral. Third, although other accounts of the transfiguration explain Christ's clarity in incarnational or eschatological terms, Thomas applies both approaches and also emphasizes the role of divine power. Thomas acknowledges that although Christ's soul was glorious, it plays no role in communicating glory to the body. Instead, Thomas repeats his position that Christ's clarity resulted from an act of divine power. The emphasis on the miraculous nature of the transfiguration is important given the overall context of this passage, which, because of Lombard's *Sentences*, needs to address not only the successive stages of the human condition and their relation to Christ's body, but also the simultaneity of glory and mortality in Christ's pre-glorified body. In this approach, Thomas is always mindful of the fact that the miracle of the transfiguration occurs in a body, which must suffer and die. Although Thomas' teaching on the transfiguration will become more complex in his later works, he will never lose sight of this important fact.

The *Catena aurea in quatuor Evangelia*

Thomas' next treatment of the transfiguration occurs in his *Glossa continua super Evangelia* or *Catena aurea*. Thomas composed this running commentary on the four Gospels in the mid-1260s at the request of Pope Urban IV.[44] The patristic retrieval Thomas accomplishes in these works is impressive. He cites twenty-two Latin authors and fifty-seven Greek authors and includes the texts of some authors who had been completely unknown in the West up to that time.[45]

Since Thomas could draw from a large body of patristic exegesis of the transfiguration narratives, an analysis of what sources he appropriated and how he arranged them will also reveal what elements of the narratives Thomas favored and how he viewed the differences between the passages in the three synoptic gospels. For this comparison, the glosses on all three synoptic gospels will be compared together in this section, and rather than explain the interpretations in these glosses, most of which the reader has encountered earlier in this study from other authors, in one form or another, the focus here will be on Thomas' exegetical priorities and his sources.

In the gloss on Matthew, Thomas divides the transfiguration narrative into three sections: the transfiguration and Peter's response, the theophany and Jesus' admonition to the disciples not to tell anyone what they had seen, and the discussion between Jesus and the disciples regarding the coming of Elijah. The *divisio textus* is notable in its stark difference from the division in Thomas' later commentary on Matthew. Thomas treats all of the elements of the first section (e.g., the six days, the significance of the disciples, the transfiguration, the presence of Moses and Elijah, and Peter's words) fairly evenly. The two elements of the narrative that interest Thomas the most, however, are in the next two sections on the theophany and the discussion of Elijah's coming.

Thomas' principal patristic authorities are Jerome and John Chrysostom, and Thomas cites them throughout the commentary (thirteen times each). The other interpreters Thomas cites in the commentary,

44. See Torrell, *Saint Thomas Aquinas, vol. 1: The Person and His Work*, 136–41.
45. See Torrell, *Saint Thomas Aquinas, vol.* 1, 139.

from Matthew 16:28 to Matthew 17:13, include Remigius of Auxerre (nine times), Origen (seven times), Rabanus Maurus (five times),[46] Hilary of Poitiers (five times), the *Glossa ordinaria* (twice), Gregory the Great (once), and Augustine (once). Despite these other sources, Jerome and Chrysostom guide the interpretation of the passage, not only because Thomas cites them more often, but also because the passages he cites tend to be longer than those of the other exegetes.

The roughly two-to-one ratio of Latin sources to Eastern sources changes from Thomas' gloss on Matthew to the glosses on Mark and Luke. The main Eastern sources Thomas draws from in the gloss on Matthew are John Chrysostom, Pseudo-Chrysostom's *Opus imperfectum* (which Thomas ascribes to Chrysostom while still distinguishing between this commentary and Chrysostom's homilies), and Origen. Some sense of dissatisfaction with the Eastern sources available to Thomas emerges in Thomas' letter to Pope Urban IV, which accompanied the *Catena* on Matthew. In that letter, Thomas not only distinguishes between Chrysostom's Matthew commentary (the *Opus imperfectum*) and his homilies, but he also notes that he had to edit some of the texts, "especially in the homilies of Chrysostom, on account of the defective translation."[47] Thomas' dissatisfaction with the translations of his Eastern sources prompted him to obtain better translations of other Eastern sources. Thomas notes this aim in his letter to Cardinal Annibald of Annibaldis, which accompanied the *Catena* on Mark: "So that the aforementioned exposition of the saints may be rendered more complete and continuous, I have had some translations made of certain expositions of the Greek doctors into Latin, which I have interwoven with many expositions from the Latin doctors, authors whose names are already known."[48]

The effect of these additional Eastern sources is noticeable in the

46. These glosses of Rabanus tend to be derived from Bede.

47. "praecipue in Homilario Chrysostomi, propter hoc quod est translatio vitiosa," Thomas Aquinas, *Catena aurea in quatuor Evangelia*, edited by A. Guarienti, 2 vols. (Turin, Italy: Marietti, 1953), 1:4.

48. "Et ut magis integra et continua praedicta sanctorum expositio redderetur, quasdam expositiones Doctorum graecorum in latinum feci transferri, ex quibus plura expositionibus latinorum Doctorum interserui, auctorum nominibus praenotatis," *Catena aurea in quatuor Evangelia* 1:429.

commentaries on the transfiguration narrative of Mark's Gospel. Although Thomas' interests in Mark's account are similar to his interests in Matthew's narrative, the appropriation of patristic citations is vastly different. John Chrysostom retains a prominent position, but Jerome practically disappears, as do Origen and Remigius of Auxerre. Thomas does not even cite Hilary, Augustine, or Rabanus Maurus. However, he does extensively cite two new sources, namely Bede and Theophylact, the eleventh- and early twelfth-century Bishop of Ochrida.

In the gloss on Luke, Thomas expands the range of patristic citations to comment on the transfiguration itself, and especially on two of his primary interests: Peter's words and the theophany. The most significant Latin author for Thomas is Ambrose, whose commentary on Luke was an important source for interpretations of the transfiguration. With respect to Eastern authors, Thomas cites Theophylact, as he did in the gloss on Mark, but he also includes Eusebius, Cyril of Alexandria, Basil, Titus of Bostra, and most importantly, John of Damascus. It is interesting to note, too, which authors receive less attention. Thomas fails to cite even once Remigius of Auxerre and the *Glossa ordinaria,* while his references to Gregory the Great, Chrysostom, Bede, Augustine, and Origen are scarce.

Although the Eastern sources, in their interpretations of the transfiguration, rarely deviate significantly from the interpretations of the Western Fathers, there are of course different theological emphases. It would be both tedious and rash, given the fragmentary nature of the interwoven exegetical passages, to speculate on or summarize assertively the differences between Eastern and Western theological emphases in these passages, but Thomas' inclusion of John of Damascus, for the first time in the gloss on Luke, merits some attention. It is not enough to say simply that Thomas cites him seven times in this passage (more than any other author except Ambrose) because, at least in this case, the number of times Thomas cites an author does not accurately reflect his importance. The length of John's extracts must be considered as well, since they are in general rather significant.

The two longest patristic texts of the commentary are from John of Damascus, and the longest one will prove influential when Thomas develops his later theology of the transfiguration. This latter addresses the relationship between Christ's transfigured glory and the hypostatic union:

Now the devil, seeing [His face] shining in prayer, thought of Moses, whose face was glorified. But Moses indeed was glorified with glory coming from without; the Lord, however, was glorified with the natural radiance of divine glory. For since, because of the hypostatic union, there is one and the same glory of the Word and the flesh, He is transfigured not as though receiving what He was not, but manifesting to His disciples what He was. Hence, according to Matthew it is said that He was transfigured before them and that His face shone like the sun; for what the sun is in sensible things, God is in intelligible things. And just as the sun, which is a fountain of light, cannot be easily seen, but its light is perceived from that which reaches the earth, so too does Christ's face shine more intensely, like the sun, but His garments are white like snow; thus follows, "And His clothing became dazzling white," that is, it was illuminated by its participation in the divine light. These things should be considered in such a way that only one Lord of the new and old covenant should be manifested, and the mouths of heretics might be shut, and faith in the resurrection might arise, and also, that He who was transfigured would be believed to be the Lord of the living and the dead, Moses and Elijah, as servants, stood by the Lord in His glory; hence it follows, "Behold two men were talking with him. And they were Moses and Elijah appearing in majesty." For it was fitting for those seeing the glory and confidence of their fellow servants, to admire indeed the holy condescension of the Lord, to love those who had labored before them, and looking to the pleasantness of future blessings, to be more strengthened for their labors. For whoever should know the reward of his labors will endure them more easily.[49]

49. "Videns autem diabolus orationibus refulgentem, recordatus est Moysi, cuius glorificata est facies. Sed Moyses quidem glorificatur extrinsecus adveniente gloria, Dominus autem ex innato gloriae divinae fulgore: cum enim secundum hypostasis unionem, una et eadem sit gloria Verbi et carnis, transfiguratur, non quasi accipiens quod non erat, sed quod erat manifestans discipulis: unde secundum Matthaeum dicitur, quod transfiguratus est coram eis, et quod facies eius refulsit ut sol: quod enim est in sensibilibus sol, hoc in intelligibilibus Deus: et sicut sol, qui est lucis fons, de facili videri non potest, lux autem eius ex eo quod ad terram pervenit aspicitur, sic facies Christi intensius refulget ut sol, vestimenta autem eius dealbantur ut nix; unde sequitur **Et vestitus eius albus refulgens;** illustratus scilicet per divinae lucis participationem. His autem ita se habentibus, ut unus ostenderetur Dominus novi et veteris testamenti, et haereticorum ora obturentur, et fides fiat resurrectionis, necnon qui transfigurabatur vivorum et mortuorum Dominus crederetur; Moyses et Elias tamquam famuli assistunt Domino in gloria; unde sequitur **Ecce duo viri loquebantur cum illo; erant**

Although this passage from John of Damascus comments on a number of elements from the first part of Luke's transfiguration story, the section of this passage that will become important for Thomas' later theology of the transfiguration addresses the glory that radiated from Christ. Christ's glory was divine, not the gift of a glorified body or a quality similar to it. Because of the hypostatic union, Christ's humanity naturally shares in the Son's glory. That is why the transfiguration merely reveals "what He was." Unfortunately, this passage fails to explain how Christ's body can share the glory of the Son and be passible simultaneously. Thomas will fully address this question, which was of primary interest to the theologians of the thirteenth century, in his later masterpiece, the *Summa theologiae.*

Super Evangelium S. Matthaei lectura

Despite some uncertainty about the precise date of Thomas' commentary on Matthew, the consensus on this work is that it derives from Thomas' second period of teaching at the University of Paris and was probably compiled between 1269 and 1270.[50] It exists in the form of *reportationes* or notes taken during Thomas' lectures and filled out into the form of a commentary at a later time. Although all the manuscripts of this work are incomplete or contain spurious material, combining the manuscripts will allow a complete edited text to be produced in the future.[51] In any case, the edition by R. Cai remains the

autem Moyses et Elias visi in maiestate. Oportebat enim videntes conservorum gloriam et fiduciam, mirarentur quidem pium dominicum descensum, zelarent vero eos qui prius laboraverant, visuri amoenitatem futuorum bonorum, et magis fortificarentur in laboribus: nam qui laborum noverit emolumenta, labores facilius tolerabit" (bold face is the editor's), *Catena aurea in quator Evangelia,* 2:131–32.

50. For a review of the evidence, see Torrell, *Saint Thomas Aquinas, vol. 1: The Person and His Work,* 55–56. See also Jeremy Holmes, "Aquinas' *Lectura in Matthaeum,*" in *Aquinas on Scripture: An Introduction to His Biblical Commentaries,* edited by Thomas G. Weinandy, Daniel A. Keating, and John P. Yocum, 73–97 (London: T & T Clark International, 2005); and Thomas Prügl, "Thomas Aquinas as Interpreter of Scripture," in *The Theology of Thomas Aquinas,* edited by Rik van Nieuwenhove and Joseph Wawrykow, 386–415 (Notre Dame, Ind.: University of Notre Dame Press, 2005), 389.

51. See H. V. Shooner, "La *Lectura in Matthaeum* de S. Thomas (Deux fragments inédits et la *Reportatio* de Pierre d'Andria)," *Angelicum* 33 (1956): 121–42; J. P. Renard, "La Lectura super Matthaeum V, 20–28 de Thomas d'Aquin (Edition d'après le ms. Bâle, Univ. Bibl. B.V. 12),"

standard text for Thomas' commentary on Matthew's transfiguration narrative.

The first thing to notice about Thomas' Matthew commentary is the *divisio textus*. Thomas asserts that the Gospel of Matthew primarily addresses Christ's humanity,[52] and he divides the Gospel into three parts: one on the entrance *(ingressu)* of Christ's humanity into the world (Matthew 1–2); one on the course *(processu)* of His humanity in the world (Matthew 3–20); and one on His departure *(egressu)* from the world (Matthew 21–28).[53] Compare these terms, which Thomas uses in this *divisio textus*, with those in his division of the second part of the *Summa theologiae*'s treatise on Christ: "We will consider those things which pertain to His entry into the world, secondly, those things which pertain to the course of His life in the world, thirdly, what pertains to His departure from the world, and fourthly, those things which pertain to His exaltation after this life."[54] The difference between the *divisio textus* of Matthew's Gospel and Thomas' outline of the second part of the treatise on Christ is that Thomas, in the latter, distinguishes between *egressus* and *exaltatio*, which is found in Matthew 28; but Thomas fails to make that distinction in the commentary on Matthew.[55] Despite this slight difference, the synoptic gospels, and the Gospel of Matthew in particular, constitute the primary lens through which Thomas views Christ's humanity.

The pericope that describes Christ's transfiguration is located within the section of Matthew pertaining to the progress of Christ's humanity in the world. This section, however, contains a number of different but

Recherches de théologie ancienne et médiévale 50 (1983): 145–90; Louis-Jacques Bataillon, "La Diffusione Manoscritta e Stampata dei Commenti Biblici de San Tommaso d'Aquino," *Angelicum* 71 (1994): 579–90.

52. See Thomas Aquinas, *De commendatione et partitione sacrae Scripturae*, in *Opuscula theologica*, edited by R. A. Verardo, 2 vols. (Turin, Italy: Marietti, 1954), 1:441–43, n. 1208.

53. *Super Evangelium S. Matthaei lectura*, edited by R. Cai, (Turin, Italy: Marietti, 1951), 1, lect. 1, n. 11 (Henceforth, *Super Matth.*). For more on the *divisio textus*, see Margeherita Maria Rossi, "La 'divisio textus' nei commenti scritturistici di S. Tommaso d'Aquino: Un procedimento solo esegetico?" *Angelicum* 71 (1994): 537–48.

54. "considerabimus de his quae pertinent ad ingressum eius in mundum; secundo, de his quae pertinent ad processum vitae ipsius in hoc mundo; tertio, de exitu ipsius ab hoc mundo; quarto, de his quae pertinent ad exaltationem ipsius post hanc vitam," *Summa theologiae*, III, q. 27, prol.

55. See Holmes, "Aquinas' *Lectura in Matthaeum*," 79.

related elements. The following is a basic outline of Thomas' divisions of this second section, including the transfiguration's place in the scheme:

I. Matthew 3–20—The progress of Christ's humanity in the world (or Christ's teaching)
  A. Matthew 3–4—Preparation for Christ's teaching
  B. Matthew 5–20—The teaching itself
    1. Matthew 5–12—Christ's teaching
    2. Matthew 13–16—The power of His teaching
    3. Matthew 17–20—The end to which His teaching leads
      i. Matthew 17—The revelation of future glory in the transfiguration
      ii. Matthew 18–20—How it is attained

The *divisio textus* of the transfiguration narrative itself, which Thomas sees as comprising all of Matthew 17, is somewhat obscured by the text of the commentary, which seems to be defective as it currently stands. According to the introduction to the commentary on Matthew 17, Thomas says that, regarding the transfiguration, Matthew's Gospel "first shows how [the future glory] was revealed in the transfiguration, and secondly, in chapter eighteen, how it may be attained. . . . Concerning the first there are two parts. First, the future glory is revealed, secondly, [Christ] orders secrecy, and thirdly [the disciples] raise a question."[56] There are two problems here. The first problem is that the text

56. Here is the opening of the commentary on chapter 17: "In parte praecedenti ostendit virtutem doctrinae evangelicae etc., hic ostenditur finis, qui est gloria futura: et circa hoc duo facit.

> Primo ostendit quomodo demonstrata est in transfiguratione;
> secundo quomodo perveniri possit ad eam, in xviii cap. . . .
> Circa primum duo.

Primo demonstratur futura gloria; secundo praecipit celationem; tertio ponit dubitationem . . ." *Super Matth.*, 17, lect. 1, n. 1417. However much one might try to make sense of this conundrum, there does seem to be a relatively small problem with the text. R. Cai tries to interpret "circa hoc duo facit," as pertaining to the two divisions of Matthew 17. The problem with that interpretation is that immediately afterward, Thomas divides Matthew 17 from Matthew 18. Cai's perplexity is apparent in his synoptic chart of Matthew 17 (415), where he places a question mark before the second main subdivision of Matthew 17 with "n. 1453" following in italics, signifying the beginning of the second half of Matthew 17. In the text of the commentary, Thomas fails to use his usual phrases to summarize a previous section, and yet it seems clear that he sees Matthew 17:14–26 as a unit distinct from Matthew 17:1–13.

seems to say that there are two parts to the transfiguration pericope, and then it lists three parts. The second problem is that the three parts constitute only the first half of Matthew 17. Thomas sees these three parts of Matthew 17 as distinct from the second half of Matthew 17, which describes Christ's healing the demon-possessed boy, Christ's announcing His crucifixion, and a question regarding Jesus paying taxes.

Since Thomas clearly seems to think that Matthew 17 has two subdivisions, the text should describe one larger division between the two parts of Matthew 17 and a subdivision of the second part of Matthew 17, as well. Regarding the two subdivisions of the chapter, the text should perhaps say, "First, the future glory is manifested in the transfiguration, and secondly the text describes 'the tranquility of glory, which is assailed by demons, and the disturbance of men.'"[57] The second subdivision of Matthew 17, like the first, has three parts, namely the healing of the boy, the prediction of the crucifixion, and the question concerning taxes.

Although Thomas considers all of Matthew 17 as pertaining to Christ's glory, only the first of the chapter's six smaller subdivisions deals directly with Christ's transfiguration. This subdivision addresses the circumstantial details pertaining to the transfiguration, the transfiguration itself, and the effect of the transfiguration, and Thomas' comments on these three parts show much dependence on the *Catena aurea*. The dependence of Thomas' Matthew commentary on the *Catena aurea*, especially the gloss on Matthew, is most manifest in the first and third smaller subdivisions, which deal with the circumstances and the effect of the transfiguration, respectively. Thomas includes roughly ten comments on the first section and approximately eleven on the third section; of these twenty-one comments, eighteen are direct quotations or paraphrases from the *Catena aurea*.

The second section, however, on the transfiguration itself, is largely independent of the *Catena aurea*. Of approximately thirty-one comments, only about thirteen come from the *Catena aurea*. One of the reasons for this difference is that in this section Thomas includes the

57. The quoted words are taken from Thomas' own words, from the opening of the commentary on Matthew 17:14ff.: "tranquillitatem gloriae, quae impugnatur per oppressionem daemonum, et turbationem hominum," *Super Matth.*, 17, lect. 2, n. 1453.

opinions of "others" as well as some short *quaestiones,* almost all of which pertain to Christ's *claritas.* The commentary, for example, on Matthew 17:2, "And His face shone like the sun," consists of an introductory explanation followed by three of these short questions. In the introductory explanation, Thomas says that, in the transfiguration, Christ

revealed the future glory, where bodies will be bright and radiant. And this clarity was not from the essence [of His body], but from the clarity of the inner soul filled with grace. Isaiah 53:8 says, "Then your light will break forth like the morning," and a little later, "and the glory of the Lord will gather you." Hence there was a certain refulgence in the body. For the soul of Christ was beholding God and was beyond all clarity from the first moment of His conception; as it says in John 1:14, "We have seen His glory."[58]

This description of Christ's clarity manifests some development from the teaching in the *Scriptum.* In the *Scriptum,* Thomas taught that Christ's soul was glorious, but it did not communicate clarity to the body because, as the form of the body, it was still passible. The clarity occurs because divine power effects a miracle. In this passage, however, Thomas argues that the clarity of the transfiguration comes from Christ's soul, which was glorified by its vision of God.[59] The glorified soul then, full of love, radiates clarity into the body.

Thomas further explains this process by comparing Christ's body and soul to those of the saints. The following is the remainder of the commentary on Christ's face shining "like the sun":

If, therefore, the clarity in the other blessed ones flows from the soul to the body, why does it not do so in Christ, who was God and man?

It must be said that because He was God, the order of human nature was in His power. This order, however, is such that its parts should communicate with one another, so that, in the case of a body having been wound-

58. "Hic futuram gloriam revelavit, ubi erunt corpora clara et splendentia. Et haec claritas non erat ab essentia, sed ex claritate interioris animae plenae caritate; Is. chap. lviii, 8: *Tunc erumpet quasi mane lumen tuum,* et sequitur, *Et gloria Domini colliget te.* Unde erat quaedam refulgentia in corpore. Anima enim Christi videbat Deum, et super omnem claritatem a principio suae conceptionis; Io. i, 14: *Vidimus gloriam eius," Super Matth.,* 17, lect. 1, n. 1424 (italics are the editor's).

59. See *III Sent.,* d. 16, q. 2, a. 2.

ed, there is shared suffering in the soul, and the body likewise is affected by the soul. But this order was subject to Christ. Thus, there was perfect joy in the superior part, which did not go beyond it; hence he was both perfect wayfarer (*viator*) and perfect *comprehensor*. Hence when He wished, there was no outpouring, but whenever He did wish, there was an outpouring, and then He appeared radiant.

But was there no gift in Christ? Some affirm that He received all the gifts while He was on earth, the gift of subtlety during the nativity, the gift of agility while He walked on the waves, the gift of clarity here, and the gift of impassibility while He administered the sacrament of the altar.

I do not believe this, however, because a gift is a certain property of glory itself. Hence it was by divine power that He walked on the sea and shone brightly, because a gift of glory is not fitting for a wayfarer, but it has some likeness since "His face shone like the sun," and Apocalypse 1:16 says, "His face was as the sun shining in its power."

But someone may object that the just will shine like the sun. Christ's splendor, therefore, will not be greater than that of others. I concur, but He is compared to the sun, because, among sensible objects, there is nothing brighter with which to compare Him.[60]

There are three distinct questions here. The first question addresses how Christ is different from the saints, since the souls of both Christ and the saints see God. Because of this vision, glory overflows from

60. "Si ergo in beatis aliis derivatur claritas ab anima ad corpus, quare non in Christo qui Deus erat et homo?

Dicendum quod quia Deus erat, ordo humanae naturae erat in sua potestate. Hic autem est ordo quod partes sibi communicent, ut laeso corpore, compassio sit in anima, et ex anima afficiatur corpus. Sed hic ordo subiectus erat Christo. Unde ita perfectum erat gaudium in parte superiori quod non egrediebatur extra: unde et perfecte erat viator, et perfecte comprehensor. Unde quando volebat, non fiebat reflexus, sed quando volebat, reflexus fuit, et apparuit splendidus.

Sed nonne dos fuit in Christo? Quidam dicunt quod sic, et quod omnes dotes accepit in via: dotem subtilitatis in nativitate, agilitatis in undarum calcatione, claritatis hic, impassibilitatis in administrando sacramentum altaris.

Ego autem hoc non credo, quia dos est quaedam proprietas ipsius gloriae. Unde quod super mare ambulavit, quod resplenduit, totum fuit ex virtute divina, quia dos gloriae repugnat viatori, sed habuit aliquam similitudinem, quia **resplenduit facies eius sicut sol;** Apoc. i, 16: *Facies eius sicut sol refulget in virtute sua*.

Sed potest obiici, quia iusti fulgebunt sicut sol. Ergo splendor Christi maior non erit aliis.

Dico quod sic. Sed quia in his sensibilibus non est clarius cui possit comparari; ideo soli comparatur," *Super Matth.*, 17, lect. 1, nn. 1425–26 (bold face and italics are the editor's).

the soul to the body; so it would seem that Christ's soul and the souls of the saints are the same in that regard. Thomas' answer here is similar to his subsequent response in the *Summa theologiae,* namely that Christ has the power to withhold the glory of the soul from reaching the body. In the *Summa theologiae,* however, Thomas will introduce the category of "divine dispensation" to explain that the glory of Christ's soul naturally proceeds to the body. In the case of Christ, a "divine dispensation" prevents that from happening. Christ nevertheless possesses the power to dispense from the dispensation, so to speak, and to allow the glory to affect His body. The teaching from the Matthew commentary is not markedly different, but in this text the passage suggests that it is simply the subjection of human nature to Christ, as God, that prevents the glory of His soul from proceeding to the body. In any case, the teaching on Christ's clarity in the Matthew commentary is more complex than in the *Scriptum,* where neither the subjection of Christ's human nature to His divinity is mentioned, nor is the outpouring of clarity from His glorified soul.

The second question is whether Christ's clarity during the transfiguration is a "gift." Thomas' teaching on this question was consistent throughout his teaching career, but his approach to it varied. In the *Scriptum,* Thomas distinguished between the acts and the habits of a glorified body in order to make sense of the teaching ascribed to Hugh of St. Victor, that Christ did assume the gifts of a glorified body while on earth. In the *Scriptum,* Thomas admitted the testimony of Hugh's teaching, but qualified it significantly, saying that in Christ the *viator* there was no habit of a glorified body. Christ assumed the acts of the gifts, but not the habits themselves.[61] In the text from Thomas' commentary on Matthew, there is no distinction between act and habit. Thomas simply says that Christ did not have the gifts of a glorified body during his earthly life. The miracles that pertained to His body were effected by divine power, and during those miracles, Christ's body possessed some "likeness" to the gifts. Although this brief passage lacks the distinctions and sophistication, which Thomas marshals in the *Summa theologiae,* this teaching, including a clear rejection of

61. See *III Sent.,* d. 16, q. 2, a. 2.

the opinion asserting the assumption of gifts by Christ, is an outline of the later teaching in the Third Part.

The third question, never explicit in either the *Scriptum* or the *Summa theologiae*, asks whether Christ's clarity will be greater than that of the saints. In the *Scriptum*, Thomas mentions that the transfiguration "manifested the clarity which He promised would be in the saints after the future resurrection, according to Matthew 13:43, 'The just will shine like the sun in the kingdom of their Father.'"[62] While Thomas does not elaborate on the implications of this verse from Matthew 13, one interpretation could be that the clarity of the transfiguration is the same as that of the glorified saints. Although other passages in the *Scriptum* seem to affirm not only this interpretation, but also that the clarity of the glorified Christ and of the saints will be equal, there is no clear teaching. One must assemble a number of related texts, which together may be interpreted in several ways.[63]

There is, however, some confirmation of that interpretation in the commentary on Matthew, since Thomas says that in the future Christ's glory will be the same as that of the saints. This interpretation is based on the fact that both Christ and the saints are compared to the brightness of the sun. In the commentary on that verse (Matthew 13:43), however, Thomas acknowledges that the brightness of the saints' bodies will be greater than that of the sun. In addition to the reason for the comparison, namely that the sun was the brightest object with which to compare the radiance of Christ's face, Thomas gives another reason: "It is fitting [to compare the just] with the sun, because just as the sun does not change, neither do the just change, as Ecclesiasticus 27:12 says, 'A holy man remains in wisdom as the sun, but a fool is changed as is the moon.'"[64] Both Christ and the saints will have bodily glory, which exceeds that of the sun, but the basis for their equality seems to be the

62. "ostensionem claritatis quam promiserat in Sanctis post resurrectionem futuram, dicens: '*Fulgebunt justi tamquam sol in regno patris eorum*,' Mat. xiii, 43," *III Sent.*, d. 16, q. 2, a. 1.

63. For related texts, see *III Sent.*, d. 15, q. 2, a. 1, qc. 3; d. 18, a. 4; d. 21, q. 2, aa. 3–4; *Commentum in quartum librum Sententiarum magistri Petri Lombardi*, in *Opera omnia*, t. 7/2 (Parma, Italy: Typis Petri Fiaccadori, 1858), IV, d. 44, q. 2, a. 4; d. 48, q. 2, aa. 3–4; d. 49, q. 4.

64. "Convenit autem cum sole, quia sicut sol non mutatur, sic nec iustus; Eccli. xxvii, 12: *Homo sanctus in sapientia manet sicut sol; stultus autem ut luna mutatur*," *Super Matth.*, 13, lect. 3, n. 1185 (italics are the editor's).

beatific vision they share. The glory of Christ's soul is the effect of the beatific vision and will overflow to the body at the resurrection; the same effect will occur for the saints.[65]

Thomas fails to provide a complete argument for this equality of bodily glory in Christ and in the saints in the Matthew commentary, and in the *Summa theologiae* he will revise this teaching significantly. No definitive hint of a change is found in the *Summa theologiae* until III, q. 45, a. 2, where Thomas associates the glory of the saints with the glory reflected in Christ's garments. While the association of garments with the saints was common in the history of scriptural exegesis, Thomas' contemporaries tended to interpret the glory of the garments to signify that the saints would receive their glory from Christ, as the garments received glory from Christ's face.[66] Thomas uses the garments to signify that, as well, but he also means to say that Christ's glory will be brighter than that of the saints, as "the radiance of the snow is surpassed by the splendor of the sun."[67] The saints are now associated with the snow rather than the sun mentioned in Matthew 13. The premises of this teaching will be examined more fully below.[68]

Several elements of Thomas' Matthew commentary are of interest. First, Thomas' division of Matthew's Gospel closely parallels the second part of the *Summa theologiae*'s treatise on Christ. Second, the *divisio textus* of Matthew 17 lacks explicit articulation in the Cai edition.

65. For more texts on this issue, see Thomas Aquinas, *Compendium theologiae*, in *Opera omnia iussu Leonis XIII P.M. edita*, t. 42 (Rome, 1979), chaps. 168, 237; *De articulis fidei et ecclesiae sacramentis*, in *Opera omnia iussu Leonis XIII P.M. edita*, t. 42 (Rome, 1979), 245–257; *In symbolum apostolorum*, in *Opuscula theologica*, edited by R. M. Spiazzi, vol. 2 (Turin, Italy: Marietti, 1954), a. 14; *Summa contra gentiles*, in *Opera omnia iussu Leonis XIII P.M. edita*, t. 15 (Rome, 1930), IV, chap. 86.

66. See Hugh of St. Cher, *Postilla super Marcum*, fol. 104rb; John of La Rochelle, *Postilla super Matthaeum*, Ms. Oxford, New College 48, fol. 180ra, and *Postilla super Marcum*, Ms. Milan, Ambrosiana D471 inf., fol. 43rb; Albert the Great, *De resurrectione*, 269, and *Enarrationes in Marcum*, 542.

67. "candor nivis superatur a splendore solis," *Summa theologiae*, III, q. 45, a. 2. Hugh of St. Cher actually says something similar in his *Postilla super Matthaeum* (fol. 59rb), but his comments refer to the superiority of the glory of Christ's divinity over that of His humanity. See also Bruce D. Marshall's comments on the role of the Holy Spirit in this passage; "What Does the Spirit Have to Do?" in *Reading John with St. Thomas Aquinas*, edited by M. Dauphinais and M. Levering (Washington, D.C.: The Catholic University of America Press, 2005), 66–69.

68. See pp. 235–36.

Third, although Thomas' discussion of Christ's clarity is incomplete, insofar as the role of Christ's divine nature in communicating clarity remains unaddressed, it nevertheless more closely resembles the discussion of the *Summa theologiae,* written shortly after Thomas gave his lectures on Matthew, than that of the *Scriptum.* Finally, and perhaps even more interestingly, is the absence of the Greek authorities, whom Thomas cited in the earlier *Catena aurea* on Luke. This omission may not be surprising, since the commentary on Matthew relies heavily in places on the *Catena aurea* on Matthew, but one wonders why Thomas did not bring insights from his research on the Eastern Fathers to bear on his later exegesis of Matthew's Gospel. Regardless of whether this was Thomas' decision or that of his scribes, Peter d'Andria and Leodegar of Besançon, the Matthew commentary lacks insights that Thomas had already gained and would later apply in the *Summa theologiae.* The textual problems, which remain in the absence of a critical edition of the Matthew commentary, coupled with an incomplete teaching regarding the clarity of Christ's transfigured body, invite us to consider Thomas' teachings in his *Summa theologiae.*

Summa theologiae

Thomas' fullest teaching on Christ's transfiguration is in the *Summa theologiae.* While his treatment is by no means as complete as that of John of La Rochelle's question in the *Summa fratris Alexandri,* Thomas considers a number of involved questions in the Third Part of the *Summa.* The simultaneous meditation on Christ's glory and suffering, which Thomas manifests in the *Scriptum,* is even more apparent in the *Summa theologiae,* and the adumbrations found in the Matthew commentary are filled out here considerably.

Although numerous scholars have discussed the structure of the *Summa,*[69] a few points are necessary to create the context for Thomas'

69. See Marie-Dominique Chenu, "Le plan de la Somme théologique de S. Thomas," *Revue Thomiste* 47 (1939): 93–107, and *Toward Understanding Saint Thomas,* translated by A.-M. Landry and D. Hughes (Chicago: H. Regnery, 1964), 297–325; André Hayen, "La structure de la Somme théologique et Jésus," *Sciences ecclésiastiques* (1960): 59–82; Ulrich Horst, "Über die Frage einer Heilsökonomischen Theologie bei Thomas von Aquin. Ergebnisse und Prob-

question on Christ's transfiguration. In addition, some effort is required to situate this question within the overall structure of the *Summa*, since, like John of La Rochelle's question on the transfiguration in the *Summa fratris Alexandri*, Thomas' question is located within a complex series of textual divisions and subdivisions. Perhaps the most elementary point to be made is that Thomas' question on the transfiguration occurs in the Third Part of the *Summa*, which is "on Christ, who, as man, is the way for us to strive for God."[70] The Third Part of the *Summa* is itself divided into three sections: the first section is "on the Savior Himself; the second concerns His sacraments, by which we obtain salvation; and the third is on the goal of immortal life, to which we come through Him by rising again."[71] Thomas divides the section on Christ into one group of questions on the "mystery of the Incarnation" and another on "those things which were done and suffered by our Savior, that is, God incarnate."[72]

Thomas places his question on the transfiguration within this latter part (III, qq. 27–59), which Jean-Pierre Torrell rightly notes should not be considered a "life of Jesus."[73] Questions 27 through 39 treat Christ's coming into the world, questions 40 through 45 pertain to Christ's life, questions 46 through 52 are on His departure from the world, and questions 53 through 59 concern His exaltation. In this four-fold schema of Christ's redemptive activity, Thomas situates

---

leme der neueren Forschung," *Münchener Theologische Zeitschrift* 12 (1961): 97–111; Ghislain Lafont, *Structures et méthode dans la Somme théologique de saint Thomas d'Aquin* (Paris: Desclée, 1961), 102–4, 190–207, 216–58, 472–84; Jean-Marc Laporte, "Christ in Aquinas's *Summa Theologiae*: Peripheral or Pervasive?" *The Thomist* 67 (2003): 221–48; Otto Hermann Pesch, "Um den Plan der Summa Theologiae des hl. Thomas von Aquin. Zu Max Secklers neuem Deutungsversuch," in *Thomas von Aquin, bd. 1: Chronologie und Werkanalyse*, edited by K. Bernath, 411–37 (Darmstadt, Ger.: Wissenschaftliche Buchgesellschaft, 1978); Max Seckler, *Le Salut et l'histoire, la pensée de saint Thomas d'Aquin sur la théologie de l'histoire* (Paris: Cerf, 1967), 28–42; Torrell, *Saint Thomas Aquinas, vol. 1: The Person and His Work*, 150–53.

70. "de Christo, qui, secundum quod homo, via est nobis tendendi in Deum," *Summa theologiae*, I, q. 2, prol.

71. "de ipso Salvatore; secundo, de sacramentis eius, quibus salutem consequimur; tertio, de fine immortalis vitae, ad quam per ipsum resurgendo pervenimus," *Summa theologiae*, III, prol. Thomas never finished the second section, and he never began the third section.

72. "incarnationis mysterio . . . de his quae per ipsum Salvatorem nostrum, idest Deum incarnatum, sunt acta et passa," *Summa theologiae*, III, prol.

73. Torrell, *Saint Thomas Aquinas, vol. 1: The Person and His Work*, 261–66, and *Le Christ en ses mysteres: la vie et l'oeuvre de Jésus selon saint Thomas d'Aquin*, t. 1, 20–22. See also Torrell, *Saint Thomas Aquinas, vol. 2: Spiritual Master*, 131–35.

the transfiguration among the questions on Christ's life in the world. First is a consideration of how Christ lived, followed by one question each on His temptation and His teaching, and three questions on His miracles. Thomas examines Christ's transfiguration in the last of these three questions, the first two of which address Christ's miracles in general as well as different kinds of miracles. Although the question on the transfiguration is the last question on Christ's life in the world and on His miracles, its placement as the last in a series before the section on Christ's departure from the world is significant. Question 46 is on Christ's passion, and it begins a series of questions on Christ's suffering, death, and descent into hell. Thus even within the framework of a scholastic literary genre, Thomas uniquely organizes his questions so that from Christ's conception to His ascension into heaven, and more specifically, from His life and teaching in the world to His passion and death, the order of theological inquiry roughly follows the Gospel narrative. Furthermore, the literary placement of Thomas' question on the transfiguration emphasizes primarily the miraculous nature of the event and secondarily, its close relationship to Christ's suffering and death, two emphases that correspond to Thomas' treatment of the transfiguration in the *Scriptum*. At least from its placement in the literary structure of the *Summa theologiae*, however, Christ's transfiguration does not possess the same eschatological orientation that it did in the *Summa fratris Alexandri* and in Albert's *De resurrectione*.

A detailed analysis of the content of this question is in order to describe not only Thomas' most definitive treatment of the transfiguration, but also its development from his earlier *Sentences* commentary and his exegetical works. Question 45 consists of four questions, which address the fittingness of the transfiguration, the type of clarity in Christ's transfigured body, the fittingness of the witnesses, and the fittingness of the testimony of the Father's voice. Each question consists of three or four objections, a *sed contra* response, and corresponding replies to the objections. There is no separate question here on whether the clarity was real or imaginary, as there was in the *Scriptum*,[74] nor any effort to adduce the same number of arguments, which Thomas listed there.[75]

74. Thomas touches on this question in the second objection and corresponding reply of *Summa theologiae*, III, q. 45, a. 2.

75. For analyses of III q. 45, see Matthew Levering, *Christ's Fulfillment of Torah and Tem-*

Perhaps what is most striking at first glance is the prominence of "fittingness" in these questions.[76] Fittingness was scarcely mentioned in the *Scriptum*,[77] but here it plays an important role in three of the questions.[78] Also, although the question on clarity is present in all of the investigations during this period, and the question of the "witnesses" is also important, Thomas is singular in devoting a separate question to the Father's voice. Indeed the proportion between the examination of Christ's transfiguration *per se* and the examination of the "circumstances" is highly unusual in the *Summa*. Most of the theological investigations of the transfiguration during the middle of the thirteenth century concentrate on Christ's transfiguration and conclude the study with a brief question or two on the circumstantial details. In the *Summa theologiae*, however, Thomas gives almost equal space to the transfiguration and to the circumstantial details.

The first article of question 45 asks whether it was fitting for Christ to be transfigured. The three objections with which Thomas begins the article are typical of scholastic questions that ask about the definition of transfiguration. The first objection alleges the inappropriateness of real bodies changing shapes; the ability to change shapes is proper only for imaginary bodies. The second objection charges that, since figure and clarity are different species of quality, as Aristotle describes it, acquiring clarity should not be named "transfiguration." The final objection argues that since a glorified body possesses not only clarity, but three other gifts as well, a simple assumption of clarity should not merit the name "transfiguration."

Although the second objection, that figure and clarity are different kinds of quality, is not included in similar questions from the middle of the thirteenth century, it is Thomas' response that really distin-

ple: Salvation according to Thomas Aquinas (Notre Dame, Ind.: University of Notre Dame Press, 2002), 96–102; Torrell, *Christ en ses mysteres: la vie et l'oeuvre de Jésus selon saint Thomas d'Aquin*, t. 1, 280–301; Joseph P. Wawrykow, *The Westminster Handbook to Thomas Aquinas* (Louisville, Ky.: Westminster John Knox Press, 2005), 157–59.

76. Although Thomas does not use the term "convenientia" in this question, the adjective "conveniens" and adverb "convenienter" occur frequently.

77. See, however, *III Sent.*, d. 16, q. 2, a. 1, where Thomas does assert that "non est inconveniens id quod est in se opacum in intrinsecis, habere claritatem in superficie vel extensione . . . ."

78. For Thomas' use of the fittingness argument in this question, see Wawrykow, *The Westminster Handbook to Thomas Aquinas*, 157.

guishes this question from similar ones. His *sed contra* simply paraphrases Matthew 17:2, "He was transfigured before them." The fact of the transfiguration as recorded in Scripture affirms the question of fittingness, and the fact that it took place in the presence of Jesus' disciples constitutes a significant detail that provides Thomas the basis for his response, cited here in its entirety:

It must be said that the Lord, having foretold His passion to His disciples, exhorted them to follow the way of His suffering. In order for someone on a journey to proceed directly, however, he must foresee the end in some way, just as an archer will not shoot an arrow accurately unless he first sees the target he is aiming at. Hence Thomas said, in John 14, "Lord, we do not know where you are going, so how can we know the way?" And this is especially necessary when the way is difficult and rough, the journey wearisome, but the end delightful. Christ, however, underwent the passion in order to obtain glory, not only for His soul which He had from the first moment of His conception, but also for His body, according to Luke 24: "Christ ought to have suffered these things, and so enter into His glory." To which He brings those who follow in the footsteps of His passion, according to Acts 14: "through many tribulations we must enter into the kingdom of heaven." And therefore it was fitting that He manifest to His disciples the glory of His clarity (which is what being transfigured is), to which He will configure them, according to Philippians 3: "He will transform the body of our lowliness and make it like the body of His glory." For this reason, Bede says, on Mark: "By His loving foresight, He made it so that, by tasting for a short time the contemplation of eternal joy, they could endure adversity bravely."[79]

79. "dicendum quod Dominus discipulos suos, praenuntiata sua passione, induxerat eos ad suae passionis sequelam. Oportet autem ad hoc quod aliquis directe procedat in via, quod finem aliqualiter praecognoscat: sicut sagittator non recte iaciet sagittam nisi prius signum prospexerit in quod iaciendum est. Unde et Thomas dixit, Ioan. xiv, *Domine, nescimus quo vadis: et quomodo possumus viam scire?* Et hoc praecipue necessarium est quando via est difficilis et aspera, et iter laboriosum, finis vero iucundus. Christus autem per passionem ad hoc pervenit ut gloriam obtineret, non solum animae, quam habuit a principio suae conceptionis, sed etiam corporis, secundum illud Luc. ult.: *Haec oportuit Christum pati, et ita intrare in gloriam suam.* Ad quam etiam perducit eos qui vestigia suae passionis sequuntur: secundum illud *Act.* xiv, *Per multas tribulationes oportet nos intrare in regnum caelorum.* Et ideo conveniens fuit ut discipulis suis gloriam suae claritatis ostenderet (quod est ipsum transfigurari), cui suos configurabit: secundum illud *Philipp.* iii, *Reformabit corpus humilitatis nostrae, configuratum corpori claritatis suae.* Unde Beda dicit, *super Marcum: Pia provisione factum est ut, contemplatione semper manentis gaudii ad breve tempus delibata fortius adversa tolerarent,*" *Summa theologiae*, III, q. 45, a. 1 (italics here and in subsequent citations are the editors').

In this remarkable passage, Thomas links the very significance of the transfiguration to Christ's passion. The notion of the clarity of Christ's transfigured body as a sign of future glory is present, of course, but the abyss between *progressio* and *exaltatio* is pronounced. Christ's glory is not merely a static sign. It possesses a hortatory and thus dynamic function; it is a sign given so that the disciples may summon the fortitude necessary to follow Christ and to be conformed to Him through suffering.[80]

The notion of being *in via* contributes to the dynamism of the passage. Thomas uses the image of a journey to describe the missions of both Christ and His disciples. The end of the journey for Christ is glory in both soul and body. As Thomas explains in a later question, "having completed this mystery of Christ's passion and death, the soul immediately communicated its glory to the body which He took up again in the resurrection."[81] Thomas reiterates in numerous places[82] that Christ's soul possessed glory from the first moment of His conception, but Thomas' teaching of the co-assumed defects of Christ's soul allows for Christ's mind to experience constant beatitude while the sensitive powers of Christ's soul experience pain and suffering. With this understanding of Christ's humanity, the idea of Christ's journey is not merely one in which Christ's body "catches up" to His soul at the end of His mission. Thomas' teaching qualifies the effects of Christ's glorious soul in such a way that He can be both beatified and suffering simultaneously; or as Thomas expresses it elsewhere, He can be both *comprehensor* and *viator* simultaneously. Thus, through His passion, Christ can cause the glory experienced by the "superior part" of His soul to be shared by the "inferior part."[83]

On account of the Savior's redemptive activity, the disciples have the same end as their Master, namely glorification of both body and soul, but they possess nothing of Christ's glory in their earthly life and

80. Torrell has rightly emphasized the uniqueness of this dimension of the article (see *Christ en ses mysteres: la vie et l'oeuvre de Jésus selon saint Thomas d'Aquin*, t. 1, 280–82).

81. "peracto hoc mysterio passionis et mortis Christi, anima Christi statim in corpus, in resurrectione resumptum, suam gloriam derivavit," *Summa theologiae*, III, q. 54, a. 2.

82. See *Summa theologiae*, III, q. 7, aa. 1, 9–13; q. 9, a. 1; q. 14, aa. 1–2, 4; q. 15, aa. 1–7, 10; q. 34, aa. 1, 4; q. 46, aa. 7–8; q. 54, a. 2.

83. See *Summa theologiae*, III, q. 15, a. 10.

have little idea of the end of their discipleship, except that it will entail great suffering. The transfiguration, as a manifestation of glory, acts as a beacon on their earthly sojourn so that they can see beyond their looming martyrdom to the fullness of the kingdom of God beyond it. Christ manifests His glory, not only so that the disciples can muster the fortitude to imitate their Master's suffering, but also so that they have a clearer idea of the end of their journey and can thus direct themselves toward it more firmly and directly.[84]

Having shown why the transfiguration was appropriate given the nature of Christ's redemptive mission and His desire to have His disciples imitate Him, Thomas returns to the questions raised in the objections regarding what "transfiguration" signifies. Thomas denies that Christ's body changed shape or lost its substance and affirms, rather, that "transfiguration" signifies merely the assumption of clarity. Judging by the parts of the word "transfiguration," one could conclude that it means to change shape, but Thomas stresses the scriptural usage of the word (and its interpretation by Jerome) to show that it refers to the changing appearance of Christ's body, wrought by the assumption of clarity, and not to a changing outline of His body. Thomas' identification of transfiguration with the assumption of clarity also answers the objection that the word should be applied to any manifestation of a gift of a glorified body. Without denying that Christ possessed the other gifts during the transfiguration, Thomas claims that other miraculous events in Christ's life, such as His birth, His walking on water, and His escaping from the Jews,[85] do not merit the designation "transfiguration" because His appearance did not change at those times.

Thomas continues his exploration of Christ's glory in article two,

84. Although Thomas here uses the image of the archer shooting an arrow to show how the transfiguration aided the disciples in imitating Christ in His suffering, that image also evokes the larger journey of Creation's return to God. In the eleven other places in the *Summa* where Thomas appropriates that image, all have to do with creation, providence, or predestination. See *Summa theologiae*, I, q. 2, a. 3; q. 19, a. 4; q. 23, a. 1; q. 59, a. 3; q. 103, a. 1; q. 103, a. 8; I-II, q. 1, a. 2; q. 12, a. 5; q. 13, a. 2; q. 66, a. 1; II-II, q. 90, a. 3.

85. Interestingly, Thomas does not list the Last Supper as one of these events but substitutes Christ's escaping from the Jews for Pseudo-Hugh's claim that Christ manifested impassibility during the Last Supper.

on whether Christ's clarity was glorious. As in the *Scriptum,* where the second article on the transfiguration also addressed whether Christ's clarity was glorious, this article also seems superfluous at first. In the first article, Thomas linked the transfiguration with the glory obtained at the end of Christ's mission, and the answer to the question of the second article in the *Summa* here is even more explicit than in the first article on the transfiguration in the *Scriptum.* In the *Scriptum,* Thomas had claimed merely that Christ's clarity was similar to that of a glorified body; in the first article here, Thomas says explicitly that it was fitting for Christ to "manifest to His disciples the glory of His clarity."[86] Although the answer to this question should seem obvious from the outset, this article, of the four that comprise Thomas' question on the transfiguration, constitutes the heart of the question, and, as Cajetan's commentary on it indicates, it is the most complex article.[87]

As in the *Scriptum,* Thomas' first objection is the gloss from Bede that claims that the clarity of Christ's transfigured body was only similar to that of a glorified body. The second objection, based on another gloss from Bede, also constitutes the second objection from the first article on the transfiguration in the *Scriptum.* It says that the glory of Christ's transfigured body was an "imaginary representation of future beatitude"[88] and so was not glorious clarity itself. The third objection is also the same as the last objection of the second article on the transfiguration in the *Scriptum.* It states that since glorious clarity inheres only in a human body and because there was clarity in Christ's garments and in the cloud, the glory of the transfiguration was not truly glorious.

Although these objections are the same as those found in the *Scriptum,* Thomas' response here differs vastly. To convey a sense of the deep patristic inspiration of Thomas' articulation of Christ's glorious clarity in the *Summa theologiae,* the *sed contra* will be quoted along with the lengthy reply:

86. "discipulis suis gloriam suae claritatis ostenderet," *Summa theologiae,* III, q. 45, a. 1.

87. In his commentary on the other three articles, Cajetan does little more than summarize the question and answer. Article two, however, merits a lengthy exposition. See his commentary on *Summa theologiae,* III, q. 45, a. 2 in the Leonine edition.

88. "imaginaria representatione futurae beatitudinis," *Summa theologiae,* III, q. 45, a. 2. See also *III Sent.,* d. 16, a. 1.

On the contrary, Jerome says, on the passage from Matthew 17, "He was transfigured before them," "He appeared to the disciples just as He will appear on the day of judgment," and on the passage from Matthew 16, "Until they see the Son of man coming in His kingdom," Chrysostom says, "Wanting to show the glory in which He would come afterwards, He revealed it to them in this present life in so far as it was possible for them to learn it so that they might not grieve over the death of their Lord."

I answer that the clarity which Christ assumed in His transfiguration was the clarity of glory as to its essence, but not as to its mode of being. For the clarity of a glorified body is derived from clarity in the soul, as Augustine says in his *Letter to Dioscorus*. And similarly, the clarity of Christ's body in the transfiguration was derived from His divinity, as Damascene says, and from the glory of His soul. That the glory of Christ's soul did not overflow into His body from the first moment of His conception was the result of a certain divine dispensation that allowed Him to fulfill the mysteries of our redemption in a passible body, as was stated above. Nevertheless, the power of allowing the glory of His soul to flow into his body was not removed from Christ. And indeed, with respect to clarity, He did this in the transfiguration; but it is otherwise in a glorified body. For clarity overflows from the soul into a glorified body like a permanent quality influencing the body. Shining bodily, therefore, is not miraculous in a glorified body. But with respect to Christ's body in the transfiguration, clarity was derived from His divinity and from His soul, not in the manner of an immanent quality influencing the body, but rather in the manner of a transient passion, as when the air is illumined by the sun. That brightness, therefore, which appeared in Christ's body then, was miraculous, as was the fact that He walked on the waves of the sea. Hence Dionysius says, in *Letter IV to Caius*, "Christ excelled man in doing those things which are proper to man: and this is shown by the Virgin conceiving Him supernaturally and by the unstable water bearing the weight of material and earthly feet."

Therefore, it must not be asserted, as Hugh of Saint Victor said, that Christ assumed the gifts of clarity in the transfiguration, agility in walking on the sea, and subtlety when He came forth from the Virgin's closed womb, because "gift" signifies an immanent quality of a glorified body. Instead, He possessed miraculously those things which pertained to the gifts. The same is said, with respect to the soul, of the vision in which Paul saw God in a rapture, as was stated in the Second Part.[89]

89. "Sed contra est quod, super illud Matth. XVII, *Transfiguratus est ante eos*, dicit Hieronymus: *Qualis futurus est tempore iudicii, talis apostolis apparuit.* Et super illud Matth. XVII,

In the *Scriptum* Thomas cited only one patristic text, the passage from Pseudo-Dionysius appropriated here, while in this response Thomas marshals for support passages from four other Fathers, including John of Damascus' interpretation of the transfiguration, which plays a central role in shaping Thomas' own interpretation.

The two exegetical passages of the *sed contra* give the transfiguration an overtly eschatological orientation. The passage from Jerome, or one like it, was well known by Thomas' contemporaries. It links the appearance of the transfigured Christ with His appearance at the Last Judgment. Other scholastics, however, did not cite the passage from Chrysostom, which adds important details not provided by Jerome's interpretation. Chrysostom also links the transfiguration with the Last Judgment, but, emphasizing the recurring theme of *synkatabasis* or divine accommodation, so prevalent in the Eastern tradition, he notes that Christ revealed His glory to the extent that the disciples

---

Donec videant Filium Hominis venientem in regno suo, dicit Chrysostomus: *Volens monstrare quid est illa gloria in qua postea venturus est, eis in praesenti vita revelavit, sicut possibile erat eos discere: ut neque in Domini morte iam doleant.*

Respondeo dicendum quod claritas illa quam Christus in transfiguratione assumpsit, fuit claritas gloriae quantum ad essentiam, non tamen quantum ad modum essendi. Claritas enim corporis gloriosi derivatur ab animae claritate: sicut Augustinus dicit, in epistola *ad Dioscorum.* Et similiter claritas corporis Christi in transfiguratione derivata est a divinitate ipsius, ut Damascenus dicit, et a gloria animae eius. Quod enim a principio conceptionis Christi gloria animae non redundaret ad corpus, ex quadam dispensatione divina factum est, ut in corpore passibili nostrae redemptionis expleret mysteria, sicut supra dictum est. Non tamen per hoc adempta est potestas Christo derivandi gloriam animae ad corpus. Et hoc quidem fecit, quantum ad claritatem, in transfiguratione: aliter tamen quam in corpore glorificato. Nam ad corpus glorificatum redundat claritas ab anima sicut quaedam qualitas permanens corpus afficiens. Unde fulgere corporaliter non est miraculosum in corpore glorioso. Sed ad corpus Christi in transfiguratione derivata est claritas a divinitate et anima eius, non per modum qualitatis immanentis et afficientis ipsum corpus: sed magis per modum passionis transeuntis, sicut cum aer illuminatur a sole. Unde ille fulgor tunc in corpore Christi apparens miraculosus fuit: sicut et hoc ipsum quod ambulavit super undas maris. Unde Dionysius dicit, in Epistola IV, *ad Caium: Super hominem operatur Christus ea quae sunt hominis: et hoc monstrat Virgo supernaturaliter concipiens, et aqua instabilis materialium et terrenorum pedum sustinens gravitatem.*

Unde non est dicendum, sicut Hugo de Sancto Victore dixit, quod Christus assumpserit dotes claritatis in transfiguratione, agilitatis ambulando super mare, et subtilitatis egrediendo de clauso utero Virginis: quia dos nominat quandam qualitatem immanentem corpori glorioso. Sed miraculose habuit ea quae pertinent ad dotes. Et est simile, quantum ad animam, de visione qua Paulus vidit Deum in raptu: ut in Secunda Parte dictum est," *Summa theologiae,* III, q. 45, a. 2.

could perceive it. The reason Chrysostom gives for this revelation of glory, namely that the disciples might not be sorrowful at the death of their Lord, hearkens back to Thomas' response in the previous article and locates the transfiguration within the framework of the narrative of Matthew's Gospel.

If the *sed contra* conveys a primarily eschatological perspective, Thomas' response broadens this perspective to include the Incarnation and the miraculous nature of Christ's transfigured glory. Thomas does not repeat the distinction in the *Scriptum* between act and habit to articulate the derivation of Christ's glorious clarity. In his response, supported by references to both Augustine and John of Damascus, Thomas' distinction is between the essence of clarity and its mode of being. Thomas uses this distinction to make two important points: first, Christ's clarity in the transfiguration represents the clarity possessed by glorified bodies, and second, that the passible, non-glorified body of Christ possesses this glorious clarity in a way quite different from how glorified bodies possess it.

To support this position Thomas combines the testimonies offered by both Augustine and John of Damascus. Augustine says that the beatitude of the glorified soul imparts clarity to a glorified body; John of Damascus maintains that the glory of the transfigured Christ is derived from His divinity. Although Augustine and John Damascene are not referring to the same type of clarity, since Augustine is referring to the physical integrity of the saints after the Last Judgment and John of Damascus is describing the transfiguration, Thomas appropriates them ingeniously to make his argument. Both passages lack the fullness and precision of expression, which Thomas would like to have, so he combines the two passages in such a way that each supplies what the other is missing. Although Augustine notes the derivation of bodily clarity from the clarity of the soul, he lacks John's emphasis on Christ's divinity, while John's emphasis on Christ's divinity fails to recognize the soul as a medium through which Christ's clarity flows. Thomas' citation of Augustine provides a fuller account of Christ's humanity than would be gained from the reference to John of Damascus alone, and it gives the transfiguration an eschatological orientation as well. John, however, supplies the notion of dispensation, so crucial to Thomas' explanation of Christ's transfigured glory as a miracle, and gives the transfiguration an incarnational orientation by linking Christ's bodily glory with His divine nature.[90]

The concept of dispensation allows Thomas to maintain that although the glory of Christ's soul naturally overflows to His body, the divine will allowed the glory of Christ's soul not to pass into His body. This understanding makes it seem at first as if the true miracle is that Christ's body was not glorious from the moment of His conception.[91] In the cases of both His transfiguration and His glorification bodies, Christ retained the power to allow the glory of His soul to enter His body, but since His transfigured body remains passible while His glorified body is not, Thomas makes a distinction to explain the difference in the appearance of Christ's glory. In Christ's glorified body, clarity proceeded from His divinity and His soul and inhered in His body as an "immanent quality," while in His transfigured body, the clarity was like a "transient passion, as when the air is illumined by the sun."[92] This distinction between immanent quality and transient passion, developed from the distinction between act and habit, which Thomas made in the *Scriptum*, allows him to claim that the transfiguration was a miracle, since bodily glory is natural only to a glorified body. In this regard, the teachings in the *Scriptum* and in the *Summa theologiae* are very similar. Although Thomas uses different concepts, terms, and arguments in the later *Summa*, he still teaches that Christ's transfigured clarity was miraculous, since glorious clarity can exist in a non-glorified body only by divine power.

The concluding argument of the response, which denies that Christ assumed the gifts of a glorified body before the resurrection, is interesting because it contrasts with Thomas' earlier articulation in the *Scriptum*. In the *Scriptum*, Thomas cites Pseudo-Hugh's ascription of gifts to Christ's pre-glorified body and interprets it in such a way that

90. For more on the centrality of Augustine and John of Damascus in Thomas' conception of Christ's bodily properties, see how Thomas uses their writings in the opening article of the question on Christ's bodily defects (*Summa theologiae*, III, q. 14, a. 1).

91. For more on this perspective, see Cajetan's commentary on this article in the Leonine edition.

92. *Summa theologiae*, III, q. 45, a. 2.

Christ possesses only the "acts of those properties,"[93] not the properties themselves. Although Thomas qualifies significantly the meaning of the text attributed to Hugh, he does cite it in support of his position in favor of the glorious nature of Christ's transfigured clarity. Here in the *Summa* he cites it as an inadmissible opinion, worthy of condemnation, "It must not be maintained, as Hugh of St. Victor says, that Christ assumed the gifts"[94] of clarity, agility, subtlety, and impassibility.

What accounts for the change from the *Scriptum* to the *Summa,* and how significant is it? The change is one of emphasis and results from Thomas' firmer insistence on the meaning of "gift." In the *Scriptum,* "gift" properly signifies a property or habit of a glorified body, but it can also signify the acts of those properties. In q. 45 of the Third Part of the *Summa,* Thomas distinguishes not between habit and act, but between "immanent quality" and "transient passion." "Gift" now exclusively means an "immanent quality of a glorified body."[95] The clarity that radiates from Christ's transfigured body is not such a quality but more like a "transient passion," like air illumined by the sun, Thomas says. What Thomas in the *Scriptum* referred to as the acts of a property is now simply "those things which pertain to the gifts."[96] Thomas likens the transfiguration to the rapture of Saint Paul as described in 2 Corinthians 12:1–4. Saint Paul saw God through the light of glory, which he possessed in the manner of a transient passion.[97] The light of glory by which he beheld God remained only in his soul and did not overflow into his body the way it will in the glorified saints. This way of possessing light in the soul in the manner of a transient passion is, interestingly, also how the gift of prophecy acts.[98] It is true that in both the *Scriptum* and the *Summa* Thomas' denial of clarity as habit is the same. However, in the *Summa,* the absence of "act" language and the more precise definition of "gift," which results in the changed at-

93. "actus illarum proprietatum," *III Sent.,* d. 16, q. 2, a. 2.

94. "non est dicendum, sicut Hugo de Sanctore Victore dixit, quod Christus assumpserit dotes," *Summa theologiae,* III, q. 45, a. 2.

95. "qualitatem immanentem corpori glorioso," *Summa theologiae,* III, q. 45, a. 2.

96. "ea quae pertinent ad dotes," *Summa theologiae,* III, q. 45, a. 2.

97. See *Summa theologiae,* II-II, q. 175, a. 3.

98. See *Summa theologiae,* II-II, q. 171, a. 2.

titude toward Pseudo-Hugh's attribution of the gifts to Christ's body, allow for a clearer and more consistent explanation of Christ's transfigured glory than articulated in the *Scriptum*.

After this richly theological response, Thomas continues his teaching on Christ's clarity in the replies to the three objections. The replies to the first two objections (regarding the similarity of the transfigured clarity to that of a glorified body and regarding the "imaginary" character of that clarity) are similar to those given in the *Scriptum*, but the reply to the third objection is, at least in articulation, vastly different from its counterpart in the *Scriptum*. The third objection argued, rather weakly, that glorious clarity pertains to a human body alone, and since clarity was manifested in the bright cloud and in Christ's garments as well as in His body, the clarity of the transfiguration in all of those objects could not be glorious. The reply to the same objection in the *Scriptum* argued simply and succinctly that the splendor of Christ's transfigured body illumined His clothes.[99] There were not two different kinds of clarity or two sources of clarity, but one clarity, which appeared differently in Christ's body and in His clothes. The *Summa theologiae* basically provides this same answer, but Thomas articulates it much differently by providing anagogical interpretations of both Christ's garments and of the bright cloud. The glory manifested by Christ's garments during the transfiguration represents "the future clarity of the saints, which will be surpassed by the clarity of Christ, just as the brightness of the snow is surpassed by the brightness of the sun."[100] The bright cloud, Thomas says, can signify three things: the glory of the Holy Spirit, the power of the Father, or the clarity of the renewed world. In all three cases, what is signified will cover or overshadow the saints in their future glory.

Thomas' description of Christ's clarity as superior to that of the saints contrasts with his teaching in the *Scriptum* and in the Matthew commentary. The only clear precedent for the position argued in the *Summa*, namely that Christ's future glory would be greater than that

99. See *III Sent.*, d. 16, q. 2, a. 2.

100. "futuram claritatem sanctorum, quae superabitur a claritate Christi, sicut candor nivis superatur a splendore solis," *Summa theologiae*, III, q. 45, a. 2. This language is also found in Hugh of St. Cher's *Postilla super Matthaeum* (see above, pp. 23–24).

of the saints, was a gloss of Remigius of Auxerre in the *Catena aurea* on Matthew.[101] Why did Thomas modify or at least clarify his position? One apparent solution seems to involve Christ's merit, by which He attained his bodily glory and which is much greater than that of the saints.[102] However, Thomas teaches that Christ's merit is just another cause of His bodily glory (in addition to the overflow of glory from His beatified soul), not the source of glory that is greater than that of the saints. A more likely possibility, however, may be Thomas' introduction of John of Damascus' testimony and its relationship to exemplary causality.

Thomas applies exemplarity in the *Summa* to explain the relationship between Christ's resurrection and that of the saints. Thomas mentions this category in his discussion of Christ's resurrection, where he says, "since the cause is greater than the effect and the exemplar is greater than what is patterned after it, how much more glorious was the glory of Christ's resurrected body."[103] This exemplarity is rooted primarily in the hypostatic union, since it is this union that allows Christ's resurrection to be a model for the bodily glorification of the saints.[104] Although John of Damascus plays only a small role in the questions on the resurrection, his inclusion of Christ's divinity as a source for the glory of the transfigured Christ is taken over by Thomas in his articulation of how the bodily glory of the resurrected Christ and that of the blessed relate to one another.

After inquiring into the nature of Christ's clarity during the transfiguration, Thomas continues to ask questions regarding the other narrative details of the transfiguration. Thomas' allusion to some of the details of the transfiguration narrative in the reply to objection three of article two (e.g., the radiant garments, the bright cloud, and the reference to Peter's words) serves as a transition to articles three and four, both of which ask questions about additional elements of the transfiguration story. Article three inquires whether the witnesses

101. *Catena aurea in quator Evangelia,* I:259.

102. See *Summa theologiae,* III, q. 49, a. 6.

103. "cum causa sit potior causato et exemplar exemplato, multo magis corpus Christi resurgentis fuit gloriosum," *Summa theologiae,* III, q. 54, a. 2.

104. See *Summa theologiae,* III, q. 56, a. 1.

present at the transfiguration were fittingly chosen. Thomas' reintroduction of the fittingness motif, which began at the opening of the question, is unexpected, especially since it is absent in similar questions in the works of his predecessors and in his own *Scriptum.*[105] Indeed the entire series of objections, from the assertions that angels would have been more fitting witnesses, or that the deception involved in their assuming the personas of Moses and Elijah was unfitting, to the arguments that it would have been better to have all the prophets or all the disciples present, is unparalleled in previous scholastic reflections, which tended to focus on how and why Moses and Elijah appeared. Thomas does cite the impersonation argument in the *Scriptum,* but there he uses it to pose an objection against the truth of Christ's clarity.[106]

The fittingness motif is not the only unique element of this question. Because Thomas is concerned with more than simply explaining how and why Moses and Elijah appeared, he is able to expand the notion of "witnesses" to include Peter, James, and John. This understanding of "witnesses," which corresponds more closely with the transfiguration narratives than did the interpretations of Thomas' predecessors, allows Thomas to integrate the question more fully into the whole complex of questions on the transfiguration than do other treatments, where the question on witnesses seems to be more of an appendix that follows the more central questions on clarity.[107] Thomas achieves this integration by recalling the reason given for the transfiguration in article one: so that Christ "could show His glory to men, and arouse them to desire it."[108]

With this motive in mind, Thomas adduces two reasons why it was fitting for the two prophets and the three disciples to be present. The first reason is that, because Christ came to bring glory to all humanity, including those who came before His entry into the world

105. See especially *Summa fratris Alexandri,* III, pt. 1, t. 6, q. 2, tit. 1, chap. 8 and Albert's *De resurrectione,* 268.

106. See *III Sent.,* d. 16, q. 2, a. 1.

107. See especially Alexander of Hales, *De transfiguratione Christi,* nn. 29–40; and Guerric of St. Quentin, *Quaestio de transfiguratione Domini,* 86.

108. "ut gloriam suam hominibus ostenderet, et ad eam desiderandam homines provocaret," *Summa theologiae,* III, q. 45, a. 3.

and those who followed, it was appropriate for witnesses who both preceded Christ and who followed Him to be present. To explain the number of witnesses, Thomas makes an interesting and unique allusion to the Law of Moses. According to the Law, evidence is confirmed by two or three witnesses.[109] In the case of the transfiguration, Christ's bodily glory is confirmed by the evidence of the two witnesses of the Old Testament and the three witnesses of the New Testament.

To explain the presence of Moses and Elijah, Thomas draws primarily from John Chrysostom, but also from Hilary of Poitiers:

> As Chrysostom says on Matthew, "Moses and Elijah are brought forward for many reasons." The first is this: "Because the crowds said He was Elijah or Jeremiah or one of the prophets, He brings the chief prophets with Him, so that in this way at least the difference between the Lord and His servants might appear."
>
> The second reason is "that Moses gave the Law while Elijah was jealous for the glory of the Lord." Thus because they appear together with Christ, the calumny of the Jews is excluded whereby "they accused Christ of transgressing the Law, blasphemy, and usurping the glory of God to Himself."
>
> A third reason is that "by bringing with Him Moses, who is now dead, and Elijah, who is still living, He might show that He has the power of death and life and that He is judge of the dead and of the living."
>
> A fourth reason is because, as Luke says, "'they were speaking with Him about His departure, which was to be accomplished in Jerusalem,' that is of His passion and death. And therefore, in order to strengthen the souls of His disciples," He leads them into the midst of those who exposed themselves to death for God's sake; since Moses set himself against Pharaoh while risking death, and Elijah set himself against Ahab.
>
> The fifth reason is "because He desired that His disciples emulate the meekness of Moses and the zeal of Elijah."
>
> Hilary adds a sixth reason, namely to show that He had been foretold by the Law, which Moses gave, and by the prophets, among whom Elijah was the chief.[110]

109. Dt 19:15. See also Mt 18:16.

110. "Ad tertium dicendum quod, sicut Chrysostomus dicit, *super Matth., Moyses et Elias in medium adducuntur propter multas rationes*. Prima est haec. *Quia enim turbae dicebant eum esse Eliam vel Ieremiam aut unum ex prophetis, capita prophetarum secum ducit: ut saltem hinc appareat differentia servorum et Domini.*

Secunda ratio est, *quia Moyses legem dedit, Elias pro gloria Domini aemulator fuit.* Unde

In all of these reasons Christ either teaches His disciples some truth about Himself, or He exhorts them to greater virtue.

Why then, as the fourth objection insinuates, did Jesus not take all the disciples? The reason lies not so much in Thomas' citation of Chrysostom, who asserted that Peter, James, and John were greater than the rest of the disciples, but rather in the Dionysian-inspired notion that "sublime mysteries should not be explained to everyone immediately, but should be handed down through superiors to others in their proper turn."[111] "In their proper turn" refers to Christ's admonition that the disciples not tell anyone about what they had seen since Christ's suffering and death might then be a source of scandal.[112] Peter, James, and John were the privileged witnesses who, as Hilary says, "were witnesses of these spiritual events" when "they were filled with the Holy Spirit."[113] Only after the resurrection could they tell the other disciples about the glory they had seen on the mountain.

The fourth article of III, q. 45 considers whether the testimony of the Father's voice was fittingly heard. By now the fittingness theme is familiar, but what is unusual in comparison to other questions that investigate the transfiguration is that Thomas devotes an entire article to this question. Among Thomas' peers and predecessors, only Albert addressed this topic in the form of a *quaestio*, and his treatment was

---

per hoc quod simul cum Christo apparent, excluditur calumnia Iudaeorum *accusantium Christum tanquam transgressorem legis, et blasphemum Dei sibi gloriam usurpantem.*

Tertia ratio est, *ut ostendat se habere potestatem mortis et vitae, et esse iudicem mortuorum et vivorum, per hoc quod Moysen iam mortuum, et Eliam adhuc viventem, secum ducit.*

Quarta ratio est quia, sicut Lucas dicit, *'loquebantur cum eo de excessu, quem completurus erat in Ierusalem,' idest de passione et morte sua.* Et ideo, *ut super hoc discipulorum animos confirmaret,* inducit eos in medium qui se morti exposuerunt pro Deo: nam Moyses cum periculo mortis se obtulit Pharaoni, Elias vero regi Achab.

Quinta ratio est, *quia volebat ut discipuli eius aemularentur Moysi mansuetudinem, et zelum Eliae.*

Sextam rationem addit Hilarius: ut ostenderet scilicet se per legem, quam dedit Moyses, et per prophetas, inter quos fuit Elias praecipuus, esse praedicatum," *Summa theologiae,* III, q. 45, a. 3.

111. "alta mysteria non sunt omnibus exponenda immediate, sed per maiores suo tempore ad alios debent devenire," *Summa theologiae,* III, q. 45, a. 3.

112. *Summa theologiae,* III, q. 45, a. 3.

113. *"cum essent Spiritu Sancto repleti, tunc gestorum spiritualium testes essent," Summa theologiae,* III, q. 45, a. 3.

very brief.[114] While Albert's primary concern was to discern the hortatory significance of the Father's testimony, Thomas' interest is primarily eschatological.

The first three objections of article four compare the theophany accompanying the transfiguration with the theophany at Christ's baptism and claim that the testimony was either superfluous or unfitting. The fourth objection focuses on the capacity of the disciples to hear the voice and claims that the fear elicited by the Father's voice demonstrates their inability to withstand it.

The opening of Thomas' response, which begins by describing adoptive sonship, seems to evade the points made by the objections and in fact seems to have little to do with the question of the Father's testimony at all. Thomas says:

> It must be said that the adoption of the sons of God is through a certain conformity of image to the natural Son of God. Now this happens in two ways: first through the grace of this life, which is an imperfect conformity, and secondly through the glory of heaven, which will be perfect conformity, according to 1 John 3: "We are now sons of God, and what we shall be has not yet been revealed, but we know that when He shall appear we shall be like Him since we shall see Him as He is."[115]

Thomas' association of adoptive sonship with grace and glory deepens as he links the latter with Jesus' baptism and His transfiguration. Baptism signifies the entrance of grace into the human soul, and the transfiguration foreshadows "the clarity of future glory."[116] Since both the sacrament of baptism and the transfiguration signify the Christian's participation in Christ's sonship, Thomas finds it appropriate that both at Jesus' own baptism and at His transfiguration the Father testifies to the natural sonship of Christ in the words, "This is my beloved Son."[117] The moments of the Father's revelation of Christ's natu-

114. See Albert, *De resurrectione*, 268–69.

115. "dicendum quod adoptio filiorum Dei est per quandam conformitatem imaginis ad Dei Filium naturalem. Quod quidem fit dupliciter: primo quidem, per gratiam viae, quae est conformitas imperfecta; secundo, per gloriam, quae est conformitas perfecta; secundum illud I Ioan. iii: *Nunc filii Dei sumus, et nondum apparuit quid erimus: scimus quoniam, cum apparuerit, similes ei erimus, quoniam videbimus eum sicuti est*," *Summa theologiae*, III, q. 45, a. 4.

116. "claritas futurae gloriae," *Summa theologiae*, III, q. 45, a. 4.

117. Mt 3:17, 17:5; Mk 1:11, 9:7; and Lk 3:22, 9:35. The Greek text of Luke 9:35 does not contain the word ἀγαπητός, but Thomas' Vulgate text has *dilectus* in all six passages.

ral sonship are then not arbitrary coincidences, but rather, in Thomas' view, they are pivotal moments in the divine economy that God uses to strengthen and teach His followers.[118]

All of the replies to the objections confirm the unique centrality, which Thomas gives to adoptive sonship and its eschatological significance as symbolized in the transfiguration. Thomas interprets the fact that the Father speaks His testimony of the Son's natural generation on two separate occasions as showing that there are "different ways by which men can participate in the likeness of the eternal sonship."[119] The different forms taken by the Holy Spirit at Jesus' baptism and at the transfiguration represent different stages and dimensions of adoptive sonship. The dove of the baptism represents the innocence of the first regeneration, while the cloud of the transfiguration, which Thomas says is the "sacrament of the second regeneration," represents "the clarity of glory and the refreshment from every evil," which the elect will have in the resurrection.[120] Thomas also finds meaningful the sequence of the disciples' terror when they hear the voice of the Father followed by Christ's reassuring words, "Rise, and fear not."[121] The fear represents the exceedingly powerful character of the glory, which was present to the disciples, and Christ's words signify the healing that occurs when Christ brings his followers into glory.[122]

Jesus' words "Rise, and fear not," are the last words of the *Summa theologiae*'s question on the transfiguration, and their place and function are fitting when one considers the whole question. Thomas began the question on the transfiguration by linking it to Christ's passion, and he reinforces this connection by treating Christ's passion immediately after the question on the transfiguration. Associating Christ's transfiguration and suffering so closely allows Thomas to develop his

118. For more on natural and adoptive sonship, see, *Summa theologiae*, III, q. 23 and Luc-Thomas Somme's exposition of it in his *Fils adoptifs de Dieu par Jésus Christ* (Paris: J. Vrin, 1997), 53–90.

119. "diversum modum quo homines participare possunt similitudinem filiationis aeternae," *Summa theologiae*, III, q. 45, a. 4.

120. "ita etiam in transfiguratione, quae est sacramentum secundae regenerationis, tota Trinitas apparuit . . . in resurrectione dabit electis suis claritatem gloriae et refrigerium ab omni malo, quae designantur in nube lucida," *Summa theologiae*, III, q. 45, a. 4.

121. Mt 17:7.

122. *Summa theologiae*, III, q. 45, a. 4.

conviction that Christ's transfiguration possesses a hortatory function. Insofar as the transfiguration occurred after Christ had foretold His passion and because of the presence of Moses and Elijah, who had suffered for their fidelity to God, the transfiguration serves to encourage Jesus' disciples to "follow in the footsteps of His passion,"[123] so that they can be configured to His glorious image. The hortatory function of Christ's transfiguration applies to all Christians in every age, as well. As Thomas succinctly explains in article three, "Christ wished to be transfigured in order to show men His glory and to arouse them to a desire of it."[124] In the transfiguration, Christ's glory is most powerfully revealed, and although Christ revealed it initially only to Peter, James, and John, those three would later relate the "sublime mysteries" revealed there.[125] Although the question on the transfiguration closes with reflections on the eschatological significance of the transfiguration, Thomas maintains his emphasis on the hortatory function of the transfiguration to the end of the question. Once the disciples have witnessed the transfiguration, once they have heard Moses and Elijah talking with Jesus about His departure from the world, once they have heard the terrifying voice of the Father, Jesus strengthens the souls of his disciples with his words of comfort so that they can endure His passion and death, which are to come.

Conclusion

In these questions and commentaries on Christ's transfiguration, Thomas has shown himself to be an insightful theologian and a skillful exegete. He provides a thorough account of Christ's transfiguration and does so by making a number of important contributions to the thirteenth-century discussions of the transfiguration. First, Thomas is the first theologian to treat the transfiguration in a *Sentences* commentary. Second, although Thomas' position on Christ's transfigured clarity, namely that it was glorious clarity in act but not in habit, is

123. "vestigia suae passionis sequuntur," *Summa theologiae*, III, q. 45, a. 1.

124. "Christus transfigurari voluit ut gloriam suam hominibus ostenderet, et ad eam desiderandam homines provocaret," *Summa theologiae*, III, q. 45, a. 3.

125. See *Summa theologiae*, III, q. 45, a. 3.

similar to the teaching of John of La Rochelle, Thomas emphasizes the miraculous nature of the transfiguration more clearly than anyone before him. Another contribution is the *Catena aurea.* Thomas' retrieval of patristic sources in his running glosses on the synoptic gospels is more extensive than that of any of his predecessors or peers, including Hugh of St. Cher. Particularly valuable is Thomas' retrieval of Eastern sources between the compilation of the gloss on Matthew and the glosses on Mark and Luke. This engagement with Eastern sources clearly manifests itself in Thomas' position on Christ's clarity in the *Summa theologiae.* Thomas also makes a contribution to his teaching on Christ's transfiguration in his *Lectura* on Matthew. In this commentary, Thomas argues that Christ's clarity was derived from his glorified soul, a position he did not explicitly hold in the *Scriptum.*

In the *Summa theologiae,* Thomas makes a series of contributions to the scholastic discussion on Christ's transfiguration. The *Summa* is the only synthetic work from this period that situates a question on the transfiguration within a body of questions on Christ's life. John of La Rochelle and Albert the Great both wrote their questions for treatises on Christ's resurrection. This emphasis on the importance of Christ's earthly life allows the transfiguration to acquire a hortatory function, since Thomas emphasizes its role in confirming the faith of the disciples before Christ's suffering and death. Of all the theologians examined in this study, Thomas links the transfiguration to Christ's passion most closely. Another contribution is Thomas' use of fittingness arguments; no other author used this method of argumentation to articulate the significance of the transfiguration.

Perhaps the most important contribution of the *Summa theologiae,* however, is Thomas' teaching on Christ's clarity. Before the teaching in the *Summa,* John of La Rochelle had emphasized the importance of the union of Christ's body with the divine nature, and Albert had emphasized the capacity for clarity that Christ would realize after His resurrection. Thomas combines these two approaches, represented in the *Summa* by passages from John of Damascus and Augustine, respectively, and teaches that Christ's transfigured clarity is from His divine nature, through His soul. It is because Christ's soul experiences the beatific vision that Christ is a *comprehensor,* and it is this vision that allows Christ to communicate the clarity of His divinity to His human body. The concept of dispensation, which Thomas uses for the first time in the *Summa*, explains why Christ's soul did not always communicate this clarity. Thomas' teaching, unique because of its explicit articulation, argues that Christ would always have communicated this clarity to His body, except that His redemptive activity required Him to assume qualities, such as passibility, which would allow Him to die for the sins of humanity.

Thomas' insights, not only into Christ's transfiguration, but also into how the transfiguration fits into the whole economy of salvation, are what make his theology unique. Like his contemporaries, Thomas sees the transfiguration as an anticipation of future glory, but it is more than just a "proof" of the resurrection. Thomas recalls, more cogently than any theologian during this period, that the transfiguration occurred before the passion for an important reason. Christ wanted to strengthen the disciples' faith and to console them as they were about to enter a period of suffering. There is more at stake than simply reflecting on the metaphysics of the transfiguration and explaining how it could happen. Thomas' emphasis on fittingness arguments shows that his concern is more about why the transfiguration occurred. All these reasons make Thomas' teaching on Christ's transfiguration the most important of the thirteenth century.

CONCLUSION

This study set out to contribute to existing literature in the field of medieval Christology. This examination of the writings of seven mendicant authors attempted to show not only their teachings regarding Christ's transfiguration, but also where those teachings occurred and how they compared to one another. Researching each author individually has shed light on the Christology, exegesis, and spirituality of the thirteenth century. Examining their reflections on Christ's transfiguration collectively, as found in several genres of scholastic literature, has allowed their full teaching to emerge. In the case of some authors, such as Alexander of Hales, an examination of disputed questions and biblical commentaries proved to be not that insightful; for others, however, especially Albert the Great and Thomas Aquinas, this comparative study has produced many insights, since the genre of literature conditions, at least to some extent, what aspects of the transfiguration these authors reflect on. Also, if the research focus had remained only on the usual scholastic genres, such as the *summa* and the *Sentences* commentary, the notable interpretations of Christ's transfiguration by Hugh of St. Cher and Bonaventure would have been omitted. Incorporating as many genres of scholastic literature as possible and studying several authors within a brief time period has allowed important questions and concerns regarding Christ's transfiguration in the thirteenth century to emerge. Also, the chronological approach pursued here allows for comparisons not only between authors but also between the generations of theologians.

Before summarizing the particular contributions of each author, something must be said about the scholastic exploration of Christ's transfiguration in general. The most important development regarding the discussion of Christ's transfiguration during this period is, quite simply, that it is discussed at all. The non-exegetical genres of scholastic literature in the twelfth and early thirteenth centuries barely touch on it, and it is discussed only infrequently in scholastic theology after 1280. When one thinks of Christ's transfiguration, the profound theological reflections of Eastern Christianity immediately come to mind, and for good reason. In general, Western medieval scholastic theology reflected little on Christ's transfiguration; and yet, in this small window, between roughly 1230 and 1280, several mendicant theologians worked on explicating the meaning and significance of this beautiful and indeed perplexing event of Christ's life. Aside from the spiritual significance of the transfiguration, these theologians wished to address a number of important questions that pertained directly to Christ and the importance of His earthly life. If Christ was truly human, how could He be transfigured? Does that not compromise His full humanity? And what is transfiguration anyway? Would this event not compromise the truth of His passible human nature? Were His passion and death only an illusion? Why did the transfiguration occur when and where it did? And why were only Peter, James, and John invited to witness this marvelous event? How could anyone know that it was really Moses and Elijah who were present with Christ? And how does the condition of transfiguration relate to the resurrection?

Many of these questions were asked, although not always in these terms, in the non-exegetical genres of scholastic literature. Some questions, however, were more central than others. The common questions, which arise in the *summae, Sentences* commentaries, and disputed questions include the meaning of the word, "transfiguration," the relationship between Christ's glory or clarity at the transfiguration and after the resurrection, and the role of the hypostatic union in providing Christ's glory or clarity. The last question is the one that provides the foundation for the others, because it establishes how the supernatural qualities manifested by Christ in His earthly life are compatible with His passible human nature. Answering this question also helps to explain how Christ could have radiated light before His death, while choosing not to do so after His resurrection. The theology of Thomas Aquinas is especially helpful in this regard, not only because of his use of fittingness arguments (e.g., why it was fitting to manifest clarity during the transfiguration, while manifesting other qualities after the resurrection), but also because of the way he uses "dispensation" as a category to explain the simultaneity of beatific vision and the "co-assumed defects" that allow Him to achieve His purpose of suffering and dying for humanity.

In addition to the more speculative dimensions of the transfiguration, which relate to the various theologies of the hypostatic union in the thirteenth century, there is a spiritual significance to the transfiguration that applies to the spiritual life of every Christian believer. In general, however, one gleans little from the non-exegetical genres of scholastic discourse regarding how the transfiguration might be appropriated by Christians to nourish and support their relationship with God, at least in any explicit way. This fact invites one to consider how scholastic theologians explained Christ's transfiguration in their sermons and biblical commentaries. The common interests and questions that arise in the exegetical literature include the relationship between transfiguration and contemplation, Christ's transfiguration as source of the individual's transfiguration and the Church's transfiguration, and the importance of the transfiguration as consolation in the face of suffering. The non-exegetical genres make only brief allusions to these themes, if at all, and yet, in the sermons and biblical commentaries, these themes receive ample attention.

While it is clear that theological emphases vary according to the literary genre, earlier theologians have accentuated different points than the later ones. Both the Christological and the spiritual dimensions of the scholastic teaching on Christ's transfiguration undergo some development during the period under consideration. First, there are alternating incarnational and eschatological emphases (both with respect to theological content and with respect to that content's placement within a larger literary context), synthesized only by Thomas Aquinas. Second, there is an increased importance given to Christ's human soul as mediating the glory of His divinity to His body. Third, there is an increased emphasis on situating Christ's transfiguration within the context of His earthly life, especially before His passion. Finally, there is an increased emphasis (in Albert and Bonaventure especially) on uniting the personal and ecclesial dimensions of the spiritual significance of Christ's transfiguration.

With these more general observations having been made, let us turn to the individual contributions of each author. Hugh of St. Cher was the first theologian of the thirteenth century to direct the compilation of commentaries on all of Scripture. His postillae on the synoptic gospels are remarkable for their interweaving patristic texts, twelfth-century commentary, and his own interpretations. The primary interpretation that emerges from Hugh and his colleagues is a spiritual one. Drawing on Richard of St. Victor, Hugh sees the transfiguration as an exemplar for personal transformation through an ascent to contemplation, but he also emphasizes how "transfiguration" refers to an advance in virtue and a transformation wrought by the grace of the sacraments. Hugh, moreover, links the transfiguration not only to the individual, but to the whole Church as well.

Alexander of Hales is the first theologian of the thirteenth century to write a disputed question on Christ's transfiguration, and he discusses it in scriptural commentaries, as well. The disputed question provides the greatest insight into Alexander's theology of the transfiguration, and it is there that Alexander asks questions regarding what transfiguration means, the nature of Christ's clarity, and how Moses and Elijah appeared. Although later theologians would ask more probing questions and introduce more sophisticated distinctions than the ones he used, Alexander's disputed question introduces some of the central questions and concerns shared by later theologians.

Although Guerric of St. Quentin wrote only a short disputed question on the transfiguration, it is important because it is the only text before Aquinas' to emphasize the role of Christ's soul in communicating glory. For Alexander and John of La Rochelle, the important fact was that Christ's body was united to the divine nature. Neither Albert, in his early *De resurrectione,* nor Bonaventure cogently explained the origin of the clarity of the transfiguration, and neither gave the soul an important role. Guerric's emphasis on Christ's soul would be reiterated later by Aquinas, although the latter would cite Augustine as an authority for this position.

John of La Rochelle marks the first important transition in the discussion of Christ's transfiguration. John's disputed question on the transfiguration is the first question of this kind to be inserted into the larger literary structure of a theological manual. Although John's own teaching on Christ's clarity stresses its origin in the hypostatic union, the literary structure of the *Summa fratris Alexandri* gives this question an eschatological coloring, since the question is situated within a treatise on Christ's resurrection. John's question on the transfiguration is also the first of this kind to pose a large range of inquiries within it. Indeed, the combination of these numerous inquiries and the lengthy arguments and *solutiones* makes this disputed question the most complete theological investigation of the transfiguration in the thirteenth century. In this question, John also makes a number of sophisticated distinctions that signal a significant development from those of Alexander of Hales and Guerric of St. Quentin. Further evidence that John's theology marks a new stage in the theology of the thirteenth century is his method of interpreting Scripture. John's *divisio textus* is not only more complex than that of the biblical commentaries of the 1230s, but there are also more *quaestiones* in his commentary, as well.

Albert the Great also situates his question on the transfiguration into a treatise on Christ's resurrection, but the content of Albert's early teaching on Christ's transfiguration has a heavy eschatological accent. Albert is unique insofar as he brings more philosophical vocabulary to bear on the transfiguration than any other theologian from this period. He is also unique for noticing the ecclesiological dimension of the transfiguration narratives, especially in the Gospel of Matthew. No other theologian from this period emphasizes so strongly the roles of the disciples and links so explicitly the transfiguration with ecclesiastical power. Albert also gives the transfiguration the deepest Trinitarian reading of any of the theologians of this period. His biblical commentaries in particular, link the role of the Trinitarian Persons in Christ's transfiguration with their role in the transfiguration of humanity. Albert's reliance on philosophers such as Aristotle and Averroes, his use of nonconventional vocabulary to describe the transfiguration, and his unique ecclesiological and Trinitarian interpretations of the transfiguration make Albert's one of the most creative treatments of the transfiguration from this period.

Bonaventure did not write on the transfiguration in any non-exegetical genre, and his only exegesis of the transfiguration narratives are from the Gospel of Matthew (in sermons) and the Gospel of Luke (in his commentary on Luke). Because his discussion of the transfiguration is confined to these two scholastic genres (leaving aside very brief discussions of the transfiguration in several spiritual writings), Bonaventure fails to ask the kinds of technical questions relating to the nature of Christ's clarity or the status of His human nature during the transfiguration, which one might find in a disputed question or *summa*. More than any theologian from this period, Bonaventure focuses on the spiritual dimension of the transfiguration. That is, rather than emphasizing Christ's transfiguration as an event located only in the past, Bonaventure seeks to show how the transfiguration relates to each person's mystical ascent to contemplation.

Thomas Aquinas' teaching on the transfiguration has both a deep spiritual current and a profound speculative dimension as well. Thomas' use of fittingness arguments in the *Summa* highlights why Christ was transfigured before the disciples and how that event relates to the cross. Of all the theologians from this period, only Thomas repeatedly reminds his readers that the glory signified by the transfiguration is attained by following Christ in His passion and death. The very fact that Thomas places his question on the transfiguration among questions on Christ's life (and immediately before his questions on Christ's passion and death) reveals his interest in preserving the narrative order of the Gospel accounts and showing the intelligibility of that order. Although Christ's followers will share in the glory of the resurrection, the clarity of the saints pales in comparison to that of their Head. Christ's clarity derives not only from His glorified soul, but also from His divinity. Although Thomas' speculation on the nature of Christ's clarity is complex, his use of patristic authorities, especially those culled from his work on the *Catena aurea* on Luke, give his theology of the transfiguration a spiritual dimension lacking in Guerric and Albert. Thomas seems to believe that the transfiguration was a sign not only for Peter, James, and John, but for all those who are *in via* and must come to the glory of the resurrection through the sufferings of this world. When those sufferings are offered in imitation of Christ's suffering, they become the means of sharing in the glory of Christ's resurrection.

Thomas' theology of the transfiguration is the most profound and comprehensive of those studied here, but it is not solely because his theology represents a synthesis and culmination of many of the themes that his peers and predecessors had raised that it is the last examined in this study. After Thomas, interest in the events of Christ's life wanes. A cursory examination of later writings, such as John Duns Scotus' *Ordinatio* or the *Sentences* commentaries of such theologians as Hervaeus Natalis or Innocent V (Peter of Tarantaise), shows that attention returned to the central Christological topics of the twelfth century, albeit with much greater complexity and sophistication. Theologians after Aquinas contributed to the developing reflection on the Incarnation and on such soteriological themes as Christ's merit and atonement in His passion and death, but little attention was given to these topics as they related to the events of Christ's life. In the late Middle Ages, reflection on the events of Christ's life would lie in the domain of spiritual writers, such as Walter Hilton and John of Caulibus.

Although the period of systematic reflection on the events of Christ's life was short, roughly fifty years from 1230 to 1280, this period was remarkable for its intense interest in all facets of Christ's earthly existence. Whether in biblical commentary or sermon, disputed question or *summa,* these early mendicant theologians worked together, the later ones learning from the earlier ones, to create a profound scholastic expression of what Christ's transfiguration was and what it meant for Christians in their day.

Bibliography

Primary sources

A. Manuscripts

Assisi, Biblioteca Comunale 355 (Alexander of Hales, *Postilla super Matthaeum, Postilla super Marcum, Postilla super Lucam*).

Milan, Ambrosiana A211 inf. (John of La Rochelle, *Postilla super Lucam*).

Milan, Ambrosiana D471 inf. (John of La Rochelle, *Postilla super Marcum*).

Oxford, New College 48 (John of La Rochelle, *Postilla super Matthaeum*).

B. Printed sources

Acta Iohannis. Edited by and translated by E. Junod and J.-D. Kaestli. 2 vols. CCSA 1–2. Turnhout, Belg.: Brepols, 1983.

Actus Petri cum Simone. Edited by R. A. Lipsius and M. Bonnet. 2 pts. Darmstadt, Ger.: Wissenschaftliche Buchgesellschaft, 1959.

Albert the Great. *De IV coaequevis*. In *Opera omnia*, t. 34, edited by A. Borgnet. Paris: Vivès, 1895.

———. *De sacramentis, De incarnatione, De resurrectione*. In *Opera omnia*, t. 26, edited by A. Ohlmeyer, I. Backes, and W. Kübel. Monasterii Westfalorum, Ger.: Aschendorff, 1958.

———. *Enarrationes in Lucam*. In Opera omnia, t. 22, edited by A. Borgnet. Paris: Vivès, 1894.

———. *Enarrationes in Marcum*. In *Opera omnia*, t. 21, edited by A. Borgnet. Paris: Vivès, 1894.

———. *Meteororum*. In Opera omnia, t. 4, edited by A. Borgnet. Paris: Vivès, 1890.

———. *Super Matthaeum. In Opera omnia*, t. 21, edited by B. Schmidt. 2 vols., Monasterii Westfalorum, Ger.: Aschendorff, 1987.

Alexander of Hales. *Glossa in quatuor libros Sententiarum Petri Lombardi*. Edited by Pp. Collegii S. Bonaventurae. 4 vols. Quaracchi, Italy: ex Typographia Collegii S. Bonaventurae, 1951–1957.

———. *Quaestiones disputatae 'antequam esset frater'*. Edited by Pp. Collegii S. Bonaventurae. 3 vols. Grottaferrata, Italy: Collegio S. Bonaventura, 1960.

———. *Summa theologica*. 4 tt. Edited by Pp. Collegii S. Bonaventurae. Quaracchi, Italy: Ex Typographia Collegii S. Bonaventurae, 1924–1948.

Ambrose Autpert. *Homilia de Transfiguratione.* Translated by John Anthony McGuckin. In *The Transfiguration of Christ in Scripture and Tradition,* by McGuckin, 293–315. Lewiston, N.Y.: Edwin Mellen Press, 1986.

Apocalypse of Peter. Edited and translated by Dennis D. Bucholz. In *Your Eyes Will Be Opened: A Study of the Greek (Ethiopic) Apocalypse of Peter,* by Bucholz, 157–265. Atlanta: Scholars Press, 1988.

Aristotle. *The Complete Works of Aristotle.* Edited by Jonathan Barnes. 2 vols. Princeton, N.J.: Princeton University Press, 1984.

Augustine. *Enarrationes in psalmos.* Edited by D. E. Dekkers and J. Fraipont. 3 vols. CCSL 38–40.

Bede. *In Lucae evangelium expositio.* PL 92, 301–634.

Biblia latina cum glossa ordinaria: Facsimile Reprint of the Editio Princeps Adolph Rusch of Strassburg 1480/81. 4 vols. Introduction by Karlfried Froehlich and Margaret T. Gibson. Turnhout, Belg.: Brepols, 1992.

Bonaventure. *Collationes in Hexaëmeron.* In *Opera omnia,* t. 5, edited by Pp. Colegii S. Bonaventurae. Quaracchi, Italy: ex Typographia Collegii S. Bonaventurae, 1891.

———. *Commentarius in Evangelium S. Lucae.* In *Opera omnia,* t. 7, edited by Pp. Colegii S. Bonaventurae. Quaracchi, Italy: ex Typographia Collegii S. Bonaventurae, 1895.

———. *Itinerarium mentis in Deum.* In *Opera omnia,* t. 5, edited by Pp. Colegii S. Bonaventurae. Quaracchi, Italy: ex Typographia Collegii S. Bonaventurae, 1891.

———. *Lignum vitae.* In *Opera omnia,* t. 8, edited by Pp. Colegii S. Bonaventurae. Quaracchi, Italy: ex Typographia Collegii S. Bonaventurae, 1898.

———. *Sermones dominicales.* Edited by Jacques Guy Bougerol. Grottaferrata, Italy: Collegio S. Bonaventura Padri Editori di Quaracchi, 1977.

———. *Sermones de tempore.* Edited by Jacques Guy Bougerol. Paris: Éditions franciscaines, 1990.

———. *Sermones de tempore, de sanctis, de B. Virgine Maria et de diversis.* In *Opera omnia,* t. 9, edited by Pp. Colegii S. Bonaventurae. Quaracchi, Italy: ex Typographia Collegii S. Bonaventurae, 1901.

Clement of Alexandria. *Extraits de Théodote.* Edited and translated with an introduction by F. Sagnard. SC 23.

———. *Les stromates: Stromate VI.* Edited and translated with an introduction by P. Descourtieux. SC 446.

De resurrectione (Epistula ad Rheginum). Edited by M. Malinine et al. Zurich: Rascher Verlag, 1963.

The Festal Menaion. Translated by Mother Mary and Archimandrite Kallistos Ware with an introduction by Georges Florovsky. London: Faber and Faber, 1969.

Gregory Palamas. *Homilia 34.* Translated by John Anthony McGuckin. In *The Transfiguration of Christ in Scripture and Tradition,* by McGuckin, 225–34. Lewiston, N.Y.: Edwin Mellen Press, 1986.

———. *The One Hundred and Fifty Chapters.* Edited and translated by Robert E. Sinkewicz. Toronto: Pontifical Institute of Mediaeval Studies, 1988.

Guerric of St. Quentin. *Quaestio de transfiguratione Domini.* In vol. 2 of *Auferstehung und Himmelfahrt Christi in der scholastischen Theologie bis zu Thomas von Aquin.* Edited by Thomas Marschler, 81–86. Münster, Ger.: Aschendorff Verlag, 2003.

———. *Quaestiones de resurrectione Christi.* In vol. 2 of *Auferstehung und Himmelfahrt Christi in der scholastischen Theologie bis zu Thomas von Aquin.* Edited by Thomas Marschler, 87–106. Münster, Ger.: Aschendorff Verlag, 2003.

Hugh of St. Cher. *Opera omnia in universum Vetus et Novum Testamentum,* 8tt. Lyons, 1645.

Hugh of St. Victor. *Hugonis de Sancto-Victore De sacramentis Christianae fidei.* Curo et studio R. Berndt. Monasterii Westfalorum, Ger.: Aschendorff, 2008.

Innocent III. *De sacro altaris mysterio.* PL 217, 773–916.

———. *Sermo XIV de tempore.* PL 217, 375–82.

Irenaeus of Lyons. *Contre les hérésies, Livre IV.* 2 tt. Edited by A. Rousseau et al. SC 100.

Isaac Israeli. *The Book of Definitions.* Translated by S. M. Stern. In *Isaac Israeli,* by A. Altmann and S. M. Stern, 3–78. Westport, Conn.: Greenwood Press 1979.

———. *The Book of Substances* [selections]. Translated by S. M. Stern. In *Isaac Israeli,* by A. Altmann and S. M. Stern, 79–105. Westport, Conn.: Greenwood Press 1979.

John Scotus Eriugena. *Periphyseon III.* Edited by E. A. Jeauneau. CCCM 163.

Leo I. *Sermo* 51. In vol. 2 of *The Sunday Sermons of the Great Fathers,* translated and edited by M. F. Toal. 4 vols. Swedesboro, N.J.: Preservation Press, 1996.

The Liturgy of the Hours. Translated by the International Committee on English in the Liturgy. 4 vols. New York: Catholic Book Publishing, 1975.

The Lorsch Gospels. Introduction by Wolfgang Braunfels. New York: George Braziller, 1967.

Novum testamentum graece et latine. 26th ed. Stuttgart, Ger.: Deutsche Bibelgesellschaft, 1991.

Origen, *In Matthaeum Commentarii* [selection]. Translated by John Anthony McGuckin. In *The Transfiguration of Christ in Scripture and Tradition,* by McGuckin, 155–164. Lewiston, N.Y.: Edwin Mellen Press, 1986.

Peter Lombard. *Sententiae in IV libris distinctae.* 2 tt. Edited by Pp. Collegii S. Bonaventurae. Grottaferrata, Italy: Editiones Collegii S. Bonaventurae ad Claras Aquas, 1971–1981.

———. *In totum Psalterium commentarii.* PL 191, 55–1296.

Pseudo-Anselm. *Homilia IV.* PL 158, 602–16.

La prière des Églises de rite byzantin, 2 tt. Edited by R. P. E. Mercenier. Monastère de Chevetogne, Belg.: Éditions de Chevetogne, 1948?–1953.

Richard of St. Victor. *Benjamin major.* PL 196, 63–192.

———. *Les douze patriarches ou Beniamin minor.* Edited and translated by Jean Châtillon and Monique Duchet-Suchaux with an introduction by Jean Longère. SC 419.

Thomas Aquinas. *Catena aurea in quatuor Evangelia.* Edited by A. Guarienti. 2 vols. Turin, Italy: Marietti, 1953.

———. *Commentum in quartum librum Sententiarum magistri Petri Lombardi.* In *Opera omnia,* t. 7/2. Parma, Italy: Typis Petri Fiaccadori, 1858.

———. *Compendium theologiae.* In *Opera omnia iussu Leonis XIII P.M. edita,* t. 42, 83–205. Rome, 1979.

———. *De articulis fidei et ecclesiae sacramentis.* In *Opera omnia iussu Leonis XIII P.M. edita,* t. 42, 245–57. Rome, 1979.

———. *De commendatione et partitione sacrae Scripturae.* In *Opuscula theologica,* edited by R. A. Verardo, vol. 1, 441–43. Turin, Italy: Marietti, 1954.

———. *In symbolum apostolorum.* In *Opuscula theologica,* edited by R. M. Spiazzi, vol. 2, 193–217. Turin, Italy: Marietti, 1954.

———. *Scriptum super libros Sententiarum.* Edited by P. Mandonnet (tt. 1–2) and M. F. Moos (tt. 3–4). Paris: Lethielleux, 1929–1947.

———. *Summa contra gentiles.* In *Opera omnia iussu Leonis XIII P.M. edita,* t. 15. Rome, 1930.

———. *Summa theologiae.* In *Opera omnia iussu Leonis XIII P.M. edita,* tt. 4–12. Rome, 1886–1906.

———. *Super evangelium S. Ioannis lectura.* Edited by R. Cai. Turin, Italy: Marietti, 1952.

———. *Super evangelium S. Matthaei lectura.* Edited by R. Cai. Turin, Italy: Marietti, 1951.

William of Auxerre. *Summa aurea.* Edited by J. Ribaillier. 4 vols. Grottaferrata, Italy: Editiones Collegii S. Bonaventurae ad Claras Aquas, 1980–1985.

Zachary of Besançon. *In unum ex quatuor.* PL 186, 11–620.

Secondary sources

Amato, Norbert de. *Doctrina Summae Fratris Alexandri de Hales de ipsa natura a Verbo assumpta.* Rome: Casa Editrice Herder, 1956.

Andia, Ysabel de. *Mystiques d'Orient et d'Occident.* Bégrolles-en-Mauges, Fr.: Abbaye de Bellefontaine, 1994.

Auer, Johann. "Die Bedeutung der Verklärung Christi für das Leben des Christen und für die Kirche Christi." In *Die Mysterien des Lebens Jesu und die christliche Existenz,* edited by L. Scheffczyk, 146–76. Aschaffenburg, Ger.: Paul Pattloch Verlag, 1984.

Baldacci, P. R. "The Significance of the Transfiguration Narrative in the Gospel of Luke: A Redactional Investigation." PhD Diss., Marquette University, 1974.

Barton, Stephen C. "The Transfiguration of Christ according to Mark and Matthew: Christology and Anthropology." In *Auferstehung-Resurrection,* edited by F. Avemarie and H. Lichtenberger, 231–46. Tübingen, Ger.: Mohr Siebeck, 2001.

Batiffol, Pierre. *History of the Roman Breviary.* Translated by Atwell M. Y. Baylay. London: Longmans, Green, 1912.

Bataillon, Louis-Jacques. "La diffusione manoscritta e stampata dei commenti biblici de San Tommaso d'Aquino." *Angelicum* 71 (1994): 579–90.

Bauckham, Richard J. *Word Biblical Commentary: Jude, 2 Peter.* Waco, Tex.: Word Books, 1983.

Berndt, Rainer. "Hugo von St. Cher." LThK: 310–11.

Best, T. F. "Transfiguration and Discipleship in Matthew." PhD Diss., Graduate Theological Union, 1974.

Biffi, Inos. *I misteri di Cristo in Tommaso d'Aquino.* Milan: Jaca Book, 1994.

———. "I misteri della vita di Cristo nei Commentari biblici di S. Tommaso d'Aquino." *Divus Thomas* 79 (1976): 217–54.

Blinzler, Josef. *Die neutestamentlichen Berichte über die Verklärung Jesu.* Münster, Ger.: Verlag der Aschendottschen Verlagsbuchhandlung, 1937.

Boobyer, G. H. "St. Mark and the Transfiguration." *Journal of Theological Studies* 41 (1940): 119–140.

———. "The Indebtedness of 2 Peter to 1 Peter." In *New Testament Essays: Studies in Memory of Thomas Walter Manson, 1893–1958,* edited by A. J. B. Higgins, 34–53. Manchester, U.K.: Manchester University Press, 1959.

Bougerol, Jacques Guy. *Introduction a l'Étude de Saint Bonaventure.* Tournai, Belg.: Desclée, 1961.

———. Introduction to Bonaventure, *Sermones dominicales.* Edited by Bougerol, 11–126. Grottaferrata, Italy: Collegio S. Bonaventura Padri Editori di Quaracchi, 1977.

———. Introduction to Bonaventure, *Sermons de tempore.* Edited by Bougerol, 7–41. Paris: Éditions franciscaines, 1990.

———. "Jean de La Rochelle. Les oeuvres et les manuscrits." *Archivum Franciscanum Historicum:* 205–15.

Brady, Ignatius. "Sacred Scripture in the Early Franciscan School." In *La Sacra Scrittura e i Francescani,* 65–80. Rome: Antonianum, 1973.

Breuning, Wilhelm. *Die hypostatische Union in der Theologie Wilhelms von Auxerre, Hugos von St. Cher und Rolands von Cremona.* Trier, Ger.: Paulinus Verlag, 1962.

Bultmann, Rudolf. *The History of the Synoptic Tradition.* Translated by John Marsh. New York: Harper and Row, 1963.

———. *Theology of the New Testament.* Translated by Kendrick Grobel. Vol. 1. New York: Charles Scribner's Sons, 1951.

Bundy, Walter E. *Jesus and the First Three Gospels: An Introduction to the Synoptic Tradition.* Cambridge, Mass.: Harvard University Press, 1955.

Cantalamessa, Raniero. *Il mistero della trasfigurazione: quale immagine di Cristo per l'uomo del duemila?* Milan: Ancora, 1999.

Châtillon, Jean. "L'union hypostatique chez les théologiens du début du XIIIe siècle: Guillaume d'Auxerre et Alexandre de Halès." *Cahiers de civilisation médiévale* 12 (1969): 161–64.

Chenu, Marie-Dominique. "Le plan de la Somme théologique de S. Thomas." *Revue Thomiste* 47 (1939): 93–107.

———. *Toward Understanding Saint Thomas.* Translated by A.-M. Landry and D. Hughes. Chicago: H. Regnery, 1964.

Coune, M., ed. *Grâce de la transfiguration d'après les pères d'occident.* Bégrolles-en-Mauges, Fr.: Abbaye de Bellefontaine, 1990.

———. *Joie de la transfiguration d'après les pères d'orient.* Bégrolles-en-Mauges, Fr.: Abbaye de Bellefontaine, 1985.

Craddock, Fred B. *First and Second Peter and Jude.* Louisville, Ky.: Westminster John Knox Press, 1995.

Cuesta Leyva, Manuel. *Salvacion y cruz, un capitulo de la soteriologia de Hugo de Saint-Cher.* Granada, Sp.: Facultad de Teologia, 1980.

Cullman, Oscar. *Le Nouveau Testament.* Paris: Presses Universitaires de France, 1967.

Dabrowski, Eugène. *La Transfiguration de Jésus.* Rome: Institut Biblique Pontifical, 1939.

Del Agua, Augustín. "The Narrative of the Transfiguration as a Derashic Scenification of a Faith Confession (Mark 9.2–8 Par.)." *New Testament Studies* 39 (1993): 340–54.

Distelbrink, Balduinus. *Bonaventurae scripta, authentica dubia vel spuria critice recensita.* Rome: Istituto Storico Cappucini, 1975.

Doucet, Victorin. *Prolegomena in librum III necnon in libros I et II "Summae fratris Alexandri."* In Alexander of Hales, *Summa theologica,* t. 4, edited by Pp. Collegii S. Bonaventurae. Quaracchi, Italy: Ex Typographia Collegii S. Bonaventurae, 1924–1948.

Etzkorn, Girard J. "How to Read the Bible According to John of La Rochelle." In *That Others May Know and Love: Eassays in Honor of Zachary Hayes, OFM,* edited by M. F. Cusato and F. E. Coughlin, 159–64. St. Bonaventure, N.Y.: Franciscan Institute, 1997.

Fauser, Winfried. *Die Werke des Albertus Magnusin ihrer handschriftlichen Überlieferung.* Monasterii Westfalorum, Ger.: Aschendorff, 1982.

Feuillet, André. "Les perspective propres à chaque évangéliste dans les récits de la transfiguration." *Biblica* 39 (1958): 281–301.

Fisher, J. "Hugh of St. Cher and the Development of Mediaeval Theology." *Speculum* 31 (1956): 57–69.

Fletcher-Louis, Crispin H. T. "The Revelation of the Sacral Son of Man: The Genre, History of Religions Context and the Meaning of the Transfiguration." In *Auferstehung-Resurrection,* edited by F. Avemarie and H. Lichtenberger, 247–98. Tübingen, Ger.: Mohr Siebeck, 2001.

Frankenmölle, Hubert. *1. Petrusbrief, 2. Petrusbrief, Judasbrief.* Würzburg, Ger.: Echter Verlag, 1990.

Fransen, Irénée. "Cahiers de Bible: Le feu de la gloire (2 Pierre)." *Bible et vie chrétienne* 33 (1960): 26–33.

Fries, Albert. "Die Entstehungszeit der Bibelkommentare Alberts des Grossen." In *Albertus Magnus—Doctor Universalis 1280/1980,* edited by G. Meyer and A. Zimmerman, 119–39. Mainz, Ger.: Matthias-Grünewald-Verlag, 1980.

Fuchs, Eric, and Pierre Reymond. *La deuxième épitre de saint Pierre, L'épitre de saint Jude.* Neufchâtel, Switz.: Delachaux, 1980.

George, Augustin. "La Transfiguration (Luc. 9, 28–36)." *Bible et vie chrétienne* 33 (1960): 21–25.

Gerber, Wolfgang. "Die Metamorphose Jesu, Mark. 9, 2f. par." *Theologische Zeitschrift* 23 (1967): 385–95.

Gerwing, M. "Hugo von St. Cher." LexMA: 176–77.

Geyer, Bernhard. Introduction to Albert the Great, *De bono*. In *Opera omnia*, t. 28, edited by H Kühle, C. Feckes, B. Geyer, and W. Kübel, ix–xxii. Monasterii Westfalorum, Ger.: Aschendorff, 1951.

Glorieux, Palemon. *Répertoire des maitres en théologie de Paris au XIIIe siècle*, 2 tt. Paris: J. Vrin, 1933–1934.

Gössmann, Elisabeth. "Alexander von Hales." LThK: 362–64.

Green, Michael. *2 Peter and Jude*. Leicester, U.K.: Inter-Varsity Press, 1987.

———. *2 Peter Reconsidered*. London: Tyndale Press, 1961.

Grillmeier, Alois. *Mit ihm und in ihm: christologische Forschungen und Perspektiven*. Freiburg, Ger.: Herder, 1975.

Haberl, Ferdinand. *Die Inkarnationslehre des heiligen Albertus Magnus*. Freiburg im Breisgau, Ger.: Herder, 1939.

Habra, Georges. *La transfiguration selon les Pères Grecs*. Paris: Éditions S.O.S., 1974.

Harrison, Everett F. *Introduction to the New Testament*. Grand Rapids, Mich.: Eerdmans, 1964.

Hayen, André. "La structure de la Somme théologique et Jésus." *Sciences ecclésiastiques* (1960): 59–82.

Hayes, Zachary. "Bonaventure: Mystery of the Triune God." In *The History of Franciscan Theology*, edited by Kenan B. Osborne, 39–125. St. Bonaventure, N.Y.: Franciscan Institute, 1994.

Heil, John Paul. *The Transfiguration of Jesus: Narrative Meaning and Function of Mark 9:2–8, Matt 17:1–8 and Luke 9:28–36*. Rome: Editrice Pontificio Istituto Biblico, 2000.

Henquinet, F. M. "Les écrits du Frère Guerric de Saint-Quentin, O.P." *Recherches de théologie ancienne et médiévale* 6 (1934): 184–214, 284–312, 394–410.

———. "Notes additionelle sur les écrits de Guerric de Saint-Quentin." *Recherches de théologie ancienne et médiévale* 8 (1936): 369–88.

Hödl, Ludwig. "Johannes de Rupella." LexMA: 598.

Holmes, Jeremy. "Aquinas' *Lectura in Matthaeum*." In *Aquinas on Scripture: An Introduction to His Biblical Commentaries*, edited by T. G. Weinandy, D. A. Keating, and J. P. Yocum, 73–97. London: T & T Clark International, 2005.

Hooker, Morna D. "'What Doest Thou Here, Elijah?' A Look at St. Mark's Account of the Transfiguration." In *The Glory of Christ in the New Testament: Studies in Christology*, edited by L. D. Hurst and N. T. Wright, 59–70. Oxford, U.K.: Clarendon Press, 1987.

Horrell, David. *The Epistles of Peter and Jude*. Peterborough, U.K.: Epworth Press, 1998.

Horst, Ulrich. "Über die Frage einer Heilsökonomischen Theologie bei Thomas von Aquin. Ergebnisse und Probleme der neueren Forschung." *Münchener Theologische Zeitschrift* 12 (1961): 97–111.

Jerman, C. "Hugh of Saint-Cher." *Dominicana* 44 (1959): 338–47.

Johnson, Timothy J. Introduction to *The Sunday Sermons of St. Bonaventure*, edited and translated by Johnson, 11–58. St. Bonaventure, N.Y.: Franciscan Institute Publications, 2008.

Kaeppeli, Thomas. *Scriptores Ordinis Praedicatorum Medii Aevi.* 4 vols. Rome: Ad S. Sabinae, 1970–1993.

Karris, Robert J. "Bonaventure's Commentary on Luke: Four Case Studies of His Creative Borrowing from Hugh of St. Cher." *Franciscan Studies* 59 (2001): 133–236.

———. "A Comparison of the *Glossa Ordinaria,* Hugh of St. Cher, and St. Bonaventure on Luke 8:26–39." *Franciscan Studies* 58 (2000): 121–236.

———. Introduction to vol. 1, Bonaventure. In *Commentary on the Gospel of Luke,* edited and translated by Robert J. Karris. 3 vols. St. Bonaventure, N.Y.: Franciscan Institute Publications, 2001–2004.

———. "St. Bonaventure as Biblical Interpreter: His Methods, Wit, and Wisdom." *Franciscan Studies* 60 (2002): 159–208.

———. "St. Bonaventure's Use of Distinctiones: His Independence of and Dependence on Hugh of St. Cher." *Franciscan Studies* 60 (2002): 209–50.

Käsemann, Ernst. "Eine Apologie der unchristlichen Eschatologie." *Zeitschrift für Theologie und Kirche* 49 (1952): 272–96.

Kee, Howard Clark. "The Transfiguration in Mark: Epiphany or Apocalyptic Vision?" In *Understanding the Sacred Text: Essays in Honor of Morton S. Enslin on the Hebrew Bible and Christian Beginnings,* edited by John Reumann, 137–52. Valley Forge, Pa.: Judson Press, 1972.

Knight, Jonathan. *2 Peter and Jude.* Sheffield, U.K.: Sheffield Academic Press, 1995.

Kraftchick, Steven J. *Jude, 2 Peter.* Nashville, Tenn.: Abingdon Press, 2002.

Kübel, Wilhelm. Introduction to Albert the Great, *De sacramentis, De incarnatione, De resurrectione.* In *Opera omnia,* t. 26, edited by A. Ohlmeyer, I. Backes, and W. Kübel, v–xix. Monasterii Westfalorum, Ger.: Aschendorff, 1958.

Kübel, Wilhem, et al. "Albertus Magnus." LexMA: 294–99.

la Chapelle, Marie Lamy de. "Fils jusque dans la chair. Le mystère de l'Incarnation dans la pensée de S. Albert le Grand, Alexandre d'Halès, S. Bonaventure et S. Thomas d'Aquin." *Doctor Communis* 33 (1980): 149–57.

Lafont, Ghislain. *Structures et méthode dans la Somme théologique de saint Thomas d'Aquin.* Paris: Desclée, 1961.

Landgraf, Artur M. "Mitteilungen zum Sentenzkommentar Hugos a S. Charo." *Zeitschrift für katholische Theologie* 58 (1934): 391–400.

Laporte, Jean-Marc. "Christ in Aquinas's *Summa Theologiae:* Peripheral or Pervasive?" *The Thomist* 67 (2003), 221–48.

Lerner, Robert E. "The Vocation of the Friars Preacher: Hugh of St. Cher between Peter the Chanter and Albert the Great." In *Hugues de Saint-Cher († 1263) bibliste et théologien,* edited by Louis-Jacques Bataillon, Gilbert Dahan, and Pierre-Marie Gy, 215–31. Turnhout, Belg.: Brepols, 2004.

Levering, Matthew. *Christ's Fulfillment of Torah and Temple: Salvation According to Thomas Aquinas.* Notre Dame, Ind.: University of Notre Dame Press, 2002.

Lohaus, Gerd. *Die Geheimnisse des Lebens Jesu in der Summa theologiae des heiligen Thomas von Aquin.* Freiburg im Breisgau, Ger.: Herder, 1985.

Longpré, E. "Bonaventure." DS 1768–1843.

Lynch, K. F. "Some Fontes of the Commentary of Hugh de Saint Cher: William of Auxerre, Guy d'Orchelles, Alexander of Hales." *Franciscan Studies* 13 (1953): 119–46.

Madigan, Kevin. *Olivi and the Interpretation of Matthew in the High Middle Ages.* Notre Dame, Ind.: University of Notre Dame Press, 2003.

Margerie, Bertrand de. *Introduction a l'histoire de l'exégèse.* 4 tt. Paris: Cerf, 1980–1990.

Marschler, Thomas. *Auferstehung und Himmelfahrt Christi in der scholastischen Theologie bis zu Thomas von Aquin.* 2 vols. Münster, Ger.: Aschendorff Verlag, 2003.

Marshall, Bruce D. "What Does the Spirit Have to Do?" In *Reading John with St. Thomas Aquinas,* edited by M. Dauphinais and M. Levering, 62–77. Washington, D.C.: The Catholic University of America Press, 2005.

Martínez Fresneda, Francisco. *La gracia y la ciencia de Jesucristo: historia de la cuestión en Alejandro de Hales, Odón Rigaldo, Summa Halensis y Buenaventura.* Murcia, Sp.: Editorial Espigas, 1997.

Marxsen, Willi. *Einleitung in das Neue Testament: eine Einführung in ihre Probleme.* Gütersloh, Ger.: Gütersloher Verlagshaus Gerd Mohn, 1964.

Masson, Charles. "La Transfiguration de Jésus (Marc 9:2–13)." *Revue de théologie et de philosophie* Sér. 3, 14 (1964): 1–14.

McGuckin, John Anthony. *The Transfiguration of Christ in Scripture and Tradition.* Lewiston, N.Y.: Edwin Mellen Press, 1986.

Miller, Robert J. "Is There Independent Attestation for the Transfiguration in 2 Peter?" *New Testament Studies* 42 (1996): 620–25.

Minnis, A. J. *Medieval Theory of Authorship: Scholastic Literary Attitudes in the Later Middle Ages.* 2nd ed. Aldershot, U.K.: Wildwood House, 1988.

Moorman, John. *A History of the Franciscan Order from Its Origins to the Year 1517.* Oxford, U.K.: Clarendon Press, 1968.

Moses, A. D. A. *Matthew's Transfiguration Story and Jewish-Christian Controversy.* Sheffield, U.K.: Sheffield Academic Press, 1996.

Mückshoff, M. "Alexander von Hales." LexMA: 377–78.

Nappo, Constantino. "La Postilla in Marcum di Giovanni de Rupella e suoi riflessi nella Summa Halesiana." *Archivum Franciscanum Historicum* 50 (1957): 332–47.

Nützel, Johannes M. *Die Verklärungserzählung im Markusevangelium.* Würzburg, Ger.: Echter Verlag, 1973.

Olsewski, Mikolaj. "St. Albert the Great's Theory of Interpretation of the Bible." In *Albertus Magnus. Zum Gedenken nach 800 Jahren: Neue Zugänge, Aspekte, und Perspektiven,* edited by Walter Senner, 467–78. Berlin: Akademie Verlag, 2001.

Osborne, Kenan B. "Alexander of Hales: Precursor and Promoter of Franciscan Theology." In *The History of Franciscan Theology,* edited by Kenan B. Osborne, 1–38. St. Bonaventure, New York: Franciscan Institute, 1994.

Pesch, Otto Hermann. "Um den Plan der Summa Theologiae des hl. Thomas von Aquin. Zu Max Secklers neuem Deutungsversuch." In *Thomas von Aquin, bd. 1: Chronologie und Werkanalyse,* edited by K. Bernath, 411–37. Darmstadt, Ger.: Wissenschaftliche Buchgesellschaft, 1978.

Petrozzi, Maria Teresa. *Il Monte Tabor e dinotorni*. Jerusalem: Franciscan Printing Press, 1976.

Potestà, Gian Luca. "I fratri minori e lo studio della Bibbia. Da Francesco d'Assisi a Nicolò di Lyre." In *La Bibbia nel medio evo*, edited by G. Cremascoli and C. Leonardi, 269–90. Bologna, Italy: Edizioni Dehoniane Bologna, 1996.

Principe, Walter H. *Alexander of Hales' Theology of the Hypostatic Union*. Toronto: Pontifical Institute of Mediaeval Studies, 1967.

———. *Hugh of St. Cher's Theology of the Hypostatic Union*. Toronto: Pontifical Institute of Mediaeval Studies, 1970.

Prügl, Thomas. "Thomas Aquinas as Interpreter of Scripture." In *The Theology of Thomas Aquinas*, edited by Rik van Nieuwenhove and Joseph Wawrykow, 386–415. Notre Dame, Ind.: University of Notre Dame Press, 2005.

Raya, Joseph. *Transfiguration of Our Lord and Saviour Jesus Christ*. Combermere, Ont.: Madonna House Publications, 1992.

Reid, Barbara E. *The Transfiguration: A Source- and Redaction-Critical Study of Luke 9:28–36*. Paris: J. Gabalda et Cie Éditeurs, 1993.

Renard, J. P. "La Lectura super Matthaeum V, 20–28 de Thomas d'Aquin (Edition d'après le ms. Bâle, Univ. Bibl. B.V. 12)." *Recherches de théologie ancienne et médiévale* 50 (1983): 145–90.

Riesenfeld, Harald. *Jésus transfiguré, l'arriére-plan du récit évangélique de la transfiguration de Notre-Seigneur*. Copenhagen: E. Munksgaard, 1947.

Rivera, Luis F. "Interpretatio transfigurationis Jesu in redactione evangelii Marci." *Verbum Domini* 46 (1968): 99–104.

Rossi, Margeherita Maria. "La 'divisio textus' nei commenti scritturistici di S. Tommaso d'Aquino: Un procedimento solo esegetico?" *Angelicum* 71 (1994): 537–48.

Rouse, Mary A. and Richard H. "La concordance verbale des Ecritures." In *Le Moyen Age et la Bible*, edited by Pierre Riché and Guy Lobrichon, 115–22. Paris: Beauchesne, 1984.

Scheffczyk, Leo. "Die Stellung des Thomas von Aquin in der Entwicklung der Lehre von den Mysteria Vitae Christi." In *Renovatio et Reformatio: Wider das Bild "finsteren" Mittelalter*, edited by M. Gerwing and G. Ruppert, 44–70. Münster, Ger.: Aschendorff, 1985.

Scheeben, Heribert Christian. *Albertus Magnus*. Cologne, Ger.: J. P. Bachem, 1955.

Schmidt, B. *Prolegomena* to vol. 1, Albert the Great, *Super Matthaeum*. In *Opera omnia*, t. 21, edited by B. Schmidt. Münster, Ger.: Aschendorff, 1987.

Schnackenburg, Rudolf. *Die Person Jesu Christi im Spiegel der vier Evangelien*. Freiburg, Ger.: Herder, 1993.

Seckler, Max. *Le salut et l'histoire, la pensée de saint Thomas d'Aquin sur la théologie de l'histoire*. Paris: Cerf, 1967.

Shooner, H. V. "La *Lectura in Matthaeum* de S. Thomas (Deux fragments inédits et la *reportatio* de Pierre d'Andria)." *Angelicum* 33 (1956): 121–42.

Sieben, Hermann Josef. "Transfiguration du Seigneur: Les commentaires spirituels." DS 1151–53.

Smalley, Beryl. *The Gospels in the Schools, c. 1100–c. 1280*. London: Hambledon Press, 1985.

———. *The Study of the Bible in the Middle Ages.* Notre Dame, Ind.: University of Notre Dame Press, 1964.

Somme, Luc-Thomas. *Fils adoptifs de Dieu par Jésus Christ.* Paris: J. Vrin, 1997.

Souza Nogueira, Paulo Augusto de. "Visionary Elements in the Transfiguration Narrative." In *Apocalyptic in History and Tradition,* edited by C. Rowland and J. Barton, 142–50. London: Sheffield Academic Press, 2002.

Spicq, Ceslas. *Les épitres de saint Pierre.* Paris: Librairie Lecoffre, 1966.

Stirnemann, Patricia. "Les manuscrits de la *Postille.*" In *Hugues de Saint-Cher († 1263) bibliste et théologien,* edited by Louis-Jacques Bataillon, Gilbert Dahan, and Pierre-Marie Gy, 31–42. Turnhout, Belg.: Brepols, 2004.

Stuehrenberg, Paul F. "The Medieval Commentary Tradition: The Glossa Ordinaria, Hugh of St. Cher and Nicholas of Lyra and the Study of the Bible in the Middle Ages." *Journal of Religious and Theological Information* 1 (1993): 91–101.

Torrell, Jean-Pierre. Introduction to Guerric of Saint-Quentin, *Quaestiones de quolibet,* edited by Walter H. Principe, 3–177. Toronto: Pontifical Institute of Mediaeval Studies, 2002.

———. *Le Christ en ses mystéres: la vie et l'œuvre de Jésus selon saint Thomas d'Aquin.* 2 tt. Paris: Desclée, 1999.

———. *Saint Thomas Aquinas, vol. 1: The Person and His Work.* Translated by R. Royal. Washington, D.C.: The Catholic University of America Press, 1996.

———. *Saint Thomas Aquinas, vol. 2: Spiritual Master.* Translated by R. Royal. Washington, D.C.: The Catholic University of America Press, 2003.

Trites, Allison A. "The Transfiguration in the Theology of Luke: Some Redactional Links." In *The Glory of Christ in the New Testament: Studies in Christology,* edited by L. D. Hurst and N. T. Wright, 71–81. Oxford, U.K.: Clarendon Press, 1987.

Vaux, Bruno Carra de. "La constitution de corpus exégétique." In *Hugues de Saint-Cher († 1263) bibliste et théologien,* edited by Louis-Jacques Bataillon, Gilbert Dahan, and Pierre-Marie Gy, 43–63. Turnhout, Belg.: Brepols, 2004.

Verger, Jacques. "Hugues de Saint-Cher dans le contexte universitaire parisien." In *Hugues de Saint-Cher († 1263) bibliste et théologien,* edited by Louis-Jacques Bataillon, Gilbert Dahan, and Pierre-Marie Gy, 13–22. Turnhout, Belg.: Brepols, 2004.

Vögtle, Anton. *Der Judasbrief, der 2. Petrusbrief.* Dusseldorf, Ger.: Benziger Verlag, 1994.

Wawrykow, Joseph P. *The Westminster Handbook to Thomas Aquinas.* Louisville, Ky.: Westminster John Knox Press, 2005.

Weber, Hubert Philipp. *Sünde und Gnade bei Alexander von Hales: Ein Beitrag zur Entwicklung der theologischen Anthropologie im Mittelalter.* Innsbruck, Aust.: Tyrolia, 2003.

Wild, Robert. *His Face Shone Like the Sun: Encountering the Transfigured Christ in Scripture.* New York: Alba House, 1986.

Young, Abigail Ann. "Accessus ad Alexandrum: The *Praefatio* to the *Postilla in Iohannis Euangelium* of Alexander of Hales (1186?–1245)." *Mediaeval Studies* 52 (1990): 3–23.

Index of Names